Mistress of Manifest Destiny

To: Archie P. MacDonald

From: Linda S. Hudson

Mistress of
Manifest Destiny

A Biography of Jane McManus Storm Cazneau, 1807–1878

Linda S. Hudson

Texas State Historical Association
Austin

For Maggie

A grandmother who told stories and a friend
who encouraged me to write them.

Copyright © 2001 by the Texas State Historical Association, Austin, Texas. All rights reserved. Printed in the United States of America.

Library of Congress Cataloging-in-Publication Data

Hudson, Linda S.
  Mistress of Manifest Destiny : a biography of Jane McManus Storm Cazneau, 1807–1878/Linda S. Hudson.
    p. cm.
  Includes bibliographical references (p.) and index.
  ISBN 0-87611-179-7 (alk. paper)
    1. Montgomery, Cora (1807–1878). 2. Revolutionaries–Texas–Biography. 3. Women revolutionaries–Texas–Biography. 4. Journalists–United States–Biography. 5. Women journalists–United States–Biography. 6. Texas–History–Revolution, 1835–1836. 7. Texas–History–Republic, 1836–1846. 8. Mexican War, 1846–1848–Journalists. 9. Messianism, Political–United States. 10. United States–Territorial expansion. I. Title.

F390.M76 H83 2001
976.4'05'092–dc21
[B]
                                                        00-048917

5   4   3   2   1   01   02   03   04   05

Published by the Texas State Historical Association in cooperation with the Center for Studies in Texas History at the University of Texas at Austin.

Book design by Holly Zumwalt Taylor. Dustjacket design by David Timmons.

FRONTISPIECE: *American Progress*, by John Gast, 1872. Oil on canvas, $17\frac{3}{4}$ x $21\frac{1}{2}$ inches. *Courtesy Autry Museum of Western Heritage, Los Angeles.*

Brooklyn artist John Gast painted this canvas to symbolize Manifest Destiny, the inevitable movement of the American empire across the West. A heavenly female figure, with the Star of Empire on her forehead, holds a school book in one hand and telegraph wires in the other, symbolically carrying civilization across the continent. Indians and wildlife recede ever westward before the oncoming miners, farmers, settlers, stagecoach, and railroad.

Table of Contents

Maps

Illustrations

Acknowledgments

*J*ANE CAZNEAU LEFT NO COLLECTION OF PAPERS, HAD SEVERAL NAMES, published under pen names, and often signed her letters with initials. Without the encouragement of friends, colleagues, family, and faculty this book would not be possible. Librarians, archivists, and others shared their time and research. Special assistance came from Patricia Crandall; Watertown, New York; Margaret Henson, Houston; and William Goetzmann, Austin. Additional help came from Doris Sheridan, Troy, New York; Kevin L. Glick, the Beinecke Rare Book and Manuscript Library, Yale University; Warren Striker, Daughters of the Republic of Texas History Research Library at the Alamo; Casey Greene, the Galveston and Texas History Center, Rosenberg Library, Galveston; Jane Pellusch, Catholic Archives of Texas, Austin; Kevin Ladd, Wallisville Heritage Center, Wallisville; Francisco Barrientos, Maverick County Historical Commission, Eagle Pass; Galen D. Greaser, Archives and Records Division, Texas General Land Office, Austin; Donaly Brice, Archives and Record Divisions, Texas State Library, Austin; Karl Kabelac, Department of Rare Books and Special Collections, Rush Rhees Library, University of Rochester, Rochester, New York; Dawn Letson, The Woman's Collection, Texas Woman's University Library, Denton; David Busseriet, the University of Texas at Arlington; Lynda L. Crist, the Papers of Jefferson Davis, Rice University, Houston; and Patrick Bryan and the Institute of Jamaica at the University of the West Indies, Mona, Jamaica.

Additional assistance came from the New York Historical Society Library; the New York Public Library; the Texas Collection, Baylor University, Waco; Center for American History, University of Texas at

Austin; the Library Company of Philadelphia; the Historical Society of Pennsylvania, Philadelphia; the Massachusetts Historical Society, Boston; Mississippi Department of Archives and History, Archives and Library Division, Jackson Mississippi; Cooperative Union, Holyoake Institute, Holyoake House, Manchester, England; the staff of the Jamaica Archives, Spanish Town, Jamaica, and the Inter-Library Loan Department of Willis Library, University of North Texas, Denton.

The Ottis Lock Research Grant from the East Texas Historical Association and the John H. Jenkins Research Fellowship from the Texas State Historical Association helped with travel. Additional thanks go to Betty Burch, Harold Weiss, Malcom D. McLean, Félix D. Almaráz Jr., Madge T. Roberts, J. F. de la Teja, Kent Biffle, Patrick L. Cazneau, and mentors, Randolph B. Campbell, Bullitt Lowry, A. Ray Stephens, Donald Pickens, Harland Hagler, Jim Lee, Rollie Schafer, and Archie P. McDonald.

Introduction

A braver, more intellectual woman never lived . . . but a
born insurrecto and a terror with her pen.
——*Henry Watterson*[1]

*W*HEN HENRY WATTERSON, EDITOR OF THE LOUISVILLE *Courier,* WON
the Pulitzer Prize for editorial writing in 1918, he attributed his success to
the woman who had taught him, as he said, everything he knew about
journalism, particularly "the value of the short descriptive phrase." Jane
McManus Storm Cazneau (1807–1878) was a friend of the Watterson family before the American Civil War, when Henry was a young man and she
was an internationally famous journalist and revolutionary. As many as
four hundred thousand people may have read her newspaper columns,
written under the pseudonym "Montgomery," during the Mexican War.
James K. Polk's Secretary of War, William Marcy, described her to
Secretary of the Navy George Bancroft as a "prodigiously smart and keen
writer for the newspapers in New York" and Cazneau herself cautioned
politicians to take her words seriously, for she could "count the beats of
the popular heart," an early form of opinion polling.[2] As the years went by,
Henry Watterson was one of the few that remembered Jane Cazneau and
her contributions as a journalist. The friends, family, and associates who
knew the facts about Jane Cazneau's remarkable career as Cora
Montgomery died, and what little information that remained about her
was based on half-truths, rumor, and innuendo.

A study of this complex woman's life is more than a saga of an adventuress rumored to have been the seventy-six year old Aaron Burr's twenty-

six-year-old mistress. Jane McManus Storm Cazneau speculated in Texas land before it was a republic, became a journalist for the *United States Magazine and Democratic Review* and New York *Sun*, journeyed to Mexico City on a peace mission during the Mexican War, and promoted revolutions in Mexico, Cuba, Nicaragua, and the Dominican Republic. From the late 1830s to her death in 1878, she published more than one hundred newspaper columns in six metropolitan newspapers, more than twenty journal articles in three national journals, fifteen or more books and pamphlets, and edited at least five newspapers and journals, including the bilingual revolutionary newspaper, *La Verdad*, which she edited for Cuban exiles in New York. Many of her publications were unsigned but she had a unique writing voice and style that may be identified through analysis of her grammatical errors. Twice-married, she had a variety of names and used several pen names, but was known best as "Cora Montgomery." The central theme of her life and work was the "Manifest Destiny" of the United States—a phrase she coined that described a foreign policy of territorial and commercial expansion. As a visionary, Cazneau foresaw the United States as a nation with equal rights for all in a world where representative government was the norm rather than the exception. Foremost, she was a nationalist who worked to preserve the Union. As a specialist in the affairs of the Caribbean and Central America, her life story represents a synthesis of United States, Texas, Southwestern Borderlands, Mexico, Central America, and Caribbean histories. Her experiences help reintegrate the fields of political, diplomatic, maritime, labor, civil war, and women's history.[3]

When Jane Cazneau died in December 1878 her death made front-page news in the New York newspapers for several days. As Cora Montgomery, she had been a national public figure for more than thirty years. She was better known and more influential at the time than many of her female contemporaries whose names are more familiar today. She was a complex person, not easily understood in her day or in ours. Often sounding like an idealist, she claimed that she could not write contrary to her beliefs, yet she frequently stood to gain financially from the courses of action that she proposed. Because she advocated gradual emancipation and the colonization of free blacks and slaves outside the United States, abolitionists considered her a pro-slavery advocate, and those in the South who advocated the divine right of slavery saw her as an enemy of their cause. Perhaps one of the most misleading articles concerning her was one written at the time of her death by former abolitionist Rev. Henry Ward

The borderland classic *Eagle Pass* is Jane Cazneau's most famous work and that by which she is most often identified. It was published after she returned to New York to coordinate the Franklin Pierce presidential campaign in the New York newspapers in 1852. *Courtesy Earl Vandale Collection, CN09569, Center for American History, University of Texas at Austin.*

Beecher (1813–1887). Beecher claimed to have played a role in her redemption from racism and portrayed her as a pro-slavery advocate—clearly something that she was not. He had met Jane Cazneau for the first time when she came to hear him preach shortly before her death.[4]

Within a few days of her meeting with Beecher, Jane Cazneau booked passage from New York to Jamaica on an aging brigantine-rigged U.S. cargo steamer, the *Emily B. Souder*. Like others of its class built during the American Civil War, the three-hundred-foot *Souder* was constructed with unseasoned timber and ten-penny nails, but it had lifeboats, safety rafts, and cork life preservers for the men and women on board—nine passengers and twenty-seven crewmen. The ship was to be retired after this voyage, and it was to be Cazneau's final trip to the tropics, where she had traveled for forty years and had resided for more than two decades. Jane Cazneau planned to exhume the remains of her husband, Boston-born William Leslie Cazneau—a hero of the Texas Revolution—for burial in Texas. Her extended plans were to spend her remaining years in Texas, where she would assist her brother R. O. W. McManus in their ongoing legal battle for possession of land claimed by others.[5]

On December 10, 1878, the *Souder* was about four hundred miles south of New York headed for the Dominican Republic in the area of the Bermuda sea-lanes when a westerly front created a line of gale-force winds from New England to Panama, the largest storm to hit the coast of the United States since record keeping began. Nothing was heard of the *Souder* until New York newspapers carried reports of the disaster at sea. By clinging to a life raft two crewmen survived and told of the ten-hour ordeal in the blowing gale; they were the only survivors. The captain had discovered the ship was leaking at sunrise and as the storm intensified the hull broke apart. Helpless at the height of the storm, the sinking ship drifted broadside in the seaway and as darkness approached the captain ordered the lifeboats launched. As the *Souder* sank into the heaving sea, the seamen could see a passenger believed to be Jane Cazneau tied to the rigging with the ship's black cook and steward. The storm mirrored one that Cazneau had experienced thirty years before when she compared the power of the sea to the force of republicanism; "Where shall the lover of the 'fierce, beautiful and free,' find anything comparable with a storm at sea."[6]

Well-educated and from a once-prosperous Hudson River Valley family, Jane Cazneau seldom took the easy path and many of her positions seem juxtaposed to one another. As a young woman she speculated in land in

Mexican Texas upon which to settle free blacks and European immigrants, and within ten years she wrote on behalf of the annexation of Texas as a slave state. The journalist worked behind enemy lines during the Mexican War to secure Northern Mexico as a free labor territory only to filibuster five years later for Cuban and Nicaraguan rebels who would extend slave territory. As a Catholic who sprinkled her writings with religious references to the Catholic Church, she lived at Eagle Pass on the Rio Grande and promoted Mexican revolutionaries who sought to end its being the official church of Mexico. Initially, Cazneau promoted gradual emancipation and colonization for the general good of the nation with little concern for the individuals involved. After a former slave nursed her back to health from a near-fatal illness, she dedicated her life to improving conditions for the black race. Cazneau urged African Americans to move to the Dominican Republic, where they would escape the prejudice that limited their potential in the United States. In anticipation of a mass migration of freed slaves financed by the federal government before the American Civil War, Jane and her husband, William Cazneau, invested in land and port facilities in the black republic. When war came, she returned to New York to rally support for the Lincoln administration. After the war, she became ensnared in the scandals of the Grant administration over the annexation of the Dominican Republic. President Grant wanted a coaling station at Samana Bay for the United States Navy and merchant steamship companies trying to recover from the devastation caused by the war.[7]

From the 1840s onward, Jane Cazneau worked with businessmen who sought to expand world trade and commerce, convert sailing ships to steam and iron vessels, and establish coaling stations in the tropics. As she traveled in the tropics promoting republican revolutions, she became an authority on the affairs of Mexico, Central America, and the Caribbean. Her influence was apparent when editors, senators, diplomats, political leaders, and foreign dignitaries singled her out for information, special favors, or criticism. She advised presidents from James K. Polk to U. S. Grant, and cabinet members in the Polk, Taylor, Pierce, Buchanan, Lincoln, Johnson, and Grant administrations. These officials did not always follow Cazneau's advice, but nonetheless through her persuasive rhetoric she helped influence the direction of American foreign relations in the nineteenth century.[8]

Jane Cazneau's public life presents a better understanding of the role professional women played in the nineteenth century. As a single parent

5

and working mother, she was recognized and accepted as an intellectual equal by New York editor colleagues who formed the New York Associated Press and made her the association's first Washington news correspondent. Although she helped organize a successful boycott of stores on Broadway in the mid-1840s that brought about women clerks for women customers, she was not part of the women's movement. Cazneau referred to the women who met in 1848 to air their grievances as the "Seneca Falls housewives." She ridiculed their complaint of a lack of suffrage because real oppression existed for women in the factories, in the needle trades, on Indian reservations, in Mexico, and in the Caribbean.[9]

Historians have formed no consensus about Jane Cazneau. In reality little is known about "perhaps the most unusual and mysterious woman in the nineteenth century." Critics have seen her as a woman behind the times, admirers say she was a woman ahead of her time, others call her a Renaissance woman. She called herself a "true woman," but in actuality she defied boundaries and categories. She was not the most beautiful, the most popular, or the most visible woman of the nineteenth century, but she was one of the more intelligent and influential women of her generation.[10]

CHAPTER I

The Early New York Years, 1807–1832

> I was born and reared on a large farm in the heart of the
> State of New York, and all my tastes are for the indepen-
> dent life and tranquil occupations of the country.
>
> —*Jane Cazneau*[1]

*J*ANE MARIA ELIZA MCMANUS WAS BORN ON APRIL 6, 1807, IN
Rensselaer County, New York, at the home of her grandparents, Hugh
and Mary McManus. Her parents were William Telemachus McManus
and Catherine Wheeler Coons. Jane's father, grandson of Irish immigrants, was a lawyer and merchant in contrast with his wife's agrarian
family. Jane's family history helps explain her liberal attitude toward
American Indians, gradual emancipation and colonization, republicanism, and the role of women in society. Her maternal Kuntz, later
Americanized as Coons, and paternal McManus families had lived near
Albany since before the French and Indian War (1756–1763). While the
McManus ancestors came from Ireland and served in the colonial militia,
the Kuntz family was not noted for its military service. In 1709, the Kuntz
family migrated from the Palatinate along the Rhine to London, where
they lived in tents. The British government shipped thirty thousand of
these religious refugees as indentured servants to Ireland, Jamaica, and
to mainland colonies in New York, Maryland, the Carolinas, Georgia,
and Pennsylvania, where they retained their culture as the Pensylvania
Dutch.[2]

In 1710, Jane's great-great-grandparents, Mathias and Margaretha Kuntz, collected naval stores of pine tar and timber for the stock company that financed their voyage to New York. The following year Jane's great-grandfather, Johann David Kuntz (1711–1788), was born at West Camp located ten miles upriver from Fort Albany, where his parents were indentured to Col. Robert Livingston. According to family lore the young couple survived that winter because they crossed the Hudson River to a native village where local Indians fed and clothed them. About two hundred Indians served as scouts for the British and paid token rent to the Dutch patroon who served as their trustee of lands granted them at the time the colony was transferred from the Dutch to the English government. By a 1670 Dutch and English treaty, the Mahican Indians remained at the confluence of the Hudson and Hoosick rivers at Scaticook, a Mahican word spelled various ways, meaning "fork of the river." The Mahican homeland once extended from the Hudson River valley eastward to the Housatonic River valley of Connecticut. In time, Europeans absorbed part of the tribe through marriage, and some Indians took Dutch names and passed into the local culture.[3]

When Jane's great-grandfather Kuntz grew up he settled fifteen miles southeast of the Indian village of Schaghticoke and he too, paid rent to the Van Rensselaer family. Johann Kuntz married Catharina Hagedorn and their son, Phillip Henry Kuntz (1758–1842), was Jane's grandfather Phillip who, as local politics dictated, changed the spelling of the German Kuntz to the English Coens, and to the American Coons. Phillip married Elizabeth Wheeler, a neighbor two farms away, and the couple had nine children, including Catherine (1784–1839), Jane's mother. Catherine was christened in the Lutheran Church at Churchtown in adjoining Columbia County, where the family had moved during the American Revolution.[4]

While her maternal Coons family were conservative and pacifists, Jane's paternal McManus family were liberal and relished warfare. Her great-grandfather Cornelius McManus (1721–?) migrated to America from Ireland, and at age twenty-five served in the Albany militia. He married Rebecca Norton sometime before Jane's grandfather, Hugh McManus (1747–1826), was born. During the French and Indian War, Cornelius served in the Albany militia and fought alongside local Indian allies. Too young to fight in the French and Indian War, Hugh was serving as a corporal in Gen. Stephen L. Schuyler's regiment of

Albany militia when Jane's father, William Telemachus McManus (1780–1835), was born during the American Revolution. Hugh had married Mary (1751–1834) about 1776, and no public or private records list Mary's birthplace or surname. She was possibly a member of the local Indian tribe fighting with the rebels against the British. Hugh may have met Mary while on campaign.[5]

While the local Mahicans had served the British as scouts and auxiliaries during the French and Indian War (1756–1763), in the American Revolution (1776–1783) they were loyal to the United States. They served as rangers, irregulars, spies, and soldiers. With their women camping with them, Mahicans fought at Lexington, Bunker Hill, White Plains, and Barren Hill. They helped defeat Gen. John Burgoyne at the Battle of Saratoga (1777), which was actually fought nearer the village of Scaticook than Saratoga. They had a personal interest in defeating Burgoyne because he, like the French in previous wars, used the Hurons and Mohawks as terrorists, thereby creating prejudice against all Indians. After the American Revolution the democratic structure and terminology of the Mahicans and their Delaware cousins became the basis of the Tammany Society. Organized by Aaron Burr, who fought alongside the Indians in the revolution, the order protected the suffrage and property rights of common soldiers from Alexander Hamilton and the Federalists, who sought to remove these rights.[6]

In the atmosphere of equality created by the new republic, the McManus family had expectations of rising socially through education, hard work, and thrift. Jane's father, William T. McManus, attended Lansingburgh Academy and studied law with John Bird in Troy. He married Catherine Coons only three months before their first child, Phillip Telemachus Coons McManus, was born in May 1805. When Jane was eighteen months old, Nicholas Wheeler Hugh McManus was born on the same leased Van Rensselaer farm as Jane. By 1812, when Robert Orson William McManus was born, Jane's family lived in Troy. Her father served in the first year of the War of 1812 as a second lieutenant in the Fourth Battery, Troy City Flying Artillery, First New York State Militia. He was a versatile man who practiced law, surveyed, was a stockholder in the Farmer's State Bank, managed the family-owned brickyard, and kept the extended family's business accounts. The surviving "William McManus Account Book, 1810–1816" provides detailed information about the family's business and daily life.[7]

Certain business activities suggest that the McManus family was connected to the local Indian tribe. In 1812, Aaron Burr represented the Van Rensselaer family against the City of Albany trying to gain possession of Indian lands held in trust by the descendants of the original Dutch patroon. That year McManus drew petitions, served subpoenas, took affidavits, and he and his mother had extensive business in Albany. The McManus family later reimbursed Van Rensselaer for legal expenses, and shortly thereafter, McManus paid for land surveys and he ceased paying the annual token rent to Van Rensselaer equaling the amount of twenty-two bushels of buckwheat, four fat hens, and one day's service. He also repaid a small debt plus compounded interest that had been held by his father-in-law, Phillip Coons, for many years.[8]

William McManus left hints that he, too, was close to the Mahican culture. The family account ledger indicated that he had business at Schaghticoke and listed Indians, disbursements for criers, rituals, and runners, as well as payments to persons with Dutch names known to have been taken by Indians. An honored position of the Mahicans was that of messenger, or crier, who spread news of danger and current events. This official tribal spokesperson was called the owl, a position gained by merit because of a strong memory and good speaking ability. The owl sat beside the sachem, the civil chief of the tribe, and proclaimed orders to the people. The sachem was a hereditary position descended through the female line and the oldest female tribal member who was in charge of the tribe's peace and diplomacy. Mahican women often married younger men and they obtained divorces through a council of women. During her lifetime Jane exhibited these same cultural traits. As a journalist she referred to herself as the "Owl of Fulton Street," she married a younger man, represented her family as their leader, counseled government leaders, and participated in diplomatic affairs.[9]

In addition to involvement in business affairs, Jane's grandmother, Mary McManus, showed a persistence of Indian folkways. For example, Mahican women owned property, spoke in council, and conducted business. Ledger entries revealed that Mary McManus made loans and dealt in real estate—an unusual circumstance. In New York everything a woman owned became her husband's upon marriage unless otherwise protected by a prenuptial agreement. Upon her death in 1834, Mary left property to family members in Connecticut and Western New York while her husband owned no real estate.[10]

Jane's most striking physical trait was her dark complexion, and Mary McManus likely passed that characteristic on to her granddaughter. Jane's skin coloring could explain an inferiority complex that was the source of her driving ambition and a career in journalism spent primarily amid the darker-skinned republicans of the Caribbean, Mexico, and Central America. Unfortunately, no photographs, drawings, or portraits are known to exist of Jane. She never considered herself beautiful. Descriptions of contemporaries, however, portrayed her as a "Spanish looking woman" with violet eyes. On official documents Jane described herself as dark complexioned. Although Jane wrote about local Indian history on her many travels she never admitted having a Native American ancestry, but it was unlikely that she would do so in an era when many people had the opinion that the "only good Indian was a dead Indian."[11]

The family account ledger also suggests that Jane was perhaps her grandmother's favorite grandchild. Whereas her brothers attended school in Troy at a combined cost of five dollars per month to their father, Mary McManus financed Jane's early education in Connecticut, where traditional Mahicans had sent their daughters to boarding school. From 1812 to 1816, when the family account book ended, Mary paid $12.50 each month to Sarah Starr for Jane's training. While attending school in Litchfield County, Connecticut, Jane lived with her father's youngest sister, Brittania McManus Sherman, and her husband, Lemuel Hawley Sherman, who owned a toll bridge. There Jane formed a lifelong friendship with Ann Sophia Winterbotham (1810–1886), the author and editor, better known as Ann S. Stephens. Ann, like Jane, also lived with an aunt, but Ann attended school in South Britain, five miles north of the Sherman residence in Brookfield.[12]

During the War of 1812, Jane's father purchased meat from the local cannery owned by Samuel Wilson, who was called "Uncle Sam" by the townspeople of Troy. During the war, Sam packed meat for the nearby army depot and marked the barrels "U.S." Workers joked that the initials stood for Uncle Sam. As the joke spread among the soldiers, a new symbol emerged for the United States and replaced that of Columbia, the Indian maiden of the Revolutionary War era, and Brother Jonathan, the republican offspring of John Bull. Uncle Sam represented the changing attitudes toward the government, women, Indians, and Great Britain. During the War of 1812, Britain again used Indian allies as terrorists and further heightened prejudice toward all Indians.[13]

Jane seemed to have a perfect childhood. She had a doting grandmother, a father who spoiled her, and a local culture that gave rise to
magical stories such as "Rip Van Winkle," "The Legend of Sleepy
Hollow," and "The Night Before Christmas." With sleigh rides, silk for
dresses, bonnets, and private schooling, Jane's childhood appeared to be
as perfect as a Currier and Ives print of a peaceful Hudson River scene.
The McManus household was not all joy. In February 1813, four-year-old
Nicholas died, less than six months after Jane left for school in
Connecticut and two months after Robert was born. The day after his
son's death, McManus shipped several books to five-year-old Jane, pre-
sumably to console her about the sad news. No clues explain why
Nicholas died, but at that same time neighbors and relatives died of
typhoid fever. In 1813, Troy had a population of less than five thousand
persons, while six thousand soldiers camped nearby. The United States
Arsenal lay across the Hudson, and Gen. Henry Dearborn's army used
Greenbush, a few miles from Troy, as a staging area for transport up the
Hudson River. With the fighting a little over a hundred miles upriver on
Lake Champlain the war seemed very near. During the war the powder
mill operated by the Indians at Schaghticoke blew up and shattered windows for miles around, but glass workers at Sand Lake provided more
windowpanes and life went on.[14]

William McManus seemed a kind and unselfish father who had his
boots mended while a shoemaker made new shoes for his family. On
Christmas Eve, 1815, McManus burned candles to Saint Nicholas. For the
first time, he made no ledger entry on Christmas Day. At no time had he
listed religious activities in the family account book, other than when his
mother attended a drowned land ritual that was a rite of passage where
Indian girls proved their marriageability by locating arrowroots underwa-
ter in winter. Although the McManus ancestors were christened in the
Episcopal Church, the Kuntz family in the Dutch Reformed Church, and
Jane, her mother, and father in the Lutheran, by 1822, William McManus
was a founder of the First Restorationist Church of Troy. The next year,
the congregation changed the name to the First Universalist Church in
honor of the Universal Friend, Jemima Wilkinson (1752–1819). In 1788,
Wilkinson had formed a colony amid the Indians in Western New York
where the British still maintained forts. She became a national hero by
establishing a United States claim to that area.[15] Jane would later become
a member of the Catholic Church.

Neither Jane, her brothers, nor her son, ever mentioned Catherine Wheeler Coons McManus. Jane described her Aunt Brittania as "the dearest guide of my youth." Catherine showed little interest in the domestic arts of home or family. Jane's father paid for a washerwoman, a cleaning woman, and paid also for flax washing, spinning, weaving, cutting, and sewing clothes. The account book showed that Catherine received cash almost daily, but seldom for necessities. McManus paid the grocer bill and his monthly tab for food and drink at Moulton's Tavern. While Jane's father worked, read, and spent his spare time at the tavern, her mother shopped and purchased patent medicine. In addition to having an unforgiving father, a dominant mother-in-law, and a workaholic husband, the family accounts suggest that Catherine showed symptoms of mental illness—a characteristic affecting her maternal Wheeler and Edwards families and one passed on to Jane's son.[16]

As Jane matured, she witnessed the process of gradual emancipation in New York and believed it was a solution that would work in all the slave labor states. Emancipation began in New York in 1799; all male slaves upon reaching age twenty-eight, and all females at age twenty-five were to be freed. No slavery was to exist in New York after July 4, 1827, and during the interim many slaveholders profited and sold their slaves for transport down the Ohio River. Although black codes were proposed, none passed, and New York allowed suffrage, jury service, and intermarriage up to 1848. With full citizenship rights, the black population of New York soared, but with the emancipation of large numbers of unskilled workers, the status of free blacks declined as trade guilds barred them from membership. Although Jane's grandfather Hugh McManus listed three slaves in 1800, the family had no slaves during her lifetime. As an attorney her father received payments for creating both indenture and bondage release papers.[17]

During Jane's teenage years her father held several local political offices. He served as Troy's first surveyor and city engineer, surrogate judge, and district attorney. William Marcy studied law under Judge McManus, and in 1816, the future governor, U.S. senator, secretary of war, and secretary of state, was elected Troy's first city recorder. Marcy once filled in for McManus at a political rally with a stirring speech that launched his political career.[18]

Beginning in 1817, the construction of the Erie Canal brought temporary wealth to the McManus family as the Farmer's State Bank paid dividends on stock and interest on deposits. When the Panic of 1819 hit, the Farmer's State Bank failed, and in 1820, Mary transferred land to William to cover liabilities. As a means of improving the local economy, in 1821, the city of Troy purchased the bankrupt Moulton Coffee House, formerly Moulton's Tavern, and converted the structure into the Troy Female Seminary. Emma Willard's school for women was the first women's college that provided women with an education somewhat comparable to that of men.[19]

A broadside promoting the institute listed Miss Jane M. McManus as one of 138 young women attending the 1824–1825 school term. Fifty-two young women listed their home address as Troy, and the majority came from New York and neighboring states. Elizabeth Cass and Catherine Sibley attended from Michigan Territory, and Jane Skinner traveled from Georgia, while the Krause and Van Brakle women lived in the West Indies. The institute emphasized manners, morals, self-help, baking, and simple dress in addition to such subjects as algebra, geometry, mineralogy, zoology, astronomy, chemistry, philosophy, history, maps, French, Italian, Spanish, German, Greek, drawing, and painting. Willard taught that women should be useful to themselves and others. She impressed upon the students the idea that well-educated mothers steeped in the ideals of republicanism formed the character of citizens. In turn, students learned that the federal government had a duty to promote the present and future prosperity of the nation. American classical republicanism stipulated that citizens should exercise public and civic virtue, subordinate their private needs to the public good, participate in government, and remain free of the will of others. In addition, all citizens were equal under a representative system of laws.[20]

Inspired by the success of Willard's Seminary, in 1824 the city of Troy purchased the bankrupt Farmer's State Bank Building to house the Rensselaer School for men. The institute was not the equivalent of Willard's Seminary but an outgrowth of the building of the Erie Canal, which had shown the need for technical training. Initially, ten to twelve boys had an intense one-year technical and science program taught by Prof. Amos Eaton and financed by Stephen Van Rensselaer. While Jane's brothers entered the school, only Philip graduated in 1826 as an agriculturalist. Robert argued with the professor over some matter and left school to become a surveyor.[21]

In the 1820s Jane's father helped organize the People's Party of Rensselaer County, a group that consisted of mostly tenant farmers and factory workers. They voted for Andrew Jackson for president in 1824, and although Jackson won the popular vote, he did not carry the electoral college and he lost in Congress when the House of Representatives settled the election. Local Rep. Stephen Van Rensselaer, a Federalist, cast the deciding vote for John Quincy Adams. Locally, the elite lost control of the government. The agrarians of Rensselaer County elected William McManus to represent them in the United States Congress (1825–1827). During his one term in Washington McManus proposed a constitutional amendment for the election of the president by a popular vote of the simple majority of the voters. His proposal attracted the attention of John C. Calhoun of South Carolina, but got no farther with politicians dependent on the patronage system. In 1826, McManus, a Mason, was defeated by anti-Masonic Federalists organized to defeat the anti-rent Indians of New York, who were trying to get titles to land held by their trustees since before the French and Indian War.[22]

Because Jane had skills she later used as a secretary and bookkeeper, it is likely she developed those skills working in her father's law office. While McManus was in Washington, the eighteen-year-old Jane became romantically involved with Allen B. Storm, who was studying law under her father's direction. Consequently, Jane did not graduate from Willard's Seminary. A marriage notice in the Troy *Sentinel* announced that on August 22, 1825, Miss McManus, daughter of Representative McManus, married Allen B. Storm, also of Troy, in the First Universalist Church. From 1826 until 1832, the Troy City Directory listed Storm as an attorney on Second Street at the same address as McManus's law office. According to the registrar's records at Rensselaer Institute, on August 2, 1826, Jane gave birth to a son, William McManus Storm.[23]

Further details of Jane Storm's life remain a mystery until 1832. After that year Allen Storm was no longer listed in Troy business directories and Jane resumed her maiden name and began keeping account books for Anthony Dey, director of the Galveston Bay and Texas Land Company, in New York. No divorce record can be found, and nothing more is known of Storm until his death in New York City in 1838. In the 1850s, Jane published "A Gauntlet for Men" in the Washington *Daily States* that provides a clue to her failed marriage. "What does a woman do who has had a bad, improvident husband?" She answered:

> She works all the harder to make up his deficiencies . . . works day and
> night . . . smiles when her heart is breaking. Grits her teeth at fate, and
> defy it to do its worst, because they chattered so . . . speaks hopeful words

when her soul is dying . . . denies herself . . . to increase her child's portion . . . and crushed neither by poverty nor lured by temptation, hopeful-
ly puts her trust in Him who feedeth the sparrows. . . . Poor fellow! . . .
fond of wine but had to drink beer, rushed out of the world and left his
wife and children to battle with the fate his coward soul was afraid to
meet.[24]

By late 1832, Jane McManus had begun to visit Aaron Burr in his apartment over his law office in Jersey City. Gore Vidal, who based the novel *Burr*
on the memoirs of Burr's associate, Charles Schulyer, portrayed Jane as a
central figure in the aging Burr's life. Vidal described Jane in the novel as a
large, blond, heavy-set woman with an Irish brogue. In reality, Jane
McManus Storm was five-feet, three-inches tall, dark complexioned, and
dark haired. Vidal portrayed Burr and Jane as lovers and insinuated that
Burr had also been intimate with Mary McManus. Jane's grandmother and
Burr likely knew one another. Burr served in the same military campaigns
as Hugh McManus, and as New York's first land commissioner he dispensed
New York's public land as payment to Revolutionary War soldiers. Also, he
aided the family in getting title to land held by Van Rensselaer. Whatever
gossip may or may not have been true, in 1831, Jane and Burr were working on a project whereby the McManus family had the opportunity to
acquire large amounts of land in Mexican Texas at little expense.[25]

The McManus family was taking advantage of an opportunity created
by Moses Austin and his son Stephen Fuller Austin. Moses Austin, a former lead mine operator in Spanish-controlled Missouri, who had been
ruined by the Panic of 1819, had received permission from Spanish
authorities in 1821 to settle three hundred former Spanish Louisiana subjects in the province of Texas. Moses Austin died of pneumonia in June
1821 and Mexico gained its independence before Austin could bring settlers to Texas. Texas Gov. Antonio Martinez, who had handled the transition from Spanish province to Mexican statehood, assured Stephen F.
Austin that the Mexican government would honor his father's empresario
contract. After a year of waiting in Mexico City for the Mexican national
government to act, Austin and other land agents received permission and
guidelines for settling vacant land in Texas. As word spread, Texas
became a magnet for men and women when as head of their household
they received title to 4,605 acres of land by paying survey and registration
fees of $192. At that time public land in the United States sold in blocks
of eighty acres for $100 paid in gold.[26]

Immigrants from the United States poured into Texas during the 1820s to take advantage of the inexpensive land. Alarmed by the growing population of Anglos and their lack of adherence to Mexican law, the Mexican national government on April 6, 1830, restricted immigration from the United States. Thereafter, only Europeans or Mexicans could settle in Texas. Anthony Dey, Jane's employer, had combined the empresario grants of an American, David G. Burnet, a German, Joseph Vehlein, and a Mexican, Lorenzo de Zavala, and formed the Galveston Bay and Texas Land Company. The purpose of the company was to promote European settlement to the thirteen million acres covering twenty present-day East Texas counties. The area stretched from the Louisiana border westward to the San Jacinto River and from the Gulf of Mexico to north of Nacogdoches. Although it was against Mexican law to do so, the company carried out the common practice in the United States of selling land scrip for five cents an acre to prospects who reserved the right to settle a certain number of acres within their designated area.[27]

Soon after she began working for Dey, in September and October 1832, Jane McManus and her younger brother, Robert, received Galveston Bay and Texas Land Company scrip. Robert's certificates were sent to Troy in care of U.S. Sen. William L. Marcy. Jane then proposed to the company trustees that she sell scrip in England and Ireland while Robert serve as company agent and surveyor in Texas. Dey, aware of her persuasive powers, issued her a power of attorney to do so, but the other trustees, William H. Sumner and George Curtis, rejected her proposal. They recommended that Robert be hired, however, as surveyor for the company in the area of Nacogdoches where Mexican land commissioner George N. Nixon represented the state of Coahuila y Tejas and authorized possession of land by settlers. Dey's records of the Galveston Bay and Texas Land Company stockholders, their addresses, the amount of stock they held, and company expenses were entered in Jane McManus's distinctive handwriting, with an incomplete upper loop on the letter "d." Whether she sold those shares listed by her hand is not clear. She also entered expenses of Dey's Florida Spanish Moss Company.[28]

The exact nature of the relationship between McManus and Burr where Texas lands were concerned may never be known, but Burr and Judge McManus were fraternal brothers and political allies. According to Dey's records, neither Burr nor Jane's father owned shares in the Galveston Bay and Texas Land Company. Jane later claimed that she and

Burr translated promotional materials into the German language. Dey had land scrip and a guidebook printed in German, and a printer's proof of the pamphlet in his records directed immigrants from LeHavre to New Orleans up the Red River and across the Texas border to Nacogdoches, where scrip would be exchanged for land. *Texas und Einlandung zu einer vortheilhaften Unsiedelung daselbt* (1835), by a Mexican citizen, offered the advantages of settlement in Texas. Burr had visited the German states during his exile in Europe and perhaps he stirred German interest in Texas.[29]

In 1832, Jane's grandmother Mary made her will, and at eighty-one years of age she did not mention her favorite granddaughter. The omission may have been to prevent Allen Storm from laying claim to his wife's inheritance as they were perhaps still legally married at that time. In Texas, Spanish law allowed married women to own separate property. At this time Robert and Jane McManus made plans to travel to Texas and acquire land for their extended family. Before she left New York in November 1832, Burr warned Jane that her enterprise had "the air of Romance and Quixotteism [*sic*]," but he added that it was not without precedent. He reminded her of Jemima Wilkinson, the young woman who had established a similiar colony in western New York shortly after the American Revolution.[30]

Around mid-November 1832, Jane and Robert McManus traveled from New York to New Orleans, where they met Burr's former partner in intrigue, Judge James Workman. Workman, an Englishman and former resident of Charleston, was a member of the Mexican Association, which he, Louis Kerr, David Clark, and Edward Livingston organized after the Louisiana Purchase did not include Texas. The three hundred-member group planned to liberate Texas from Spain. Burr, Workman, Burr's secretary Samuel Swartwout and others were among those who had been tried for treason in 1807, but then acquitted for lack of evidence. Burr's recruits had received land in Arkansas and Louisiana that had been acquired by Phillip de Neri, the Baron de Bastrop. In 1821, the baron assisted Moses Austin in obtaining the empresario grant in Texas for three hundred Louisiana settlers, which led to the Anglo settlement of Texas. Officially, Judge Workman translated Louisiana Spanish laws written in French into English for American judges to interpret. Unofficially, he directed immigration into Mexican Texas.[31]

In his letter of introduction to Workman, Burr introduced Jane McManus as "A Lady!" and "a woman of business." Burr assured Workman that she could "send out one or two hundred substantial settlers in less time . . . than any man or half a Dozen men whom I this day Know." Burr explained that Jane McManus was her family's pioneer and agent, and he requested that Workman write letters of introduction to Colonel Austin. In glowing terms Burr invited Workman to form his opinion of "her talents and of her competency." Burr thought she was "eminently qualified" and had "that peculiar discernment or tact in the Character and disposition of men—a talent peculiar to her sex." According to Burr, Jane "also had (which is more rare) courage, Stability and perseverance. . . . But enough," Burr advised, "Judge for yourself and act accordingly." Impressed by Burr's introduction of his protégé or by Jane's charm and intelligence, Workman wrote contacts in Texas to expect the potential buyers from New York. In December 1832, Jane and Robert McManus sailed from New Orleans to Mexican Texas.[32]

Sir,

In applying for the privilige of locating my claim in whole or in part in the Coast-Colony, I have two distinct objects in view — One is to secure if possible some land (and the more the better) on the Peninsula of Matagorda — as I intend to reside there — The other is to obtain at least one league not deficient in wood and water and if possible on or near some of the streams that empty into [...] da Bay that emigrants may get it even in the rainy season without being subjected to long and expensive delays after reaching Matagorda — These points as well as the business in general are however confi-ded absolutely to the judgement of J. M. Lewis Esq who is fully possessed of the very imperfect views I have been able to make up from the data within my reach —

Very Respectfully
Jane M. McManus

N. Orleans July 29. '34

Jane McManus became involved in Texas emigration schemes in the 1830s and was well connected to the Anglo-Texan leadership. Jane McManus, New Orleans, July 29, 1834, to Saml. M. Williams, Esq., New Orleans. Jane Cazneau papers, box 2B141. *Courtesy Cazneau Papers, CN01474, Center for American History, University of Texas at Austin.*

CHAPTER II

Texas, 1832–1840

∾✼∿

As a female—I cannot bear arms for my adopted country—but if the interest I possess in her soil, will be a
guarantee for any money, I will with joy contribute my
mite to the purchase of arms for her brave defenders.
—*Jane M. McManus (1836)*[1]

*W*HEN JANE AND ROBERT MCMANUS ARRIVED IN TEXAS IN DECEMBER
1832, the Mexican government was in turmoil, and conflicts that would
escalate into revolution had begun. In June, Texans clashed with Mexican
troops at Anahuac and Velasco. For defying Mexican authority and organizing a Mexican militia, Kentucky-born Mexican Col. Juan D. Bradburn
had arrested William B. Travis and Patrick Jack. The Battle of Velasco
occurred when friends coming to the aid of Travis in Anahuac encountered Mexican resistance at the fort at the mouth of the Brazos River. Jane
and her brother came to Texas for a fresh start and to take advantage of
the liberal land policies of the Mexican government, but instead, they
became caught up in the forces of revolution and in the aftermath of conflict over land claims. Jane did not find wealth in Texas, but returned to
New York and found her place as a journalist and political analyst.[2]

The conflict between the Texans and the Mexican government
emanated from more than a clash of cultures as Jane McManus suggested
in her first book *Texas and Her Presidents* (1845), a history, geography, and
guidebook that she wrote for investors and settlers. The issues involved
Mexican centralists, federalists, Anglo immigration, and slavery. A federalist Congress had created the Constitution of 1824, which gave Mexican

states the right to dispose of public land within their borders. Because of its sparse population Texas was combined with Coahuila and the vast territory governed from Saltillo. Stephen F. Austin and other Texas empresarios then received additional contracts for settlement from state authorities under the state colonization law of March 1825. At first settlers from the United States brought their slaves with them with no adverse consequences, but Mexican liberals disliked the American form of slavery with no way out. Austin protected the labor supply of his colony when the issue came up in the state legislature in 1828, and his settlers brought slaves to Texas as indentured servants for life. Meanwhile, the national government also took action against slavery. As a symbolic gesture, in 1829, President Vicenté Ramón Guerérro abolished slavery by executive decree. By 1830, federal law abolished slavery. After eight months in office, opponents removed Guerérro, and the centralist Vice President Anastacio Bustamente served two years before Antonio López de Santa Anna called for a revolt that coincided with the 1832 Anahuac disturbances. Consequently, in July 1832, when federalist Col. José Antonio Mexía arrived at Anahuac with Mexican troops from Matamoros to put down the revolt led by Travis, he celebrated Santa Anna's victory with the Texans. In support of Santa Anna, the Anglo settlers issued the Turtle Bayou Resolutions in which they pledged their lives and their fortunes to uphold the Mexican Constitution of 1824.[3]

To further complicate Texas matters, in February 1831 authorities in Saltillo had granted the sparsely settled area of the Robert Leftwich Grant, or Nashville Colony, to Austin for settlement. The area extended two hundred miles upriver from Austin's four other colonies that lay between the Colorado and Brazos Rivers. Austin instructed his assistant Samuel May Williams to locate three eleven-league grants for Austin, but otherwise left development to Williams in lieu of salary. To keep his services, Austin made him a partner in the venture, and the area was renamed the Austin and Williams Colony, but simply called the upper colony in their correspondence (see Map 1).[4]

By the time the McManuses arrived in Texas in December 1832, Austin had sold his interest in the upper colony and in some other areas to Capt. John Austin, a distant cousin. A month before the McManuses' arrival in Texas, Williams had ordered the survey of nineteen eleven-league grants in the new colony. After checking several possibilities, the McManus siblings agreed to purchase one of these grants. Unbeknownst

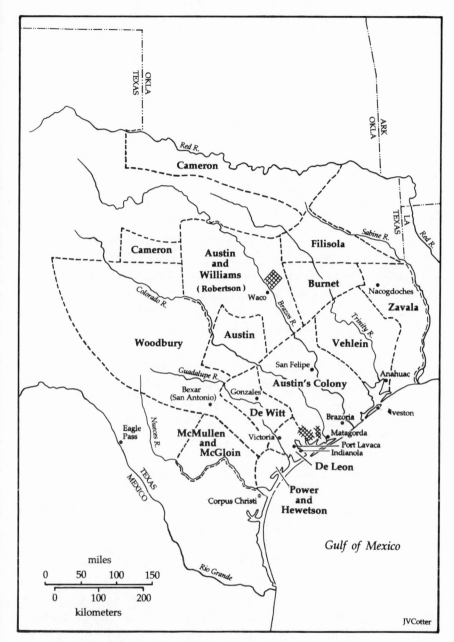

MAP 1: Texas Land Grants. The shaded areas near Matagorda and Waco represent the approximate location of the McManus land claims.

TABLE 1

SPANISH LAND MEASUREMENTS AND THEIR EQUIVALENTS

Eleven square leagues=48,712.4 acres
One square league=4,428.2 acres=25 labors=5,000 varas
One square labor=177.1 acres=1,000 varas
One square mile=640 acres
One vara=33.3 inches
One acre=208.71 square feet
One statute mile=5,280 feet

SOURCE: General Land Office of Texas.

to them, however, Sterling C. Robertson, representing the Nashville Company, had arrived from Tennessee in December 1832. In an attempt to regain control of the area Robertson was taking depositions from settlers to prove that it was not unsettled when reassigned to Austin.[5]

Williams and John Austin located the eleven-league state land grants of 48,712 acres for fifty pesos per league plus surveying fees (see Table 1). On January 22, 1833, Charles Sayre, who had come from New York the year before and owned a store in Brazoria, informed Williams that the "New York Commission" had arrived. Two weeks later he wrote to Williams that Jane McManus was visiting San Felipe to finalize a purchase. He was "much pleased with her" and described her as "a very intelligent Lady." Sayre urged Williams to hurry the forms because Jane McManus wished to return to New Orleans with Capt. Samuel Fuller, who transported trade goods regularly to Texas and hides and cotton back to New Orleans on the schooner *Nelson*.[6]

It is not clear at this point if the McManus siblings were part of a larger plan to settle Texas for the Galveston Bay and Texas Land Company or its satellite companies. It appeared as if they were merely seeking cheap land for speculation and for their extended New York family that had not recovered from the panic of 1819, plus those Indians forced by Congress to leave New York after 1830. Regardless of their motives, by February 8, 1833, Jane and Robert had arrived in San Felipe, the headquarters of Austin's colonies up the Brazos River from Brazoria. About thirty single and double log cabins were located on a high bluff. Williams operated the land office out of his home, where he lived with his wife and children. Austin's original headquarters had been sold and enlarged into

Whiteside's Hotel operated by Jonathan Peyton and his wife Angelina, who were two of Austin's first colonists. They, too, invested in an eleven-league grant in the upper colony. Jane McManus probably stayed at the inn, for she became friends with Angelina. Jane wrote fondly of the Texas pioneer for the next twenty years.[7]

The day the McManus family representatives arrived in San Felipe, Williams transferred an eleven-league grant held by Samuel Sawyer to Doña Jane M. McManus. Sawyer had a position similar to that of Anthony Dey—Jane's New York employer—with several Texas land speculation companies. The transfer document contained the signature of Luke Lessasieur, the local alcalde, or mayor, and Isaac Jones and W. Barret Travis witnessed it. Travis then resided in San Felipe where he practiced law, gambled, and kept a tally of female conquests. As his surviving diary does not begin until the following August, it is not known if Jane McManus was one of his "amorous adventures." She never mentioned meeting Travis in any of her correspondence.[8]

Although Jane McManus had converted to Catholicism in New York sometime after her marriage failed and before she came to Texas, she declared her faith and loyalty to Mexico. As a Mexican citizen, she received the maximum amount of land a Mexican citizen could own. Land possession in Mexico was a more complicated process than in the United States, and a situation requiring clarification. The national Law of April 6, 1830, limited Anglo settlement and stated that only Mexicans could own land—the reason McManus declared herself a Mexican citizen. Coahuila y Texas state law set the maximum amount of land that an individual could own at eleven square leagues. In 1830, the state had issued a number of the large grants to finance the state government. The intention was that Mexicans would purchase and locate the grants on unoccupied land or issue a power of attorney to others to do so. After paying survey and registration fees, local land commissioners granted possession of the land to the holder of the grant. These land grants became a source of speculation in the United States, and were passed from speculator to speculator. Because the new colony of Austin and Williams had less than one hundred families no land commissioner had been appointed, and the nearest alcalde, or magistrate, certified the documents. Jane and Robert McManus probably paid two thousand dollars for the grant because a week earlier Robert McAlpin "Three Legged Willie" Williamson quoted that amount to his client in Montgomery, Edward Hanrick, director of the Alabama Land

Company. Williamson informed the syndicate administrator that only four of the large grants were left.[9]

The eleven-league grant that Jane McManus purchased had originally been issued to Perfecto Valdez by the state of Coahuila y Tejas on July 13, 1830. Within two weeks, on July 29, Valdez transferred his power of attorney to Samuel Bangs and Isaac Donoho. Bangs was an associate of Benjamin Lundy, who planned a free black colony in Texas, and Donoho was a Santa Fe trader from Missouri. Samuel Sawyer had purchased the Perfecto Valdez grant from Bangs and Donoho a month before Jane's arrival. Williams had ordered it surveyed on the Brazos River a month before their arrival in Texas. Field Notes in the Spanish Collection of the Texas General Land Office show that William Moore and his assistants surveyed the grant the following May specifically for Jane McManus exactly where Williams had previously instructed, slightly above the Waco Indian Village and across from the mouth of the Bosque River.[10]

Jane and Robert possibly visited the Waco area before they purchased the grant. Although most buyers of eleven-league grants were speculators and did not normally inspect their land, Williams later testified in court that some did. The grant at Waco was not as remote as it appeared. Settlements existed along the two hundred miles up the Brazos River from San Felipe to the Waco Indian village. Above Austin's headquarters lay Groce's Landing at the Coushatta Indian crossing. Next, Andrew Robinson had a ferry near the mouth of the Navasota River on the Spanish La Bahía Road. Farther upstream, a trading post identified the abandoned Mexican Fort Tenoxtitlan at the crossing of the Old San Antonio Road. At the falls of the Brazos, Francis Smith had a trading post where the Comanche Trail ran eastward to Nacogdoches. Another twenty-odd miles upriver was what remained of the Waco Indian village. In 1829, mixed-blood Cherokee farmers from Tennessee, including the Chisholm family, had killed most of the Waco and Tehuacano Indians after the Waco Indians had raided the farms of the mixed bloods living along the Red River. John Boyd, one of the Cherokee half-breeds, remained on the Brazos and had a blacksmith shop in the Cherokee settlement about four miles below the Waco village. Perhaps Jane McManus had planned to settle her extended family alongside the civilized Indians all along; a possibility that would explain Burr's comparing her venture to that of Jemima Wilkinson in western New York.[11]

Before Jane left San Felipe, Williams created a power of attorney for Robert McManus to act in his sister's absence. Robert had loaned Jane the money to purchase the large grant in her name as the head of their family household. The brother and sister were to share their land purchase and each of their headrights as settlers. Robert began surveying with John Austin in the area of the Trinity River for the Trinity Land Company, one of the satellite companies created out of the Galveston Bay and Texas Land Company holdings. Jane returned to Brazoria and presumably sailed to New Orleans with Captain Fuller. By May 20, 1833, she was in New York and entered expenses in Dey's ledger.[12]

McManus was not the only woman to hold an eleven-league grant in Texas. A grant in the name of María de la Concepción Márquez was located in present-day Leon County. Moreover, of the 4,313 first class headrights of one league and one labor, or 4,605.5 acres, issued by the General Land Office of Texas for heads of households who settled in Texas prior to independence, 4 percent, or 176, were women. Women came because of cheap land, or to control their own destinies under *Las Siete Partidas*, the thirteenth-century Spanish law that allowed married women to own and control separate property. Mary Austin Holley, propagandist for her cousin's colonies, urged women to come to Texas where "more Dianas and Ester [*sic*] Stanhopes than one" existed, and women could be "free spirits" and have a "capacity for greatness."[13]

While Jane was in New York and making arrangement to return with settlers, William H. Wharton presided over a convention of Texans held in April 1833. The repercussions altered forever Jane McManus's plans. Delegates drew up a petition to be presented to the Mexican national government in Mexico City in which they asked that the tariff exemption be extended another year, and they requested separate statehood. In addition, they asked for repeal of the section of the Law of April 6, 1830, forbidding Anglo immigration. Stephen F. Austin, who understood the political atmosphere in the capitol more than any other Anglo in Texas, agreed to carry the petition to Mexico City. He journeyed by way of Matamoros, where he remained for some days because he contracted cholera. While recovering Austin learned that land speculations in the upper colony had ruined his reputation with Mexican authorities. On May 31, 1833, Austin wrote to tell Williams to locate no more eleven-league grants and "keep clear of *all* speculations." He was concerned about any publicity over slavery. In Austin's letter to Williams he specifically named Jim Bowie and Ben Fort Smith. The latter had been caught trying to smuggle slaves into Texas. Austin's anguish is apparent as he condemned that "cursed foolish trip" to Cuba for slaves that had called attention to Texas.[14]

While Austin carried the petition for statehood to the Mexican capital, Williams traveled to Mobile. He met with Edward Hanrick, director of the Alabama Land Company—a syndicate financed by the Bank of the United States to develop cotton land on a commercial scale in Texas with slave labor. Hanrick introduced Williams to James W. Fannin—a man Hanrick described as "desperate," and with "nothing to lose and all to gain." Fannin would smuggle slaves from Cuba to Texas for the planters. In Mexico, Austin presented the Texans' petition to Santa Anna, who agreed to all the requests except separate statehood. The Mexican Congress had adjourned because of the spreading cholera epidemic. To cover additional expenses, Williams sent Austin two thousand dollars in letters of credit from Samuel St. John, who was married to Williams's sister Sophia, and who had banking interests in New York.[15]

Back in Texas, on July 14, 1833, Samuel Sawyer wrote to John Austin that Robert McManus was staying with Sawyer on the San Bernard River. In bad health and planning to return to New York, McManus wanted Austin notified that Williams's surveyor, Frank Johnson, was requesting payments for surveys he had not made in the upper colony. Robert also asked that John Austin locate his sister's headright claim as head of the McManus family—4,605.5 acres—on the Trinity River. That summer, John Austin and his children died of cholera, as did Lessasier, Sawyer, countless Texas settlers, six thousand in New Orleans, and sixteen thousand in Mexico City, as an epidemic spread from India to Europe to America. Because of these complications Jane's headright claim was not located. On the last day of August, Williams billed her $150 in fees for the survey of the Valdez grant at Waco. When paid, he would issue her a title of possession, the grant would be finished, and she could bring her family to Texas. Meanwhile, Williams carried her note, presumably, as he did that of others at 5 percent interest plus a service fee.[16]

Because of fraud and traffic in counterfeit eleven-league grants, Jane McManus took her copy of the Perfecto Valdez Grant to the Mexican vice-consulate in New York. On September 21, 1833, August Radcliff certified it to be true and valid. Jane McManus then began indenturing unidentified German immigrants for twelve dollars per year for two years service in return for passage to Texas. In general, Germans came to America at this time because of high unemployment, bad harvests, marginal-sized farms, and a romantic vision of America after republican reforms failed in Germany in 1830.[17]

Since 1821, Germans had migrated to Texas, and by 1826, more than two hundred residents had German surnames. In 1831, fifteen thousand Germans came to the United States, and that year, the Galveston Bay Company had one shipload of almost sixty settlers turned away by Mexican customs officials because of the ban on Anglo settlement and the ship had sailed from New York. Most Germans entering New Orleans settled in Missouri, but a few came to Texas. One group camped near Anahuac. On Mill Creek, in present-day Austin County, Germans had a colony, later named Industry, where they raised tobacco and manufactured cigars. In Matagorda, F. W. Grasmeyer operated a general store with William Leslie Cazneau, a Boston cotton buyer. Germans also settled on Cummins Creek in the Frelsburg community. Lorenzo de Zavala, Mexican minister to France, promoted European migration to Texas, as did José Antonio Mexía in Matamoros. Since December 1832, newspapers in Germany had advertised Texas land for sale. In a venture unrelated to that of the McManus family, in June 1833 Johann von Racknitz sailed from Le Havre with two hundred Germans to settle an eight-league grant on the Colorado River near Bastrop. The colony failed because of the cholera epidemic then sweeping the Texas coast and a lack of funds for supplies and transportation inland.[18]

In late September 1833, Jane McManus chartered a vessel to transport her German indentures and supplies from New York to Texas. Charles Sayre, who also was bringing Germans and supplies to Texas, was to share the cost of the ship, but he was delayed and withdrew his freight and passengers. In panic, Jane McManus wrote to her mentor, Aaron Burr, for an additional $250 and pleaded, "I cannot go home, you are aware it drained their means to pay for the land." Burr did not supply the funds, perhaps because his new wife saw the letter before he did. In July, the seventy-seven-year-old Burr had eloped with the fifty-six-year-old widow Madame Eliza Jumel after a whirlwind courtship. Jumel had a questionable reputation and a nasty disposition, but she was rumored to be the richest woman in America. Her fortune had come from her husband's smuggling wine and spirits from France into New York during President Thomas Jefferson's Embargo, a policy that forbid United States vessels to visit French ports. New York marriage laws gave Burr immediate control of Jumel's wealth, and their honeymoon consisted of a tour of her possessions. Before the wedding trip ended, Burr began selling his bride's assets and investing the money in Texas real estate.[19]

Contrary to Eliza Burr's later charges in divorce proceedings, McManus did not receive the funds to carry on with her project from Burr. Jane swallowed her pride and returned to Troy. On October 2, 1833, she deeded five hundred acres of an unidentified and unlocated eleven-league grant to Justus Morton for $250. Although the land was not hers to deed, Morton had a paper deed that he later sold and that eventually appeared in the deed records of Matagorda County, Texas. Morton was Grand Commander of the New York Commandery of Knights Templar and a fraternal brother of Jane's father, William McManus, a thirty-second-degree Mason.[20]

In November 1833, Jane, Robert, Judge McManus, an undisclosed number of German indentures, auctioneers, Logan and C. H. Vandeveer, and unidentified settlers from Kentucky arrived in Matagorda. Elias Wightman and William Selkirk had established the town in 1829 with fifty-two families from New York and New England. Because of a shortage of timber and poor anchorage, the town had grown little.[21]

Although Jane McManus left no memoirs, Annie Fisher Harris recalled when she arrived in Matagorda less than six months before the McManuses. The harbor was not deep enough for ships, so small boats, called lighters, transported freight and passengers to and from the deep water to the landing on the Colorado River. A seven-mile logjam blocked the river's mouth and created a giant marsh. The McManus pilgrims walked two miles into town along a path newly cut through the six-feet-tall marsh grass from which the town derived its Spanish name—a place of reeds. While some settlers lived in sheds, tents, and in the open because of a shortage of timber and lumber, Harris recalled that her mother and siblings shared a room with Judge McManus and his daughter at Grasmeyer's store. Annie described Jane McManus as a "woman adventuress" who was "young and handsome" with letters from important people. According to Harris, Jane McManus was "useful and agreeable," "possessed of much fascination," and she disclosed that Grasmeyer's partner, the Boston cotton-buyer William Leslie Cazneau, was romantically in love with Jane McManus. The countryside around Matagorda was untamed. Karankawa Indians still lived less than a mile from town, and when the women came to trade, they camped beneath the store, which was raised on stilts. The Indian women had Spanish names, yet they wore only animal skin skirts and wreaths of leaves around their necks. During the full moon,

Matagorda residents could hear the Indians singing, and as the Karankawas danced and beat their drums, coyotes howled in the distance.[22]

The German indentures broke their contracts with Jane McManus and refused to go inland. Perhaps they were frightened by Josiah Wilbarger, the local schoolteacher, who was scalped by Comanche Indians while on a survey party upriver and lived to tell about it. They may have gotten word that Robertson was successful in his efforts and the Mexican state government had granted him control of the area of Jane's Waco grant, and Robertson refused to honor transactions made by Williams. Perhaps the Germans learned that they could have land simply by filing a claim at the land office and they preferred to live in the German settlements already established.[23]

Jane's father had additional business in Texas besides accompanying his daughter. Judge McManus served as Samuel Swartwout's Texas agent for his land speculations after Sawyer died of cholera. Swartwout, once Burr's private secretary and in 1833 the United States customs inspector for the Port of New York, held shares in the Galveston Bay and Texas Land Company and in those formerly under Sawyer's direction—the Arkansas and Texas, the Rio Grande and Texas, and Colorado and Red River land companies, which were speculative ventures for marketing land in Texas. Presumably, Judge McManus also handled the preliminaries for the development of the New Washington Association, in which Swartwout also invested. First discussed in 1829, this project was the work of Dr. Thomas Cooley, a social architect, and John R. Bartlett (1805–1886), later founder of the American Ethnological Society. They visited Matagorda in 1833 and selected the 1,600-acre site of Clopper's Point on Galveston Bay for a social experiment to blend Europeans and free blacks in an agricultural and a commercial venture. The directors were Lorenzo de Zavala, John P. Austin, James Treat, Stephen Sicard, James Watson Webb, editor of the New York *Courier and Enquirer*, and Mordecai Noah, editor of the New York *Star*. Joseph L. Joseph was a financier involved in the project, and the general manager was James Morgan, who operated a store at Anahuac for Union and Trinity Land Company settlers. Impressed with his economic development, on March 31, 1834, the city of Matagorda deeded Judge McManus twelve acres of city lots in return for his building a sawmill. In April 1834, Jane and her father returned to New York and she again worked for Dey and entered expenses in his ledgers. In October, the New Washington Association was chartered in New York and began plans for development in Texas.[24]

31

Because of New York's liberal laws, the state's black population had grown by 65 percent in the last decade. In 1830, New York had 44,870 African Americans, or one-third of the black population of all the northern states. Until 1848, blacks with $250 in property could vote and Whigs labeled them "Jackson whites" because they voted Democratic. Free blacks were encouraged to migrate to Liberia and create a black republic in Africa, but British abolitionist George Thompson, funded by the London-based World Anti-Slavery Society, toured the United States and declared the American Colonization Society, "the enemy of the people of color." In Catholic countries and Europe, no stigma was attached to being black. Thus, the New Washington venture, which proposed relocating New York's growing population of unskilled blacks and European immigrants on agricultural land in Mexican Texas, was a viable solution to New York's growing race and immigrant problems.[25]

In July 1834, Jane McManus experienced additional difficulties that delayed her Texas settlement. Grandmother McManus died the first week of July, and within two weeks, on July 12, Eliza Jumel Burr filed for divorce. In the divorce plea Mrs. Burr labeled Jane McManus a divorced woman, and named Jane as the correspondent in the bill of complaint filed against her husband. Burr had sold bridges, land, and buildings, but selling her fine carriage and matched pair of high-stepping horses was the last straw. Ann Stephens, Jane's best friend, later explained that divorce was the only way Mrs. Burr could regain control of her finances. While Mrs. Burr could have used the name of a servant girl, Burr requested that she name someone who would do him honor. Thus, because her letter requesting funds gave proof of his involvement with another woman, Jane McManus became a part of the Burr divorce scandal.[26]

Eliza Burr's attorney was Alexander Hamilton Jr., the son of Burr's famous nemesis. Young Hamilton was a leader of nativist Whigs who formed in opposition to Burr's Tammany Hall Democrats. Using the divorce scandal to their advantage, by association the Whigs connected Burr and the Democrats to an Irish Catholic divorcée, and the seventy thousand Irish Catholics who controlled a growing proportion of New York votes, lower government offices, and street vendor licenses. According to Burr's friends, Eliza Jumel had played a part in the Burr-Hamilton duel by spreading the rumor that Burr's daughter, Theodosia, was also his lover. The elder Hamilton had used the gossip in a nasty political campaign to destroy Burr and the Chase Manhattan Bank, which Burr created as a rival to Hamilton's Bank of the United States. Thus, Burr's marriage was not one of romantic love but provided an opportunity to gain control of a large fortune at a time of rampant speculation in Mexican Texas, where possible fortunes awaited the investors.[27]

By late July 1834, Jane McManus wrote to Williams from New Orleans that her agent, Ira Randolph Lewis of Matagorda, would select eight leagues of land for her along the coast that did not have the problems of the upper colony. The new leagues were not substitutes for the Brazos River land. They were additional ones that Jane and Robert financed by selling their share of the McManus family estate near Troy to their brother, Phillip McManus.[28]

Meanwhile, relations between the Mexican government and the Texans deteriorated. Since January 1834, Austin had been held in prison and under house arrest in Mexico City because in a moment of despair he had requested that officials in San Antonio make plans for separate statehood even though the Mexican government had not approved the request. Austin was caught in the power struggle between centralists and federalists that spread from the capital to the states. By March 1834, the legislature of Coahuila y Tejas had moved from Saltillo, which had many centralists, to federalist Monclova, and sold four hundred unlocated eleven-league grants to arm a state militia. John T. Mason, agent for the Galveston Bay and Texas Land Company, purchased all four hundred of these grants. Meanwhile, President Santa Anna assumed control of the government from federalist Vice President Valentín Gómez Farías when federalist reform policy became unpopular with conservatives. Santa Anna then ordered new state elections, named his brother-in-law, Martín Perfecto de Cós, commander-general of the Mexican Army, closed Congress, and suspended all liberal laws passed by his federalist predecessor.[29]

In November 1834, Jane and Robert McManus planned to return to Texas, but their father was in poor health. On January 18, 1835, William McManus died of a heart attack. Word quickly spread about his death and by the end of January, Swartwout wrote to East Texas surveyor José María Carbajal that Col. Frost Thorn of Nacogdoches had assumed McManus's former duties. In March at the San Felipe land office, Jane's agent Ira Lewis filed for her eight leagues of land near Matagorda. When Jane arrived in June to inspect her acreage she was furious; the land had no timber. She wrote to Williams and explained that she could not attract settlers to land without timber. She complained, "not one has a stick of timber—not even large enough for a walking cane or poles for a mosquitoe [*sic*] bar." One can imagine her outrage as she examined the marshy leagues west of the Colorado River. As for the payment of the survey fees, she wrote to Williams that her brother would handle that when he was done surveying on the Neches River.[30]

At the start of 1835, the political turmoil in Mexico increased at the national and state level. President Santa Anna had ordered the customs houses in Texas reopened in defiance of the Texan's petition that he had previously approved. Meanwhile, two state governments now existed in the state of Coahuila y Tejas; centralists governed from Saltillo and federalists from Monclova. The Monclova federalists sold eight hundred additional eleven-league grants to finance resistance to Santa Anna's arbitrary actions. Three Texans—Samuel May Williams, William Durst, and Dr. James Grant—purchased these particular grants. Santa Anna then ordered the Monclova government closed and the federalists arrested. At that point, federalist Gov. Augustín Viesca pleaded for Anglo support in establishing a true republic in Mexico. While most settlers in Texas wanted peace, in defiance of Santa Anna Travis organized a militia at Anahuac and obtained the surrender of Mexican troops at the local customs house. Preparing for the inevitable, in early July 1835 Williams left for New Orleans and began raising funds and recruiting armed men. Only a month after she arrived to inspect her eight-league grant, Jane McManus returned to New Orleans on July 29, where she sarcastically listed her occupation on the custom and immigration form as "traveler." After almost two years of travel and expense she had nothing tangible to show for the investment of her time and money. Her claims remained unfinished because she had not paid Williams for the survey of the grant that had reverted to Robertson or the eight coastal leagues, and her headright claim was not yet located.[31]

In August 1835 friends secured Austin's release in Mexico City and he returned to Texas. After twenty-eight months of prison and house arrest, he no longer advised cooperation with Mexican officials. Austin urged the formation of a militia to protect Texans and their property from General Cós. Santa Anna ordered Cós to remove those Anglos who had settled since 1830 from Texas. Fighting began on October 2, 1835, when General Cós ordered a detachment to Gonzales to recover a cannon that had been loaned to the colonists for defense against Indians. Texans defied the troops with a flag picturing a cannon, a lone star, and the challenge, "Come and Take It," painted by Naomi DeWitt on a scrap of silk cut from her wedding dress. From November 3 to 14, Texans held a consultation and called for the restoration of the Constitution of 1824, which favored federalism. Delegates ordered the land offices closed because confusion and arguments about land claims distracted the participants from the immediate problems at hand. During Williams's absences from San Felipe to New Orleans and elsewhere, Gail Borden Jr., the son of the local blacksmith, maintained the land records, but primarily he coordinated the committees of correspondence that had been set in motion. Therefore, many claims in the San Felipe land office were not processed and remained unfinished. In Nacogdoches, land commissioner George Nixon issued titles beyond the closing date, which were later denied. In all, fourteen hundred claims in the Spanish Collection of the General Land Office were "unfinished," including the claims of Jane McManus.[32]

Jane McManus had more difficulties than unfinished land grants and the Burr divorce scandal to contend with. As later court proceedings would show, at some point Williams altered the land office copy of the Perfecto Valdez Grant. He erased the name Perfecto Valdez on the first page and inserted Rafael de Aguirre. Years later, Williams claimed that Perfecto Valdez was inserted in error on subsequent pages, but, as Galen Greaser, translator of Spanish documents in the General Land Office explained, mistakes were never erased on these grants, but lined through and explained at the end of the documents in a way similar to endnotes. The best explanation for his duplicity is that Williams needed four grants for members of Hanrick's Alabama Land Company in April 1833 when they came to inspect the land for which they had made a deposit in the form of drafts that Williams had cashed. In Williams's haste to locate the cotton lands in the upper colony for the planter syndicates with whom he dealt before Robertson reclaimed the area for the Nashville Company, Williams accepted payment for more grants than he had available. Williamson, the syndicate's agent, stalled the planters by his participation in the convention of April 1833. It was at this time that Robert McManus had alerted Sawyer and John Austin that Frank Johnson was making the fake field notes. With the three grants of Tomas de la Vega, Rafael de Aguirre, and Jose Maria Aguirre still unlocated and with that of Jane McManus altered as a second Rafael de Aguirre grant, Williams had four of the large grants for the members of the visiting land syndicate. Williams showed the grants as finished, although the Alabama syndicate had not paid in full for the forty-four leagues or the survey and location fees. Land company investor Asa Hoxey located the altered grant on the San Gabriel River in present-day Williamson County.[33]

In New York and unaware of Williams's deception, in October 1835 Jane McManus offered a thousand acres of land at an undisclosed location to Joseph D. Beers, of Beers, St. John and St. John for arms and ammunition for the Texas Revolution. Joseph D. Beers was president of the North American Trust and Banking Company, with advertised capital of fifty million dollars. With paper claims showing land holdings of more than eighty thousand acres, McManus appeared to be a wealthy woman, but she had no money to pay room and board. She turned to her father's last employer, New York Customs House Inspector Samuel Swartwout, who agreed to pay her living expenses in exchange for land. When Mrs. Fisher and the children arrived from Matagorda, where they had once shared living quarters, Jane McManus discreetly visited them on their way to stay with Mrs. Fisher's parents in Philadelphia.[34]

Jane McManus did not want to attract any undue attention. The gossip about her alleged affair with Burr was spreading, as the divorce proceeding grew more caustic with each court hearing. Toward the end of December 1835, the court awarded Mrs. Burr full control of her assets because of the testimony of her maid. Whether the court testimony was the cause of his health problems is unknown, but that month Burr had a massive stroke, from which he never recovered. Friends moved him from his Jersey City apartment to a New York boardinghouse where they could care for him. With Burr unable to defend himself, Eliza Burr continued her public tirades against Jane McManus and him as she walked the streets of New York rather than ride in her former aristocratic splendor.[35]

As 1836 began, Jane McManus was discouraged and had doubts of ever returning to Texas. Santa Anna would soon enter Texas with the Mexican Army. She was still in default on her note for survey fees, and Williams, who was temporarily staying in New York on business, dunned her for payment of the survey and location fees. He notified her that he located her headright claim near Matagorda. McManus replied thanking Williams for his advice to sell her claims for what she could get. Apparently he had a buyer in mind for she explained that she was playing one side against the other of those who wished to purchase her land. At that moment she only wanted to "settle down to a much neglected, though dearest duty, the care of my child's education." William was then nine years old and presumably had been living with his grandmother and uncle on the family farm near Troy. Jane was perhaps teaching school or caring for children because she explained to Williams that she was not thinking too clearly because the children had been noisy and distracting.[36]

In Texas, Robert joined the Texas Volunteer Army on March 6, 1836, four days after the signing of the Texas Declaration of Independence. He served in Capt. William M. Logan's Spy Company and with Erastus "Deaf" Smith at the Battle of San Jacinto. Their flag was a bare-breasted Spanish-looking Liberty painted by Kentuckian James Austin Sylvester and proclaimed "Liberty or Death." While her brother fought for their Texas land claims and became a hero, Jane McManus gave land away and became notorious. Details of the Burr divorce became public on September 14, 1836, the same day as Burr's death. Court records of the proceedings revealed that the Lewis sisters, Ellen and Hannah, gave depositions stating that Mrs. Burr's maid told them that Dr. Ezekiel Johnson had told the maid he had seen Burr in his room with his trousers lowered standing before a seated Mrs. McManus. McManus hired a lawyer and won a perjury indictment against the maid, Eliza Johnson, who was later found "not guilty" for lack of evidence. The indictment did not end the gossip nor erase the scandal that has since immortalized Jane as Burr's young paramour.[37]

While Jane McManus was having legal problems in New York, Sam Houston became president of the Republic of Texas in October 1836. Although Texans overwhelmingly supported annexation, the United States government did not extend an offer. The government of Mexico did not recognize the independence of Texas, and annexation would mean war. John Quincy Adams, William Lloyd Garrison, and Benjamin Lundy claimed that the Texas Revolution was part of a plot to extend slavery. The Republic of Texas government made it appear that slaveholders had enacted a constitution for their benefit. Instead of Texas being a refuge for free blacks as the anti-slavery reformers once planned, or as an outlet for slaves whose children would be free as the Mexicans proposed, the Texas Constitution made slavery perpetual and free persons of color were denied residency without the approval of the Texas Congress. The Texas government refused to automatically honor eleven-league grants because many were fraudulent and counterfeit. Some Texans believed that the eleven hundred grants issued by the Monclova Legislature in 1834 and 1835 had been the reason for Santa Anna's march north and the subsequent war. Section 10 of the Constitution of the Republic essentially denied the claims of the Galveston Bay and Texas Land Company, whose agent was John Mason. In addition, the General Land Office shows that claims by the company's settlers were denied. Furthermore, only Texas residents could own land, and claimants had to register in local county offices, where conflicts over land claims would be settled in local courts.[38]

In New York, on September 20, 1837, Jane McManus paid expenses incurred during the revolution and the extended legal battle to clear her name. She deeded one-half of League No. 4, Carancahua Survey, in what was then Matagorda County, to James Morgan to hold in trust for Swartwout. The land was the headright Williams located for her as the head of the McManus family. Although Morgan bonded the deed for ten thousand dollars, he wrote to Swartwout that it was worth more as a possible port.[39]

Three days before Christmas in 1837, Jane and Robert McManus returned to Texas to establish their residency and register their land claims. Although she was thirty years old, Jane listed herself on the ship's manifest as J. Maria McManus, age twenty-seven, a Texas resident, occupation, spinster. She gave her description as "5ft. 3 in," but lined through and wrote above, "complexion dark." She also signed for Robert, age twenty-four, a surveyor, described as five-feet-seven-inches tall and dark complexioned. With free blacks prohibited, the shade of one's skin had become important. Jane McManus also signed for her servants, Betsy Stewart, age thirty-eight, and her son, William H. Stewart, age ten, both listed as colored. Nothing more is known of the Stewarts, but they were not slaves. Slaves were listed under a master's name and last names were not listed.[40]

In January 1838, Jane McManus registered the eight leagues that Lewis had selected for her with the Matagorda County Land Board clerk, Thomas E. Davis, who was also a shareholder in the Galveston Bay and Texas Land Company and the New Washington Association. County commissioners recognized as valid her eight leagues of claims, her one league and one labor as a colonist, and the eleven-league Perfecto Valdez grant that was in limbo because the Williams and Robertson feud would have to be settled in court. In February, Thomas Morewood, of the Texas Land Board at Houston, certified that the claims of Jane McManus, her brother, and the William McManus heirs were valid. Robert surveyed around the Houston area, and in July married Sarah Spinks, whose parents came from

Mississippi as some of Austin's first colonists. Robert brought his mother, Catherine, and his sister's son, William, to live with him on his smaller headright claim established as a single man on the Trinity River. Twelve-year-old William helped his uncle run survey chains. That fall, Catherine McManus died of yellow fever.[41]

Meanwhile, Jane McManus lived in Matagorda with her agent, Ira Lewis, his wife, and their four daughters, Laura, Louisa, Cora, and Stella. Others had filed claims against the eight leagues that would have to be settled in court. Morton had sold the $250 deed to an unlocated Mexican land grant to Charles Howard, newly elected president of the Matagorda Land Board, for $100, who then sold the claim at a profit. Although a deed was merely a piece of paper, survey notes helped produce a clear title when recorded at a courthouse and recognized by a local jury as valid.[42]

Jane McManus's Perfecto Valdez claim was in legal flux because the Texas Congress had authorized Robertson to sue Williams for control of the area. The former Leftwich grant had shifted from Williams to Robertson and back in 1831, in 1834, and in 1835. Added to the suits of Robertson and Williams were those of Thomas Chambers for town sites located at the junctions of major rivers, plus the Mississippi, Alabama, Galveston Bay and Texas Land Company clients, their settlers against the companies and other settlers. Texas was a lawyer's paradise. President Houston ordered that the land offices remain closed until the land records were gathered, sorted, and organized. The chaos explains why the Texas Congress voted to allow local juries to award titles to settlers in adverse possession of their land, meaning persons living on the land had a valid claim against someone with a paper deed. Land wars began, family feuds developed, and many means were used to sway juries to award clear titles to deeds.[43]

When Jane asserted her claim for land at Matagorda, her rivals used the Burr divorce scandal against her. After all, she was the protégé of Aaron Burr, a man three times her age and noted for his political intrigues and "libidinous passions." When Jane McManus arrived at the Matagorda City Ball with the Lewis family in late November 1838, the managers of the ball turned her away because rumors of the Burr scandal made her unacceptable for respectable society. McManus was crushed and Lewis was angry. The Virginia gentleman and protector of his family honor demanded an apology or that he be met on a field of honor by the manager of the ball, a noted duelist, Col. Volney Howard, former Mississippi state representative and then a reporter for the Mississippi Court of Errors and Appeals. Lewis issued a formal challenge the next day in which he wrote, "the laws of society precluded her from adjusting her own wrongs." As Jane McManus was a guest in his home, and a member of his household, he too was insulted. Lewis had "heard the rumors that had turned her into a recluse, investigated, found them false, and to be based on political motivations." William Cazneau and Maj. Charles DeMorse, later editor of the Clarksville *Northern Standard,* agreed to serve as Lewis's seconds.[44]

Colonel Howard left town, and Lewis challenged the next person on the list, George W. Collingsworth, son-in-law of newly elected Matagorda Mayor Harvey Kenrick. Collinsworth, a hero of Velasco and Goliad, decided that he had urgent business in Houston at the inauguration of President Mirabeau B. Lamar. No one wanted to face Lewis. The matter was resolved without a duel, but Jane's honor was not avenged. An article appeared in the Matagorda *Bulletin* the first week of December reporting that Justice of the Peace Silas Dinsmore presided over a public meeting where the matter of Jane McManus's lack of an invitation to the ball and Lewis's challenge was settled. A resolution passed, which stated that the situation was not within the code of honor. On New Year's Eve 1838, Jane and Robert McManus, as heirs of William McManus, deeded twelve acres of Matagorda city lots to J. T. Belknap. Jane McManus left town, for she stood little chance of receiving a title to her land claims by a jury of her peers.[45]

A Matagorda County map drawn by County Surveyor James H. Selkirk in 1839 showed the eight leagues that Jane McManus claimed as vacant. The person who later patented the land explains the politics she faced. League No. 6 went to planter John D. Newell. Collingsworth patented League No. 12 on Trespalacios Bay. League No. 20 went to three members of the Yeamen family, one of whom at the time served on the Matagorda County grand jury. Silas Dinsmore, the justice of the peace, received a portion of League No. 25. And the league from which Mrs. McManus had deeded James Morgan half for the Swartwout debt went to Nancy A. McFarland, wife of local salt works operator Dugold MacFarland.[46]

Ironically, Matagorda, the town that rejected her, has the only known monument that honors Jane McManus Storm Cazneau. The Texas State Historical Commission marker is within sight of Grasmeyer's store, where Jane first met William Cazneau. While Jane went on to live a life of adventure, R. O. W. McManus (1812–1885) settled on the Trinity River with his wife and sons and operated a sawmill. He received all land due him as a settler and a soldier of the Republic of Texas and as one who served at the Battle of San Jacinto.[47]

From 1838 until 1847, Swartwout and Morgan gossiped about Jane McManus as they corresponded about the deed that she had issued Morgan for Swartwout's paying her expenses during the revolution. While Swartwout called her that "Bitch of an Angel, the Copper Captain," Morgan labeled her "Captain Copperhead," which in that era meant those who made false claims about themselves—and also perhaps Indians who represented themselves as white. According to Morgan, McManus could have gotten title to her land had she married Anthony Butler, the former minister to Mexico who had settled in Washington County, or a wealthy New Orleans man worth $300,000—both of whom wanted to marry her. Morgan did not explain whether they desired her or her claims totaling some eighty thousand acres of cotton land and coastal frontage. To Swartwout and Morgan it was practical for Jane to marry and secure her land claims. Like Cora in James Fenimore Cooper's novel, *Last of the Mohicans* (1826), however, when faced with the allegorical choice of marriage or worse, McManus did not choose marriage to a man old enough to be her grandfather. The "Copperhead" could not compare, however, to a "Swartwouter"—a new term that was coined for a swindler when the Port of New York was found short in customs receipts. Swartwout then spent several years in Europe because he had allegedly used public funds for private purposes.[48]

Just as her failed marriage led Jane McManus to Texas, her failed Texas venture led her to perform what she termed her "mental gymnastics"—a strengthening of resolve—to go on and "grit her teeth at fate." Although the ideal of the Republican mother and wife had begun to dominate prescriptive literature, many women worked. Jane's friend Ann S. Stephens wrote to supplement her husband's income as a New York customs house clerk. In "Woman of Genius," published in *The Hesperian* in 1839, Stephens explained that a woman of genius must write as a bird must sing, but Fanny Fern, a contemporary wrote, "No happy woman ever writes." An established serial writer in newspapers and magazines, Stephens perhaps helped McManus find work as a journalist.[49]

From 1839 until her marriage to Cazneau in 1849, Jane McManus again used the name Storm, either to avoid the Burr scandal or because she now had responsibility for her son William. She enrolled William in Rensselaer Institute in Troy while she traveled to the Mediterranean as a journalist for Horace Greeley, editor of the *New Yorker*, a weekly magazine of literature and current events. She wrote "Letters From An American Lady," signed, "Josephine." Because she traveled to Aleppo in the Ottoman Empire with a group including New Washington Association member, John Bartlett, she likely visited United States Consul Cmdr. David Porter in Izmir. Porter's extended family lived with him in the ancient port of Smyrna. She wrote later that she once worked as a governess for a diplomat. Porter's daughter had married the brother of Jane's classmate at Willard's Seminary, Cornelia Van Ness, who then lived in San Antonio. As Mexican naval commander (1826–1829), Porter had received land grants in Texas as payment for his services. Jane Storm was close to the Porter family and later intervened on behalf of a state department job for Porter's secretary and nephew George Porter.[50]

Jane Storm also visited Consul Horatio Sprague and his wife in Tangier. It was Mrs. Sprague who suggested that William be placed in the College of San Augustin in Cadiz. The boy was exceptionally bright, but Jane labeled his condition as "peculiar." William Storm's second wife's family called him "eccentric and unpleasant" and stated that he was "in and out of institutions" most of his life.[51]

While on her travels in the Middle East, Jane Storm met an independent and self-reliant woman who changed her life. In Syria, where the Knights Templar had their origins, Lady Hester Stanhope (1776–1839), the daughter of British nobleman and inventor Charles Stanhope, lived with Druse tribesmen near Aleppo on the trade route between Baghdad and the Mediterranean Sea. Jane Storm later published details of Aleppo and of meeting the famed eccentric in the *United States Magazine and Democratic Review* and in the journal *Our Times*. Lady Hester had an extensive library of Masonry, told fortunes, and predicted that the United States was "to cut a great figure" in the millennium. She encouraged Jane Storm, who considered her aspiring nature a liability. Lady Hester told Jane that God had given her ambition for some great purpose.[52]

Returning to New Orleans in May 1840, signing her letter as J. Maria McManus, Jane Storm wrote to Sam Houston from New Orleans. She requested letters of introduction to the minister of France and to his Holiness the Pope [Gregory XVI], then a friend of Masonry, that showed her father's rank and her Texas citizenship. She explained that she wanted to enter William in an exclusive European school and claimed that she had letters from New York Gov. William L. Marcy and the bishops of New York and New Orleans, John T. Hughes and Antoine Blanc. The coy and flirtatious letter suggests that she and Houston were acquainted and knew one another very well.[53]

With Jane McManus gone from Texas, Williams declared the Waco area of the Perfecto Valdez grant vacant. The legal battle between Robertson and Williams was not easily settled, and legal battles over land claims continued until after the Civil War. Only in the late 1840s did Williams's alteration of Jane McManus's grant and Johnson's fake surveys come to light in Williamson County court cases involving suits of possession by subsequent buyers of Asa Hoxey's land. Hoxey went bankrupt in 1837 and the land reverted to Hanrick. Upon his bankruptcy, the land went back to the Bank of the United States. The Ufford brothers of Connecticut bought the land from the bank and thought they had acquired a bargain in rich cotton lands. The Uffords then sued settlers for possession of the land in Williamson County local courts. Jane and her brother continued their legal battle for the Perfecto Valdez grant until their deaths.[54]

CHAPTER III

Manifest Destiny, 1840–1846

I have the satisfaction of believing myself useful and acceptable in my own circle, and if that is not quite equal to the attractions of Matagorda and Galveston it is at least as good as New York has to show and suits me admirably.

—J. M. Storm to Mirabeau B. Lamar (1845)[1]

*A*FTER MEETING HESTER STANHOPE IN 1839 AND BEING ENCOURaged to follow her ambitions, Jane McManus Storm had a new sense of purpose. Instead of allowing the Burr scandal to turn her into a recluse or to cause her to seek escape abroad or rush into marrying someone whose wealth and prestige would insulate her from reproach, she became more quixotic than before. Between 1839 and 1846 she wrote for the *New Yorker, The Daily Plebeian,* the *Workingman's Advocate,* and the New York *Sun.* Storm also wrote for the *United States Magazine and Democratic Review,* edited by John L. O'Sullivan. From the time she left Texas to when the Mexican War began, J. M. Storm, as she signed most of her letters, would grow from being an anonymous staff writer to the respected journalist, "MONTGOMERY." After it became known that MONTGOMERY was a woman, she wrote as Cora Montgomery. Although her name was "Storm," she signed her correspondence, "Storms." Whether the spelling was a misprint because of her poor handwriting, to shield her from the Burr scandal, or to provide a degree of anonymity is unknown. She was popular and effective because she had a natural talent for expressing the expansionist goals of the Democratic Party known as Manifest Destiny. The phrase was one of the most important emotional and intellectual precepts of the nineteenth century. Furthermore, and contrary to what has been written, analysis of the grammatical errors of Storm and O'Sullivan indicate that she created the phrase and wrote the editorials credited to O'Sullivan (see Appendix B). By using a computer grammar checker and tabulating the results, Jane Storm had 100 percent identical errors to the famous July-August 1845 article, "Annexation," with the phrase "manifest destiny," and O'Sullivan had none.[2]

Most likely, Gov. William L. Marcy provided Jane Storm with her first opportunity to publish in the *Democratic Review*. In January 1839, O'Sullivan published an article critical of Marcy after his defeat by Whig candidate William H. Seward. After being reprimanded by President Martin Van Buren, O'Sullivan offered Marcy, or someone of his choosing, equal pages in the magazine. Anonymous articles published in the September and November 1839 editions resembled in tone Marcy's letter to O'Sullivan, but textual analysis indicates it is likely that Jane Storm wrote the articles.[3]

Marcy had reminded O'Sullivan that all in the party were in a line of march, some faster than others. After traveling abroad and being aware of Stanhope's optimism for America, Storm saw the United States as the harbinger of the future. "The Course of Civilization" in the September 1839 issue follows Marcy's line of thought in Storm's voice and style: "The history of humanity is the record of a grand march, more or less rapid." In a November 1839 article titled "Great Nation of Futurity," Storm asked, "Who will, what can, set limits on our onward march?" She portrayed the nation "in its magnificent domain of space and time" as "the nation of many nations destined to manifest to mankind . . . the sacred and the true . . . a union of many republics." She declared, "America had been chosen for a blessed mission to the nations of the world to carry freedom of conscience, freedom of person, freedom of trade and business pursuits."[4]

After an 1840 fire burned the Washington facilities of the *United States Magazine and Democratic Review*, O'Sullivan's brother-in-law, Samuel Daly Langtree, withdrew from the magazine. New Yorker O. C. Gardiner thereafter published the journal, which was printed by H. G. Langley. Publication resumed in New York in July 1841 with O'Sullivan listed as editor. The journal's motto, "The best government is that which governs least," explained its Jeffersonian stance against the Whig view of a strong central government. From the beginning, the magazine had the patronage of Andrew Jackson and Martin Van Buren to provide democratic literature for the middle class. In New York the Tammany Society supported the magazine.[5]

Textual analysis identifies Jane Storm as the author of three 1841 economic articles in the *Democratic Review*. In October, she introduced a report of the "Select Committee of the House of Commons." Titled "Free Trade," the article began with her prose style written as if in step with the marching feet of progress. "Our subject is free trade," she began, and launched into the ways free trade was a world-embracing revolution of political and social improvement that would lead to universal peace. She portrayed the United States as being composed of twenty-six sovereign states that lived in peace as a model for other nations. In November, "Hurrah for a War with England" represented a sarcastic response to calls for war over encounters between English and American logging companies in Maine. "By all means. Let us have a war," she jeered, "Let us read or hear again some daily new tale of battle and blood." Instead, she urged, "The true glory of a nation is to be found in the great moral principles which govern its conduct and mould its character." In December, she explained that the protective tariff policy of "The Home League" was an outdated approach scorned by Adam Smith in *The Wealth of Nations* (1776).[6]

The stated aim of the *Democratic Review* was to create an American literary culture and spread democratic ideals at home and abroad. The magazine published the works of Nathaniel Hawthorne, Walt Whitman, Edgar Allan Poe, Ralph Waldo Emerson, and Herman Melville. Not all the writers were Democrats, but the magazine was designed for a broad readership. It also included women authors and articles of interest to women. Mrs. E. D. E. N. Southworth, the most prolific woman writer in American publishing history, was divorced and wrote about abandoned women who became strong and self-reliant. She remained popular well into the twentieth century; as late as 1929 some of her novels were still in print, and fifty of her novels each had sold a hundred thousand copies. Jane Storm's childhood friend, Ann S. Stephens, wrote some twenty-five historical romances, one exposing working conditions of women was described as a "book no father would allow his daughter to read." Stephens's 1840s serial, "Maleska, the Indian Wife of the White Hunter," became the first Beadle paperback in 1860 and sold three hundred thousand copies, thereby launching the American genre of the dime novel. Elizabeth Ellet, wife of Columbia University professor Henry Ellet, wrote women's history and translated

French and German democratic literature, and Lydia Sigourney's poems were found in most publications. These were but a few of the "damned mob of scribbling women," whose publications outsold those of the men in the 1840s and 1850s. Jane Storm wrote about popular government and the expansion of commerce and democratic ideals in the *Review*, but, unlike George Bancroft, Lewis Cass, Samuel J. Tilden, William Cullen Bryant, and other leaders, she did not receive credit for her work until March 1845, and then it was under the generic pseudonym, "C. Montgomery."[7]

Jane Storm's distinctive writing style, best described as utilitarian or modern, was a sharp contrast to the verbosity of the Romantic style of the era. She used short words and with a haughty tone delivered messages that more resembled stump speeches than formal essays. Critics point out that her sentences carried the reader directly to the point with themes of unity, peace, and progress achieved through republicanism. Her style was simple and to the point with arguments based on research and knowledge of economics. Her newspaper columns were filled with opinions and predictions; they were highly critical of politicians, yet complimentary of statesmen.[8]

Storm made frequent grammatical errors in punctuation and verb tense. Although her work did not show the educational polish of other contributors, her messages appealed to the patriotism of readers. When comparing the grammar, mechanics, style, and substance of signed articles by Jane Storm with those signed by O'Sullivan, textual analysis suggests that articles previously attributed to O'Sullivan on commercial and territorial expansion were actually written by Storm (see Appendix B). Researchers using the *United States Magazine and Democratic Review* have considered the unsigned articles a problem, but failed to compare the style and substance of articles with O'Sullivan's signature to those written on expansion. Authorship is significant because Storm's contributions to the magazine have gone unrecognized. O'Sullivan wrote editor's notes and sentimental fluff, for example, "Seeing a Friend off in a Packet," about his fiancée, and "Poor Esther, the Jewess—a Reminiscence of Morocco," about his wet nurse. Hawthorne's first impression of O'Sullivan was that he was "charming, but superficial." O'Sullivan was a social butterfly who avoided editorial responsibilities when possible.[9]

For much of 1842, Jane Storm was concerned with family matters, and no major articles in the *Democratic Review* reflected her style. According to James Morgan, who kept up with her until the matter of Swartwout's deed was tended to, she traveled to Europe and to Mexico that year. In May

1842, Philip McManus's wife, Eliza, died of consumption and William Storm graduated from the College of San Augustin at the head of his class in the Castilian language. Upon his return from Europe, William lived with his uncle Robert McManus in Texas, but soon moved to Troy, where he lived with his uncle Philip on the family farm after his aunt's death. On Christmas Day, Jane's grandfather Philip Coons died at age ninety-five. Although the McManus siblings were named in his will, no records reveal what they received from their grandfather's estate; however, Storm's next address was in Park Place, a gated complex in lower Manhattan.[10]

In July 1842, William Cullen Bryant, editor of the New York *Evening Post*, criticized O'Sullivan in the *Post* for neglecting the *Democratic Review*. Since early 1841, O'Sullivan had served in the New York Assembly where he worked to remove the death penalty and in support of married women's rights. He also courted Annie Ward, younger sister of Julia Ward Howe, and wrote lengthy and intricate laws as well as a book on corporal punishment. Beginning in 1841, Jane Storm possibly worked as O'Sullivan's bookkeeper or secretary. As no body of papers exists for either Storm or O'Sullivan, the exact nature of their business arrangement may never be known, but O'Sullivan has been called a "con artist," and described as urbane, ambitious, vain, impulsive, and highly susceptible to fads, with an air of mystery and unanswered questions about him. In 1839, O'Sullivan left the magazine and tried to establish a law practice in New York, asked for a diplomatic post, and even sought the New York U.S. marshal position. Thus, with Jane Storm absent in 1842, perhaps because O'Sullivan failed to pay her an equitable salary, it was not out of character for O'Sullivan to hire Orestes A. Brownson, former editor of the *Boston Quarterly Review*. Later, when Storm left O'Sullivan to have her own column in the New York *Sun*, two well-known editors replaced her.[11]

Brownson was an intellectual and elitist with a negative view of "the people." A November 1842 article on President John Tyler titled "A Political Portrait With Pen and Pencil," is an example of Brownson's style.

> The invaluable practical services recently rendered by Mr. Tyler to the cause of those principles which have always been advocated by this Review, and sustained by its political friends, have attached to his position an interest which necessarily extends in no slight degree to his person also.[12]

The article contrasted sharply to a filler that followed, written by Storm. In "The Coup-De-Grace," she asked, "Has the reader ever seen a Spanish bull-fight? Probably not!" she answered. She compared Daniel Webster's latest speech with the matador who killed the bull after everyone had weakened the beast. After outlining Whig disasters, she predicted the death of the party. After letters of complaint and dropped subscriptions because of Brownson's subject matter and elitist attitude, O'Sullivan let Brownson go, and the journal again reflected Storm's clear and distinct style. As several of O'Sullivan's rambling letters to President James K. Polk were in her handwriting, it appears that Storm was O'Sullivan's assistant. As she next became the political editor of the *Sun*, and O'Sullivan hired John Bigelow as political editor, she was probably the political editor of the *Democratic Review*.[13]

Jane Storm wrote for a living and not for fame, but seeing her name in print was not an option for her or her publishers. Furthermore, unsigned articles were more the rule than the exception before the American Civil War. From 1841 to 1846, the years Jane worked there, the *United States Magazine and Democratic Review* had its most successful years with the largest circulation of any of the political and literary journals. Monthly, its 112 pages went to six thousand patrons in all parts of the United States and Europe. The second largest journal, the *Southern Literary Messenger*, had a circulation of 5,500. Because of the success of the Democratic journal, Whigs revamped the *American Whig Review*. Therefore, Storm's work was influential, but her name was unknown to the public.[14]

In the increasingly conservative atmosphere promoted by the Whig party, no woman should be concerned with the political sphere and no man would take a woman's opinion seriously. Therefore, it was to Jane Storm's advantage to remain anonymous when O'Sullivan paid $2 per manuscript page, or about $25 an article, at a time when working women in New York, primarily employed in the needle trades, made on average $2.50 for a six-day week of twelve- and fourteen-hour days.[15]

Jane Storm represented the radical, or Locofoco faction of Democrats with a tradition of sexual equality. In the 1830s, working women had a champion in Frances Wright (1795–1852), the Scottish heiress who migrated to the United States in the early 1820s and helped organize the People's, or Workingmen's, party in which Jane's father, William McManus, had been active. Wright established the Hall of Science in New York City for evening educational lectures, and by day, the former Methodist Church building was a school for children of working mothers. By 1840, Whigs denounced Wright as the "petticoat leader" of the

Locofoco Democrats, so named because they once used Locofoco matches to carry on their political caucus after a faction of Tammany Hall conservatives turned off the gas lighting in the meeting hall. Locofocos called for honest friendship with the American Indian and popular sovereignty for all adult males regardless of property ownership. By 1842, the "Cult of True Womanhood," with its admonitions to piety, purity, submissiveness, and domesticity, was the prescriptive behavior for women, and while literature was an acceptable profession for single and widowed women, journalism was not.[16]

In April 1843, the *Democratic Review* published an expansionist editorial connecting the Oregon Territory with Texas annexation. The article focused on Britain's interference with the expansion of the United States, Washington's lack of initiative, and the duty of the people to act. "The importance of the Oregon Territory has not been duly considered, nor its value properly estimated by the people of the United States," the article began. The tone and speech patterns resounded as if written by Jane Storm. As a habit, she took long walks each day and wrote after dinner. When books, magazines, and newspapers were read aloud, one could almost hear her words echoing through homes, on the boardinghouse steps, and in the saloons. She appealed to the people, she wrote, "because narrow-minded politicians" would "give England all it demanded." Britain had no legal claim, she asserted, only an agreement to hold the territory jointly with the United States. "What constituted a valid title?" she asked. "Possession," she answered, "Britain pressed its claim for the territory north of the Columbia River only by right of possession." Her Texas experience with the law of adverse possession enabled her to foresee the loss of Oregon as the Hudson's Bay Company encouraged French Canadian trappers to marry into native tribes, take possession of the land, and establish farms and communities.[17]

Although Oregon was 150 sailing days out of Boston and New York, farms and missions to the Indians would secure the land, Storm advised. She scoffed at those who said, "Britain will rise up in wrath and threaten us with annihilation." She argued, "The question is not what will England do? but what ought the United States to do?" A little over a month later, the great migration to Oregon began, and two thousand settlers established a United States presence that secured ports on the Pacific for United States trade with Asia. Storm did not originate the surge to the Pacific, but her publication was in support of the commercial expansionists in the

Democratic party. In 1844, Caleb Cushing negotiated the Treaty of Wanghia, which opened five Chinese ports to American ships. Britain had won the Opium War and acquired Hong Kong as its trade base and was moving to secure the exclusive control of Chinese ports. The editorial verifies Norman Graebner's thesis that expansion to Oregon had commercial aspects.[18]

In May 1843, Samuel Swartwout, William L. Marcy, John C. Calhoun, Robert J. Walker, and Mirabeau B. Lamar were members of a committee formed to promote Texas annexation in the press. Andrew Jackson directed the campaign, and circulated letters to Sam Houston, Senator Walker, and Duff Green. Jackson feared Britain would "place an iron hoop around the United States" and prevent its growth to the Pacific. In the New York press, Storm tied British interest in Oregon to Texas. She knew three members of the committee very well and communicated with Lamar, Green, and Mayor William Havemeyer of New York.[19]

Also in 1843, Storm sent pro-annexation letters to James Morgan that he forwarded to Dr. Francis Moore, editor of the Houston *Telegraph and Texas Register*. Morgan replied that he preferred independence because settlers from Europe would pay cash for their land, increase his land values, and help end slavery. Morgan claimed that he was no abolitionist but that one need only to compare the prosperity of Ohio with the poverty of Kentucky to see the weakness associated with slavery. Storm also inquired about old beaus. Morgan lied that he knew nothing about William Cazneau or Anthony Butler. He knew, however, that Butler had become a planter in Washington County and had married a grandmother of his own age. After the Matagorda incident, Cazneau had moved to Austin, where he represented Travis County in the Republic of Texas Congress and was a warden in the Royal Arch Chapter of Free and Accepted Masons, Lone Star Lodge No. 3. He was also Commissary General for the 1841 Texan Santa Fe Expedition that failed to establish trade between Texas and Santa Fe.[20]

As of 1843, Samuel Swartwout still considered Jane Storm a "Copper Captain" because he did not yet have a clear title to the deed she issued Morgan for him in 1837. In January 1844, Morgan assured Storm that she could get a good lawyer to handle her land problems if she came to Texas. "Texas owes you a debt of gratitude and if she don't pay it *I Will*," he vowed. Morgan, now a widower and seeking a helpmeet, described property he had on Galveston Bay with a frame dwelling and brick chimneys, "*Do* come," he purred, "and 'claim my hospitality'—*I dare you to do it!*" Storm had more important tasks than catering to Morgan's illusions of her settling down as his spouse amid the quiet solitude of Morgan's Point.[21]

In the April 1844 edition of the *Democratic Review*, Storm summarized the thirty-two-page pamphlet, "Letter of Mr. Walker, of Mississippi relative to the Annexation of Texas: in reply to the Call of the People of Carroll County, Kentucky, to communicate his views on that subject." Her seven-and-one-half-page summary titled "The Texas Question" coincided with the United States-Texas annexation negotiations between Secretary of State John C. Calhoun and Texans Isaac Van Zandt and James P. Henderson. She began, "Que sara, sara—what must be, must be—and in general, the sooner therefore it is, the better." The position of the magazine was neutral, she stated, "We are neither Southerners . . . nor Abolitionists. We occupy a position midway between the two, and . . . overlooking both." She used Walker's argument that Texas was the key to the defense of the Mississippi Basin because the Sabine River was too near New Orleans for adequate defense, and the uppermost boundary of Texas was "only twenty miles from South Pass, the overland route to Oregon and the Pacific." To refuse Texas, she quoted, was "to lower the flag of the union to the red cross of St. George," and "surrender Florida Pass, the mouth of the Mississippi, the gulf, and Texas into the hands of England." Parts of Walker's letter issued by the annexation committee resemble her style, and she possibly composed the passages that she quoted.[22]

To counter objections that Texas meant the extension of slave territory, Jane Storm quoted, "The question of slavery is not a federal or national, but a local question." She ignored Walker's pages of statistics and fearful predictions of the cost of abolition when hordes of free blacks would descend on the north to compete for work and fill asylums and prisons. Instead, she emphasized the positive "safety-valve" aspect whereby slavery would drain through Texas and end as peonage in Mexico. Later, as she witnessed its destruction, she would change her opinion about peonage, but at this time she repeated. "We do not regard the question as a *federal* but a *local* one." Her viewpoint reflected that of New York merchants and shippers dependent on Southern business. Other parts of the Walker letter reflected the Van Buren faction of Democrats, who feared abolition would inundate the north with free blacks who would be "paupers, beggars, thieves, assassins, and desperadoes; all, or nearly all, penniless and destitute, without skill, means, industry, or perseverance to obtain a livelihood."[23]

Storm assured readers that Texas could be annexed without a war. "Surely Mexico could be induced to surrender title to territory already lost," she argued. She claimed Mexican officials had mortgaged Texas and California to British holders of Mexican bonds. In 1839, Bernard Bee, Texas minister to the United States, had met with the British Lizardi and Co., holders of the bonds, and proposed five million dollars for recognition of the Rio Grande as the Texas boundary.[24]

With annexation a national topic of discussion in April 1844, Storm traveled to Texas and engaged an attorney to handle her land claims. She also wrote about annexation from Galveston. In May 1844, Morgan wrote Swartwout, "Do you see the New York Sun and the letters of the Copper Captain from Galveston . . . if Texas should be annexed you will be a rich man yet." Morgan urged Swartwout to hold his Texas bonds, sure to be funded at full value upon annexation. Marginal investors, and those like James Watson Webb who faced bankruptcy, sold their bonds for a fraction of their value. Financiers bought the bargains and pushed for annexation. When arranging for a lawyer, Storm paid Morgan a brief visit. Morgan soon advised Swartwout that the matter of the deed would be handled. William Cazneau had agreed to help Storm with her land business. She possibly swapped land for attorney fees as she deeded the other half of her headright claim to Thomas J. Chambers, Cazneau's commanding officer in the Texas Revolution. Needless to say, Robert, who was to share in the claim, was upset with his sister.[25]

From at least 1843, or about the time O'Sullivan hired Brownson, Storm had written occasionally for the New York *Sun*. Benjamin Day had established the Locofoco paper in 1833 with Robert Owen and Frances Wright. Since 1835, Moses Y. Beach, a self-made man, had been publisher and owner. An orphan of a Danbury hatter, Beach indentured himself as a cabinet maker's apprentice and eventually had his own business. He married Nancy Day, his future partner's sister. He sold his cabinet works, but when his next business failed, he moved his family to New York and ran the press department of his brother-in-law's newspaper. He purchased Day's interest in the *Sun* in 1835 and was one of the first to use paperboys, which provided orphans with work. He used a pony express, carrier pigeons, and the telegraph to deliver news first to the streets of New York. Although Beach was a director of four banks, his working-class background and lack of formal education made him an outsider in New York society.[26]

From 1840 to 1855, the *Sun* also published directories of the wealthiest citizens of the city as a credit rating for New York merchants. *The Wealth and Biography of the Wealthy Citizens of the City of New York*, edited by Beach, exaggerated his wealth, omitted others, and was not an accurate list. Storm may have compiled parts of the publication noted for establishing the literary genre of the pioneer compendium and for providing a social doctrine to the poor about the value of virtue and honest effort.[27]

The *Sun* was independent in that Beach received no political funding or government printing contracts, but profited from classified advertising and steamship notices. Thus, readers looked to the *Sun* for unbiased information as opposed to the slanted news of Horace Greeley's Whig *Tribune* and J. Gordon Bennett's Democratic *Herald*. While no leading Democrats or Whigs advocated Texas annexation, Storm kept the issue before the public in the independent *Sun*.[28]

Since 1843, Storm's letters in the *Sun* had been written as if from the public and sometimes signed "Storms." Whether she added the "s" to alter her identity, or because typesetters mistook her scribbled "m" as plural is unknown, but Storms was her public identity until she married Cazneau in late 1849. The *Sun*, like the *Democratic Review*, supported free trade and commercial and territorial expansion. She identified the policy as that of the Free Trade Democrats and the Young Democracy—programs thought to help the working poor, New York merchants, shipping, and the shipbuilding industry. In a March 1845 editorial she summed up the lengthy annexation campaign by saying that Texas would provide a balance of power between north, south, and west; a safe southern boundary, a carrying trade in American bottoms and new markets for manufacturing; and an opportunity to extend the doctrine and principle of free institutions.[29]

The Van Buren-Albany Democrats opposed Texas annexation, however, and labeled the urban New Yorkers as "hunkers," or those hankering for the rewards of office through their alliance with southern Democrats. In turn, hunkers labeled the upstate faction "barnburners," who would destroy the party to get rid of slavery like the Dutch farmer who burned the barn to get rid of the rats. Storm was determined to maintain a middle ground in the independent press until the slavery issue was resolved, which she believed would happen as European labor replaced slaves drawn into the tropics of Africa and the Americas.[30]

In 1844, the U.S. Senate did not approve annexation as Whigs and Van Buren's Democrats defeated the treaty that became entangled with the presidential election of 1844. In October, Morgan wrote to Storm thanking her for copies of the *Sun*. Morgan thought it a joke that the Mexican navy had claimed to blockade Galveston as a means to discourage the senate from confirming annexation when he thought they only put into port for repairs. Although Morgan said he had no interest in politics, and a stage ran to the Texas capital, he invited Storm to ride horseback with him and attend the Anson Jones inauguration. Morgan was perhaps still seeking Jane as a wife. "I have a fine ladies saddle horse at your service" and "your friends Cazneau and McLeod will be there," he cooed. She did not accept his invitation.[31]

In November, New York was the key state that voted for James K. Polk as a pro-annexation president and created a mandate for annexation. Although the Liberty party pulled votes from Henry Clay and allowed James K. Polk to carry New York and the election, Beach boasted that his press had secured the annexation of Texas. O'Sullivan also took credit for the victory in the New York *Morning News*, a campaign paper for which he and Samuel J. Tilden were listed as editors. Beach, O'Sullivan, Senator Walker, and members of the annexation committee received public congratulations for their success. Her New York editor colleagues, Greeley at the *Tribune*, Thurlow Weed at the Albany *Whig*, Colonel Webb of the *Courier and Enquirer*, Bennett at the *Herald*, and Erastus Brooks, editor of the *Express*, by this time knew that Jane Storm was the political editor of the *Sun* and the *Democratic Review*. Thus, she achieved a level of respect and power experienced by few women of her era.[32]

In his 1844 state of the union address, President John Tyler urged Congress to annex Texas by joint resolution, and when Congress convened, annexation was the foremost topic of discussion. On February 28, 1845, Congress passed a joint resolution inviting Texas to join the Union. "The Presidents of Texas" by C. Montgomery appeared in the March issue of the *United States Magazine and Democratic Review*. It was a history of the Texas Republic as told through the administrations of the presidents. Why Storm chose "Montgomery" as a pseudonym is a mystery unless she did so in honor of Gen. Richard Montgomery, who captured Montreal during the American Revolution. She began:

The four men who, in turn, have been called to the highest place in
the Land of the Lone Star, are as diverse as men can well be in mind and
lineaments, but they are agreed on three points—in their strong love for
Texas—in a devout faith in the glories of her future destiny—and in the
extraordinary littleness of their faith in each other.[33]

Storm presented the presidents of Texas as folk heroes and not as noble
or faultless men of an earlier era. She described the "True Texians" as
"fearless, witty and affable, open of speech, and prompt in generous
deeds" but also said they had "a quick relish for scandal" and could "out
gossip an army of old women." She portrayed David G. Burnet as an elegant and forceful orator with a fiery temper. She described Mirabeau B.
Lamar as an impractical dreamer who mounted huge debts and
involved Texas in wars with Indians and Mexicans, but also brought education and foreign recognition to Texas. Anson Jones was a practical
man, like Houston in many ways, but a speculator. Houston had the
most detailed biography as she described his voice, his manner, his
charm, his lovely wife, Margaret, and his drinking habits. Lamar's biographer thought that the poetic Lamar inspired her to write the article
and believed their relationship more than a casual one. Her letters to
Lamar were friendly, but businesslike, and less suggestive than those
written to Houston or others.[34]

When Lamar traveled to Washington in February 1845, Jane Storm
and Ann Stephens met with him. Returning to New York, Storm wrote to
Lamar while she and her friends waited for the train in Baltimore. While
Stephens was pregnant and complained about the cigar smoke, Storm
mimicked her friends' writing styles. She admitted she valued Lamar's
"fame, which came from duty done." One can empathize with Storm as
she returned to New York to do the work for which her editors took credit. She channeled her disappointment, however, into a project to help
other women less fortunate than she.[35]

Upon her return to New York in March 1845, Jane Storm directed
her energy into a project to improve the conditions of workingwomen.
Ann Stephens, Carolyn Sawyer, Mrs. E. D. E. N. Southworth, and others
joined with her in organizing the Female Industrial Association with
Elizabeth Gray as president and Mary Graham as secretary. Storm publicized meetings in the *Sun*, attended rallies at City Hall, made speeches in
the Hall of Science, and helped organize benefits. Stephens and
Southworth agreed to write stories about workingwomen. Storm did not

advise women to form combinations or withhold their labor from the market, as did Horace Greeley and his feminist writer, Margaret Fuller, in the *Tribune*. In basic economic articles in the *Sun* and *The Workingman's Advocate*, Storm explained that if women formed combinations to increase wages, they would attract more workers and lower wages or would be replaced by others willing to work for less. She suggested that women educate themselves, improve their skills, and enter professions that paid more money. She wrote that low pay "drove many virtuous females to courses which might, otherwise, have been avoided" as they "supported families, aged parents, and younger siblings." The women of the association were dressmakers, shirt makers, cap makers, straw workers, fringe and lace makers, book folders, and book stitchers. The workingwomen, Storm wrote, were the true "Women of the Nineteenth Century," and not those of wealth and prestige found in Margaret Fuller's book by that title.[36]

While Greeley advised women to go west where they could find husbands, Storm advised women to enter men's professions. As clerks and bookkeepers, she jeered, they would hardly be taking "a real man's job," and, she said, women could "surely sell lace and ribbons." The association organized a boycott, and the *Sun* reported that by May 1, 1845, New York stores would begin hiring young ladies to sell ribbons, lace, and other notions to women customers. The result of the boycott was a small victory, but it started a trend for the acceptance of women in the public workplace.[37]

Not only did the *United States Magazine and Democratic Review* publish works by female authors, it addressed women's issues. In May 1844, O'Sullivan had endorsed "The Legal Wrongs of Women," as an article worthy of consideration. It appeared as Storm traveled to Texas on land business and reflects her writing style. The "woman problem" was not one of equal faculties, political suffrage, or divorce, because, as she said, children needed both parents. She explained that a laboring woman supporting aged parents or children or the wife of a drunkard needed special consideration under the law for protection of their children and wages. Married women in New York had no power over their property, earnings, or children—a situation that led to the 1848 women's convention in Seneca Falls, New York.[38]

After the final congressional vote on annexation, Lamar traveled to New York and attended one of Mrs. Greeley's Saturday afternoon teas where the literary elite met. He snubbed Margaret Fuller, the feminist who had declared a war of the sexes and bragged she knew everyone worth knowing. Lamar greeted, however, Ann Stephens, Carolyn Sawyer, and Southworth. Sawyer wrote children's literature. Stephens then edited *Peterson's Magazine*, which had a larger circulation than *Godey's Ladies Book*. Storm also attended these gatherings, much to the chagrin of Fuller, who called Storm's group the "Ionian *distingués*."[39]

The literary women formed two factions. Storm and her friends were Democrats who advised self-reliance and concrete solutions for women. The activists ridiculed Fuller and the Whig feminists with their attitude of *noblesse oblige* as the solution for society's ills. In 1843, Greeley had hired Fuller, former Boston editor of *The Dial*, as music critic for the *Tribune*, but she soon earned a reputation as an outstanding literary critic. Fuller and Storm were both journalists, aided revolutions abroad, and died at sea, but they had little else in common. Fuller was an elitist, racist, ethnocentric who advocated same-sex love. Storm identified with the working class, treated everyone the same whether newsboys or presidents, urged racial tolerance, and believed other races and ethnic groups were capable of republican government. Storm could be termed a coquette, if not a *femme fatale*.[40]

"Annexation," an article in the July-August 1845 issue of the *Democratic Review* long attributed to O'Sullivan, was Jane Storm's response to the continued abolitionist agitation against Texas annexation. David Lee Child, who with Benjamin Lundy and George Thompson had planned a colony of free blacks in Mexican Texas, titled a pamphlet:

THE TAKING OF NABOTH'S VINEYARD, OR HISTORY OF THE TEXAS CONSPIRACY, AND AN EXAMINATION OF THE REASONS GIVEN BY THE HON. J. C. CALHOUN, HON. R. J. WALKER, AND OTHERS, FOR THE DISMEMBERMENT AND ROBBERY OF THE REPUBLIC OF MEXICO.

The tirade was first published in the Northampton *Gazette* in 1842, then printed at Washington in 1843, and reprinted in 1845.[41]

In the anonymous article Storm chastised those who stirred up the sectional debate in "Annexation":

It is time now for opposition to the annexation of Texas to cease, all further agitation of the waters of bitterness and strife, at least in connexion with this question . . . It is time for the common duty of Patriotism to the

Country to succeed; . . . it is at last time for common sense to acquiesce with decent grace in the inevitable and the irrevocable. Texas is now ours.[42]

Storm called for common sense to resolve the slavery issue. The real enemy was "England, our old rival and enemy," she wrote, and "France, strangely coupled with her," whose object was one of "thwarting our policy and hampering our power, limiting our greatness and checking the fulfillment of our manifest destiny to overspread the continent." She urged tolerance for "one of the most difficult of the various social problems." The greater adjustment, she believed was "the coexistence of the races with social equality as it existed in Mexico, Central and South America." Furthermore, "Until a still deeper problem shall have been solved than that of slavery," she wrote, it was best "to guard against its abuses, to mitigate its evils, . . . by prohibiting the separation of families" and "the licentiousness of mastership." She concluded by predicting that the Mississippi River valley would soon be connected to the Pacific by rail. It was an effort to refocus national attention on commercial expansion.[43]

Since 1927, John L. O'Sullivan has been thought the author of the phrase "manifest destiny." Almost every history of the United States in the two decades before the Civil War has the phrase that named an era and a foreign policy. It was thought that O'Sullivan authored the phrase because he was editor of the *United States Magazine and Democratic Review.* Historians were not cognizant of Jane Storm's association with O'Sullivan or the magazine. Those who knew her well were aware that Beach hired her away from O'Sullivan at a time when Thomas Ritchie of the Washington *Daily Union* also sought her talents for his paper. Her protégé, Henry Watterson, winner of the second Pulitzer Prize awarded for editorial writing in 1918, wrote, "whatever I may have attained in that line I largely owe to her for she had learned the value of the short descriptive phrase." O'Sullivan's obituaries in 1895 did not mention his being the editor of the *Democratic Review, Morning News,* nor contain the term "manifest destiny."[44]

Comparing the grammar, mechanics, and style of signed articles by O'Sullivan and Storm with "Annexation" strongly suggests that she wrote the article. By comparing the first three hundred words of "Annexation" and those articles signed by O'Sullivan and Storm using "Grammatik," a

ANNEXATION.

It is time now for opposition to the Annexation of Texas to cease, all further agitation of the waters of bitterness and strife, at least in connexion with this question,—even though it may perhaps be required of us as a necessary condition of the freedom of our institutions, that we must live on for ever in a state of unpausing struggle and excitement upon some subject of party division or other. But, in regard to Texas, enough has now been given to Party. It is time for the common duty of Patriotism to the Country to succeed ;—or if this claim will not be recognized, it is at least time for common sense to acquiesce with decent grace in the inevitable and the irrevocable.

Texas is now ours. Already, before these words are written, her Convention has undoubtedly ratified the acceptance, by her Congress, of our proffered invitation into the Union ; and made the requisite changes in her already republican form of constitution to adopt it to its future federal relations. Her star and her stripe may already be said to have taken their place in the glorious blazon of our common nationality ; and the sweep of our eagle's wing already includes within its circuit the wide extent of her fair and fertile land. She is no longer to us a mere geographical space— a certain combination of coast, plain, mountain, valley, forest and stream. She is no longer to us a mere country on the map. She comes within the dear and sacred designation of Our Country ; no longer a "*pays*," she is a part of "*la patrie ;*" and that which is at once a sentiment and a virtue, Patriotism, already begins to thrill for her too within the national heart. It is time then that all should cease to treat her as alien, and even adverse—cease to denounce and vilify all and everything connected with her accession—cease to thwart and oppose the remaining steps for its consummation ; or where such efforts are felt to be unavailing, at least to embitter the hour of reception by all the most ungracious frowns of aversion and words of unwelcome. There has been enough of all this. It has had its fitting day during the period when, in common with every other possible question of practical policy that can arise, it unfortunately became one of the leading topics of party division, of presidential electioneering. But that period has passed, and with it let its prejudices and its passions, its discords and its denunciations, pass away too. The next session of Congress will see the representatives of the new young State in their places in both our halls of national legislation, side by side with those of the old Thirteen. Let their reception into "the family" be frank, kindly, and cheerful, as befits such an occasion, as comports not less with our own self-respect than patriotic duty towards them. Ill betide those foul birds that delight to 'file their own nest, and disgust the ear with perpetual discord of ill-omened croak.

Why, were other reasoning wanting, in favor of now elevating this question of the reception of Texas into the Union, out of the lower region of our past party dissensions, up to its proper level of a high and broad nationality, it surely is to be found, found abundantly, in the manner in which other nations have undertaken to intrude themselves into it, between us and the proper parties to the case, in a spirit of hostile interference against us, for the avowed object of thwarting our policy and hampering our power, limiting our greatness and checking the fulfilment of our manifest destiny to overspread the continent allotted by Providence for the free development of our yearly multiplying millions. This we have seen done by England, our old rival and enemy ; and by France, strangely coupled with her against us, under the influence of the Anglicism strongly tinging the policy of her present prime minister, Guizot. The zealous activity with which this effort to defeat us was pushed by the representatives of those governments, together with the character of intrigue accompanying it, fully constituted that case of foreign interference, which Mr. Clay himself declared should, and would unite us all in maintaining the common cause of our country against the foreigner and the foe. We are only as-

"Annexation," an article in the July-August 1845 issue of the *United States Magazine and Democratic Review* long attributed to John L. O'Sullivan, was likely written by Jane Storm. The phrase "manifest destiny" is halfway through the paragraph that begins on the second column on the page.

computer grammar-checking program, flags of errors provided data. The differences and similarities in mechanics and style between the three articles were significant. While O'Sullivan showed a 41.5 percent overall similarity to the anonymous article, Storm showed a 79.6 percent overall similarity to "Annexation." When comparing the grammatical errors the differences are dramatic, with Storm having 100 percent of the same errors and O'Sullivan having none (see Appendix B: Textual Analysis). O'Sullivan, who received a preparatory education in France, attended Westminister School in London, and earned a master's degree from Columbia University, made no punctuation and few stylistic errors. Storm, on the other hand, made the same types of errors found in "Annexation." Their styles differed also in that O'Sullivan consistently used the nominative case "we" to refer to national matters or the magazine and Storm more often used the possessive pronoun "our." Moreover, O'Sullivan wrote in a formal style, but used jargon, whereas Storm wrote informally and used slang and metaphors.[45]

In the same July-August 1845 issue as "Annexation," O'Sullivan contributed "Seeing a Friend off in a Packet." The thirty-two-year-old editor married Susan Rogers the following year and honeymooned in Cuba at his sister's home. "One of the commonest incidents in life for a New Yorker," he began, "is to find himself occasionally at the foot of Marketfield Street, in the midst of a crowd of mail bags, trunks, porters, and poultry, making his way to a friend about to sail across the Atlantic." O'Sullivan's mind was not on annexation or the magazine that summer. In September 1845, when Jane Storm moved to the *Sun*, O'Sullivan tried to hire Alexander Everett, Whig editor of the *North American Review*. Evert Duyckinck, who had been literary editor of the *Morning News* since 1844, took over literary and miscellaneous duties while John Bigelow, as political editor, contributed twenty pages per issue. O'Sullivan then departed for Europe, and did not return until late December. He had not made arrangements for the *Morning News*, but claimed later that Bigelow was supposed to do that. Nelson Waterbury, one of the investors, filled in at the newspaper, and Storm wrote a few editorials on territorial and commercial expansion from October through December.[46]

During the summer of 1845, Storm expanded "The Presidents of Texas" into her first book, *Texas and Her Presidents with a Glance at Her Climate and Agricultural Capabilities*, published in September. Writing as Corinne Montgomery, in one short volume she outlined the exploration and settlement of Texas, summarized the Texas Revolution, and included a short history and geography of the republic. The book was not popular with everyone in Texas. In November, Houston wrote to his wife, Margaret, not to read the publication from the pen of "the *elegant* Mrs. Storm." The appendix contained biographies of Texans with a pen portrait of Houston that was not flattering. The fine print at the beginning of the appendix stated "the writer claims the notice of Doctor [Branch T.] Archer as her own, and true to the letter." It was someone else who described Houston as "a portly man of six-feet-two and fifty-four winters, twenty of which have been spent in whiskey drinking and opium eating." The notice in *DeBow's Commercial Review* was negative as well, but the reviewer admitted that he had not read the book. In *Prominent Women of Texas* (1896), however, the book was listed as one of the most reliable accounts of early Texas history.[47]

After Congress voted to annex Texas in March 1845, Storm kept the *Sun's* readers informed of Mexican reaction. When Mexican Minister Juan Almonte immediately broke diplomatic relations with the United States and declared annexation tantamount to war, she explained that Mexico did not recognize the Texas Republic nor accept that Texas was no longer part of Mexico. In the *Sun*, she urged the United States to purchase from Mexico territory between the Nueces River and the Rio Grande. Although the French had claimed the Rio Grande as the Louisiana border, Spain and Mexico considered the Sabine River as the national border and the Nueces River as the southern boundary of the Province of Texas. When Mexico refused to negotiate on any terms, Secretary of State James Buchanan used Storm's columns in the *Sun* as trial balloons to test reactions and leaked that the Polk administration had offered to lend Mexico fifteen million dollars to pay its debts and thus be free of European interference in internal affairs. In August 1845, Storm reported that the Mexican government regarded the public offer of a loan as an insult and had called for volunteers to defend the honor of Mexico.[48]

Earlier, in the May 1845 issue of the *United States Magazine and Democratic Review*, Storm had minced no words in an article titled, "The Mexican Question." "It's an ill bird that fouls its own nest," she warned. The Texas Revolution came about, she explained, because the Mexican leaders set aside the Constitution of 1824. Furthermore, Mexico could not recover Texas, and it was recognized as a nation among sovereign nations. "Texas was no revolted province," she attested, "Away with this Mexican gasconading about pretended rights and pretended wrongs."[49]

In October 1845, Storm wrote to Lamar that the Polk administration had offered her a place on the administration's organ, the Washington *Union*. She was flattered to be offered a staff position under editor Thomas Ritchie, but obtained a full-time position with a regularly scheduled column at the *Sun*. She explained to Lamar that she preferred the independent press where she was "free to write" as she had for "the U.S. Magazine." As she supported the Whig position that the western boundary of Texas did not include the Rio Grande or Santa Fe, she explained, "My loyalty is most uncertain I think, indeed they say, they would do something handsome if I will let certain vexed questions alone." She thanked Lamar for the invitation to join him in Texas, presumably as his wife, "This is my proper home, I have the satisfaction of believing myself useful." She added, "I would dearly love to see the Maffitts and Mrs. Eberly," and she sent news of Ann Stephens's new baby, Edward Lamar Stephens. She also explained that Polk's cabinet represented shipping and canal interests that desired to expand into Texas, Lower Mexico, Oregon, Cuba, and California. She complained, "There is not a man in the cabinet who could not be blackballed in a month for his stupid unstatesmanship."[50]

On December 12, 1845, Storm officially began a biweekly column called, "Correspondence From the Sun," signed, "MONTGOMERY." With her name in capitals, there was no mistaking the authorship. While Congress was in session, she commuted about every three weeks between New York and Washington, where she lived with the family of the assistant postmaster general, William J. Brown. At thirty-nine years old, she earned her byline and became the national news editor of the world's largest penny press.[51]

When O'Sullivan returned from his ill-arranged trip to Europe, he found unhappy investors and disgruntled associates. In January 1846, O'Sullivan was surprised by the furor that "his editorials" had caused on "manifest destiny," but he immediately used the phrase in a published letter summarizing Storm's expansionist articles. O'Sullivan's investors were not impressed, and he was removed as editor of the *United States Magazine and Democratic Review* and the *Morning News*. Through his social connections O'Sullivan became a regent of State University of New York and continued his courtship of Susan Rogers. In November 1845, his sister, Mary, the widow of his former partner Langtree, married the wealthy Cuban,

Cristobal Madan y Madan, who then supported the aristocratic but impoverished O'Sullivan and his mother.[52]

In the *Sun*, Storm informed readers about the changes taking place in the Democratic party. She explained that the Congress was passing through a period of realignment. She predicted that senators Thomas Hart Benton of the West, John C. Calhoun of the South, and Daniel Webster of New England would oppose President Polk's foreign policies in Orgeon and Mexico. As December ended, MONTGOMERY announced that Secretary Buchanan, Senator Benton and Sen. Lewis Cass had declared their interest in being presidential candidates in 1848. In addition, Secretary of War William Marcy and others were contemplating the possibility of entering the race.[53]

"MONTGOMERY" announced on December 17, 1845, that the Mexican government had agreed to receive a minister from the United States. She next published the diplomatic instructions from Secretary of State Buchanan to John Slidell, Polk's appointee. She was not impressed with Slidell and thought that Cornelius Van Ness, former minister to Spain and most recently collector of the Port of New York, should handle the negotiations. She promoted Buchanan's plan—a cash settlement with Mexico for sale of the Rio Grande border and California. She promised, "Tomorrow, the other side of the political triangle." On December 18, she identified those she called the "war-panic makers" as "contractors who wish to make fortunes in building forts, . . . green lieutenants burning for promotion" and "high tariff people" who need a war to justify higher rates. As December ended, her column reflected the growing impatience of the Polk administration to buy California; "Mexico sells because she knows if she does not it will be 'annexed' at no price at all in five or six years." She suggested that Mexicans expected British support because of investment and trade and the unresolved Oregon question. She warned, "England will not interfere," or "the Republican banner will go up in Canada." Britain respected the fighting ability of the Americans and distrusted the Canadian republicans. Britain encouraged the Mexicans to avoid war and started a fort-building campaign in Canada.[54]

Mexican officials faced a dilemma. "MONTGOMERY" explained that any leader negotiating with the United States for the Rio Grande border could expect removal from office. In 1845, the current Mexican leader, Gen. José Joáquin de Herrera, realized that Texas was not recoverable.

Previously, he had met with Samuel May Williams, an agent during Houston's second administration, and negotiated the recognition of Texas if it remained a republic. Herrera was unable to maintain his leadership, however, and comply with Slidell's public demands for action, she explained. On December 29, 1845, the United States Congress accepted the Texas State Constitution and the next day a conservative junta overthrew Herrera.[55]

In January 1846, Polk faced a more hostile Mexican government than before. In March, "MONTGOMERY" counseled Slidell to "bide his time in Mexico." She cautioned that "the new triumvirate of Mexico," wanted neither a monarchy nor "a downright, serious war." They would negotiate, but "with great caution because of the angry prejudice of the people." She suggested: "There may be a brush on the borders; just enough to prove to the Mexican people that peace and a treaty is desirable." As the prospect of war with Mexico increased, she played down the possibility of war with Britain over Oregon.[56]

In March, "MONTGOMERY" warned readers, "We have a class of politicians that are anxious to bathe the country in blood to win notoriety and office for themselves." She feared "men who would make powers of all the States of the union, and play them for peace or war . . . in their presidential game of chess." That same month, Storm wrote to Lamar, "Polk is a base, narrow souled man and would sell his mother's grave to buy up a Senator." It is not clear to what she was referring, but she opposed the "Ten Regiment Bill," which would create ten permanent regiments and a ten thousand-man army. Also, Polk had ordered Gen. Zachary Taylor to leave Camp Marcy on the Nueces and proceed to the Rio Grande.[57]

While Taylor camped on the Nueces River awaiting further orders, a group of federalists met in Northern Mexico and considered declaring their independence from Mexico. They suggested that Gen. Mariano Arista serve as president of this Republic of the Rio Grande. At the end of January 1846, Col. José María Carbajal, educated in the United States and a former surveyor for the Nacogdoches district, represented Gen. Antonio Canales of Camargo when he met with General Taylor. Canales had lived for a time in Cincinnati and he was willing to use his men in support of the United States in return for weapons, ammunition, and pay. Taylor wrote to Washington for instructions, and Secretary of War William L. Marcy replied that Taylor should make full use of the Mexicans if war came.

Taylor, not wanting to get involved in Mexican politics, later faced the men in battle who had proposed an alliance.[58]

Negotiations with Britain had settled the Oregon boundary dispute, and the forty-ninth parallel was far short of the bellicose slogan, "Fifty-four-Forty or Fight." Storm had been "Calhounized," she explained, and like him, she understood that with no real navy, the United States could not win a war with Britain. Merchants, shipping companies, and the working class who pushed for all Oregon would suffer in any embargo or blockade Britain established.[59]

In Mexico, the conservative monarchist Lucas Alamán raised one million pesos from the Mexican clergy to finance a war against the United States. They ordered war steamers from Britain and prepared for war. When Taylor and his army arrived opposite Matamoros on March 28, 1846, he attempted negotiations. Gen. Mariano Ampudia notified Taylor that arms alone must decide the question. On April 24, Capt. Seth Thornton's patrol was attacked by soldiers who were part of a Mexican force of five thousand men led by Gen. Mariano Arista moving across the Rio Grande. On May 8, the two sides fought an artillery duel at the Battle of Palo Alto, and the following day, at the Battle of Resaca de la Palma, 547 Mexicans and 33 Americans died. A volunteer army had defeated the Mexican professional army, and war had begun.[60]

In *Notable American Women*, Jane Storm was described as "a dim figure on the fringes of the journalistic circles of her day." The true identity of "MONTGOMERY" was unknown to all but a few colleagues, and only by comparing her writing with that of O'Sullivan and identifying her handwriting would one know of her work for O'Sullivan or her political contributions to the *United States Magazine and Democratic Review* during its years of greatest fame. While Storm wrote for the *Sun*, from 1843 to 1847, the newspaper grew to have eight editors and reporters, sixteen pressmen, twelve female folders, one hundred newsboys, and its daily circulation rose from thirty-eight thousand to more than fifty thousand. With the largest daily circulation of any newspaper in the world during the Mexican War, editors of other papers nationwide quoted her columns. Three or four pages of the eight-page *Sun* were devoted to news, poems, book reviews, police reports, and serials while the balance was in advertisements. It is believed that each newspaper reached an additional eight readers as it passed from person to person and family to family. Therefore, as many as four hundred thousand persons may have read her columns daily at a time when the penny press joined the pulpit, the pamphleteer, and the politician as a sphere of influence. The *Weekly Sun* reprinted her columns as a recap of the news on Saturday as did *The American Sun*, the first United States newspaper printed abroad, and sold for two pence on the streets of London. MONTGOMERY was a well-known journalist at the time of the Mexican War.[61]

CHAPTER IV

Behind the Battle Lines of the Mexican War, 1846–1848

> In the course of the summer a "*female*" fresh from Mexico, and with a masculine stomach for war and politics, arrived at Washington, had interviews with members of the administration, and infected some of them with the contagion of a large project—nothing less than the absorption into our Union of all Mexico, and the assumption of all her debts.
>
> —*Sen. Thomas Hart Benton*[1]

*J*ANE STORM WAS THE "FEMALE" SEN. THOMAS HART BENTON CRITICIZED in his memoirs. Benton suggested that she advocated the Mexican War and led the movement to absorb all Mexico into the United States. An examination of forty-three of Storm's columns in the New York *Sun* and more than twenty personal letters to members of the James K. Polk administration do not support Benton's allegations. The peace mission to Mexico lasting from December 1846 to April 1847 that Storm undertook with her publisher, Moses Y. Beach, was the best-known episode of her career and propelled her into a nationally known public figure. She lost her anonymity to a certain degree when it became know that MONTGOMERY was a woman, and thereafter the name Cora Montgomery became synonymous with revolutions in Mexico, Cuba, Europe, Central America, and the Caribbean. Her revolutionary ardor was not motivated purely by civic virtue, but reflected her financial interests and those of her friends and business associates. As her mentor Aaron Burr said, political affairs should yield "fun, honor, & profit."[2]

Benton was not a disinterested observer of Storm's activities, nor was she one of his supporters. Benton had opposed Texas annexation, and Jane Storm criticized his Mexican policy in her columns that would keep the Mexican people under their same leaders. She wanted a Republic of the Rio Grande that would benefit the people and her investments along the border. In 1856, when Benton completed his memoirs as his version of politics, he was a bitter man who had lost his U.S. Senate seat because of sectional politics in his home state of Missouri. At that time, Jane Storm, as well as pro-slave advocates, promoted a southern rail route to the Pacific and filibuster operations into Mexico—policies that would not benefit Missouri. Thus, Benton's claim that a *"female"* led the All Mexico movement was one way of repudiating the southern rail route and what he called, "the scheme" of "Mr. Calhoun and his friends."[3]

Benton's "view" of history was not accurate. John C. Calhoun and Jane Storm both opposed the Mexican War and the absorption of Mexico, but for very different reasons. Calhoun was a racist and thought the Mexicans incapable of republican government, and Storm opposed the war because she thought diplomacy could accomplish the same goals. Furthermore, she believed the Mexicans were capable of republican government. When war with Mexico came on the Rio Grande, she insisted that the moral aim of the war be the establishment of a republic and that it not be a war of conquest. Her view of the Mexican War from behind closed doors and from behind the battle lines is not the one of bravery and valor as told by the participants or that of war correspondents written from official reports at headquarters behind the front lines. Her view of the war was one of personal experience and an intimate knowledge of backroom politics. She witnessed the actual conditions of war as she passed through the lines of combat to and from Mexico City. In her columns and personal correspondence, she criticized leaders on both sides of the Rio Grande and exposed the betrayals, ambitions, and greed of the war makers and those who would use the war to gain profits and glory for themselves.[4]

In January 1846, as Mexican conservatives installed a regime favoring war and chances of a peaceful settlement with Mexico diminished, Storm wrote of her frustrations to Robert Owen (1771–1858), the labor reformer and co-founder of the New York *Sun*. She confided that she was in an ill-tempered mood and she was not sure the world was worth mending. She proposed that she and the elderly English reformer run away together where she could scold comfortably and he could carry out his improvement in human nature by teaching her common sense. Jane was avoiding Washington, she said, because she "never had a taste for mad houses." Jokingly, she added, "They say those who of right belong to them never have."[5]

Beginning with her first signed column in the New York *Sun* in December 1845, Jane Storm, writing as "MONTGOMERY," had advocated a peaceful solution to differences between Mexico and the United States. She warned about those who stood to gain from such a war. She also was aware of Mexican federalists along the Rio Grande who had from before the time of the Texas Revolution opposed the centralist government of Mexico.[6]

After President James K. Polk ordered Gen. Zachary Taylor to march from Camp Marcy at Corpus Christi on the Nueces River to the left bank of the Rio Grande, Storm, writing as "MONTGOMERY" in the *Sun*, accused the president of "withdrawing from the vulgar sympathy of the people." She opposed having ten permanent army regiments created in the spring of 1846, because Polk would have "a standing military force to do his bidding." Storm saw an all-volunteer army as "the strength of republicanism expressed through support or rejection of the executive's call to military action." In April 1846, she reminded readers, "This republic should teach the world that it will owe nothing to the sword." She advocated that the United States was "the guiding star to liberty," and should help others in obtaining republican government. During her career, she called herself the Argus-eyed press, the pilot of the Fourth Estate, the warden in the watchtower, and the Owl of Fulton Street. She believed it was her duty to inform the public about corruption. In a letter to Secretary of the Navy George Bancroft, she labeled unidentified cabinet members as "demagogues" who "would corrupt the Republic." She had advised Mirabeau B. Lamar that the cabinet represented steamship interests intent on territorial expansion.[7]

Through informants, Storm knew that certain Mexicans did not support a war with the United States, and she was possibly the link between the Polk administration and the Mexican peace groups. Jane was a friend of both Gen. Mirabeau B. Lamar and William L. Cazneau, who communicated with Mexican Freemasons and traded illegally with the republican merchants who wanted independence and peace with the United States.

71

Her Catholicism and support of the working class put her in contact with New York Bishop John Hughes, who corresponded with Mexican bishops. Hughes's best friend, Peter A. Hargous, operated a steamship line to Mexico and served as United States consul at Vera Cruz. Hargous was then negotiating in Mexico for a Mexican land grant across the Isthmus of Tehuantepec that would establish a transit connection for United States steam lines operating on the Gulf and Pacific coasts.[8]

On May 13, 1846, after word arrived in Washington of the April 24 ambush and capture of Capt. Seth B. Thornton and his men on the left bank of the Rio Grande, President Polk requested funds from Congress to defend the United States against Mexican aggression. That day, Secretary of State Buchanan wrote to Bishop Hughes, who was then attending a Catholic conference in Baltimore, about parties in Mexico that were willing to recognize Texas, cede California, and have peace. Hughes conferred with colleagues and came directly to Washington. After several meetings with Buchanan and Polk, Hughes refused to undertake the task unless Polk granted him plenipotentiary status with full powers of negotiation. According to Hughes's biographer, Polk refused Hughes's request because of anti-Catholic prejudice.[9]

Once hostilities began, Polk ordered Col. Stephen Kearny to occupy New Mexico and General Taylor to move deeper into Mexico. Taylor lingered a month near the mouth of the Rio Grande before he moved upriver to Camargo. Polk and Secretary of State William L. Marcy ordered Taylor, like Kearny, to take advantage of republican allies, but Taylor again hesitated to accept the overtures of the republicans. "MONTGOMERY" criticized the administration, "We would not have had a war had Polk not sent Taylor to look one up." In the independent *Sun*, she took the Whig point of view concerning the Rio Grande as the border of Texas. She asserted,

> Our children's children will blush at the overbearing injustice of this year's history. But today the man does not stand in a high place that has the boldness to tell the truth . . . . Neither Polk, his party in Congress, nor his cabinet will explain the exact nature of *the jurisdiction of Texas over the country beyond the Nueces.*[10]

Jane Storm wanted William Cazneau appointed a secret agent to negotiate with the peace factions along the Rio Grande. Before war began, she had informed readers that the northern states of Mexico had rebelled with the Texans in 1835 and in 1840 declared their independence as a Republic of the Rio Grande. As the war with Mexico began, Hugh McLeod, the Texas adjutant general, set up a newspaper in Matamoros titled the *Republic of the Rio Grande*. Taylor, however, would not negotiate with the republicans, nor would the administration appoint Cazneau as an agent to do so. Storm was furious. She accused Buchanan of having a secret agent on the border, "If I am right—I shall have him shot—I mean that exactly." With a fury she warned Buchanan, "A great cause and true men were not to be endangered by untrustworthy rulers." Storm cautioned against making Taylor a war hero, predicting that he would become the next Whig presidential nominee. She concluded her letter by saying, "Taylor is a good soldier," but "Cazneau is worth forty of him in border negotiations."[11]

Jane sought to use what influence she had to have Cazneau appointed to a position of responsibility and power. He had helped keep her Texas land claims open and they had become engaged earlier in the year. Cazneau was a public figure in Texas politics and represented the Western or pro-Lamar expansionist faction. He had served as Travis County delegate in the Constitutional Convention of 1845 and in the First Texas State Legislature. In 1845, he became general of the Grand Royal Lone Star Chapter of Texas Free and Accepted Masons—the source of the honorary title of general that he carried the remainder of his life. He also became a partner of Henry Kinney at Corpus Christi and supplied contraband goods to merchants in northern Mexico. The business and fraternal ties in Mexico did indeed make Cazneau more qualified to conduct border negotiations with the Mestizo republicans than Taylor, a Louisiana plantation owner and Indian fighter. Cazneau would help set up a republic based on the Texas model, but without slavery—something Cotton Whigs and Calhoun Democrats opposed as did racially prejudiced Free Soil Democrats. Not getting a diplomatic appointment, Cazneau served on General Lamar's staff of the Lone Star Contingent of Texas Volunteers.[12]

Jane Storm had made a public display of her differences with the administration's border policy for she sought to make amends while exploring other avenues for creating a Republic of the Rio Grande. As she commuted between New York and Washington, Storm gossiped with fellow travelers. One such trip at the end of June 1846 was with Cornelia J. Randolph, Thomas Jefferson's granddaughter and sister-in-law of Nicholas

P. Trist, chief clerk of the State Department. The week after Storm's tirade against Buchanan, the women took the train from Baltimore to Havre de Grace, Maryland, then traveled by ferry to Philadelphia, where they took a steamer to New York. Storm gave Randolph her version of the disagreement with Buchanan and informed Randolph that she wished to speak with Trist, a close friend of the secretary of state. Randolph promised to arrange a meeting.[13]

Storm was certain the Polk administration would create a new republic on the Rio Grande before the end of autumn and worked to make it a reality. On June 29, 1846, she wrote to Robert Owen that all of Mexico north of twenty-five degrees would soon establish an alliance with the United States. She assured the reformer, a native of England, that he was not to be concerned because the United States would protect the economic interests and safety of British citizens in Mexico.[14]

Storm had created gossip by her public display against the administration. On July 4, 1846, Trist contacted Sen. Robert Dale Owen of Indiana, son of the English reformer. In reply Owen explained to Trist the source of Jane's anger. Once frequent correspondents, Owen and Trist had not written for six years when Owen remarked that women had a very different political style from men. Owen explained that Storm and Cazneau had been engaged for some time but they had not married because she doubted his attachment was strong or that their characters were compatible. Cazneau had recently traveled to New York and pressured her about marriage, and she had again declined. Owen explained that Cazneau managed her Texas property and refused compensation although his financial situation was not good. She sought a position that repaid him and knew that he was worthy of the appointment. Her failure to obtain Cazneau an appointment was the source of her bitterness, Owen explained. Apparently Trist and Owen knew of the informal talks with Mexican republicans and plans for further negotiations, for Owen advised Trist to judge for himself if she should be part of the mission.[15]

When General Taylor began his march toward Camargo on July 9, 1846, Secretary Marcy wrote to Taylor, reminding him that President Polk had ordered him to take advantage of any independence movements in Northern Mexico. Through July, "MONTGOMERY" pressed for recognition of a Republic of the Rio Grande in the *Sun* as if it actually existed. In her column of July 7, Storm wrote that Polk had two paths, he could hew Mexico to fragments and take what he wanted, or plant "a new and grateful republic." She implored, "I would not see our eagle merely a bird of prey!" She further suggested, "a republic with stable laws, fostered industry, liberty of conscience, and proper education of all the children" would be a redeeming act of the war. She claimed the area would become Americanized through trade and commerce. In one column, she assured Horace Greeley, editor of the *Tribune*, that the republic would not extend slavery; "*That region is written free by the finger of its Creator.*" On July 17, "MONTGOMERY" challenged, "The President may make war. . . . He may kill the inhabitants, plunder the churches and desolate the towns of the friendly States of the Rio Grande," but he cannot "call a republic into being."[16]

In July, Storm continued her quest for a new republic. She wrote to Secretary of the Navy George Bancroft that she was returning to Washington to speak to him and Marcy about her intelligence from the border. She was confident that it was more reliable than the cabinet's information. Storm urged Bancroft to remain in the cabinet and continue his work on naval reform. Later that month, hearing rumors of his resignation, she wrote to the secretary that if Slidell was his successor, "as there is a Sun on earth and in heaven it will be a costly whim if Mr. Polk takes it into his head to put that man in the Cabinet." She claimed she could "count the beats of the popular heart" and warned Bancroft that the Democratic party was fragmenting. She claimed to control over half the country's daily circulation, and if he had doubts, he should ask Marcy or Robert Owen. The secretary passed her letter to Marcy, writing at the bottom, "Who is Storm?" Marcy scribbled below his note, "a prodigiously smart and keen writer for the newspapers in New York. . . . I studied law with her father when *she* was some 8 or 10 years old."[17]

Meanwhile, Polk sought ways to end the war with Mexico. In July 1846, he sent Alexander Slidell Mackenzie to Havana to negotiate with the exiled Gen. Antonio López de Santa Anna. John Slidell's brother had taken the name of an uncle after a navy scandal had blackened his reputation. Mackenzie arranged for the dictator's cooperation in ending the war and delivered orders that Bancroft wrote for Santa Anna's passage through the United States naval blockade. After Taylor's capture of Camargo on July 14, the Paredes pro-war regime had fallen from power. Storm informed readers that the past three Mexican administrations knew the right of the United States to annex Texas. Ignoring that the Mexican government had refused to meet John Slidell, Polk's special negotiator, she criticized, "Had a good diplomatist been sent . . . in the first place, Mexican pride could have been soothed and war avoided." She blamed Slidell for his public demands for action and his disregard for Mexican pride and sensibilities. She predicted, "Mexico will debate," while our Congress votes appropriations.[18]

As Storm observed the House of Representatives on the evening of August 8, 1846, Congress debated war expenditures. She described it as "A day of fearful significance" and "danger to the Union." Rep. David Wilmot of Pennsylvania made "slavery the test of party" with his rider that banned any new lands acquired from becoming slave territory. Wilmot and his supporters were not abolitionists, but racist Free Soil Democrats who believed in containing slavery within its present limits and limiting the power of slaveholders until slaves and free blacks could be transported out of the country. As Wilmot blurted in the House chambers, "By God, Sir, men born and nursed by white women are not going to be ruled by men who were brought up on the milk of some damn negro wench." Although it did not pass, Wilmot's "The White Man's Resolution" split the Democratic party further. Storm wrote, "The moderate and independent press must now stand forth the vigilant and faithful conservator of its country's peace." She reminded readers that the forefathers decided that each state should govern its own and answer for its domestic sins. "Shall we keep faith?" she asked, or "allow the ultraist to dash the Union to fragments."[19]

By the first of September 1846, Storm saw no victors in the war with Mexico because, "Much treasure, much integrity and much harmony have been wasted." Polk had "blemished the hitherto spotless fame of our mother land" by "coveting our neighbor's soil." The people were the "deep losers," she lamented, "for they must pay the cost in tax and blood." She again promoted "a free and independent republic beyond the Rio Grande." On September 21, she sent Trist recommendations from Sam Houston about negotiations with Mexican officials during his second presidential term. The Mexican national government had secretly agreed that Texas was independent. Evidence such as this would "never cease coming," she warned, "while I live and the press is free."[20]

After Taylor's victory at Monterrey on September 25 still did not bring peace negotiations, Polk increased military pressure. He ordered Gen. John E. Wool from San Antonio to Chihuahua and Gen. Winfield Scott to lead a military force into the heart of Mexico from Vera Cruz. As a preliminary to negotiations, Buchanan made Moses Yale Beach, publisher of the New York *Sun* and a representative of New York bankers, a special agent to travel to Mexico City on a secret mission to end the war.[21]

The mission was a joint effort of the United States, Great Britain, and the Mexican peace factions. Mexicans who wanted peace were clerics, a faction within the Conservative Party, Liberals, and Moderates. The clerics had helped install the Conservative Paredes regime that viewed the church as a source of income. Clerics were the official record keeping and educational bureaucracies of Mexico and charged fees to register and legalize baptisms, marriages, and burials. The church made loans for the fees and when the loans were not repaid, the debtors became peons kept in perpetual servitude by Conservative masters. The church also made loans to Liberals and Moderates, whose foreclosures created enemies determined to break the power of the church. Liberals were European-educated professionals who wished to industrialize Mexico and Moderates sought closer ties with the United States.[22]

The cover for the peace mission was for Moses Beach, Jane Storm, and Beach's daughter Drusilla to pose as an English family traveling to Mexico on business. Officially, they were to evaluate the political climate in Mexico City, arrange for the sale of the Rio Grande border and California, and get verification of a land grant across the Isthmus of Tehuantepec. In September, Manning and Mackintosh, of London, had sold the José de Garay land grant across the Isthmus of Tehuantepec to Hargous Brothers of Philadelphia. Ewen C. Mackintosh was British consul at Mexico City and Manning and Marshall was the company in charge of collection and readjustment of the Mexican debt owed British bankers. Besides publishing the *Sun,* Beach was a director of several New York banks, and he carried fifty thousand dollars to establish a National Bank of Mexico. Such a private bank would make banking independent of the church and their conservative allies. Storm was interpreter and guide because neither Beach nor Drusilla spoke Spanish or had been to Mexico.[23]

Buchanan issued Beach formal diplomatic instructions as a secret agent on November 21, 1846. If possible, Beach was to make peace on just and honorable terms. He was also to communicate all useful information that he might acquire. That same day, Buchanan wrote to Rev. Jonathan Serretta of St. Louis, in care of Rt. Rev. Dr. Antoine Blanc, the Archbishop of New Orleans. Buchanan authorized passports for the reverends Serretta, Jonathan B. Figerola, and John Buguet of the Order of St. Vincent de Paul in St. Louis. Under the direction of Rev. John Timon of St. Louis, they were to go to Mexico and aid fellow priests of the order and the Sisters of Charity. They would travel to Vera Cruz via Havana as auxiliaries of the mission. Three days later Storm attended a White House reception on November 24. That day, Trist wrote to her concerning the Tehuantepec route and the spread of rational principles into Mexico—something he did not foresee happening in her lifetime. Polk jotted in his diary that it would be a good joke if Beach made a treaty. The agents steamed from New York on November 27, 1846, on *The Southern*, a new steamer put into operation by the New York-based Spoffard and Tileson Shipping Company, which was then converting its sailing fleet to steam vessels. While Beach's sons, Alfred and Moses S., were left in charge of the *Sun*, Henry served as cashier of the Plainfield New Jersey Bank from which Beach took the money to finance the mission and to establish a bank in Mexico. Beach failed, however, to document the loan.[24]

Because newspapers had better newsgathering techniques than the government, President Polk and government officials received the war news through their daily newspapers. Thus a series by MONTGOMERY titled "Tropical Sketches" in the *Sun* unofficially reported the mission's progress. She promoted a winter vacation of steam travel, hotels, and sightseeing in the "Sunny South." Dated from December 1, 1846, to January 9, 1847, fifteen sketches appeared in the daily and weekly *Sun* from December 11, 1846, to March 26, 1847.[25]

The agents arrived in Charleston, South Carolina, on December 1, and remained two days before they sailed by schooner to Matanzas on the north shore of Cuba. They then traveled to Havana by small Cuban steamer because the road across the mountains was impassable. After a week of Cuban hospitality and tours of Catholic institutions, on January 9, 1847, the secret agents steamed by a British mail steamer from Havana to Vera Cruz. Buchanan and Polk knew Mexican officials would meet with Beach.[26]

What readers did not know was that Storm and Beach had met with Buenaventura Aroujo, the Mexican minister in Havana, who wrote the agents a letter of introduction to liberal Vice President Valentín Goméz Farías. Aroujo introduced Beach as editor of the New York *Sun* and Storm as an editor and writer of importance. He described them as "apostles of peace" for the American government. The designation linked them to an international movement that was designed to end warfare in the world.

Aroujo gave Goméz Farías the proposed plan by which 200 to 250 Mexicans were to foment a rebellion in Vera Cruz and lay siege to the fortress of San Juan de Ulloa guarding Vera Cruz. Aroujo complained of a lack of pay, but explained that he survived through speculations with the English minister in Havana and the governors of Nassau and Jamaica. Aroujo wrote to Goméz Farías about slave dealings of British officials per-haps to explain how Beach and party came to operate under British pass-ports—by using this knowledge to get British cooperation. Aroujo explained that British officials fitted out privateers in Nassau and bought slaves as indentures. They then seized their own ships and sold the cargo as slaves in Cuba and then smuggled them into the United States.[27]

The British Consulate in Havana provided Beach and Storm with pass-ports and arranged passage to Vera Cruz on a British mail steamer. In addition to Aroujo's letter, Beach carried letters from Catholic officials in the United States and Cuba to clergy in Mexico—all in a British diplomatic pouch. Beach later wrote that Britain wanted to prevent France and Spain from establishing a monarchy in Mexico, and therefore was helping the United States end the war.[28]

On January 13, 1847, Beach, Drusilla, and Storm arrived in Vera Cruz. The priests from St. Louis were on the same steamer. In her col-umn, "MONTGOMERY" described Vera Cruz with Spanish, English, and American houses stretched along the beach. She assured readers that the blockade was effective and that Vera Cruz had been defenseless for seven months, but the navy under sail was dependent on favorable winds and tides to land an expeditionary force. "The inefficiency of the navy added a year to the war," she complained. She blamed Congress for not having a steam navy. "I know what I am talking about," she wrote, "I have been to sea fourteen times and on every class of ship." In June, Storm had pro-moted Secretary Bancroft's proposal, based on the British model, to subsi-dize mail steamers run by auxiliary naval personnel that could have deck guns added in time of war. Instead, Congress voted to build ten war steamers that she claimed cost as much as one hundred mail steamers and they would not be self-supporting as the merchant ships would be. The Oregon crisis had made the weakness of the navy apparent when Britain threatened to close the Straits of Florida, but she also promoted a steam navy because working conditions were more humane and democra-tic. "We shall return home in a few weeks by way of Tampico or New Orleans," she informed readers. Later that evening, the governor of Vera

Cruz called at their hotel and talked privately while soldiers searched their baggage. A resident of Vera Cruz also met with the agents.[29]

It took eleven days for the agents to travel some 250 miles inland from Vera Cruz to Mexico City, a normal journey of six days by stagecoach. They did not take the most direct route, but followed the Old Spanish National Highway through Jalapa. Hernàn Cortéz took the same route in 1519 when he defeated Montezuma, and muleteers still used the road for trade goods. Persons carrying large sums of money traveled with the muleteers for safety. At Perote, soldiers threatened the agents with arrest and again searched their baggage. At Puebla the agents met with moderates who knew of their coming from General Lamar, an unnamed Mexican commander in the field, and others. The moderates presented the terms under which they would agree to end the war. Beach labeled their proposal the "Three Points." The United States would occupy California and all territory above 26 degrees north latitude. They would pay citizens' claims with an additional three million dollars for California. The United States would restore forts and public buildings to the Mexican government, and no forced loans would be placed on the Mexican people.[30]

The moderates' proposal was similar to one Storm had published a year earlier in the *Sun* in December 1845. Their condition for acceptance of the plan contained a way for the Mexicans to save face. The United States should capture Vera Cruz and show their superior power and full preparation of a march to the capital while Santa Anna was engaged with the army in the north. At that point, Santa Anna could declare "a crisis," that would end the war by honorable terms. Moderates informed the travelers of the best procedure for completion of the mission. The Americans learned that baggage searches and threats of arrest at Vera Cruz and Perote were to prevent suspicion of moderates in those cities. According to Catholic sources, Storm met with the Bishop of Puebla, and he agreed to support the Americans in return for protection of church property.[31]

The agents arrived in Mexico City on January 24, 1847. On January 11, Vice President Farías had the Mexican Congress pass a law calling for raising fifteen million pesos by the sale or mortgage of church property. Church officials refused to comply, and moderates supported the clerics and demanded a change in government. United States Consul John Black arranged for Beach to meet with individuals in congress, the administration, and the church receptive to their mission. Beach, a self-made man, did not play the role of the English businessman effectively. On February

4, 1847, Storm and H. B. Sutton of the Louis Hargous Company in Mexico City signed an affidavit stating that Beach was a British citizen who lived in the United States. That day Beach sent a written proposal to Farías for a National Bank in Mexico City capitalized and controlled by Beach and his associates. The bank would assume the debts of the Mexican government and serve as the depository of the treasury. It appeared that Beach and his associates were taking over the debts and responsibilities of Manning and Marshall. Thus, Storm's letter to Owen a year before about British debts being honored suggests that the project had been in the making for at least a year. Beach began talks on the government's recognition of the Hargous's land grant across Tehuantepec that had been pending, but learned that the transfer had to be approved by the Mexican congress.[32]

On February 27, 1847, a civil uprising led by Santa Anna's elite National Guard began in Mexico City. Beach wrote that the purpose of the revolt was to bring about a change in the government to support the "Three Points," protect church property, and end the war. The revolt became known as the "Revolt of the Polkos," because the regiments of Santa Anna's elite National Guard danced the polka. The rebels occupied the convents and shelled government buildings, but "a crisis" did not develop—General Scott did not attack Vera Cruz on schedule. As Scott pondered tactics, a norther blew in and rough seas further delayed landing. In Mexico City, clerics, leery of their new allies, began rejoining the Conservatives. While waiting for Scott to attack, the peace coalition dissolved.[33]

On George Washington's birthday, apparently according to a pre-arranged plan, Santa Anna had attacked General Taylor's forces at Buena Vista some six hundred miles to the north of Mexico City, captured battle flags, and withdrew claiming victory. On March 8, 1847, Scott finally landed at Vera Cruz, and Storm wrote from Mexico City, "For three weeks we have been expecting 'the crisis.'" That same day the rebel generals met in Mexico City, changed their strategy, and demanded the resignation of Farías. With the coalition failing, friends wrote to Santa Anna that he should return to Mexico City. Although Santa Anna had returned to Mexico under an agreement to secure peace with the United States, he changed his position and warned that cooperating with Beach was against the best interests of Mexico. Perhaps transit rights to Tehuantepec had not been part of the original pact with Santa Anna or the British.[34]

When Scott landed at Anton Lizardo some twelve miles below Vera Cruz and began a landward approach to the city, Moderates and their remaining cleric allies in Mexico City thought Scott should know which Mexicans would cooperate with United States officials. Members of the peace faction were listed in a certain order on a program printed for a Grand Ball. Beach decided Storm should travel to Vera Cruz and deliver the key to the ball program to General Scott while Beach continued negotiations. Thus, around March 13, Jane left Mexico City with "fleeing citizens of many nationalities." Beach remained at the capital awaiting Scott's capture of Vera Cruz, and the peace commissioner he thought accompanied Scott.[35]

After a six-day journey by stage, Storm reached the battle lines at Vera Cruz. Since March 9, Gen. William Jenkins Worth and his New York regulars had been fighting sand fleas and blowing sand as they dug trenches on the landward side of the city. The day after her arrival, March 22, General Scott, not knowing of any arrangements and paying little heed to Storm's fantastic scheme, demanded the immediate surrender of the city and when it was not forthcoming began a cannon barrage.[36]

Two days after her arrival in Vera Cruz, the words of Storm's column reverberated with the sound of cannon fire. "The destiny of Mexico trembles in the balance," she wrote, because Mexico "lacked determined purpose and honest leaders." She explained that a revolt had not occurred in Vera Cruz, and the National Guard had betrayed the peace effort in Mexico City. Yet, she wrote, "All the way down from Mexico City the road was strewn with houseless families blaming the Americans for their misery." For three nights, from a British vessel crowded with British citizens, she watched the city burn. She described an array of sailing and steam-powered ships anchored beyond the sand bar that lay between the city and the gulf. From her description, one could almost hear the cannon fire, see the pounding surf, and smell the gun smoke as she pictured the scene of small boats filled with civilians paddling from ship to ship in search of refuge. The Spanish and French ships took care of their citizens, she wrote, and she was on the English man-of-war *Daring* because the U.S. Navy could not keep women and children on board. Exhausted after months behind enemy lines and days without rest on the stage from Mexico City, she directed her frustration at a Captain Bennett, who refused her refuge on the *Indiana* "unless she could pay in dollars." The Yankee merchant captains were "already well-paid with contracts for supplying U. S. troops," she fumed.[37]

With no knowledge of events occurring in Vera Cruz or Washington, Beach waited in Mexico City for a peace envoy now two months late.

General Scott acted as if he was unaware of any plan for cooperating with the Vera Cruz or Mexico City republicans. Possibly, like his Whig colleague General Taylor, Scott ignored Polk's orders to cooperate with Mexican factions. Meanwhile, Scott blasted homes and businesses along a path to the fort guarding the harbor.[38]

In Washington it was politics as usual. Presidential aspirants fought among themselves for the opportunity of conquering the Mexican peace and gaining political advantage. Benton checked Buchanan's move for power in the administration. By his gossip to the press and unapproved leaks, Buchanan lost Polk's confidence, and Benton became Polk's unofficial adviser. When Polk tried to make Benton his chief of staff to negotiate peace, Benton's senate rivals, Lewis Cass and John C. Calhoun, thwarted his plans. Thus, while Beach waited in Mexico City and Storm waited on a British man-of-war, Santa Anna returned triumphant to Mexico City.[39]

On March 24, 1847, Santa Anna, with captured American flags from Buena Vista, entered Mexico City a hero and the staged revolt of his personal guard ended. Santa Anna declared the moderates traitors, and they went into hiding while Farías went into exile. Upon his demand, clerics gave Santa Anna additional funds to continue the war. On March 25, Beach wrote from the Mexican capital that the "woman's revolution" had failed and he predicted that Mexico would soon be under "a nation who could appreciate its value." Within days Beach received a message to meet with Santa Anna. U.S. Consul Black suspected treachery and convinced Beach that his life was in danger. In the middle of the night, Beach and Drusilla, leaving all their possessions behind, set out by horseback with a party of moderates who were leaving for Tampico. Under control of the United States, Tampico was three hundred miles to the northeast on the Gulf of Mexico.[40]

Storm remained on HMS *Daring* and sent daily observations on the war to the *Sun* by supply ships that steamed daily to and from New Orleans. On March 29, the Mexican commander Gen. Juan Morales surrendered the fortress guarding Vera Cruz. For the first time, Storm revealed what she called, "The Plan of La Playa" as put forth by "the citizens and clergy of Mexico." The plan was similar to Beach's "Three Points," but in addition, she said the United States was to protect the border against Indian raids, ports would remain with the Americans, a tariff would pay all claims, and the United States would get a right of way across the Isthmus of Tehuantepec. She added, "no doubt General Scott has been consulted." The latest news in Vera Cruz was that Polk would appoint Benton to negotiate the peace. "This is so much better than anything Benton can do with his millions of bribe money," she announced. "The United States has to decide whether it will save or destroy the last hope of the Mexican people," she wrote. She did not mean the "30,000 officers who have devoured her wealth and strength," but, "her long suffering . . . working class." The next day she repeated, "The appointment of Benton with money paid to their corrupt rulers, means chains for the masses."[41]

On March 31, 1847, Storm claimed that Mexicans first raised the issue of annexation. "I have had convincing proof, that the northern provinces of Mexico," she wrote, "would have declared in favor of annexation to the United States to escape the miseries of their present conditions." Storm again urged Scott to adopt the system Kearny used in New Mexico to take advantage of local republicans. Yet "If like old Rough and Ready, Scott will use no argument but the sword," she predicted, "it will cost many lives; much treasure, and much time to conquer peace."[42]

On April 8, 1847, the day after her fortieth birthday, Storm sent a column on the "Plan of La Playa" to Horace Greeley at the New York *Tribune*. The plan also called for creating three Mexican republics of the Rio Grande, Vera Cruz, and Yucatan and ending the civil wars that had destroyed the "fine, but terrible abused country." She described the Mexican people as "generous to their friends and brave in a good cause." Greeley printed her letter with its warning, "There is danger of a strong military ascendancy in the United States and it will expand to control the destiny of the republic."[43]

Also on April 8, Scott ordered his army inland to a healthier climate. On April 10, a government vessel transported Beach and Drusilla from Tampico to Vera Cruz. The transport carried the Beaches, plus two military companies and 280 mules. Upon their arrival in Vera Cruz, the Beaches found Jane Storm quartered in the city. As Beach told the story, Scott had been slow to accept Storm's statement about cooperation with peace factions and "uttered an epithet regarding her" which "had it found its way to the public press, would have become a by-word." When Beach located Scott, the general listened, but lectured, "Never send messages of such importance by a plenipotentiary in petticoats." Storm described Scott as "Old Fuss and Feathers" in her column, and of his victory at Vera Cruz wrote, "European papers will say more women and children killed than soldiers . . . unhappily is true." Foreign consuls had raised a white flag and asked if women and children could leave the city, but Scott had continued the shelling of the city.[44]

After Beach conferred with Scott, Storm returned to Puebla through enemy lines around April 13, 1847. She perhaps carried a message to the bishop from Scott. Outside Puebla, a handsome messenger, whose bridle and saddle were covered with silver and gold, rode alongside the stage and delivered a message. Storm described the equestrian as a Mexican Robin Hood who robbed the rich and gave to the poor. General Worth recommended that Insp. Gen. Ethan Allen Hitchcock use the local hero Manuel Dominguez. Conservatives had destroyed the business of the once respected merchant. As a highwayman, Dominguez took revenge on wealthy conservatives. Hitchcock estimated Dominguez controlled some ten thousand men along the trade routes of Mexico. His men communicated by sign and issued passports that allowed merchants to travel safely. Hitchcock made Dominguez a U.S. Army officer over a regiment of his men who served as guides, couriers, and spies. Thus, it was probably through Dominguez that Lamar and Cazneau knew of the peace factions, and the Bishop of Puebla and the Vera Cruz merchants were prepared for Beach's arrival. It is likely that Dominguez's men escorted Beach, his daughter, and Storm in their travels to and from Mexico City and Tampico. Not everyone had the same view of Dominguez and his men. John Kenley described the spy company as "the worst-looking scoundrels I ever saw."[45]

While Storm remained to await the results of Scott's meeting and further bribery of Santa Anna, on April 14 Beach and Drusilla sailed aboard the USS *Massachusetts* for New Orleans. Upon his arrival in the city, Beach wrote, "I am once more, thank heaven, . . . among white folks." Drusilla did not enjoy the mission and wrote unfavorably of the Mexican people in the *Sun*. Beach wrote of his travels in the *Sun* and immediately returned to New York up the Mississippi and Ohio rivers. Unfortunately for Beach, during his absence New Jersey officials investigated his Plainfield Bank and found that it had questionable transactions and missing assets. Beach's son, Henry, and a brother, Asabel Beach, had shifted funds between banks, and with the public investigation and withdrawals by depositors, the bank went into receivership while Beach was in Mexico. Thus, Beach found a scandal and disappointed financial associates upon his return.[46]

Jane Storm remained in Mexico and on April 16, 1847, wrote that the Polk administration had three options. The United States could recognize the independence movements in each section of Mexico and allow the republicans to handle their own affairs; U.S. troops could occupy all of Mexico until a stable government could be established and maintained for an estimated five years; or, Polk could take what he wanted and leave the rest for some European prince. If unwilling to recognize any new republics, she wrote, the United States "must control Mexico to the Isthmus of Tehuantepec or let some European power do it." If yielded to a foreign friend, she predicted, the United States could expect perpetual war in Mexico.[47]

By mid-April, Storm had been part of the daily life of Mexico for nearly four months. She had compassion for the people and predicted that Scott would face little opposition because of the tyrants that ruled Mexico. She warned, "This war lays a deep and nervous responsibility on the American nation. They decide the fate of Mexico." On April 20, Storm left Vera Cruz with news of Santa Anna's defeat at Cerro Gordo. "The plan was for Jalapa and Puebla to declare independence when Scott took Vera Cruz," she explained, but like Taylor, Scott had "rejected the people as allies" and "turned them back to their enemies."[48]

While Jane's friends such as Cazneau and Lamar would benefit financially through trade had a republic come into being, she stood to gain as well. A weakened Mexico would be more likely to grant Hargous Brothers the right of transit across the Isthmus of Tehuantepec, an enterprise in which both she and Cazneau had a financial interest. In addition, she owned one of the few waterholes between Corpus Christi and Eagle Pass on a trail linking the Gulf of Mexico to the Chihuahua Trail. However, she truly believed the Mexican people capable of republican government, and saw the area as a possible area to relocate free blacks from the United States. As she would later inform Beach, it was impossible for her to write contrary to her convictions.[49]

On May 6, 1847, more than a month after Scott captured Vera Cruz, President Polk appointed Nicholas Trist, the state department clerk, as peace negotiator. Vice President George M. Dallas and Treasury Secretary Robert Walker, representing shipping and canal interests, insisted the Tehuantepec route be part of a treaty. Nevertheless, Polk, now influenced by Senator Benton, who favored a land route through Missouri to California, was adamant; the canal route had nothing to do with the objective to secure the Rio Grande boundary and obtain California.[50]

As Trist traveled to Mexico, Storm returned to New York by way of Havana. There, she met with her former employer, John L. O'Sullivan,

U.S. Consul Robert Campbell, and Cuban republicans. The Cubans hired her to promote Cuban independence from Spain in the New York press. On May 11, 1847, Beach reported to Polk and Buchanan in Washington. Two days later, at Buchanan's insistence, Polk had a private interview with Storm. Although the president wrote that he was impressed by her intelligence, he claimed she told him nothing he did not already know. Polk did not reveal the source of his next diary entry, but stated that Scott had taken Jalapa without resistance.[51]

After the Mexico mission, Jane Storm no longer worked for Moses Y. Beach. Perhaps he blamed her for involving him in the Mexican fiasco, his financial losses, and the bank scandal. Drusilla Beach and she had lasting differences. Also, while in Mexico, Beach and Storm had developed different views of Mexico. While Jane promoted the creation of three Mexican republics, with annexation possible by future generations, Beach urged the occupation and annexation of all of Mexico in his letters to the *Sun*. As early as March 31, 1847, Drusilla wrote that annexation would help end the anarchy in Mexico. Beach urged annexation to prevent Britain from reaping "the harvest we have planted." While Storm wrote that the Mexican people probably would be better off under a republican government and reported that an annexation party existed in Mexico, she supported the Moderates' plan for the creation of the republics of the Rio Grande, Vera Cruz, and Yucatan. Beach, not Storm, led the All Mexico movement in the *Sun*. On April 5, 1847, Beach wrote, "Every foot of territory and every Mexican citizen . . . by coming under the United States government" would be a "great profit." Jane stood to gain as well when her property and transit routes became even more valuable along the shortest route from the Gulf of Mexico to the Pacific through the republics of the Rio Grande and Yucatan.[52]

The letters by "MONTGOMERY" from behind the battle lines created a sensation in New York and circulation of the *Sun* rose to fifty-five thousand per daily issue. Young Beach reprinted Storm's letters in the *Weekly Sun* of April 24, along with those of his father and sister, signed "M. Y. B" and "D. B. B." Somehow it became known that "MONTGOMERY" was a woman and demand to read her letters brought another round of their printing on May 1 and in an extra edition on May 8. In the reprints, signatures were often omitted, but on May 15, "MONTGOMERY" asked, "What is the government of the United States to do with or for the people of Mexico?" and continued her crusade for a Republic of the Rio Grande.

Because young Beach printed and reprinted the "All Mexico" letters of his family alongside those by Storm advocating three republics, the paper presented no clear policy. Therefore, after the senior Beach's Washington conference with Polk and Buchanan, an editorial appeared on May 17, 1847, titled, "Our Position on Mexico." Beach urged the United States to take possession of Mexico and let their customs pay the cost of the war, and he added, "Let the people remain under our starry flag." On May 22, 1847, Beach advocated that the United States "occupy Mexico and let the future determine how long." The editorial was reprinted again on May 29. Although the original letters by Storm, Beach, and his daughter were reprinted in each *Weekly Sun* and *American Sun* for the balance of May, none of these carried a byline nor did those printed earlier by Storm appear that mentioned the three Mexican republics.[53]

After her return from Mexico in May 1847, Storm wrote no more editorials in the *Sun*, but increased her correspondence to Buchanan, Marcy, and Bancroft. In May 1847, she wrote Buchanan to take care in dealing with the Yucatan people who wanted to trade recognition of their independence for a canal route. The cabinet should accept no undated instruments, she warned, since the Mackintosh Company still held the Garay land grant and canal rights with the conservative government that Santa Anna had returned to power. She also informed Buchanan, "the people who went for 'annexation' are now for the occupation of Mexico." Thus, New York financiers, steamship owners, and merchants advocated the "All Mexico" movement.[54]

Jane Storm, like many soldiers, "had seen the elephant," a popular saying that arose during the war to describe "one unduly disappointed by great expectations." When Buchanan asked her to return to Mexico in July, she suggested that he send her brother Philip McManus, although he had simple country manners, or as "a paid messenger," her son, William, who was a gentleman and fluent in Spanish. In May, June, July, and November she advised Buchanan to send Naval Lt. Richard Meade, a Pennsylvania Catholic and a Freemason, who would work with fraternal brothers to end the war. Storm also advised using Father Ellet in Rome, or Bishop Hughes. She wrote Marcy an angry letter because she had received a department form letter stating, "your letter is received and will be duly considered." Marcy sent an apology and explained the chaos in his office caused by the war.[55]

Storm did not break all contact with the Beach family and sought to make amends for their financial difficulties. On July 8, she wrote Buchanan of Beach's disappointment that Buchanan did not appear at a reception prepared for him when he was in New York. In her next letter, she apologized, "I shall call with Beach's brother, Asabel Beach, looking for a job in Washington. It will be the last demand the Beach's will make on the administration." Beach had requested an appointment for Henry and begged the president to attend another son's wedding in Boston. Storm tried to get the Democrats to subsidize the *Sun* with printing contracts, but after the bank scandal Beach had become a political liability. While their father was in Mexico, Alfred Beach had sold his share of the *Sun* to his brother, Moses S., and bought the *Scientific American*. Alfred escaped the scandal that tainted other members of the family.[56]

From June 1847 to February 1848, while the senior Beach promoted "All Mexico" in the *Sun*, Storm wrote about Cuba. Young Beach published a series of ten "Letters from Cuba," by "MONTGOMERY." In August 1847, Storm arranged for prominent Cuban leaders to meet with President Polk. Although Scott's forces captured Mexico City on September 14, 1847, still no peace came. Senator Benton later claimed in his memoirs that "the '*female*' had gone back to Mexico, with high letters from some members of the cabinet to the commanding general, and to the plenipotentiary negotiator." Storm wrote from Havana on September 1 and again on October 26, during which time she could have traveled to and from Mexico for Buchanan. She wrote to Buchanan that every officer in Mexico that spoke Spanish and knew how to act like a gentleman was worth a company of soldiers. No special friendship had induced her to request Meade be sent to Mexico, she added, as if Buchanan had inquired about her personal life. Meade likely wanted to serve with General Worth and his volunteers who were rumored to be organizing to aid the Cuban separatists once the war was over. Buchanan probably chuckled as he read her next line stating that she did not meddle in affairs beyond her comprehension and had "avoided as much as possible the matter" of Mexico.[57]

In Mexico, Trist ignored the recall orders from Polk and Buchanan on the advice of Edward Thornton of the British legation in Mexico. With help from Charles Bankhead, British minister to Mexico, Trist brought the Mexican factions to the negotiation table with the threat that they had two choices, deal with Trist and have a chance for a republic, or fight with General Scott and lose their national identity. Meanwhile Scott's generals declared in favor of the permanent occupation of Mexico. Benton wrote of the difficulty in dissuading Polk from including the proposal in his December 1847 State of the Union address. In her December letter to Buchanan, Storm was more concerned about the fate of the transit company in Tehuantepec than in affairs of state. She had an interest in the Hargous Company, which was attempting to establish a freight line across the isthmus in the area of the Garay Land Grant. The civil war in Yucatan between whites and mestizos had disrupted that enterprise.[58]

In January 1848, Storm set up the New York Cuban revolutionary paper *La Verdad* [The Truth] in conjunction with Cuban exiles, and as Cora Montgomery served as editor of the bilingual newspaper. Each edition cost six cents and was distributed in the United States, Mexico, Cuba, the Caribbean, and South America by George Law's U.S. Mail Steamship Company. The purpose of *La Verdad* was to help teach both Spanish and English and distribute news of republican activism in the Western Hemisphere and Europe.[59]

M. S. Beach, with full editorial responsibility for the *Sun*, perhaps had respect for Jane Storm's ability and work ethic, and they remained friends for the remainder of their lives. Several times she mentioned to the younger Beach her indebtedness to the Beach family. Thus, the *Sun* printed *La Verdad* on its new Hoe steam press purchased at the apex of the *Sun's* popularity. The *Sun* printed notices of *La Verdad,* and the editors exchanged news clippings. The *Sun* also published three of Storm's Washington columns in early 1848.[60]

As "MONTGOMERY," Storm analyzed the Mexican policies of the presidential aspirants. She reported that General Scott had dashed his hopes by arguments with his officers, that General Worth was for taking and keeping the whole country, and that General Taylor favored returning troops to the line of his victories. She still advocated Buchanan's proposal of making peace with each state, but "From the first our military men have thrown every obstacle in the way of such adjustment." She warned, "If they can prevent it, the pen will steal no laurels from the sword."[61]

On February 8, 1848, Storm advised President Polk, "The Democracy will mourn in 1848." She explained her method "of tracing public opinion" and how she was able to "feel the pulse of the nation." The hundred or more news carriers of the *Sun* in New York, Brooklyn, and Jersey City were trained to report the results of each week's question for the public. "We have but to frame a simple inquiry," for example, "At this time, New York would go for Taylor" and "All Mexico." Thus, she used a form of polling to report current public opinion, but she did not necessarily advocate that position.[62]

In *La Verdad*, Storm opposed ratification of the Treaty of Guadalupe Hidalgo, which was arranged by Trist on February 2, 1848, and arrived in Washington on February 19. Within four days, the treaty went to the Senate Foreign Relations Committee and by the end of February it reached the Senate floor for discussion. From February 28 to March 10, senators debated the treaty. Storm did not think it was a legitimate treaty because it favored British interests and ignored Tehuantepec and republicans on the Rio Grande. As she explained in a letter to President Polk, "the fruits of the war remain with the Whigs." She advised Polk to stall confirmation until after the presidential election in the fall. In *La Verdad*, she criticized the "closed door" discussions of the Senate. She wrote to Polk, "New York and the West are for a very larger slice of Mexico and will count the country defrauded by this treaty. The people want results."[63]

Storm wrote to Bancroft while the Treaty of Guadalupe Hidalgo was under Senate discussion. Although Bancroft had resigned as Secretary of the Navy in September 1847 and became the Minister to the Court of St. James, she kept him informed about politics. He was not to be surprised, she wrote, when he read of her support and admiration for Sam Houston. Houston opposed the treaty as a matter of principle and supported incorporating Mexico as far as Tampico and Mazatlan—the area she had promoted as a Republic of the Rio Grande. "There is a fluent grace in Old Sam's morality that is perfectly irresistible. I am completely captivated," she confessed. The masses want to keep the whole of Mexico, she reported, "They paid for it in blood and treasure!" Our leaders, she wrote, "cannot compute the volcanic force, the onward, self-relying, fearless, grasping, ambition of our republicans." She predicted, "The masses will feel the loss of Mexico and woe to the party that tears it from them."[64]

When John Quincy Adams, who opposed the treaty, collapsed in the House chambers and died of exhaustion on February 23, Storm's tribute was to a great republican. She described Adams as "the president descended into citizen and the general who took his place in the ranks for the benefit of the commonwealth." On March 10, 1848, the Senate ratified the Treaty of Guadalupe Hidalgo by a vote of thirty-eight to fourteen. She reported in *La Verdad* that senators had drunk "the finest wine ever seen in Washington" and "Mexican doubloons and British sovereigns were as plentiful as snowflakes." When discussion began, she wrote "only fifteen

Senators had supported it." She quoted a western senator who, "as he reached for his seventh glass of brandy and water," revealed to her the secrets of the closed door senate sessions. "Half the 'uncertains' never knew when or where they went to bed," she quoted him as saying.[65]

In *La Verdad*, Storm tried to console the confused veterans who had won the war but had to turn the country back to their enemies. She tried to make the war one of republican ideals and not one "of a predatory nation upon a weak or treacherous one." She insisted it was the destiny of the United States to help in raising up the temple of freedom in the world. In March, she reported on republican revolutions spreading through Europe. "We are the reserve corps . . . a light and fire illuminating their sails and warming their hearts . . . until they have dared to shout, we too are men . . . we will be free!"[66]

The *Sun* republished Storm's column in which she urged that George Washington's home, Mount Vernon, become an asylum for soldiers disabled by the war. She used the example of Patrick Walker, who lost both arms in battle and had applied for a pension. Storm could not resist a jab at politicians. She wished the "nation could but have heard the cold arithmetic, the heartless calculation" of those "who were so eager to present Mexico with fifteen millions and resign the Isthmus of Tehuantepec," but "voted against giving $480 to one of our own for one year." She failed to reveal her personal investment in Tehuantepec, however.[67]

In May, the cabinet voted to recognize the independence of Yucatan, but the Senate refused to hold hearings. Britain continued to influence the region, republican activity ended, and the Hargous Transit Company ceased operation. As Storm had predicted, Europeans filled the void left by the United States. Storm used fear tactics in *La Verdad* in an article titled, "England is about to take possession of Yucatan." She explained that British arms dealers supplied the natives, incited them against white leaders, and then sold arms to the white authorities to protect themselves. When both sides were weakened, Britain offered the white administration protection. The scheme was similar, she explained, to that used by the British to take over India and other areas of the world where they achieved dominance.[68]

Jane Storm believed that war with Mexico could be avoided. Then, when war came, she worked to end it through cooperation with the Mexican republican factions who wanted to curb the power of the church and of the conservatives to create a true democracy in Mexico. Her mission to Mexico and letters written during the war provide a view of activities behind the battle lines and of backroom politics that help further explain the war and its consequences. Her activities during the Mexican War show the complexity of politics in Mexico and the United States that led to the war and illustrate the ongoing negotiations that led to the Treaty of Guadalupe Hidalgo. She would not forget the republicans along the Rio Grande, but just then, a revolutionary movement in Cuba showed more promise of fulfillment.

CHAPTER V

Cuba, 1847–1850

Cuba belongs to the Cubans, and they have a right higher than human condition—a right directly from the
throne of Divine Justice—to govern themselves.

—*Cora Montgomery*[1]

$\mathcal{B}$EFORE THE MEXICAN WAR BEGAN, ON DECEMBER 22, 1845, JANE
Storm first raised the subject of Cuban annexation in the New York *Sun.*
Writing as "Montgomery," in a column that focused on the purchase of
California and the settlement of the Oregon dispute, she predicted that
the United States would soon republicanize Canada, followed by "no more
excitement until Cuba and Dominica give us a call." In conjunction with
the secret mission to Mexico with Moses Y. Beach in December 1846,
Storm wrote fifteen numbered travel pieces on Cuba titled "Tropical
Sketches," which appeared between December 11, 1846, and March 26,
1847. Her aim was to acquaint readers with conditions in Cuba and the
Cuban people. She provided information on transportation, types of
money in circulation, Spanish soldiers and fortifications, and other political, economic, and social data. The "Sketches" were designed to create
sympathy for the Cuban republicans and illustrate the economic and social
benefits of annexation.[2]

Storm was not merely a hired pen that lobbied on behalf of the
Cubans; she was firmly committed to extending the area of freedom. Yet,
like the men who subsidized her publications, she stood to gain from
annexation because of her investments in transportation and transit routes
in South Texas and the Isthmus of Tehuantepec. With Cuba under control

of the United States, shippers would have coaling stations and warehouses in Havana and the steamship and land routes to California would became profitable. Upon the completion of her Mexico mission in May 1847, Storm wrote almost exclusively on behalf of the Cuban revolutionaries. From 1847 until 1850, the name Cora Montgomery became synonymous with the Cuban independence faction in New York. She campaigned openly until the first Narciso López expedition failed and she was threatened with fines and prosecution for breaking the neutrality laws of the United States. Surrounded by political enemies, she married William L. Cazneau and moved to Eagle Pass on the Texas frontier. In this remote setting, she did not forget the Cubans, nor cease her revolutionary activities.[3]

In the 1840s and 1850s, the Cuban separatists thought they could best gain independence from Spain through annexation to the United States. In the United States Cuban annexation was both welcomed and feared. Storm's point of view reflected a coalition of businessmen, politicians, and journalists who came to be called the "Young Americans." The acquisition of Cuba was but one part of their foreign policy agenda, which also included free trade, a subsidized merchant marine, and support of republican revolutions in Europe. In the increasingly fierce competition on the high seas for trade and commerce, financial and military strategists saw Cuba as essential to the protection of domestic shipping that connected the Atlantic, Gulf, and Pacific ports. The Cuban matter was complicated by slavery. To some, Cuba was a means of extending the political power of slaveholders that would balance the growing economic and political power of the free labor states. Others saw it as a way to remove slaves from the United States, and still others opposed Cuban annexation because it would help end slavery.[4]

The Havana Club of Havana, Cuba, the New York Cuban Council, the Young Democrats of Tammany Hall, and the Friends of Cuba and the Union financed publications by Jane Storm that promoted Cuban independence. Writing as Cora Montgomery, she stressed the importance of Cuban annexation to the United States. The theme of her publications was that slavery was being replaced by free immigrant labor and that slavery would end in the United States as slaves were deported to Cuba. From 1846 to 1853, she published at least thirty-eight signed news columns on Cuba in the New York *Sun*, the New York *Herald*, and the New York *Tribune*. Between January and June 1848, Cora Montgomery was listed as editor of *La Verdad*, the official newspaper of the New York Cuban Council, the governing body of Cuban exiles. In December 1849, she published "The King of Rivers" anonymously in the *United States Magazine and Democratic Review.* The Democratic Republican Young Men of Tammany Hall financed its expansion into a pamphlet. Charles Wood in New York and William Adam in Washington published *The Queen of Islands and the King of Rivers,* financed by New York merchants and shippers as the "friends of Cuba and the Union." In February 1850, Freeman Hunt, editor of *The Merchant's Magazine,* published "The Union of the Seas," by Cora Montgomery, in which Storm promoted Cuba as essential to steamship routes to the Pacific. In addition, she advised cabinet members and presidents about Cuba and introduced prominent Cubans to United States officials.[5]

The publicity campaign for annexation followed the Texas model with its appeal to patriotism and profits by giving the economic and social benefits of Cuba. Storm emphasized that Cuba was essential to national security and to the expansion of trade and commerce into the Caribbean, Central and South America, and the Pacific. She sought to enlighten readers about the realities of international trade warfare. She explained that Cuba lay fifty nautical miles across the Florida Straits midway between New York and New Orleans and separated the Gulf of Mexico from the Atlantic Ocean. In wartime, the sea-lanes could be closed and devastate the economy. She told of the Cuban struggle for independence that began in the 1820s when Cuban republicans thought they could achieve independence as had Spain's other colonies. Cuban rebels had sought annexation to the United States at that time, but fearing war with Spain's protector, the John Quincy Adams administration established a "no transfer policy" with Great Britain. Because of its proximity, naïve Americans thought Cuba would gravitate to the United States and fall like ripe fruit from a tree.[6]

With the coming of steam-powered merchant ships and the acquisition of California and Oregon, the need to control the Florida Straits and have secure coaling stations became more vital. During the Oregon border dispute, the James K. Polk administration realized Her Majesty's Royal Navy could shut down the coastal trade between New York and New Orleans—the first- and second-ranked export and import points in the United States. Until the United States controlled the Florida Straits and Cuba, the nation did not control its destiny. Therefore, the Polk administration, backed by shippers and merchants, made the acquisition of Cuba a priority. Cuban republican planters pledged a hundred million dollars toward the purchase of Cuba.[7]

Because Cuba was the chief source of wealth for the Spanish royal family, Spain had no intention of selling its colony or allowing it to fall to the United States. Besides tariffs that supported the crown and made payments to the Rothschild bankers who had financed the First Carlist War (1833–1839), two-thirds of Spain's merchant marine depended on the Cuban trade. Also, importation fees on African slaves, smuggled illegally and imported as emancipated persons indentured for life, netted an additional three to four million dollars each year for Spanish officials. Some eighty wealthy Cubans purchased titles that offered them immunity from arrest and produced additional funds for the royal family. Therefore, the Spanish monarchy did not want to sell Cuba and lose some ten million dollars in annual net revenue, and Britain did not want to lose the ports she controlled. United States imports from Cuba increased from six million dollars in 1845 to more than eighteen million dollars annually in 1855, of which 89 percent came from sugar. During the decade, United States exports to Cuba increased by less than $1.5 million, creating an imbalance of trade. In 1847, more than two thousand United States vessels entered Cuban ports, compared to 819 Spanish, 563 English, and less than one hundred French ships.[8]

Although naval strategists saw Cuba as a key to the defense of the Gulf of Mexico, it was also a stepping stone toward control of the Antilles, the island chain that linked North and South America and separated the Caribbean Sea from the Atlantic Ocean. Britain had no intention of losing control of the area and regarded Havana as vital to the Gulf of Mexico as Gibraltar was to the Mediterranean. After the defeat of the French fleet at Trafalgar in 1805, Britain had increasingly controlled the seven sea-lanes of the Antilles that led to ports on the Gulf of Mexico and the three land bridges of Panama, Nicaragua, and Tehuantepec—the most direct sea route from Europe to China and Australia, and between North and South America.[9]

Not all Cubans were in favor of annexation to the United States, however, and Cuban separatists were divided into republican annexationists and liberal nationalists. After the 1820s rebellion failed, republicans fled to New York and Santo Domingo. In 1843, Cuban liberals, educated in Europe, attempted an uprising to establish independence, but Spanish authorities put down their revolt. The liberals then went into exile in France or New Orleans. Thus, two Cuban exile groups found refuge in the United States.[10]

In the "Tropical Sketches," Jane Storm described conditions in Cuba. She illustrated Spain's neglect of essential services. She and her companions could not travel the forty miles from Matanzas to Havana because the road would not accommodate wheeled vehicles. The railway from Matanzas connected to the other side of the island, but not to Havana. Therefore, the only transportation was one steamer that traveled irregularly between Matanzas and Havana. During the trip, a norther blew in and rough seas made the passengers ill. Undaunted, Storm extolled the value of smoking cigars as a remedy for seasickness. Because the Havana customs house closed at two in the afternoon, the passengers were delayed another day. She described the bay as narrow with a wharf a half-mile in length and thirty to sixty feet wide constructed of new mahogany planks six to eight inches thick and held with copper bolts. In Havana, twenty-five thousand soldiers, paid from tariff receipts, were present on all public streets, in front of the churches, and guarded the mental asylum that she visited. She also provided information about caves, vantage points, and a shortage of money in circulation.[11]

Storm also described street scenes and daily life. She observed that Cubans lacked the "power of fusion" for joint action. They had not learned to pool their resources, she explained, but she believed that this would be corrected with republican laws. Upon hearing of the 1843 arrest, imprisonment, and beating of a free black American the Tyler administration had ignored, as "Montgomery," she wrote to Horace Greeley at the New York *Tribune* and asked, "Where do I look for an honest politician? Is our Eagle, after all nothing but a vulture in borrowed plumage, a vile bird of prey?" In reply, the Whig editor asserted, "had the author not consorted with Locofocos all his life, he would know where to look."[12]

As a female from the United States in 1846, Storm felt restricted by her gender. Cuban ladies never walked, so she hired a carriage to drive her, "an hour's walk from Havana," to the village of Guanabaco, where she walked to the mineral baths. There, she found no soldiers to question her walking the streets. Not only did Cuban ladies never walk, they did not read, nor attend lectures, she wrote. Nevertheless, she added, they danced, smoked, went to church, and reared sons to be gentlemen instead of republicans.[13]

What Storm did not report in the newspaper was that she met with members of the Havana Club, a group formed by wealthy sugar planters in 1837 to separate Cuba from Spain, abolish slavery, and encourage white immigration. In April 1847, when she left Vera Cruz for New York, Storm returned by way of Cuba and met with John L. O'Sullivan, her former editor; Robert Campbell, the United States consul at Havana; and members of the Havana Club. Campbell wrote to Secretary of State James Buchanan that he had arranged the meeting of two Americans and two Cubans when they planned the revolutionary newspaper, *La Verdad.* The South Carolina native also advised that he knew more about the Cuban dissident groups than they knew about each other. Beach did not attend these planning sessions, and O'Sullivan later wrote to Secretary of State James Buchanan that Beach was not involved in the initial plans. Storm's letters and those of colleagues confirm that her role in the Texas annexation campaign was well known, and O'Sullivan, most of all, knew of her editorial abilities. Therefore, perhaps upon O'Sullivan's advice, the Cubans hired her to handle their press campaign in New York.[14]

Before she opened the formal campaign for Cuban annexation in the New York *Sun* on July 19, 1847, Storm had consulted with Secretary Buchanan. Her letters indicate that she maintained a personal and working relationship with the politician who had served in Congress with her father. Like Storm, Buchanan believed colonization was a solution to slavery. He relied on Storm's personal observations and intelligence from abroad and provided her with selected leaks for her columns. In a July 1847 personal letter, she advised him about changing attitudes in Mexico and in the United States in regard to Cuba. Between July 19 and August 25, the New York *Sun* printed six numbered "Letters From Cuba," by "MONTGOMERY," dated June 20 to July 4, 1847. In the opening letter, Storm explained that for the next several months she would make Cuba known to the people of the United States as the fulfillment of her promise, "when in Havana last winter" to "lay the matter before the people of the United States." The "Letters" were not in the casual style of the "Sketches," but concise reports designed to inform readers of the causes for independence and annexation to the United States. She defined a Creole as a Cuban-born Spaniard, not one of Negro blood as many in the northern states thought. She explained that Spain taxed, through tariffs, the Cuban population an average of thirty-eight dollars each per year, while in the United States each person paid about two dollars in taxes. In addition, she illustrated that soldiers allowed the Cubans no freedom of movement, speech, press, or assembly.[15]

Storm described slavery in Cuba. Unlike enslaved persons in the family system of the southern United States that replenished themselves,

Cuban slaves were primarily men imported directly from Africa. As slavery ended in Haiti and Jamaica and their sugar production declined, the Cuban slave trade and sugar production increased. The Spanish government confiscated church lands and sold them to absentee landowners who hired overseers to operate the plantations. Thus, like the clergy in Mexico, the Catholic Church in Cuba sought protection of its property. Although prohibited under a treaty with England, the slave trade continued. Cubans who questioned the policy were imprisoned or exiled, as was the liberal Don José Saco in the 1830s. According to Mexican Minister Buenaventura Aroujo in his 1847 letter that Beach carried to Vice President Valentín Gómez Farías, corrupt British authorities in Havana, Jamaica, and the Bahamas profited from the slave smuggling.[16]

The Spanish government used slaves to intimidate the Cuban separatists. Storm reported that Spanish authorities threatened to arm the slaves if the Cubans tried to establish independence. Slave trading had increased the slave population of Cuba from 32 percent of the total population in 1774 to 58 percent by 1842. She visited the eastern part of the island where privateers smuggled male Africans into Cuba or brought others into port legally where authorities taxed them as emancipated persons indentured for life. When authorities heard rumors of slave revolts, they flogged or executed slaves, or released them to their owners after paying heavy bribes to officials. Planters had to resupply their labor force with more slaves because Spain discouraged European emigration, claiming that only Africans could work in the tropics. Thus, planters wanted annexation to end the slave trade and blackmail, she asserted. Cuban republicans wanted the more humane form of slavery as practiced by the southern United States, and they intended to make gradual emancipation a feature of their proposed state constitution. Until then she asserted that Cuba would be an outlet for slaves drained from the United States.[17]

After publishing the first six "Letters from Cuba," in July and August 1847, Storm wrote four more columns from Havana. She explained that Britain, in a strategy similar to that used against the Republic of Texas, offered to guarantee Cuba independence on the condition that it did not join the United States and agreed to abolish slavery. Free blacks and liberal Cubans supported the official British plan that would someday make Havana the capital of a Republic of Antilla in the West Indies and block United States territorial and commercial expansion.[18]

In August, Storm reported that because of her previous letters in the *Sun*, Spanish authorities had banned American newspapers in Cuba. As if answering a series of questions, she explained that Spain discouraged European emigration because European emigrants empathized with the Cuban republicans. Also, she countered the apologists' justification of slavery—she had witnessed white men working in the tropical climate. Some one thousand Americans lived and worked in Cuba. Thomas B. Smith, for example, was an American who used free white labor in his copper mine. Cuba was then the world's largest producer of copper, which made it a valuable possession.[19]

At the time Beach was calling for the occupation of "All Mexico," Storm campaigned for Cuban annexation. She wrote to Secretary Buchanan, "The Cuba fever you see is rising and sooner or later will stir the all embracing appetites of the nation." In London, Lord George Bentinck had urged in Parliament that Spain be asked to sell Cuba to pay its debts to British bondholders. Tory opposition to the Carlist War (1833–1839) had forced Whig Foreign Secretary Lord Palmerston to finance the ten regiments of the voluntary British Legion with loans from the Rothschild bankers. Thus, Storm advised Buchanan to "establish our country in the market." She asked that he grant a passport to a Cuban gentleman more valuable than "the blockheads you sometimes employ." Two days later, she introduced Don Gaspar Betancourt Cisneros to President Polk. He was a member of the Havana Club and had purchased his title for twenty-five thousand dollars. He was also a member of the New York Cuban Council. Other Havana Club and Council members were John L. O'Sullivan and his brother-in-law, Cristobal Madan y Madan, president of the New York Council.[20]

The Havana Club committed thirty thousand dollars for three newspapers established in the United States. Presumably, each had a budget of ten thousand dollars. In New York, Storm set up the most successful, *La Verdad*, and wrote most of the copy for the bilingual newspaper herself. She rented an office across the street from in the Sun Building at 124 Fulton Street, arranged for printing on the *Sun* press, and for distribution by George Law's U.S. Mail steamers. The lesser-known *La Aurora* [The Light] promoted Cuban annexation in Washington, and in New Orleans, the *Picayune* printed *La Patria* [The Mother Land], which reflected liberal sentiments.[21]

On January 9, 1848, the first issue of *La Verdad* appeared with Cora Montgomery listed as editor. The banner letters with fringe reflected the popularity of Latin styles made fashionable by the Mexican War. Reflecting the Young American agenda, the "Prospectus" stated that *La Verdad* would compile news of republican activity worldwide. Under Storm's leadership, the newspaper carried news of republican progress in Europe and Latin America. She listed New York wholesale prices and provided shipping and immigration news. The paper's format and content were similar to the *Sun,* and it provided an example of a free press under a republican form of government. The newspaper favored Cuban annexation by purchase.[22]

In January and February 1848, *La Verdad* had news of Mexico, but when the war ended, focus shifted to Cuba. One article repeated rumors that Cuban taxes had financed an attempt to place a monarchy in Mexico. In an article titled "Disinherited Cuba," Storm traced Cuba's demise from a province with self-government to a colony under martial law. After her letters in the *Sun* brought about a ban on American newspapers in Cuba, Law's employees, John Lyttle and William Bush, smuggled the *Sun* inside casks of beans to persons in Cuba she described in Masonic terms as the "good and true." The "beans were excellent" and "copies of the *Sun* faithfully distributed." Because Freemasons participated in republican activities, Spain had outlawed Masonry in Cuba. When Gen. William S. Wetmore, the naval agent overseeing steamer construction in New York, asked William Marcy's opinion of Storm's work on behalf of the Cubans, Marcy replied that he "highly appreciated her talents and political principles."[23]

In February 1848, Storm had complained to Buchanan that U.S. Consul Campbell opened her correspondence to Cuban dissidents. "It is not for my sake alone that I desired the consular protection, for I shall write what when and to whom I please." She was concerned for the safety of her friends in Cuba. Buchanan discounted her fears, and she warned him in Masonic terms, "the word of a true woman is worth as much as a cabinet member if not more."[24]

Polk agreed to the purchase of Cuba but he would not aid a revolution with United States troops. In March 1848, O'Sullivan, the business agent of the Cuban Council, had suggested to Buchanan that Thomas Hart Benton's son-in-law, John C. Frémont, be appointed an agent to negotiate with Spain about the purchase of Cuba. In May, O'Sullivan and Campbell both warned Buchanan that uprisings would soon begin. During the previous year, the Havana Club had dispatched Rafael de Castro and Sedano y Cruzat to Mexico to recruit Gen. William Jenkins

Worth to aid the Cubans. When the Mexican War ended, Worth was to lead five thousand veterans to Cuba for payment of three million dollars. If the purchase of Cuba were arranged, Worth's men would replace the Spanish soldiers. If not, Worth was a fighting general whose men would follow him anyway. On June 2, 1848, O'Sullivan wrote to Polk that revolution was imminent and sought aid from the United States. Jefferson Davis accompanied the Cubans José Iznaga, Gaspar Betancourt Cisneros, and Alonzo Betancourt to the White House to request that troops be stationed at Key West in support of the rebellion. Polk refused. He was no Andrew Jackson, and Cuba was not Texas. Polk would only agree to the purchase of Cuba and instructed the navy that no veterans returning from Mexico were to land in Cuba.[25]

Independent of the Havana Club and the Cuban Council, Narciso López, former liberal Cuban governor, planned an uprising scheduled for June 24, 1848. Word spread of his plot and the Havana Club urged López to wait until General Worth and his volunteers could be transported back to Cuba from the United States. Two weeks later, Spanish authorities knew of the plot called the "Conspiracy of the Cuban Rose Mines" where López owned the copper mine and where the uprising was to begin. Campbell had informed Buchanan about López's plans, and Buchanan, in an attempt to win the trust of Spain, purchase Cuba, and become the next president, passed the information to the Spanish minister in Washington, Angel Calderón de la Barca. The administration wanted to acquire Cuba but not chance a war with Britain and have the Florida Straits blocked or have African slaves released less than one hundred miles from the coast of the United States. López was warned of his imminent arrest. He escaped from Cienfuego by horseback, traveled by train to Càrdenas, and caught a steamer to Matanzas and escaped to the United States. By the end of July 1848, López was in New York and the hero of the exiles.[26]

The republican revolutions of 1848, then sweeping Europe, temporarily diverted European attention from Cuba. British Minister Sir Henry Bulwer insisted that Spain "liberalize," which meant abolition. Spain temporarily broke relations with Britain and was receptive to the sale of Cuba. The foreign minister asked if Spain could expect United States protection against Britain. Having just ended one war, Polk did not want to start another during the presidential campaign summer. British control of the Florida Straits thwarted United States plans. Strategists in Britain and the

United States knew that Cuba was a stepping stone to the control of the West Indies and the land bridges of Central America that were vital to British and French plans for trade with China. With the collapse of the 1848 republican uprisings in Europe, Britain united with France and Spain in a cooperative effort to prevent the spread of American influence in the tropics—the repercussions of which Jane Storm would become acutely aware of in later years.[27]

With the failure of the Polk administration to purchase Cuba in June 1848, the Havana Club withdrew its financial support of the New York Cuban Council. The planters favored annexation, but only through purchase. Betancourt and Madan continued as liaison between the New York Cuban Council and the Havana Club, while John S. Thrasher, Havana editor of *El Faro Industrial*, represented exiles in New Orleans. O'Sullivan remained the business agent for both groups. Without the financial backing of the Havana Club, the New York Cuban Council could not afford the eight-page *La Verdad*, and Storm was suddenly unemployed. The council sold ships and supplies, but retained the business office and occasionally Don Gaspar Betancourt and José Teurbe Tolón published *La Verdad* as a single-page newssheet. Tolón designed the Cuban flag as it is today and hung it in the office window. The Spanish consul in New York protested the public display, and later that year Spain established *La Cronica* [The Times] across the street to counter the propaganda of *La Verdad*.[28]

Confident of success, the New York Cuban Council continued plans to liberate their homeland. From Havana, Campbell wrote to Buchanan that the revolutionaries did not believe the administration had betrayed them, and Buchanan's duplicity was not widely known until the 1856 presidential campaign. A month after López fled Cuba, however, Storm wrote to Buchanan about the impact the failed revolution had in Cuba. The republicans were disheartened, and as she explained, "Our enemies circulate rumors that the U.S. turned informer. It is time some friendship and protection reaches them." She implored, "I appeal to you to do something." She suggested that Buchanan "show the broad seal of state to those blood thirsty wretches. . . for heaven's mercy, let your habitual excess prudence keep you from an error." She requested naturalization papers for J. M. Iznaga, who was imprisoned for treason because *La Verdad* and other United States newspapers were found in his possession. His subsequent naturalization papers showed that he applied for citizenship when he was a student in the United States. She ceased correspondence with Buchanan until early 1853, when she again wrote on behalf of the Cubans and asked which officials in the Franklin Pierce administration could be trusted on Cuba.[29]

The New York *Sun* openly promoted the efforts of the Cuban republicans to the dismay of O'Sullivan and the Polk administration, who wished to keep negotiations with Spain as secret as possible. Consequently, the administration and O'Sullivan distanced themselves from Beach, who was still embroiled in the Plainfield Bank scandal. After the bank's closure by New Jersey bank examiners in February 1847, the scandal still made news during the political campaign in June 1848. The bank failure cast doubts on all New Jersey bank notes, and state authorities made Beach an example. A New Jersey legislative report suggested the bank was a cover for questionable operations. James Gordon Bennett, the pro-slavery editor of the rival New York *Herald*, kept the scandal in the news and challenged Beach's claim that the *Sun* had a fifty-five thousand daily circulation.[30]

Bennett also questioned the credibility of a *Sun* article titled "Insult to the American flag." The article, a reprint from *La Verdad*, claimed Spanish officials opened United States diplomatic pouches. He added that when he inquired at the *Sun* office, Beach claimed only to be the business manager and said that Storm was responsible for the article. Bennett explained that Storm was a literary lady who lived in Park Place and had traveled through Mexico and Cuba with Beach. Bennett then lectured Storm for advocating a revolution that could unleash another Santo Domingo off the coast of the United States. The 1796 slave revolt had spread from neighboring Haiti and resulted in an estimated 780,000 whites being killed or driven from the Spanish colony. Consequently, Santo Domingo became a symbol for those who advocated perpetual slavery.[31]

The *Herald* article revealed that Beach, like O'Sullivan, took credit for Storm's work when it brought accolades, but blamed her when things went wrong—a pattern repeated by two of the Beach children. Storm later wrote to her publisher about a "capricious" Drusilla, and other family members who threatened to "drag her from the office," while Alfred accused her of abandoning his father and using the *Sun* "only for personal objects" when she established *La Verdad*. Possibly Alfred was irritated because his partner, Orson D. Munn, at the *Scientific American*, was one of those smeared by the Plainfield Bank scandal. In December 1848, Moses Y. Beach retired from the newspaper business because of his "shattered health," but Storm remained friendly with Beach's son, Moses Sperry Beach, who continued as editor of the *Sun*.[32]

During these developments, Storm kept George Bancroft, Minister to the Court of St. James, informed of political happenings. She attended the state and national political conventions in 1848 and informed Bancroft that "Neither nominee was suitable," but General Taylor "stands for firmness, honesty, and *progress*," and on "that last instinctive idea . . . rests his chance of winning the votes of the masses." Acquisition and progress was "the ruling passion of the masses," she explained, and had become "the platform of the Progressives." She described the Democratic presidential nominee, Lewis Cass, as timid and unreliable. She saw Van Buren's Free Soil party as a "new conservatism" because it opposed slavery and the spread of free blacks. She predicted the ideology would sweep the country for the next eight to twelve years. "Whoever is elected," she entreated, "take care of Cuba and come home to be president."[33]

Polk removed O'Sullivan from Democratic party patronage because he would not support the Democratic presidential candidate, Lewis Cass of Michigan. Storm possibly wrote the lead article, "Principles, Not Men," in the July issue of the *United States Magazine and Democratic Review* as it reflected her style and attitude. "The destiny of the country at this moment hang trembling in a fearful balance," she wrote. She claimed that the Democratic schism would plunge the country in the "fiery furnace of a desolating feud." She blamed "professional politicians" with "a lust for power" who created parties with "geographical distributions whose object was the weakening of the bonds of the nation."[34]

After the Whig Zachary Taylor was elected president in November, the New York Cuban Council planned an invasion of Cuba. General Worth was on leave from the army in Rhode Island assisting the new head of the New York Cuban Council, Ambrosio José Gonzales, with invasion plans. In January 1849, Storm introduced Gonzales to New York Democratic Sen. Daniel S. Dickinson, who in turn, introduced Gonzales to President Polk. Before Taylor's inauguration, Polk transferred Worth to Texas, where he contracted cholera and died. After Worth's death, Gonzales appointed Narciso López head of the invasion force. In Havana, Spanish authorities arrested Law's employees, Lyttle, a free black, and Bush, the steward on the *Childe Harold*, who had smuggled the *Sun* into Cuba with the dry beans. With difficulty, Consul Campbell secured their release.[35]

In February 1849, at the onset of the California gold rush, Storm wrote young Beach to develop a "*policy of telling your readers the truth*." The *Sun* editor had advised immigrants to take the Missouri route to California instead of a steamer-land route that passed through Havana. "In fourteen years of enquiry and nine trips to and from and through Texas I *know* what I am talking about," she lectured. "During my contribution for the paper I have never been found mistaken in a position operating on facts." She confessed that she had investments along the Texas route, but explained that it would benefit his family as well. Furthermore, the route from Corpus Christi was an all-weather route five hundred miles shorter and 50 percent cheaper than the route through Missouri, she attested. If he continued to mislead the public, she threatened to contradict him through other newspapers. In January, one of Storm's long-standing Texas land claims was resolved. Storm received a cash settlement of five thousand dollars on her headright claim. That claim was the one that she had deeded half to James Morgan for Swartwout in 1837, and half to Thomas Chambers in 1844 as a legal fee to secure title to her land claims. She then speculated in more land along the Rio Grande, which would increase in value as that area became the preferred route to California.[36]

By March 1849, Storm had purchased an interest in the New York *Morning Star*. During the presidential campaign she had formed new alliances with expansionist Whigs including J. Watson Webb, owner of the New York *Courier and Enquirer*, and newly elected New York Sen. William H. Seward. Seward favored government aid to develop a steam merchant marine to compete with British subsidized shipbuilders and shippers. Webb's brother owned one of the largest shipyards in New York. Webb, a former director of the experimental New Washington Association in Mexican Texas, was present in May 1848 when representatives of the *Tribune, Herald, Journal of Commerce*, and *Express* met at the *Sun* office and organized the New York Associated Press to share a common telegraphic wire service and a press boat. Storm became the first Washington correspondent for the group. Webb contacted Seward and called twice at the *Sun* office trying to reach Storm, thinking she was still editor. Webb located her and informed Seward that Jane lived with the family of Assistant Postmaster General W. J. Brown near the capitol when she was in Washington. Webb encouraged Seward to contact her and explained, "She is a managing dame and a past friend—just the woman to cultivate with a bow." Like Storm, Seward was part of the political web created by George Law, president of the U.S. Mail Steamship Line. Within a week, Storm and Seward were in communication, and Seward, although he had met her many times at Thurlow Weed's family gatherings in Albany, did not realize J. M. Storm was a lady, or the famous "Montgomery." Amazingly, she had kept her private and public lives separate. Through Seward, she tried to have Mirabeau B. Lamar appointed to a diplomatic post in Latin America on behalf of Taylor's Texas supporters loosely organized as the Union party.[37]

The next month, while on an assignment for New York businessmen calling themselves "Friends of Cuba and the Union," Storm traveled to Texas with William Cazneau's sister, Mary Eliza Cazneau Holden. The women traveled as far as Eagle Pass, a newly formed tent city on the Rio Grande that William Cazneau and John Twohig, a San Antonio merchant, had established within sight of Fort Duncan. California Camp was nearby as a rest stop for westward migrants. Cazneau provided supplies to emigrants and shipped goods for California through Mexico to the Pacific port of Matzatlan. Mary Eliza traveled west to join her other brother, Thomas Cazneau, a Pacific marine insurance claims adjuster, and her father, Capt. W. L. Cazneau Sr., in San Francisco.[38]

Storm's assignment on behalf of the Young Democrats of Tammany Hall and the Friends of Cuba and the Union resulted in articles, pamphlets, and books on the importance of Cuba to gradual emancipation. In December 1849, the *United States Magazine and Democratic Review* published "King of Rivers" without her signature. This publication was based on an adventure that began in June 1849 when she steamed from Corpus Christi to New Orleans and traveled up the navigable length of the Mississippi River by steamboat, a trip she described as lasting three weeks. Her writing was optimistic, joyful, and romantic as if she were on holiday. "We left the bright and lovely banks of Corpus Christi where the flowers never cease to bloom" and "the fresh breeze never forgets to play in the fairy groves that dot the green savannah." In sharp contrast was the "dreary expanse of black mud of lower Louisiana." There, the "stupid, vicious, refractory slave drainage of all states," she wrote, have created "the harshest discipline and least kindly bonds." She looked not upon the "justice or injustice of slavery," she told readers, but dealt "simply with the facts."[39]

Traveling the length of the Mississippi River to the northern terminus of navigation, St. Anthony Falls, Minnesota, a popular spot for honeymooners, Cora Montgomery described the river as a great teacher that linked the nation's four economic sectional interests of agriculture, mines, manufacturing, and commerce. She listed state by state the oppression that existed against Africans, Indians, sailors, and factory women. These evils were seen only by critics in other sections—a condition she termed, "geographical morality."[40]

The theme of the pamphlet and article in the December *Democratic Review* was that slavery was ending in the United States and flowing southward just as the Mississippi River. As the north sold their slaves south, European immigrants would replace slavery in the transition states. In the last three quarters of the previous year, three hundred thousand immigrants had arrived in the United States. In New Orleans, emigrants had replaced slave drivers, maids, and porters at the St. Charles Hotel where she lodged. She did not advocate relocation of all blacks. The African families in New Orleans were developing their moral and intellectual powers, and as she explained, "The race among us will go rapidly forward."[41]

Once, every state was a slave state, Storm reminded readers, and now five states "trembled in the balance of transition." Were it not for a wall of prejudice on each side of them, she asserted that slavery would have departed. "Where are 150,000 souls to go?" she asked as did Sen. Henry Clay of Kentucky when he served as President of the American Colonization Society. "Why arrest the mighty wheel of progress, and endanger the noble machinery of the confederation?" she reasoned. The total percent of slave population had fallen from one-fifth of the population in 1800 to one-seventh by 1850, she added. She appealed to the common sense of readers and reasoned that any schoolboy twelve years of age could see that by 1870, slavery would only be found in South Carolina, Georgia, and the Gulf states.[42]

In a letter to George Bancroft, Storm called the coalition of New York Democrats and Whigs the "Progressives." The idea of resolving the slavery issue by getting rid of slaves was popular, and according to many who supported as well as opposed Cuban annexation, a feasible solution. Storm probably knew that some two-thirds of the New York slaves had not been freed but were sold south. With Brazil and Cuba importing thousands of slaves yearly the plan was plausible. As Senator Clay had reminded the nation and his colleagues, a statesman's purpose was to preserve the nation, not preserve slavery. Storm and her employers struggled to prevent the rupture of the union. They supported Taylor for president in 1848 and in 1850 organized a New York state Union ticket. The Union Safety Committee had one hundred merchant and shipping members, such as William B. Astor, E. K. Collins, George Law, Paul Spoffard, and Marshall O. Roberts. Their aim was to strengthen Union forces in New York, and from there, consolidate Union sentiment throughout the country. They were not pro-slavery, but realistic businesspeople who realized that the eradication of slavery would take years and that immediate abolition would wreck the economy.[43]

Cora Montgomery advised that Cuba had three choices: independence, becoming a protectorate under England as part of the proposed Republic of Antilla, or annexation to the United States. Just as the South provided an outlet for northern slavery, and Britain established Sierra Leone to rid the London slums of blacks, she proposed that Cuba would be a depository for slaves from the United States. Furthermore, annexation would improve the conditions of Cuban slaves. She added, "Were Cuba under the United States, the African slave trade and the horrors of the Spanish system of slavery would be replaced by the more humane family system of the Southern states." In an appeal to antislavery forces she stated that annexation would stop the importation of eight thousand enslaved Africans into Cuba each year. She defended gradual emancipation and did not "seek to prove slavery was good or the race incapable of better things," but "hasty emancipation has it evils." Albert Brown and John A. Wilcox of Mississippi expressed similar views, but perhaps the best endorsement of her policy was that of pro-slavery North Carolina Rep. Abraham Venable. He opposed Cuban annexation because it would drain slaves away where they were in short supply.[44]

Cuba was about more than slavery or removing free blacks from the United States, it would aid the expansion of trade and commerce. "If Cuba is ours," she wrote, "we would soon cut the narrow band that parts the ocean at Panama or Nicaragua, and trade of the world would flow into our sea." The shortest route from New York to the Pacific, she maintained, was through Corpus Christi. She warned, "In 1845, England enfolded us on every side, like a coil of a serpent." She reminded readers, "We broke that circle and tore from her grasp Texas, California, and Oregon, with Cuba, the last bond is broken."[45]

While Storm continued the Cuban campaign in 1849, the New York Cuban Council finalized plans to invade Cuba and create an island republic that could be annexed on the Texas model. In September, the six hundred Cuban exiles in New York and New Orleans were united under Gonzales with O'Sullivan as their business agent. They had money, ships, and trained Mexican War veterans with arms, ammunition, field pieces, and elaborate plans to coordinate departures from Boston to New

Orleans. The leaders met with John C. Calhoun, Jefferson Davis, and Stephen A. Douglas in Washington. While Davis and Douglas supported the Cubans, Calhoun did not think the Cubans were ready for republican government. On August 11, 1849, President Taylor issued a proclamation that persons breaking the neutrality laws were subject to arrest, a $25,000 fine, and three years in prison. The republican revolutionaries did not believe the proclamation would be enforced.[46]

On September 7, 1849, the United States Navy turned back the Cubans and their allies as they left ports in Boston, New York, Philadelphia, Baltimore, and New Orleans. While the Cubans and their supporters had friends in the southern ports, those in the North faced political enemies. Federal authorities impounded their ships for cost of repairs and other excuses, and held leaders for breaking the neutrality laws of the nation. Abolitionists considered the movement an attempt to extend slavery, Free-Soilers saw it as a means to increase the political power of slaveholders in Congress, while Conscience Whigs wanted nothing to interfere with plans to develop jointly an isthmian canal with Britain then being discussed by Secretary of State John M. Clayton and Sir Henry Bulwer.[47]

As the voice of the movement, Storm was a target of investigations and was threatened with arrest unless she implicated others. Jane later wrote her publisher, Charles Wood, from the safety of Eagle Pass that the attack came from Wall Street and targeted him, her, the Beach family, and even her brother Philip. In September 1849, Jane wrote to Seward seeking a favor for her nephew by marriage, Samuel Francis Storm. He had been dismissed from the Navy Department as had Charles Wood from the customs house. She did "not feel inclined to waste ink and paper on an administration," she warned, that "could cut down an unoffending clerk, neglect the border, throw away Cuba, and refuse to make good their five election pledges." She assured Seward, "The evil will cure itself, for the people are intelligent and the press is free." By December, Seward had found employment for her nephew, and she signed her letter of appreciation as J. M. Cazneau.[48]

Sometime between September and late December 1849, Jane Storm and William Leslie Cazneau married. No records have been found as to when or where, but it was his first marriage and her second. Both were forty-two years old. Storm wrote to Charles Wood that she left New York "in a fit" when she tried "to ferret out the plan and names" of Wall Street enemies. Political enemies had destroyed the Cuban crusade for annexation, and with it plans for gradual emancipation. She feared possible criminal charges, fines, and imprisonment. Cazneau, who had pushed the letter and spirit of the law to its limits for most of the years she had known him with his infiltration of trade into Mexico, seemed to be involved in legal activities in 1849. He had a legitimate trade business into Mexico and was in the process of acquiring more than fifty thousand acres of ranch land bordering the Rio Grande. Surrounded by enemies and without work, she found that Cazneau and Eagle Pass offered her an opportunity to renew her crusade for a Mexican republic on the Rio Grande and promote the transit route through Texas.[49]

Before she left New York for Eagle Pass, however, the new Mrs. Cazneau found herself distracted by her husband's latest scheme. She wrote at least two books about the adventure, but both were attributed to Joseph Warren Fabens (1821–1875), Cazneau's business partner. *The Camel Hunt; a Narrative of Personal Adventure* (1851) and *A Story of Life on the Isthmus* (1853) cover the period from September to December 1849 at the height of the California gold rush. In *The Camel Hunt,* the heroine, named Jane Eddington, used her inheritance to purchase the *Double Eagle,* a clipper-brig seized for non-payment of repairs by the sheriff at Boston—probably in connection with the failed López expedition. The thinly disguised autobiographical travelogue had characters called Jane and Tom Eddington, instead of Cazneau, William Douglas Wallach and his wife spelled Wallack, and Fabens was called Joseph Warrener. They sailed to Morocco, where they traveled into the desert on camels and purchased a herd of the beasts, which they delivered to Panama for transport to California for use in the southwestern desert. As she described herself and her husband, she catalogued their business failures and told of his father's prediction that he "would be lucky to steer clear of the State prison," while hers was sure that she would end up in the poor house. She described Cazneau as careless, nervous, angry, and always "so full of anecdotes, yet never inquired into the correctness of them." He saw his wife as an angel, idealized her, and placed her on a pedestal.[50]

The *Camel Hunt* depicted life at sea, and Jane Cazneau wrote about a storm that made a lasting impression on her. She felt a sense of awe surrounded by sea billows "capable of taking us down at a swallow, and closing over our grave without adding another sigh to the mournful rushing of the winds." William Cazneau tied himself to the mast to savor the excitement or in fear of being trapped below deck. During the night she had a chilling premonition: "Who has never been suddenly possessed with the knowledge, in the midst of gaiety and unbridled enjoyment, that a certain point could not be passed?" No doubt, she had misgivings about her marriage and had learned more than she wanted to know about Cazneau's business dealings. The camel hunt may have disguised a slave-running operation. The sequel to *The Camel Hunt* was *A Story of Life on the Isthmus,* in which she described the sights and sounds and smells of Panama. As she sat on the veranda of the Empire City Hotel in Chagres, through her lorgnette she watched the mass of humanity that passed going to and from the California gold fields.[51]

In late December 1849, Moses Y. Beach contacted Jane Cazneau about editing the New York *Morning News,* which he and John L. O'Sullivan again owned. She thanked him, but queried, "What range do you allow your contributing corps? . . . It is impossible for me to write contrary to my convictions." Also, she reminded him that she was not "over inclined to be dainty with the weak or corrupt in high places," for "all my sympathies are with the people."[52]

Beach replied immediately: Jane Cazneau had left for Washington, where his letter caught up with her. She wrote that her husband was there pressing a claim for the loss of trade goods in Mexico—a suggestion that all was not well with his Mexican business. On January 8, 1850, she wrote that her plans were to leave for New Orleans and the Mexican border on the first of February, "Unfortunately my obligation to proceed to the South, prevents my availing myself of the editorship of your name." Apparently Beach again wanted her to do the work while he got the credit. She replied that she regretted the demise of the *Sun,* and its loss to creditors. With sadness, she added, "my heart has been set on a close relation with the editorship of *a paper for the people.*" Tersely she added, "for the next three or four years, I shall not have my turn." She proposed writing from Washington, and then, "as many letters as possible."[53]

Jane Cazneau offered Beach advice for hiring an editor and alerted him as to what she considered "the greatest political problem at hand— the great sectional struggle." As the issues that would be termed the compromises of 1850 were then being debated and some in the South were calling for a convention of slaveholding states, she saw the need for a "constitutional union praising journal," one that "can discern the right through the mist and smoke of sectional prejudice and demagogue sophistry, my art itself in an hour." She suggested that he contact Mr. *Dispatch*, then added, there was "danger from his enthusia; seled, "We must not strengthen the popular prejudice." ; Beach, "When Mr. Cadie had the editorial and Mr. Connelly was the leading contributor, it [*Sun*] was in the summer noc perity." She could not resist a barb, "It was also the period o ̖⌣ independence and was never dismayed at being alone and foremost in its news making." She warned, "I have no strong partisan feelings, I shall continue to do as I see or think."[54]

In February, Freeman Hunt published Cora Montgomery's "Union of the Seas" in *The Merchant's Magazine*. She analyzed sea and land routes to the Pacific and promoted the Topographical Corps surveys of the west. Communication, she wrote, was as vital to the states as circulation of blood to the heart. She still promoted the Corpus Christi route as the shortest route to the Pacific, but wrote, "Let no line be omitted, by land, sea, or telegraph." In conclusion, she urged, "Let no peevish sectional discontent provoke a wayward child to raise a hand against our mother the union."[55]

Politically, Jane Cazneau can be categorized with George Bancroft, Robert Walker, Stephen A. Douglas, Sam Houston, and William Seward as nationalists These nationalists also believed it their duty to assist others in establishing political freedom. They thought slavery should not be disturbed within states, but saw it "a dangerous distraction that could be healed by focusing on foreign policy." They had a sense of mission and purpose, and that "Great mission," said Douglas, was the "great mission of progress." While she labeled the coalition group "Progressives," others would call them the "Young Americans." Historians have identified various aspects of its leadership: Edwin de Leon, a South Carolina editor, named the group; Douglas was its soul; Seward gave it the commercial thrust, with Law its financier. Edward Duyckinck, as literary editor of the *United States Magazine and Democratic Review*, promoted its literature. Unrecognized as a member of the group, Cora Montgomery was the voice of Young America up to 1850—a pivotal year. Up to then, Young America had been unionist, manifest destiny had been a national movement, and the gradual emancipation and emigration of free blacks into the tropics was a solution to slavery that would bring expansion of trade and commerce. That year, because of political pressure, the base of Cuban operations shifted from New York to New Orleans, and with that shift the Cuban independence movement altered its focus.[56]

The Cubans first sought refuge in Washington at the time Jane Storm was there, then migrated on to New Orleans in February when she left for Eagle Pass. With the shift to New Orleans, the movement mutated from one of gradual emancipation to one of slavery preservation, and from republican annexation to liberal independence. The national manifest destiny that Jane Cazneau envisioned as the peaceful spread of republican ideas through trade and commerce, and which would incorporate a confederation of many peoples, creeds, and colors, for some, became the single-minded extension of slave territory with the perpetuation of slavery. James Dunwoody Brownson DeBow, editor of *DeBow's Commercial Review*, became the reactionary voice of the Cuban independence movement. As if using back issues of the *Democratic Review* as a guide, DeBow twisted Storm's words into Southern nationalism. In August 1850, he wrote, "We have a manifest destiny to perform over Mexico, South America, West Indies, and Canada." While Storm had written of gradual conquest through commerce, DeBow exhorted, "The Eagle of the republic shall pass over . . . and . . . by war conquer," and "by commerce and trade civilize." Year by year, DeBow borrowed her phrases until manifest destiny became synonymous with slavery. Not understanding the subtle politics that drove the Cubans to New Orleans or Jane Cazneau to Eagle Pass, historians have assumed that she was an apologist for slavery. As Hiram Ketchum of the New York Union Safety Committee said of their efforts to unify the New York Democrats, the nation, and end slavery by gradual emancipation and relocation, it was "a beautiful dream and for awhile it almost seemed to be fulfilled."[57]

In February 1850, when the Cubans shifted their base to New Orleans, Jane Cazneau would put her failures behind her, once more grit her teeth at fate, pack her books and belongings, pick up her birdcage with a pair of white doves, and head for the Mexican border. She would not forget her Cuban friends, or their quest for freedom.[58]

CHAPTER VI

Eagle Pass, 1850–1852

> I have learned to comprehend the charm of a pastoral
> life, so hard to be understood, like the freedom of the
> sea, by those to whom it is not congenial. . . . This calm
> monotony would not suit the eagle soul who feels a high-
> er but more troublous mission beating at his heart.
> —*Cora Montgomery,* Eagle Pass *(1852)*[1]

*W*HEN JANE CAZNEAU RETURNED TO TEXAS IN 1850, SHE WAS NOT
the naïve young pioneer of twenty years before. As she said, she did not
have the "ugly eyes of that hideous demon failure looking into her soul."
Jane Cazneau was the well-known journalist Cora Montgomery, who was
dedicated to her Young American generation's mission—the expansion of
trade, commerce, and republican ideals. She had published in major newspapers and national publications on behalf of free blacks, women workers,
and Mexican and Cuban republicans. She had worked to maintain neutrality on the slavery issue in the New York press. Although Jane Cazneau once
believed peonage was an improvement over chattel slavery, she changed
her mind when she learned about the system. She published a series of ten
articles in the New York *Tribune* to prevent its continuation in the territory
acquired from Mexico. In *Eagle Pass; or Life on the Border,* she portrayed the
hardships of peons in Mexico and told of their precarious existence on the
border as she promoted the area's potential for economic development.
She did not go into seclusion at Eagle Pass, but continued to support
expansionist causes and widened the scope of her personal mission to
bring republican government to more groups at home and abroad. The

borderland classic *Eagle Pass* is Cazneau's most famous work and that by which she is most often identified. It was published after she returned to New York to coordinate the 1852 Franklin Pierce presidential campaign in the New York press.[2]

Much of what is known about Jane Cazneau's Eagle Pass years comes from her letters to politicians, editors, and publishers; columns in the *Tribune,* New Orleans *Delta,* and [Austin] *Texas State Gazette;* and *Eagle Pass; or Life on the Border.* Published on September 29, 1852, by George P. Putnam, the volume was no. 18 of Putnam's "Semi-Monthly Library for Travelers and Fireside"—a paperback series. Putnam published works by Washington Irving, Herman Melville, Francis Parkman, Margaret Fuller, and Susan Warner, but was best known as the editor of *Putnam's Monthly.* Jane Cazneau dedicated *Eagle Pass* to her aunt Britannia Sherman, "the dearest guide of my youth" because Sherman had allegedly requested that Cazneau write "what she saw and what she thought of peon slavery on our border." The false humility was a literary device often used by married women to excuse their writing.[3]

Cazneau's *Eagle Pass* and Teresa Griffin Viele's (1831–1906) *Following the Drum* present similar views of border life. *Eagle Pass* is sometimes compared to Harriet Beecher Stowe's *Uncle Tom's Cabin* (1852). Stowe's book was created to rouse public indignation against chattel slavery and promote colonization to Africa. Whereas the novelist created romantic composite characters to achieve sympathy, Cazneau wrote as a journalist about the reality of individuals who escaped from peon debt servitude. Peons, however, were Indians or mestizos, a Spanish-Indian mixture abhorred by racists, and they failed to elicit sympathy. *DeBow's Commercial Review* merely stated that the author had "much material on the peon slavery of Mexico." Cazneau also advocated fair treatment of American Indians at a time when that was an unpopular position. Cazneau mentioned women as boarding-house operators, pioneers, factory workers, army wives, peons, and those married to abusive husbands. As she predicted, *Eagle Pass* did not rouse public indignation against those abuses.[4]

When Jane Cazneau left New York in February 1850, the north was still experiencing winter weather. Moving was a sad time for her as she packed her books, pictures, and specimens of natural history into trunks, baskets, valises, carpetbags, and other types of packages. In Galveston, she, along with a dozen or so passengers, transferred from the oceangoing steamer *Galveston* to the coastal steamer *Palmetto* and continued on to

Indianola. She was in awe that spring had come to Texas. She described Indianola as sitting on "a belt of white sand that separated the ocean of green prairies from the ocean of blue water." To her, the "line of wooden buildings" resembled "a string of overgrown packing boxes set out on the beach to dry."[5]

In Indianola, Cazneau lodged with her old friend, Angelina Peyton Eberly, whom she had known since her first trip to Texas in 1832. Eberly had operated boardinghouses in San Felipe, Austin, and Galveston, and since 1848 in Indianola. She had private rooms for families at the American Hotel. Cazneau stayed in a private snuggery that had been vacated for the night by a southern gentleman, possibly the local editor, John Henry Brown, whose books and firearms filled the attic nook. The travelers dined on fresh oysters, turtle soup, fish, venison, turkey, biscuits, and coffee. Cazneau had never referred to food previously and praised Mrs. Eberly's food. Mrs. Eberly was legendary; she had once banned William B. Travis from her boardinghouse in San Felipe because he switched the better food of the women's table for the coarser food that was served to the men.[6]

While at Mrs. Eberly's, Cazneau wrote that slavery in Texas was "accepted as a part of the constitution" and "black men were called boys whether they were nine or ninety years old." She used traveling companions, whose names she possibly changed, as examples of "geographical morality." A Mr. Grey, of Pennsylvania, had come south "with his head full of whips and chains," and as he came further south, he changed his views until by the time he reached New Orleans, he was "indifferent to the spread of slavery." Another character was a Mr. Jobson, who Cazneau described as the son of an English factory owner and whose notions of right and wrong would never change. "At all costs," she wrote, he desired "instant emancipation and perfect equality for the blacks in marriage relations, social influence and political rights." Jobson tried to convert everyone he met to his way of thinking, and Cazneau cautioned him not to be rash, for Southerners feared "the tiger that sleeps by their hearths." Jobson decided the hot sun had addled Southerners' brains as he set out to find a mythical Texas town he had purchased.[7]

Jane Cazneau saw abolitionists and Free-Soilers as hypocrites. "My test of a sincere anti-slavery man is very simple," she wrote, "will the disciple of equal rights give a place at his table to his hired domestics?" She had "found two such persons in her lifetime." She considered one a fanatic

119

while the other was a Methodist she admired. While Henry Ward Beecher claimed to have converted her from a pro-southern attitude before her death, in *Eagle Pass,* as in other publications, Cazneau stated her position clearly, "I do not say we should, and I know in this age we cannot, keep alive the slave trade, or unduly retard the liberation of the bondsman."[8]

Jane Cazneau chartered a stagecoach to carry her baggage to San Antonio. As she traveled on what would become the San Antonio-San Diego mail line, she noted that Port Lavaca resembled Indianola in its box-like appearance. She described the terrain extending from Victoria to Matagorda as resembling Belgium and made the flat marshy plain seem attractive. She described a natural road that wound like a serpent across a carpet of grass and flowers, but turned to mud when it rained and made it difficult for the horses. At thirty to thirty-five miles a day, the four-horse stage entered San Antonio five days later. March in Texas was like June in New York, she explained. William Cazneau met her and with friends they visited the local sites with their "park-like tranquil beauty," and saw the springs from which the San Antonio River flowed.[9]

At the San José Mission, Jane Cazneau was dismayed that United States soldiers had used the religious statues for target practice during the Mexican War. She praised the Spanish missionaries who had tamed the wild Indian. She considered United States policy a disgrace:

> Our Indian tribes will drink our fire-water and die, but they will not give their limbs to our service, nor bequeath to us their children for slaves— stubborn creatures that they are—so we have to be content with killing them off and taking their lands.[10]

She proposed that Indian children be trained in manual labor schools, "They must accept civilization or death—they have no other choice at our hands." The Locofocos had advocated fair treatment of Indians, as did Lydia Maria Child and Lucretia Mott before they became obsessed with slavery.[11]

The author retired to her room after dinner, leaving her husband to talk with friends. She wrote until twilight, as she said was her usual daily custom. At one such sunset, a time she once described as "the hour of better angels," she heard a familiar voice and saw that Victor Espeta, General Cazneau's employee, had arrived to escort them to Eagle Pass.[12]

By St. Patrick's Day, March 17, 1850, the Cazneaus had packed a mule-drawn wagon for the journey farther west. They traveled to Eagle

Pass with James Campbell and his wife, with a wagon of goods. San Antonio friends, perhaps the George Van Ness family, or Robert B. Campbell, former consul at Havana, then residing in San Antonio, rode with them as far as Rosita Creek, where they had a picnic of fried chicken and biscuits Mrs. Campbell had cooked that morning. The morning's ride was a "holiday of delight." Victor, a full-blood Indian, and Severo Valdez, a Mexican Creole hired in San Antonio, served as scouts and guards. The travelers passed near Castroville, where Jane Cazneau commented that Germans had come to that region from the fatherland to make free soil.[13]

Beyond the German settlements, Jane explained, the land belonged to the Indians. Thus, they did not travel by the most direct route to Eagle Pass, but south toward Laredo. At night, the travelers unloaded their wagons, stacked the boxes underneath, and slept on the wagon floor. The men kept loaded guns under their heads. They passed the remains of burned carts where a Mrs. Horn and her children, colonists in the John Charles Beales colony, had been taken captive by Comanches at the start of the Texas Revolution. "Years later, with a blaze of trumpets they will be rescued and their families will be ashamed of them," she asserted, as if she spoke from personal knowledge. She thought it more merciful to leave women with their captors. Near Chacon Creek in present-day Webb County, the travelers buried two soldiers from Fort McIntosh who had strayed too far from the fort and were killed by Indians.[14]

The travelers turned toward the Rio Grande and followed the old River Road past irrigated crops and orchards to Eagle Pass, which Jane Cazneau described as "the lone and remote border sentinel of Texas." Victor rode ahead to arrange for her arrival as it had not been known for certain that Mrs. Cazneau would come. As the travelers rounded a bend, they saw Eagle Pass "on a vast tree sprinkled plain, between the hills and the gleaming river." They were welcomed by a herd of sheep and cows heading for the milking pen, whereas the year before, "a single white tent recessed in the lap of a hill" had greeted her when she visited with Cazneau's sister. William Cazneau's warehouse was beyond Fort Duncan perched on the edge of the highest of the three stairstep banks of the river. Eagle Pass was "full of promise," she sighed. For dinner, Fabian Valdez roasted a kid goat, which they dipped in fresh mesquite honey. Valdez's wife, Francesca, served as maid. For two weeks, the Cazneaus lived in the tent, a dugout cut into one of the upper banks of the Rio Grande. Far from a crude dwelling,

Victor had the earthen walls lined with light blue printed muslin for the general's wife. They had a full view of the river and the hills of Mexico as they sat on stools and used traveling boxes for tables. One to make the best of any situation, Jane Cazneau called those days "a calm, contented, indolent period, which I shall always remember as a sweet, half-waking dream of fairy-land." She described Eagle Pass as a commercial depot with the reputation of being the driest and least beautiful spot in Texas, but, it was healthy, and the river was "as wide as the Hudson at Troy." With snow melt from the Rocky Mountains and before New Mexico landowners drained the river for irrigation, the river ran high and wide for several months each year. Immediately, William Cazneau had stonemasons, adobe makers, and thatchers begin building a house for his wife within sight of his warehouse between the California Camp and Fort Duncan.[15]

Eagle Pass was 260 miles west of Indianola, more than three hundred miles up the Rio Grande from the Gulf of Mexico, and 140 miles southwest of San Antonio. There was no stage or mail service. Across the Rio Grande lay the infant Mexican community of Piedras Negras, which supported a Mexican military post. Two miles below Eagle Pass was the original site of Camp Eagle Pass at the old river crossing. Fort Duncan was a United States infantry post with three skeleton companies assigned to protect the five hundred miles of United States border between Eagle Pass and El Paso. California Camp, two miles beyond the fort, provided those bound for the gold fields a place to rest their stock, repair their equipment, and restock for the trek across the edge of the Chihuahua Desert to Coon's Ranch [El Paso], the midpoint along the lower route to California.[16]

In 1850, Gen. William Leslie Cazneau, his brother, Gen. Thomas N. Cazneau, and their father, Capt. W. L. Cazneau Sr., had warehouses in Texas and Sausalito, across the bay from San Francisco. The Cazneaus, a French Huguenot family, had lived in Boston since 1688. Cazneau's grandfather, also named William Leslie, had a shop in Boston where he sold retail and wholesale goods in brass, copper, steel, and iron. He was a staunch American rebel and personal friend of Paul Revere. Jane's father-in-law, Captain Cazneau, once survived 191 days on a raft, and upon his rescue immediately returned to sea as a privateer in the West Indies against the British in the War of 1812. While Jane's husband operated warehouses and lived a life of adventure on the Texas frontier, his younger brother entered the New York business world of marine insurance, married, and had children. While he was captain of the New York Fusiliers in 1842, the

"Cazneau Quick Step" became the company song. William Cazneau, then commissary general of the Republic of Texas, became responsible for two hundred thousand dollars in goods lost in the failed Santa Fe Expedition. Charles DeMorse, editor of the *Northern Standard*, described William Leslie Cazneau as dashing, handsome, and diplomatic, while others described him as a man of energy, capacity, and integrity. His political enemies were less gracious, as Cazneau was a member of the Mirabeau B. Lamar camp, which promoted the interests of West Texas, as opposed to the Houston faction, which promoted those of East Texas.[17]

After serving one year under Lamar in the Mexican War, William Leslie Cazneau transported United States goods into Mexico duty free. After the war, he continued operating under Article VII of the Treaty of Guadalupe Hidalgo, which allowed free border trade for eight years. In 1849, Cazneau laid out a wagon route from Corpus Christi to Monterrey that connected with the Chihuahua Trail at Saltillo. From Saltillo, the trail converged with others extending southward into central Mexico, northward to Chihuahua City and Santa Fe, westward to Durango, and ended at the port city of Mazatlan on the Pacific. The Corpus Christi-Matzatlan route was the shortest distance by land from the Gulf of Mexico to the Pacific Ocean and provided trade with northern Mexico. The republicans preferred to trade with the Americans and resented paying duties to the government of central Mexico. Jane Cazneau, Sam Houston, Stephen A. Douglas, and Zachary Taylor had wanted the area included in the Treaty of Guadalupe Hidalgo.[18]

Cazneau and Dr. Levy Jones, a founder of the Galveston City Company, received city lots in Corpus Christi for organizing the eighty-wagon train expedition Jane Cazneau publicized in her publications. In October 1849, the Mexican government closed the border, and in November seized United States goods in Mexico, including those belonging to Cazneau. After the United States withdrew from Mexico in June 1848, British officials supervised tariff collection with 25 percent being applied to the 1824 government debts owed London financiers. In addition, the Mexican government held the monopoly for cotton goods, and British merchants had exclusive rights to sell tobacco. According to historian J. Fred Rippy, smuggling became a respectable profession on the border. Traders moved their steamer landings up the Rio Grande from the customs port of Matamoros. Mexico claimed the right to ignore Article VII, which allowed free trade, because the United States did not uphold

Article XI and prevent Indian raids into Mexico. The political climate provided General Cazneau with business at Eagle Pass and Jane Cazneau with
the ingredients, as she wrote her editor, "to cook up a revolution."[19]

Jane Cazneau's first days in Eagle Pass were spent exploring on
Chino, her black Mexican pony. Chino threw her off at every opportunity
until she had Victor switch from a Spanish to an American bit. Victor,
whom she called, "our spoiled man of all work" and "a mint of useless
accomplishments," was her constant guide and bodyguard. Although an
Indian, Victor had attended a mission school in Guadalajara before he
was forced into debt peonage along with his parents. He came to
Matamoros as the young servant of a military officer from whom he fled
across the Rio Bravo to Corpus Christi, where he met William Cazneau,
and had worked for him ever since. Victor was "slight, rather well-formed,
easy and lithe in his movements, but with the serious, self-contained air
that characterizes his race." His face was "seamed with the small pox," but
showed "intelligence and courage." She compared Victor to the Roman
orator Cicero when he contrasted Eagle Pass to his native Guadalajara
with fruits and flowers, or to the magnificent scenery of Yucatan where
they both had traveled. Mexico had everything, Jane Cazneau said, but
good government. As she and Victor rode daily, Victor became "a fixture
in the family." He taught her to shoot a rifle—a feat of which she was very
proud. She described Victor as poetical and tenderhearted as he went
about "singing as merrily as a lark." Victor took her on an overnight trip
to the painted rocks, a day's ride upriver, and the site of an ancient
Indian civilization. With irrigation and windmills, she could see the
Quemado Valley as an oasis once more. As she and Victor wandered with
the shepherds and herds of sheep and goats, she wrote, "Wherever I am, I
like to know the features, character, and capabilities of the region; what it
has done, and what it can do."[20]

After two weeks in the calico-lined dugout, the Cazneaus moved into
their unfinished, and as she described it in Know-Nothing terms, "wide-
awake looking house" without windows or doors. "I had never given much
thought to the adornment of person or house beyond the essentials," she
confessed. For the next two weeks she was busy with boxes and calico. "A
tack hammer [was] never out of my hands," she bragged, as she converted
boxes into furniture covered with cloth.[21]

With her house in order by May, Jane Cazneau was bored. She tried
gardening, but her vines, flowers, and vegetables died from lack of water.

The Campbells had made their home nearer the river and irrigated their garden and had vegetables to spare, but Cazneau preferred to buy her fruits and vegetables from the vendors in Piedras Negras. Her choice, she explained, was to water the beans or write. While at Eagle Pass, she completed the book about their African adventure. Perhaps she worked as a ghostwriter or hid her identity because Joseph W. Fabens was listed as author of *The Camel Hunt* (1851).[22]

One day while she and "The General," as she called her husband throughout the book, were sipping chocolate, they saw a procession of horsemen approaching from the direction of the hills where "only Wild Indians roamed." She described "well mounted male and dark female riders followed by all manners and sizes of animals mounted by all ages, sexes, and sizes of Negroes." Wild Cat, the Seminole chief, with Creek, Cherokee, and Kickapoo allies were moving from their reservations in the Indian Territory to where they could be useful. In addition, they wished to move away from professional slave catchers who caught and sold their people as runaways in Arkansas and Louisiana. The entourage stopped and parlayed with General Cazneau and the commander of Fort Duncan. Later, Wild Cat came to call in state, Jane Cazneau reported, dressed in Indian costume complete with scarlet turban and attended by his cousin, Crazy Bear, and other braves. John Horse, a full-blood Negro and chief of his people, was Wild Cat's interpreter. Jane Cazneau was amused that he had received his nickname, Gopher John, because he resold the same gopher turtles numerous times to a United States Army officer in Florida. Wild Cat saluted the ladies and addressed the men through John Horse. For six months, Wild Cat had been passing from tribe to tribe on his way to the border urging them to cease hostilities. Jane Cazneau suggested, "A seven-year war would not teach our officers what the chief had learned in six months." She believed Wild Cat could rid the frontier of "Wild Indians." Staffed with infantry, the fort was more a presence than a force, she complained.[23]

As summer began, Cazneau's book promoting Eagle Pass was not progressing as planned. After all, she could only write as she believed, and she had difficulty believing in Eagle Pass. The Cazneau home, located between the fort and a miner's camp, was not a safe place for a woman alone in a house with no windows or doors. In a letter to the New York *Tribune*, she complained of seeing a slave boy whipped. One afternoon in search of shade, she rode Chino toward the river. "A lonely mesquite beckoned," and when she had ridden that far, she could see "deep green shade downriver." She rode to a mulberry grove where their employees camped at the old river crossing opposite the mouth of the Mexican Escondida River. "I pined for shade, and fruit trees," she confessed. "It is only under foliage that I can entirely possess myself and live—untrammeled by the tedious weight of society—with my thoughts, my books, and my birds," she swooned. Her turkey, ducks, geese, and spotted chickens had already found solace in the shade, so she had Victor build her a reed house in the mulberry grove like those of tropical Mexico. With difficulty, Victor found large canes downriver and built what she described as "an enormous bird cage." The structure was twelve feet wide, twenty feet long, with a thatch roof, and lined with calico curtains for privacy when needed. "With a table for writing, embroidery, and other feminine helps to idleness disguised in form of work," she listened to the Mexican women talk about their escape from peonage across the Rio Bravo as they went about their daily chores.[24]

On June 18, 1850, Jane Cazneau wrote to Sen. William H. Seward requesting that mail service be established to Fort Duncan because it was 150 miles from a post office. She suggested that soldiers carry the mail by regular express from San Antonio. Local citizens had sent a petition to their Democratic senator, Gen. Thomas J. Rusk. She wanted the true Whig, Thomas K. Wallace, who was their store clerk, to be made postmaster. She was glad the "administration was for the admission of California without mixing it with that swindling proposition to pay Texas some millions for New Mexico." When she had mail, she said, she would write some things to please him. The next year, Eagle Pass had postal service and a stage line with Wallace as postmaster, but Cazneau would not support the Whigs for long.[25]

Jane Cazneau wrote for several newspapers and the *United States Magazine and Democratic Review* while she lived in Eagle Pass. Horace Greeley needed a new female correspondent and published Cazneau's letters (written as Cora Montgomery) on peonage in the *Tribune* from July 15, 1850 to August 2, 1851. While in Europe, Margaret Fuller, Greeley's literary critic, had a flagrant affair with an Italian revolutionary ten years her junior, and when Fuller become pregnant, Greeley dropped her column.[26]

Cazneau sent her letters about peonage and conditions on the border to Sen. William H. Seward, who reviewed them before sending them to the *Tribune*. Greeley, in introducing the first letter of the series, credited Cora

Montgomery with playing an important role in Texas annexation. The correspondence came about because "The Senate recently refused to decreee the abolition of Peon Slavery in New-Mexico because no information was at hand." The letters would educate readers on the reality of the debt-labor system and prevent its continuation in the territories acquired from Mexico.[27]

On September 7, 1850, the *Texas State Gazette* published Jane Cazneau's editorial on the Texas-New Mexico boundary dispute. While she did not support the Texas claim to part of New Mexico, in "Texas and Her Duty," she advocated that Texas retain its public lands. While Thomas Hart Benton opposed Texas retaining its public land, she urged cooperation between New Mexico and Texas because "Sectional politicians for their own petty and personal ends would make them rivals and enemies." They both had a right, she urged, to demand that the overland mail route pass through their areas.[28]

By the end of September 1850, Cazneau wrote to Moses S. Beach, who she thought still edited the New York *Sun*. She reproached him because she was not receiving the *Sun*. His father was supposed to send the *Weekly Sun* to Indianola in care of J. Brown, who would forward it to her. She tried to interest Beach in investing in the Santa Rosa Silver Mine some seventy miles into Mexico that only needed modern extraction methods. William Cazneau was not interested, she complained, because his business kept him in Mexico. She further grumbled that she could not get windows or doors for her house, "It must be done. It is a month or more before I can stir from this unproductive Texas property that eats of itself." Jane Cazneau had received some news, for she quipped, "I see the Tehuantepec treaty, a miserable business, has been cooked up of late." She suggested that the elder Beach "come out with the secret history of its origin." She would do it, but she did not have the data on the latest claimant [A. G. Sloo]. If Beach wanted drawings of the country, or of Wild Cat, he should ship her canvas by the first vessel bound for Port Lavaca and consigned to Pryor, Adams and Company for General Cazneau. Beach was no longer editor of the *Sun*, however, and her letter was passed to Charles Wood, the new business manager.[29]

William Cazneau's business in Mexico of which Mrs. Cazneau wrote concerned an 1848 arrangement Cazneau had made with the heirs of Antonio Rivas to acquire a deed to the family Spanish land grant of approximately 125,835 acres on the left bank of the Rio Grande below the

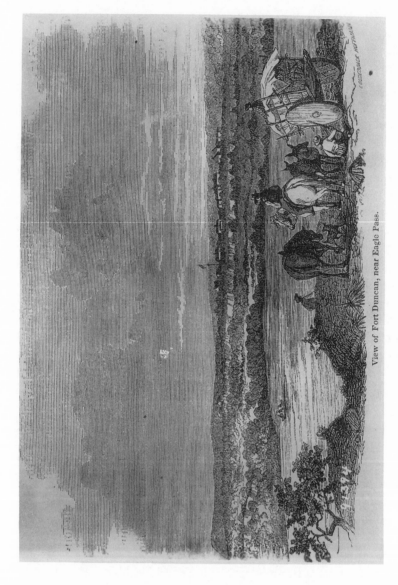

View of Fort Duncan, near Eagle Pass.

View of Fort Duncan, near Eagle Pass (1852). From William H. Emory, *Report on the United States and Mexican Boundary Survey . . .*, I, Pt. 1, 79. Courtesy Texas Collection, CN02444a, Center for American History, University of Texas at Austin.

old Eagle Pass crossing. After the Mexican War, Texas gained the area as part of its public lands, and the legislature voted to recognize Spanish land grants between the Nueces and the Rio Grande on a case-by-case basis. Vicente Garza represented the Rivas family, and William L. Cazneau acted as their agent to recover the grant for one-half the claim. Before the claim could be considered, Cazneau had to gather the signatures of the Rivas heirs. During his delivery of goods to the mines and elsewhere in Mexico, Cazneau located the heirs and obtained their signatures. It is unknown who paid the application fee of five dollars per league.[30]

Because she requested drawing materials and mentioned the scenes and people portrayed, it is likely that Jane sketched the "View of Fort Duncan, near Eagle Pass" (1852), published in William H. Emory's, *Report on the United States and Mexican Boundary Survey . . .*, Pt. 1. The surveyors came through Eagle Pass, and the sketch depicts Fort Duncan, but also a black pony [Chino] with a sidesaddle, an American on a white horse [Cazneau], a man with a turban [Wild Cat], a Mexican cartman, a boat with occupants on the Rio Grande, and a seated woman holding a rifle. Cazneau's house and warehouse are shown to the left of Fort Duncan (see page 128).[31]

Although Jane Cazneau wrote that Eagle Pass was in Kinney County, a county government was not yet organized. In October 1850, the Bexar County census taker listed William L. and Jane M. Cazneau as living between the households of James Campbell and Fabiano and Francesca Valdez. Others she immortalized in the book were on the Eagle Pass census: Alexandro and Maria Ruiz, Antonio Sanchez, Jesus Martinez, Pedro and Barbara Aquila, Juanita Hernandez, Manuel and Saloma Rios, as well as a household with Victor Espeta, age thirty-five, and Guadalupe, age twenty-six. Although, she and Cazneau were forty-three years old, she told the census taker they were thirty-seven.[32]

The Cazneaus were the wealthiest members of the community—he having $16,000 in merchandise and she with unnamed assets of $12,500. Cazneau's partner, Virginia-born San Antonio merchant Ludovic Colquhoun (1804–1883) and his wife, Frances, were then living in Eagle Pass and were the next wealthiest with $15,000 in assets. The Scotland-born dry goods merchant John Brown and his wife, Margaret, had $8,000 in merchandise. Dennis Meade, an Irish dry goods merchant, had $2,000 in assets, while Irish merchant Frederick B. O'Shea and his wife, Hanora, had only $1,000 in dry goods, the same amount as the Missouri-born baker

William Brown and his wife, Mary. Aside from merchants and traders, the community had one eating house, a butcher, a cooper, two shoemakers, a tailor, a bar keeper, a Mexican liquor maker, carpenters, stonemasons, cartmen, and laborers of mixed nationalities. The number of traders, merchants, and cartmen suggests the economy of Eagle Pass depended on the Mexican trade.[33]

Jane Cazneau wrote that people settled opposite the Escondida River for commercial reasons. It was, she explained, on "the right side of the fords and paths precious to contrabandists." The natural crossing was the original Paso de Aquila, where an eagle once nested and gave the crossing its name, near the Spanish Mission San Juan Bautista del Rio Grande. Spanish explorers, French traders, missionaries, and runaways from both sides of the border used the crossing. She liked the clear drinking water and the bathing rapids of the Escondida "where the timid bather might recline at careless length . . . and enfold and lave his indolent limbs with its watery delights." Using the German carpenter's boat, she had gypsy dinners in quiet nooks on the river, whether with Victor or the general she did not say, nor did she mention a bathing costume. Her reed cottage was next to the brush and hide shelter of Pedro Aquila, the adobe maker, and his wife, Barbara, the tortilla maker. Victor and the shepherd families also lived in the mulberry grove. Francesca's story, overheard in the reed house, inspired Jane Cazneau to include the peon sagas in her book promoting the commercial aspects of Eagle Pass. The stories brought meaning to her work and gave her another form of tyranny to slay.[34]

While Jane Cazneau was in Eagle Pass, Bvt. Maj. W. W. Chapman, assistant quartermaster, ordered Capt. Harry Love to explore the Rio Grande to see if the river forts could be supplied by steamers rather than by land from Lavaca. Love ascended the river 967 miles and reported that steamers could operate as far as Kingsbury's Falls near Rio Grande City and that for five hundred dollars the channel could be improved to allow small steamers to ascend the river to above Eagle Pass. The army paid $92 in freight to deliver a barrel of flour from Lavaca to El Paso, whereas if the forts could be supplied by river to Eagle Pass, and then by land, the cost fell to $32 per barrel. Mrs. Cazneau mentioned Love, who was not exaggerating about the river being navigable at that time. For the past twenty years, she explained, unusual rains had come to the area. The shepherds believed the Americans had brought the rains along with their government. She chided Victor for encouraging their superstitions.[35]

Major Chapman suddenly reversed himself after receiving real estate and a warehouse in Brownsville from Charles Stillman. Stillman controlled trade and shipping on the lower Rio Grande and sought to destroy competition upriver. Chapman, after becoming a partner, gave Stillman, founder of Brownsville, and his partners, Miflin Kenedy and Richard King, the government contract to supply the river forts without taking bids.[36]

Stillman was a merchant of the Cornelius Vanderbilt style of cutthroat competition. He encouraged the Carbajal revolt, or Merchant's War, which began in September 1850. Stillman persuaded and backed José María Jesús Carbajal (1823–1874) in an attack on Matamoros and his declaration of a Republic of Sierra Madre. Rangers, soldiers, ranchers, merchants, and peons joined the popular revolt. Carbajal was born in San Antonio, educated in Kentucky and Virginia, surveyed for the Galveston Bay and Texas Land Company, fought in the Texas Revolution, and was with Antonio Canales and Antonio Zapata when they declared a Republic of the Rio Grande in 1840, and he had approached Gen. Zachary Taylor about an alliance before the Mexican War. Using the disruption along the border, Stillman sent an estimated million dollars worth of cotton goods across the border and destroyed his former competition upriver. To Jane Cazneau, it was a "Calico War," and she compared it to "elections in the United States—they had the same principle at stake, spoils." The Comanches, although motivated by hunger, she explained, were "too ignorant to dress up their motives," and "said their object was plunder." Jane Cazneau had invested in one thousand acres of land where a channel would be dug to open steam navigation of the river to Eagle Pass. With the border in turmoil, there was little chance of the river's development.[37]

The Calico War involved more than Stillman's destruction of competition on the Rio Grande. Jane Cazneau's $12,500 in assets listed on the census in October was perhaps her share of the Hargous Tehuantepec Transit Company at last recognized by the Mexican government. Since the 1840s the Hargous Brothers had sought rights of transit across the Isthmus of Tehuantepec. Steamship interests sought confirmation of that grant in conjunction with the Treaty of Guadalupe Hidalgo. In 1850, the Hargous company sold its assets to Judah P. Benjamin, president of the Louisiana Tehuantepec Company. Hargous Company stockholders, represented by William H. Seward, then had the option of selling or transferring their stock. In August 1850 the Fillmore administration had opened negotiations in Mexico to renegotiate the Treaty of Guadalupe Hidalgo to include the Tehuantepec transit route. American support of the Carbajal revolt in September, however, made it appear that the United States was trying to retake Mexico. Thus, by January 1851, Mexican officials opposed any change in the treaty, and the United States was still without a land bridge to connect steamer traffic from the Gulf to the Pacific. When Stillman had destroyed rival trade and commerce, he negotiated with the army commander of northern Mexico, a General Avalos, and goods entered Mexico by special permit obtained through a fee paid to the general. Stillman then abandoned Carbajal, who continued a guerrilla war out of the Sierra Madre.[38]

From 1851 onward, William Cazneau supplied the Santa Rosa and other silver mines by special Avalos permit. Silver bullion trains out of Mexico passed through Eagle Pass to Indianola for transshipment to New Orleans and the United States Mint—some shipments were as much as three hundred thousand dollars. In 1850, traffic between Indianola and Eagle Pass had processions of 150 wagons pulled by six mules or oxen, or trains of 250 Mexican carretas. By summer 1850, some five or six hundred wagons were outfitted in Indianola for the Mexican trade. The Santa Fe trade was at last diverted through Texas because the distance between the gulf ports and Chihuahua was four hundred miles less than the distance between Chihuahua and Independence, Missouri. Eagle Pass was a booming, but lawless, frontier town.[39]

In November 1850, Jane Cazneau wrote to Charles Wood, the manager of the New York *Sun*. She proposed to write anonymously all year for $850, but wanted the money in advance. She supposed the Beaches would drag her from the office, and wrote mocking the elder Beach, "if this revolution don't come off." But, she vowed, "I shall come along to Washington to cook up some excitement."[40]

Jane Cazneau was concerned about her investments in Eagle Pass and wrote to Seward about the Whig plan to develop the Rio Grande for a thousand miles of steam navigation. The area was rich in minerals, and coal deposits gave Piedras Negras its name in Spanish, "black stones." Lead and silver deposits also dotted the area. In Piedras Negras, Mexican women plastered their adobe walls with gypsum. Her workers and others brought her samples of pottery and porcelain clay. She said that she applied "the Golden Rule" to their relationship and taught those who desired to learn to read and write; "Everyone thought it was a fair exchange in trading silver ore for tutoring."[41]

During the Carbajal revolt, Wild Cat, John Horse, and a former slave escaped from Cuba whom she identified as part Arab, sought General Cazneau's advice. The Mexican government that had given Wild Cat refuge in return for protecting the border had ordered him and his men downriver to help defeat Carbajal. Wild Cat was concerned that his people would be unprotected from raids. As they talked, Jane Cazneau realized that four men from four continents sat in her living room and discussed their mutual problem of "how to subdue the restless Indian that raids and plunders." With Wild Cat gone, she did not ride more than two or three miles from the house, and then only in the presence of six-shooters. One day, she and her employees climbed onto the roof of the wide-awake house to watch Comanches raid the ranch of Don Felipe Garcia across the river. One can imagine her shading her eyes with one hand and peering through her lorgnette and saying, "We must have the justice to feed and civilize these famishing outlaws, or we must have the hardihood to exterminate them."[42]

Jane Cazneau knew that her workers were runaway peons and that the old crossing at the mulberry grove was used by fugitives from both sides of the border. Slaves belonging to Wild Cat were "accommodated" in Mexico, a term, she explained, that peons used to describe their being bound to an owner for food, clothing, medicine, and religious rites. She invited Bishop John Odin to Eagle Pass, where he performed marriages and baptisms and legalized the common-law relationships of the former peons who refused to have their children born into peonage. The bishop of the Texas Diocese established Our Lady of Refuge Catholic Church in Eagle Pass in 1852.[43]

Jane Cazneau cautioned that unskilled runaway slaves were soon bound into peonage in Mexico and did not find the freedom they expected. One exception was Dan, who became Don Dionisio Echavaria when he married into a prominent border family. Wealth, rather than race, determined class in Catholic countries. Although the Treaty of Guadalupe Hidalgo made Mexicans on the north bank of the Rio Grande United States citizens, the runaway peons were not safe—"a dealer in cards, calico, cheap rum, and kidnaping," operated "under the very eye of Fort Duncan." She identified the man-catcher as Dennis Meade, a forty-year-old dry goods merchant with a Mexican wife.[44]

One Sunday morning in September 1850, during the Carbajal revolt, a professional man-hunter chased Manuel Rios into Mrs. Cazneau's kitchen and captured him at gunpoint. Caught and bound like Mazeppo, as she described the scene, Rios was carried into Mexico. The general got up a petition, and Jane Cazneau wrote to Secretary of State Daniel Webster about the kidnapping of a United States citizen. Webster replied that Rios "must make good his claims to freedom, before the judicial tribunals of Mexico." In discussing the issue, one Eagle Pass Whig said that if Webster became a presidential candidate, he must vote for him because of party. Jane Cazneau wrote a scathing comment: "So faded and effete has become the preserving salt of republican virtue that sensible men, . . . make no scruple to avow that party over-rides principle." She further raged:

> What an abyss of mire and corruption; what a stinking depth of moral decadence; what a departure from the lofty spirit of '76 there is in that perverse cry! It loads the air, it taints the moral health of the nation, and makes every returning election day more vilely opposite to what it should be, a jubilee of sacred duties.

She then wrote to Seward about the kidnapping, and Greeley published her letter on February 1, 1851. Seward brought the matter before the United States Senate on February 26, but no action was taken. Rios, a United States citizen, remained in bondage in Mexico.[45]

Kidnappers next seized her precious Victor in Piedras Negras during the festival of San Diego, where he went to celebrate with his newest "coquettish flame," Jesusa. The holder of Victor's three-dollar debt demanded either the full payment or use of the peon for labor. With Victor jailed, General Cazneau decided to use the case as another example of border injustice. Victor's debt was contracted on the side of the border where United States law prevailed, and so, using Webster's logic, Cazneau said, "I think I shall bring home Victor this day." Jane Cazneau described what happened next: One friend and another joined in "and as in as brief time, and as lightly as I have written it, were they armed, in saddle, and under spur." They were "not like that dead, spongy excrescence of the popular will—no, of party intrigue—a partisan cabinet," she fumed. Before sunset Victor was home and chanting his ballads, but border troubles continued.[46]

Throughout the spring Greeley published Jane Cazneau's letters about peonage. She lambasted a do-nothing Congress and Whig administration in her usual caustic style. She accused the partisans and fame hunters of using the New Mexico slave issue as "a convenient football for the players in the political circus at Washington." Meanwhile, peons made into citizens by the Treaty of Guadalupe Hidalgo were kidnapped from United States soil and two-thirds of the citizens of New Mexico remained in peon servitude. Three types of slavery existed like colored layers on a riverbank or beads on a string, she wrote. The red race were held in debt-bondage or peon slavery, white immigrants were held as wage slaves, and blacks as chattel slaves. She traveled to Washington in late spring 1851 and personally chastised President Fillmore about "the terrible state of the frontier" with only infantry stations to guard against the wild Indians. She proposed a national system of border protection headed by Wild Cat. If the government would "assign his band a home and rations," he would create "a humane, politic, and economical border militia of the friendly tribes." She admonished, "We owe something very different to the Indians than the mockery of gifts of rum and treaties of specious promises."[47]

Jane Cazneau perhaps had another reason to return to Washington, one concerning the Cubans. The year she moved to Eagle Pass, Narciso López and volunteers had landed on the north shore of Cuba and planted the Cuban flag. When no uprising occurred, López narrowly escaped to Florida. John L. O'Sullivan, López, and others were arrested and charged with violating the neutrality laws of the United States. Judah P. Benjamin represented the revolutionaries in trials in New Orleans, and none were convicted. In April 1851, authorities seized the steamer *Cleopatra*, and again arrested O'Sullivan along with the Hungarian republican refugee Louis Schlessinger.[48]

On July 4, 1851, in Washington, López declared Cuban independence. Women made Cuban flags, and one hung in the window of the Sun Building. On August 3, López and 420 men steamed from New Orleans and other southern ports to liberate Cuba. Duncan Smith, one of the participants, posed as Dr. Henry Burtnett, acquired knowledge of the invasion plan, and reported to the Spanish minister in Washington, Calderon de la Barca. López and his volunteers walked into a trap. López was garroted on September 1, 1851, some sources claim as he clutched a miniature likeness of Cora Montgomery. A Spanish firing squad in Havana shot William S. Crittenden, nephew of the attorney general of the United States, and fifty other American volunteers. Witnesses wrote that Crittenden refused a blindfold and declined to kneel, saying, "An American kneels only to God, and always faces his enemy." The remaining prisoners were transported to Spain. Riots erupted in New Orleans, and the Spanish consulate was looted and burned. Gov. John A. Quitman of Mississippi was then rumored to have become the next leader of the revolutionaries. Jane Cazneau was strangely quiet in the press about Cuba and wrote on melon sugar production in the Rio Grande Valley for the *Tribune*.[49]

Ironically, no letters or publications are known to reflect Jane Cazneau's reaction to the executions in Cuba. Perhaps she made an agreement with New York prosecutors in 1849 that she would be silent on Cuba. An anonymous article published in October 1851 in the *United States Magazine and Democratic Review* was probably written by Jane Cazneau, and defended López and his companions against charges that they were outlaws. Jane Cazneau's whereabouts is unknown between July 8 and November 1851, but in August of that year she sold the Carrizo property to J. B. Shaw, comptroller of Texas, for an undisclosed sum.[50]

On December 12 and 14, 1851, the New Orleans *Delta*, a backer of Lopez, published two editorials written by Montgomery from Eagle Pass about Carbajal's continued efforts to establish a Republic of Sierra Madre. Carbajal would end peonage and provide the second best land route to the Pacific, she asserted. She did not propose that the United States annex the area, but suggested instead a purchase of the transit route that would help finance the new government. The large landholders opposed a republic, she explained, because it meant the liberation of the peons to whom they would have to pay wages. By the end of December 1851, Jane Cazneau wrote to Seward that peonage must be stopped and included another article for him to review before sending it on to Greeley. She and Seward had no further written communication until the eve of the American Civil War.[51]

While she lived at Eagle Pass, Jane Cazneau realized that she preferred the women of the frontier to those of the city where "the set of hat and the length of a skirt were gossip." She cared little for fashion, and she was glad there were too few women in Eagle Pass to form cliques and "hear Mrs. Snooks' criticism on Mrs. Smith's last lace, last party, or last flirtation." She mentioned the fort commander's wife and Mrs. Campbell. Most of the merchants had wives and families, but Jane Cazneau seemed more content amid her Indian and Mexican friends than at any time of her life.[52]

As she watched Barbara grind corn, Martha preserve food, Madalina play the harp, and Francesca sew, Jane Cazneau had nothing but disdain for the Romantic poets. "The bread-baking, blanket-weaving period, in which woman walks out her tread-mill round of life in mental torpor and laborious usefulness," she challenged, "reads well in Arcadian poetry." She observed, "Man was not high where woman was so low . . . and he cannot rise without taking woman with him." In this pastoral world idealized by romantics, she witnessed "domestic strife, fraternal wars, neighborly deceit, and mutual injustice." She thought the Women's Rights Convention could do more good by "inducing the Cabinet to define its position on Mexico" and in preventing women from being sold into peonage. In the sketches, she wrote about the peons' whippings, hunger, and neglect. The peons slept on hides and blankets and some had never seen a mattress. They had grass bags to hold their possessions of a gourd, a kettle for cooking and eating, and they had only the clothes on their backs. She told stories of sacrifice, sorrow, and bravery as peons risked their lives to escape across the Rio Bravo to freedom.[53]

In defense of frontier justice, Cazneau told about a local murder and community justice. She also repeated the story of an East Texas woman whose husband had squandered her inheritance, physically abused her, and gambled and drunk away the family's money. "The men of the community held a common law court and meted out 100 lashes to the offender of the community standards," she wrote approvingly. "The brutal coward who can raise his hand against a woman is exactly of the mould to yield to fear and brute force." Her telling the story suggests that she identified with the woman in some way. Perhaps Allen Storm was intemperate and abusive, or William Cazneau, who seemed to spend most of his time in Mexico and left her alone in the lawless border town, was not the knight she thought she married. It is likely he discovered that the angel he idealized was demanding and had a fiery temper. She saw them as a "strange couple"; he "so full of anecdotes" while she was "somewhat of a hermit." Their mutual friend Lamar said their marriage was a partnership and inferred it was more a business than romantic relationship. In *Our Times*, she reviewed the psychology book, *Love and Marriage*, and quoted a passage that meant something to her. She quoted, "Never idealize a woman to her face, because she needs to look up to the man she loves . . . if scorned, a true hero . . . will not seek consolation in . . . the light love of inferior women, or in animal dissipation and coarser excitements."[54]

Throughout *Eagle Pass*, with few exceptions, the general seemed to be in Mexico, and Victor was her protector and companion. Aside from his supplying the mines and guarding silver shipments, William Cazneau secured the documentation for recognition of the Antonio Rivas Spanish land grant. On February 10, 1852, a special act of the Texas legislature awarded the grant to the Rivas heirs. Garza, representing the Rivas family, then deeded Cazneau one-half of the grant. While Garza recorded the family's deed in the Bexar County Courthouse in San Antonio, Cazneau did not record his deed. R. O. W. McManus, his brother-in-law, said that he was careless about things like that, but he likely had a judgment against him for previously lost goods assigned to him in Mexico.[55]

By June 1852, Jane Cazneau left her husband in Eagle Pass and returned to New York and her former world of newspapers and politics— her eagle soul feeling a higher calling than Eagle Pass. Colleagues needed her expertise in the upcoming presidential campaign. Early in 1852, Col. J. L. Curtis, an associate of U.S. Mail Steamship Company President George Law, hired Mrs. Cazneau to help unite the New York Democrats for the presidential campaign.[56]

The New York politicians had been divided since the 1844 presidential campaign of James K. Polk, when Martin Van Buren's followers resented the New York appointments made by President Polk. In 1848, the Van Buren "Barnburner" and the William L. Marcy "Hunker" factions held separate state conventions and sent two delegations to the national convention. The Van Burenites formed the Free Soil party, which drew votes from the Democrats and helped elect Whig Zachary Taylor as president and Hamilton Fish as New York governor. In 1852, Jane Cazneau's old friend, Marcy, lured the Free-Soilers back into the Democratic party with promises of patronage. Marcy probably arranged Cazneau's return to New York as she was the logical peacemaker, having been an independent throughout the fray. In addition, she had written in support of George Law's U.S. Mail Steamship Company, and Law controlled the expansionist Seward Whigs and both factions of New York Democrats with political contributions.[57]

At the national Democratic party convention of 1852, steamer interests dominated politics. Law supported Sen. Stephen A. Douglas of Illinois for the nomination. Douglas and Jane Cazneau had similar ideals. They were Anglophobic and held a common view that time would resolve the slavery issue. Douglas was a member of the Tammany Society, the organization that financed her publications on Cuba. In "The Union of the Seas," she had promoted Douglas's idea of binding the three sections of the nation with rails and steamers to California and Oregon. Despite Law's efforts, the presidential nomination went to Franklin Pierce, a rival steamship company's candidate. James Buchanan and Marcy aligned with Pierce, who was also backed by Jefferson Davis. Thomas W. Pierce, the candidate's brother, was president of Bacon and Pierce Shipping Company, a major transporter of cotton from southern ports and an investor in southern railroads. August Belmont of the American branch of the Rothschild family financed the Pierce campaign.[58]

Jane Cazneau helped organize the Pierce presidential campaign around themes of neglect and corruption. On July 7, 1852, she wrote to Sen. Thomas J. Rusk of Texas about the neglect of the border. When she had left the border the month before, two skeleton companies of fifteen men each were on duty at Fort Duncan. She was "not going back to Eagle Pass to be murdered," nor was she going to "let the matter rest as long as a paper was printed in New York." Later that month, she wrote to Douglas about their conversation on making the Clayton-Bulwer Treaty (1850) the major issue of the campaign. She encouraged him to "strike a bold blow" against "corrupt influences" and "force the Whigs to define their position." In closing, she pledged the support of the newspapers that she represented; "the campaign paper [New York *Morning News*], the independent press [New York *Star*], the New York *Sun*, its satellites, and Tammany Hall."[59]

Douglas called for Senate investigations, and in July, hearings documented Jane Cazneau's assumptions about corruption. The companies that made up the U.S. Mail Steamship Company owned by Law, William Aspinwall, and Edward Collins were subsidized by the government, but operated at a loss. Isolationist Whigs demanded an end to the steamship mail subsidy. The Senate investigation showed that the Whig administration paid a British steamer company $529,341.04 to carry the mail to and from California and Oregon, while Law and Aspinwall received only $9,896. In addition, the British Cunard Steam Line operating between New York and England received $536,000, while the Collins Line received around $10,000. In addition, the scandal illustrated that the Clayton-Bulwer Treaty (1850) favored British companies at the expense of those of the United States. The treaty was to end Anglo-American rivalry in Central America and allow the joint construction of a canal across Panama.[60]

Cornelius Vanderbilt was responsible for the Clayton-Bulwer Treaty because he planned a canal through Panama. Construction required more financing than he had available, and he joined with the British Rothschild, Baring Brothers, and Hudson's Bay financiers and cemented the agreement with the treaty neutralizing Central America to further United States advancement. When a re-survey found a Panama canal beyond current technology, Vanderbilt shifted his focus to Nicaragua. There, he secured exclusive rights of transit, and some ten thousand of the thirty thousand annual immigrants to California by sea took the Nicaragua overland route.[61]

Jane Cazneau's *Eagle Pass; or Life on the Border* was published in September 1852 as part of the expansionist Young America literature of the Pierce campaign. As Cora Montgomery, she also edited and wrote the September and October issues of *Our Times*, subtitled "a monthly review of Politics, Literature, and etc." The October journal featured articles on foreign policy and trade with Japan and gave the history of the fisheries problem in the North Atlantic. Shorter articles were on nature, inventors, and mining. She had book reviews, patriotic songs, and poems. "Events of the Month" were news summaries where she featured Law's troubles with steamer access to Havana. In "The Cuba Junta," she declared: "Cuba and the Cubans are resolved to wage incessant war with the tyranny of Spain until Cuba has achieved independence." "The Editor's Portfolio" was Cazneau at her wittiest. She convicted Daniel Webster of neglect of the border, and sentenced him to read all Benton's speeches. She sentenced General Scott, for giving away Tehuantepec, to read the life of Jackson three times, while he kept Webster company. Benton was to prove that all routes to the Pacific passed through Missouri, or he had to have dinner with Fillmore and Scott on the same night. One can see her seriously asking the British minister at a Washington reception if Prince Bobo, the heir of the Majesty of Hayti, was a candidate for the hand of the Princess Royal of England. "The doctrine of the amalgamation of the races is only intended for Americans," she was told by the distinguished English gentleman. She concluded that "next to honesty, perhaps, the rarest commodity at Washington is courage."[62]

When Pierce was elected president, Marcy secured political printing contracts for the New York Free-Soilers and Jane Cazneau's usefulness ended. In January 1853, she wrote to James Buchanan, newly appointed ambassador to the Court of St. James, about her betrayal. When Colonel Curtis hired her, she explained, she had bought into the New York *Morning Star*, but "the majority owners, the ultra Free-Soilers, threw me out without one cent return." In addition, Thomas Childs and the Williams Brothers had stopped printing her expansionist journal, *Our Times*. "One honest word would choke them to death if by chance such a strange thing should get in their throats," she blurted. She further fumed, "A cooler act of plunder was never perpetrated." She asked Buchanan about the incoming

As Cora Montgomery, Jane Cazneau edited and wrote the September and October issues of *Our Times*, an expansionist journal that printed articles, book reviews, patriotic songs, and poems. "The Editor's Portfolio" was Cazneau at her wittiest.

administration. The Cubans wished to know who they could trust on Cuba. While her husband's business faltered, and she was without work, the California Cazneaus were a highly visible couple at the Pierce inauguration. Phoebe Cazneau, the wife of Gen. Thomas Cazneau, led the grand march at the inaugural ball.[63]

Encouraged by Britain's success in stopping United States expansion with the Clayton-Bulwer Treaty, France and Spain launched campaigns to recover investments and colonies in the Western Hemisphere. Louis-Napoleon set out to expand industry and trade with Mexico, Latin America, and to Southeast Asia by way of the Caribbean and Central America; the most direct route to China from France. In Mexico, Antonio López de Santa Anna became president and again allowed French troops to seize silver mines to repay debts. In Mexico, authorities seized Cazneau's trade goods and jailed his employees in Saltillo and Parras. Cazneau secured the release of his men, left his sheep and goatherds with his shepherd, Desiderio de Luna, and traveled to Washington. He expected to return, and left the warehouse and house as they stood, and with the Rivas deed still unrecorded. In the Caribbean, Spain made plans to recover its former colony of Santo Domingo, which had existed as the Dominican Republic since 1844.[64]

Looking for work, Jane Cazneau wrote to Senator Douglas for the subscription list of the *United States Magazine and Democratic Review.* Upon the death of his wife earlier in the month, however, Douglas had left for Europe on a six-month tour. George Sanders of Kentucky, the former editor of the *Democratic Review,* was determined to purge the party of reform elements, and prevented Cazneau from resuming control of the journal. Sanders also opposed Marcy's appointment as secretary of state.[65]

In Eagle Pass, William Stone, a San Antonio store clerk, acquired the power to seize William Cazneau's property and herds, claiming that Cazneau took goods belonging to San Antonio merchant Enoch Jones into Mexico without permission. Judge T. J. Devine, newly elected Bexar County District Judge, witnessed Stone's deed of lien to a tract of property Cazneau owned on the edge of Eagle Pass. Stone also began trading in Mexico, but supplied the French mining interests and conservative landowners. In Washington, unaware of these events, William Cazneau filed a $235,500 claim with the United States government for the "Illegal detention of persons and goods imported into Mexico under the Avalos tariff."[66]

Two years after the Cazneaus left Eagle Pass, the town was bypassed by the San Antonio-San Diego mail line. In 1854, New York Free-Soiler Frederick Law Olmsted traveled to Eagle Pass by a more direct but more desolate route than Jane Cazneau had described. He saw none of the orchards or sights she mentioned on the river road. Olmsted found Eagle Pass desolate and deserted. The runaway camp was beyond the river and deeper into Mexico. On his brief visit, he decided that Cazneau had exaggerated the hardships of peonage. As a Free-Soiler opposed to other races incorporated as citizens into the United States, Olmsted had nothing good to say about Jane Cazneau, Eagle Pass, or Mexicans.[67]

Jane Cazneau had failed to "cook up a revolution" in Mexico, but the revolution that she predicted in *Eagle Pass* eventually came to Mexico. Carbajal was raising another army in 1855 when Texas Ranger James Callahan raided into Mexico after runaway slaves, burned Carbajal's home, and looted Piedras Negras. In 1861, Benito Juarez, an Indian educated in the United States, brought about the separation of church and state in Mexico with the help of his ally, Carbajal. By the 1870s, Wild Cat's tribe served as U.S. Army scouts and helped control the Indians on the border. The peons were not released from debt servitude, however, until Francisco Madero, also educated in the United States, triggered the Mexican Revolution of 1910. Over a million Mexicans died in their civil war in an attempt to establish true republican government in Mexico. Perhaps, it was destiny, or merely coincidence, that Madero entered Mexico to begin the revolution at the old Eagle Pass crossing where Jane Cazneau had lived in the reed house amid her peon friends and, as Cora Montgomery, wrote *Eagle Pass* as a tribute to their courage and love of freedom.[68]

CHAPTER VII

"In The Tropics," 1853–1861

> I say this on data not learned in a day, but slowly and
> surely acquired in a nine year's faithful apprenticeship
> to the cause and a clearer insight into the heart of affairs
> than is commonly attainable . . . the issue of Cuba is
> entangled with the Central American complication.
> —*J. M. Cazneau to James Buchanan* (*1857*)[1]

*I*N 1853, JANE CAZNEAU COMPLETED *A Story of Life on the Isthmus* AS A
sequel to *The Camel Hunt*, with Joseph W. Fabens again listed as author.
George Putnam paired the travel piece that described the Panama cross-
ing at the height of the California gold rush with a second edition of *Eagle
Pass; or Life on the Border*. The books provided Fabens with immortality and
Cazneau with an income, but led bibliographers to attribute her unsigned
works on the tropics to Fabens. From 1853 to the onset of the American
Civil War, Jane Cazneau promoted expansion into the Caribbean and
Central America. By this time in her career, she was an internationally
known republican revolutionary whose activities were closely monitored by
British officials concerned that she would bring revolution and United
States territorial expansion to the tropics. She and her husband, as well as
the businessmen and politicians with whom she associated, invested in
inter-ocean transit, property, and mining ventures in the areas they infil-
trated. She still hoped that colonization would solve the sectional dispute
over slavery and worked on behalf of the Cubans, backed William Walker
in Nicaragua, supported Benito Juarez in Mexico, and encouraged republicans in the Dominican Republic. If successful, slavery would be ended in

145

the continental United States, areas of national security would be secured, and commerce and trade boundaries would be extended. When secession by slaveholding states interrupted these plans, Secretary of State William H. Seward hired Jane Cazneau to rally the New York press behind the Abraham Lincoln administration. With support for the Union firmly established, she returned to the tropics in 1861 and continued her work on behalf of colonization and commercial expansion.[2]

By May 1853, Secretary of State William L. Marcy had begun the process by which Manuel Rios, the Cazneaus' kidnapped employee, was released from peonage in Mexico. Therefore, Jane Cazneau and Secretary Marcy were in communication when Marcy first received dispatches from United States Commercial Agent Jonathan Elliot in the Dominican Republic saying the French and the Spanish were intriguing to annex the country but that Dominicans wished to negotiate a United States treaty of amity and friendship. The United States had recognized the republic in 1844 when it broke away from Haiti and Jane Cazneau first mentioned the Dominicans in December 1845 while writing for the New York *Sun*.[3]

Jane Cazneau saw the fate of Cuba and the Dominican Republic linked with "the independent use of the Isthmus highways to the Pacific." While in Eagle Pass, she had written about the Anglo-American rivalry in the tropics in the *United States Magazine and Democratic Review*. In 1849, she wrote about the British protectorate over the Mosquito Indians of Nicaragua. "The foreign policy of the United States" was "no policy at all," she asserted in 1851 as she again ridiculed the Mosquito Kingdom. In "British Aggression in Central America," she quoted the Monroe Doctrine, "'We consider any attempt on the part of European nations to extend their system to any portion of the American continent, as dangerous to our peace and safety.'" As late as February 1853, she had written about the Dominican Republic's continued struggle to remain independent.[4]

From 1853 onward, Jane Cazneau focused exclusively on United States expansion into the tropics and played a role in the undeclared diplomatic, trade, and commerce war that existed between the United States and Britain and her allies, France and Spain. More than simply to exert control, the United States wanted Havana for a harbor that could not be closed at the whim of a foreign power. British foreign policy reflected a statement made by Sir Walter Raleigh (1552–1618):

He who commands the sea commands the trade routes of the world. He who commands the trade routes, commands the trade. He who commands the trade, commands the riches of the world, and hence the world itself.[5]

The American Revolution was partly about freedom of trade, and during the Napoleonic wars, United States shipping expanded with little competition. After the War of 1812, Britain sought to regain its lost commerce. As she became enmeshed in the affairs of the Caribbean and Central America, Jane Cazneau realized that European powers were determined to prevent the extension of the United States maritime frontier.[6]

An editorial in the [London] *Times* stated Britain's official position shortly after the execution of Narciso López and fifty Americans: "Possession of Havana by the Americans would be to the Gulf of Mexico what Gibraltar was to the Mediterranean." Also, the editor explained, "Traffic which more and more connects the eastern and western oceans" would be "placed under the gun of the Americans." In addition, "if the southern states are allowed to incorporate Cuba," the north will insist upon Canada, which would "result in the expulsion of Europe from North America and the West Indies." The Pierce administration was dedicated to the expansion of trade, commerce, and republican ideals that challenged British hegemony and French and Spanish plans to regain colonies and investments in the Western Hemisphere.[7]

By 1851, American sailing ships exceeded the tonnage of British merchant ships under sail, but the British steamer trade exceeded that of the United States. As United States industry grew and shippers converted to steam vessels and iron hulls, Britain feared they would gain control of the world's commerce. Under the Pierce administration, steamship production tripled to 583,000 tons annually, but steamers required coal depots, warehouses, and repair shops at central points. Cuba was more than an outlet for slavery—it challenged Britain's control of trade and sea-lanes, but the British Navy had 650 warships and the French, 328, while the United States had 70 vessels. Historians have downplayed the nineteenth-century Anglo-American rivalry. While one stated that Britain shook off an American challenge by switching from sail to steam and from wood to iron ships, and another believed that the United States was not unduly alarmed by the strength of British merchant shipping. Jane Cazneau's experiences show the true extent of Anglo-American rivalry in the tropics.[8]

Jane Cazneau had no illusions about British intentions. Britain had made loans to Spain and her former colonies in the 1820s and 1830s, and then collected those debts by imposing port regulations, taking a percentage of tariffs favorable to British goods, and selling Welsh coal at British coaling stations. With its superior navy, Britain supervised almost all the ports in the Caribbean except those of the Dominican Republic, where France and Spain vied for control. Covering the eastern two-thirds of the island of Hispaniola, the second largest island in the island chain stretching from Florida to South America, the Dominican Republic shared the island with the Republic of Haiti.[9]

The two countries had a history of warfare. In setting themselves free of French control, the Haitians had invaded Santo Domingo and brought a bloody slave uprising. Britain helped Spain recover its colony in 1814, and the Dominicans won independence in 1821. The following year, Haiti invaded again, and controlled the country up to 1844, when the Dominicans regained independence. In 1852, France encouraged Haiti to invade the Dominican Republic, and then offered protection to the Dominicans in return for the lease of Samana Bay. The Spanish agent in Cuba then offered five thousand Spanish troops to aid its former colony.[10]

The international focus on the Dominican Republic lay in its strategic location and control of Samana Bay, considered the best natural harbor in the Caribbean. Seven deep water passes allowed commercial vessels to pass from the Atlantic Ocean to the Gulf of Mexico, the Caribbean Sea, and the land bridges to the Pacific across the fifteen hundred miles of islands, atolls, and coral reefs that make up the Greater and Lesser Antilles stretching from Florida to the northern coast of South America. The Straits of Florida represented the gateway to the Gulf of Mexico, the Mississippi River basin, and the Isthmus of Tehuantepec. The Windward Passage, between Cuba and Haiti, funneled traffic from the Atlantic to Jamaica, Nicaragua, and Panama. The forty-mile-wide Mona Passage between the Dominican Republic and Puerto Rico guarded sea-lanes from Northern Europe to Panama. Samana Bay faced the Mona Passage that was the North-South American sea route through the Lesser Antilles passes of Anagada, Guadeloupe, Galleons, and St. Vincent. United States merchant vessels used the passes for traffic between ports on the Gulf of Mexico and Atlantic, and to Europe, the Mediterranean, Africa, and South America.[11]

From May until June 1853, Jane and William Cazneau were in Washington and in contact with Secretary of State Marcy. After having

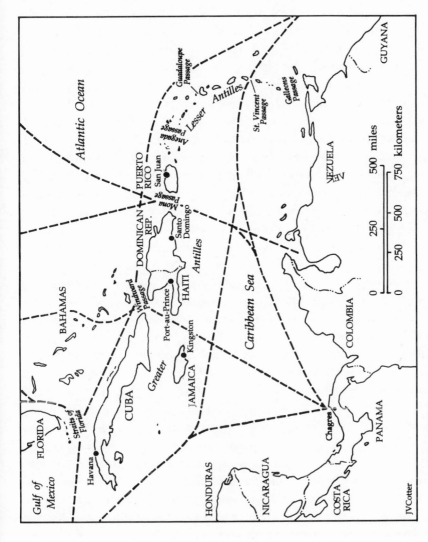

Map 2: Caribbean Islands and Sea-lanes.

149

been named secretary with the backing of the New York Union Committee within a day of the Pierce inauguration, Marcy was still getting settled. While William Cazneau was trying to get his Mexican claim paid by congress, Jane Cazneau wrote about the Isthmus of Tehuantepec hearings for the New York *Herald*. Perhaps, because of the "True Woman" idea that a widow but not a wife could have a professional life, or because of her reputation as a "filibustera," J. Gordon Bennett published the articles without a byline. As an investor in the Hargous Company with her stock transferred to the Louisiana Tehuantepec Company, Jane Cazneau had a personal interest in the hearings. She gave the history of Mexican grants issued between 1826 and 1852. The latest was that of A. G. Sloo and a London-based company arranged under the Clayton-Bulwer Treaty in 1851. James Sykes of England would construct the railway, and the Louisiana Tehuantepec Company would provide maintenance. The acquisition of the Isthmus of Tehuantepec as a land bridge would allow United States shipping from New Orleans to the Pacific through the Gulf of Mexico, but did not solve the need for a coaling station near Cuba. In late June she wrote in the *Herald* about Cuba as a national security matter and claimed that free trade would draw Cuba closer to the United States.[12]

Previous agents to the Dominican Republic, Benjamin Green, Mike Walsh, and J. T. Pickett, had seen the Dominican Republic as secondary to Cuba. Because Marcy trusted Jane Cazneau's "talents and political principles," in November 1853 he named William Leslie Cazneau as special agent to the Dominican Republic. Perhaps, New York Archbishop John Hughes was involved because the archbishop of Santo Domingo preferred American intervention to that of Spain or France. By appointing Cazneau a special agent, Marcy avoided any problems with Senate confirmation.[13]

Historians have credited Jane Cazneau with securing the assignment for her husband, but they incorrectly assume that she was the *de facto* agent. The Cazneaus needed employment, and Marcy needed accurate reports. Upon his appointment, critics ridiculed William Cazneau as the husband of a more famous wife. In February 1854, John Bigelow, the Free Soil "Barnburner" and political editor who John L. O'Sullivan had hired to replace Jane at the *United States Magazine and Democratic Review* in October 1845, was editor of the New York *Evening Post*. Bigelow claimed that the Cazneaus were to annex the Dominican Republic as part of a papist plot and identified Cazneau as the "husband of 'Cora Montgomery,' . . . famous as a filibustera." In a letter to Secretary of War Jefferson Davis,

James Gadsden, the South Carolina nullifier and minister to Mexico, called the Cazneaus, "General and Mrs. Flora Montgomery." Primarily, historians have identified William Cazneau in derogatory terms based on questionable post-Civil War testimony given during congressional hearings on the purchase and annexation of Samana Bay.[14]

William Cazneau was qualified for the position as special agent to the Dominican Republic. He spoke and wrote fluent Spanish, understood the nature of Latin business culture, and had experience in commercial infiltration. His Masonic ranking of general assured the confidence and respect of the Freemasons who had established the republic in 1844. As five hundred pages of dispatches indicate, he was the special agent, while Jane Cazneau handled public relations. She mingled with the people, assisted with a newspaper, and wrote about the Dominican Republic. With her knowledge of foreign affairs, she surely advised her husband, but reports were made in his excellent penmanship in a formal style and not in her hurried style and scratchy scrawl.[15]

In early November 1853, Secretary Marcy mailed William Cazneau's commission to Jane Cazneau in New York while her husband remained in Washington, still trying to get his claim paid for the trade goods lost in Mexico. Jane Cazneau departed in early December and traveled by British steamer, because none from the United States called on the Dominican Republic. Her journey was from New York to St. Thomas, a free port in the Danish Virgin Islands that British shippers used to avoid the reciprocity treaty of 1815. She then sailed to Samana Bay by schooner. In *Our Winter Eden* (1878), she described the thirty-mile-long bay surrounded by verdant green mountains rising steeply in natural terraces to cave-lined rocky crests some two thousand feet above the bay. The arm of the peninsula that protects the bay from the Atlantic Ocean slopes downward from Mount Duarte, the highest peak in the Caribbean at 10,417 feet, to below the waves until it becomes the Puerto Rico Trench, the deepest point in the Atlantic Ocean at 30,238 feet below sea level. Jane Cazneau described small islands in the five-mile-wide bay as well as a cove the pirate Jean Laffite once used as a base.[16]

Upon her arrival, Jane Cazneau contacted a "benevolent mutual aid society of about seventy immigrants from the United States." She reassured the former Virginia slaves of their continued freedom. In the 1820s, they had migrated to the area as part of an emancipation and colonization program of the Methodist church. As she made her way across the island, she countered European rumors that the United States wanted to annex the country and enslave the blacks. Officially, William Cazneau was to develop trade relations, ascertain the extent of Dominican independence, and, if possible, lease Samana Bay for a naval station and a coaling depot. In his first report, Cazneau credited his wife's calming effect for his warm reception in January 1854.[17]

William Cazneau explained the Dominican situation in official dispatches. As a guarantee of its independence, Haiti paid France annual indemnities for damages incurred in 1795 in Haiti's war of independence. When the Dominicans established independence from Spain in 1821, the Haitians invaded and forced the Dominicans to help pay the debt, but Dominicans did not feel that they owed the Haitians anything. Haiti had raided tobacco barns and warehouses since that time, until a wide swath of territory along the border was deserted. Previous agents described the Dominican leaders as corrupt mulattos, but Cazneau made no reference to their morals or racial identity in dispatches.[18]

In February 1854, William Cazneau sent Marcy copies of Dominican commercial treaties with the Netherlands, Denmark, Britain, and France. He explained that Europeans had a monopoly on goods transshipped from St. Thomas. At Santo Domingo, non-treaty nation's ships paid $1,500 per ship in annual port fees, but, Cazneau assured Marcy, proximity favored U.S. vessels that were capable of making six annual voyages while European ships could make only three. Liverpool was over four thousand miles away, compared with New Orleans and New York at twelve hundred and thirteen hundred miles away, respectively. Cazneau urged "economic penetration to sustain the only American power in the Caribbean." In February, Jane Cazneau advised Marcy that the general needed credentials to negotiate a commercial treaty. By May 1854, the Cazneaus were back in Washington.[19]

While William Cazneau waited for the proper credentials to be drawn up at the department of state, Jane Cazneau wrote for Moses S. Beach, who had resumed editorship of the New York *Sun*. She believed the acquisition of Cuba was certain and would help end African slave trading because, as she said, Spain was "an outlaw, a slave trading pirate." Jane Cazneau promoted Cuba as an outlet for slavery and the Dominican Republic for colonization of free blacks. She sent editorials to Beach that she had cleared with the cabinet in which she claimed that "four, if not six border states proposed to enter upon emancipation if they could find an outlet for their surplus colored population." As "foreign labor has made slave labor of little or no profit," she asked, "what do we do with the large class who are incapable of self-government?" She urged slave holders to "move to the new colonies and set free the southern states." The editorials were designed to persuade people to accept a program of territorial expansion for slaves and free blacks. Both black and white groups linked colonization with emancipation. Black Masons had promoted Liberia as a place of opportunity, and after 1850, even Frederick Douglass and other blacks considered colonization in the Western Hemisphere because of discrimination in the United States.[20]

On June 17, 1854, Marcy issued William Cazneau the credentials to negotiate a commercial treaty of recognition and trade with the Dominican Republic and to arrange a lease on Samana Bay. Capt. George McClellan, U.S. Army Engineers, accompanied Cazneau on the *Columbia*, a Spoffard and Tileston Shipping Company steamer. McClellan surveyed Samana Bay and soon determined the best location for a coaling station.[21]

Not everyone in the Pierce administration had the same goals for the Dominican Republic. In July 1854, in the letter in which he ridiculed the Cazneaus, Gadsden wrote to Secretary Davis from Mexico that "slavery as practiced by the United States" would "regenerate Haiti and Santo Domingo." If Davis would provide a Navy escort, he would go on "an inquisitorial cruise," because "the president of St. Domingo might consult with me in his negotiations." He saw Samana Bay as a possible rendezvous point for trade with South America by "one homogenous American system" that would be "free from those conflicts at Washington." He cautioned, "We can not begin the work too soon."[22]

In September 1854, Cazneau and the Dominican leaders negotiated a treaty that gave the United States access to all ports except Samana Bay. The British consul and geographer, Sir Robert Schomburgk, contacted the Foreign Office. He wanted British and French men-of-war sent to "prevent the realization of American projects."[23]

On October 9, 1854, the Dominican Congress met in executive session and signed the United States commercial treaty. Cazneau sent Marcy a copy of the letter written to Dominican officials, in which Schomburgk expressed his concern for the safety of the Dominicans whose republic would be "immediately endangered" by their association with the United States. Bigelow at the New York *Post* reported that Britain threatened to unleash the forty-thousand-man Haitian army on the Dominicans and "not a drop of white blood would be left on the island." Cazneau protested to the British and French consuls of their interference with President James Monroe's "principle of 1823." To invoke Monroe, Schomburgk reported to superiors, "was only what could be expected of a person of little education, and of much less experience in the transactions of questions of national importance." When James Buchanan, the United States minister to Britain, passed the protest to Lord Clarendon, the British foreign secretary replied, "The Monroe Doctrine is merely the dictum of its distinguished author."[24]

That same October, Lord Crampton, the British minister at Washington, questioned Marcy about the Cazneaus. "Was it true," Crampton inquired, "that the mission was to establish a rendezvous, a retreat for a Cuban invasion force? Were they planning to establish a coaling depot and fortifications?" he queried. Marcy answered he did not know what was in the treaty recently negotiated, but the United States needed a coal depot for steam vessels passing to and from the Caribbean. Crampton explained his alarm and that of Foreign Secretary Lord Clarendon: "Cazneau and his Lady, by whom he was accompanied, were very notorious in favor of annexation by any means of Cuba to the United States." In an earlier dispatch to the foreign secretary, Crampton identified "Mrs. Cazneau as an Irish Lady who under the name Corah [*sic*] Montgomery, founded and for a time edited a newspaper in the Spanish language called 'LA VERDAD.'" Aside from supporting republicans in Europe and Latin America in the Cuban revolutionary newspaper, Jane Cazneau promoted an Irish republic while Clarendon was the Lord Lieutenant of Ireland.[25]

Lord Clarendon was more concerned about Jane Cazneau's activities in Spain that summer than those of her husband in the Dominican Republic. Two different sources state that Jane Cazneau arranged a treaty with Queen Christina, regent for Queen Isabella II, for the sale of Cuba to the United States. Only a revolt in Spain prevented its fulfillment. No official records confirm that Jane Cazneau was in Spain, but the military revolt in June 1854 resulted in the permanent exile of the Queen Mother from Spain.[26]

At the mention of Jane Cazneau's name by Lord Crampton in October 1854, "Marcy smiled and replied, 'I assure you, Mr. Crampton, I have no dealings of any sort with that Lady.'" Marcy, the irreverent democrat, shabbily dressed and with snuff perpetually dripping out the corners of his mouth, played the diplomatic game with the British lord by using Jane Cazneau's reputation as a revolutionary. Marcy was a strong advocate of democracy and ordered U.S. ambassadors and ministers abroad to appear at official functions in American business dress rather than court uniforms. He was not intimidated by royalty and knew that in Europe the American ministers, James Buchanan, John Mason, and Pierre Soulé, were meeting with August Belmont in Ostend, Belgium. The Americans were discussing a strategy to purchase Cuba by assuming the British-guaranteed Spanish debt that the London Rothschild bankers demanded be paid. The Palmerston government had been drawn into the Crimean War with France against Russia and needed additional funds. The American ministers created a policy statement, known as the Ostend Manifesto, which stated that if all else failed, the United States would seize Cuba.[27]

Back in the Dominican Republic, Schomburgk reported to the Foreign Office that William Cazneau had "employed every intrigue to induce the Dominicans to throw their selves to the support of the United States." United States currency was everywhere, he charged. He confided that he and the French consul "used every effort to prevent the scheme." In November 1854, the French fleet arrived and lay at anchor at Santo Domingo City. The French consul-general from Haiti, a Monsieur Raybaud, arrived and threatened the Dominicans with a cannon barrage similar to that dealt Sebastopol in the Crimean War, "if they gave 'even one inch' of territory to the Americans."[28]

The Cazneaus had planned to return to Washington in December with the October treaty, but it took six weeks for the document to be translated. When the treaty arrived, notations by the British and French ministers filled the margins and it contained an amendment stating that all Dominican citizens would have equal rights as U.S. citizens when traveling in the United States. Cazneau withdrew the treaty because he knew that in its altered form it would not be ratified by the United States Senate. In the Dominican Republic, all races were equal citizens under the law and in practice. The government officials were racially mixed.[29]

Cazneau called on the British and French consuls and returned a lesson in international law. He threatened that "under the laws of nations, the United States had the right of redress." The British, French, and some Dominicans feared they would suffer the same fate as Greytown, which had been shelled by an American gunboat in protecting American interests in

Nicaragua earlier in July. Schomburgk wrote to the Foreign Office and demanded that a force be sent at once to protect British interests.[30]

After Cazneau withdrew the treaty, the Dominican cabinet provided him with more proof of European interference. Minister of Interior Felix Delmonte, Minister of Justice José Debrin, and landowner Alphonse Gundi, revealed that the British brought the warship, *Devastation*, to the capital, and the French consul announced, "We have now conquered Sebastopol, we will now throw our attention to the Yankees." Schomburgk told the Dominicans that Lord Clarendon "was astounded of their negotiations with the United States without British knowledge and sanction." In their letters to Secretary Marcy, Delmonte and Debrin begged for help from the United States in remaining an independent nation. The Dominicans explained that the Europeans' chief objection was to the United States leasing Samana Bay. A French company similar to the East India Company wanted the bay, and "with a private company," Cazneau wrote, "they elude the principles of 1823." Also, Cazneau explained, they intended to retain the Dominicans' dependence on European trade.[31]

By Christmas, Jane Cazneau wrote to Beach from the Dominican Republic about her views on territorial expansion: "*We must end right here. . . .* but the independent press must stand by the Dominicans, the Monroe Doctrine, and American interests in general or the Congress will stem the whole future as sure as you live." She included a letter of introduction for Anguelo Gundi, the son of Alfonse Gundi, a Cuban republican who had migrated to the Dominican Republic after one of the many purges following the republicans' attempts to liberate Cuba. She explained that the younger Gundi needed a cheap press and type for around five hundred dollars because, "Europeans had twice destroyed his printing presses and type." Gundi was going straight to Washington then to New York. He would tell Beach everything that she could not write, because, she said, "the French and British 'lose' letters in the mail or they meet with 'accidents' and are lost."[32]

In February 1855, Lord Clarendon notified Schomburgk that he did not have the authority to declare war on the United States. He added that he had conferred with the French foreign minister, who concurred. It was March 1855 before Gundi returned to the tropics and June before the Cazneaus traveled back to Washington. Before they left, they purchased Esmeralda, a forty-acre bankrupt and burned-out estate at San Carlos near Palenque Point on the southern coast between the capital and the Haitian border. They were determined to return and fulfill their mission.[33]

As a result of the Ostend Manifesto, made public by the New York *Herald* in February 1855, more than a hundred rebel leaders in Cuba were arrested and executed. Secretary of War Davis summoned Gen. John Quitman, former governor of Mississippi and leader of Cuban activity, to Washington. After an April 30, 1855, meeting with President Pierce and the Spanish minister, Quitman resigned as leader of the Cuban junta. By then, Spain had declared a state of siege in Cuba and armed a black militia force, while Britain blockaded the coast with four men-of-war. The Cuban refugees felt betrayed and wanted vengeance, but they did not know who to blame. They turned to the one person they knew they could trust—Jane Cazneau.[34]

On June 20, 1855, Jane Cazneau wrote to Moses Beach about the Cubans. They thought that Secretary of War Davis and the Southerners were their enemies, but, she explained, "My own idea is that Davis and the Southerners are sound, but you have been an observer while I have been afar and out of communication with the world in general for a whole year." The next week she urged Beach to mediate in the dispute between the Cubans and Davis. She advised, "I do not mean that Quitman, Davis, or any other names ought to be spared, if the evidence against them can be proved," but "the major point is *not to waste your powder.* We want a new cabinet and keep the good men and even beneficial ones and drive out the evil ones." In her opinion, Pierce had been "the betrayed rather than the betrayer." In regard to Dominican affairs, she admitted, "There is nothing men or women know about what our cabinet think of doing on the matter." She also advised, "The *Sun* has a great work before it in the pacification of these terrible sectional disputes which are endangering the Union." Popular sovereignty in Kansas had led to bloodshed, and the acquisition of Cuba had become a secondary matter to the administration. Three days later, Jane Cazneau wrote Beach a terse reply to his note suggesting that "official diplomats were playing a game over her shoulders." She challenged, "I know my data . . . I was thinking of the conscience and undeniable lead which the *Sun* may or may not take in *the* question of the day—Shall the Union endure?"[35]

In September, Jane Cazneau wrote to Beach about his attack on the New York junta. Beach took the administration's side. She thought that the public feud "destroyed the prestige of the cause and killed the last chance for seeing Cuba free and American." She informed Beach, "England, France, and Spain are pledged to the status quo of Cuba. Our cabinet have had these instructions since last May and will fight the Cubans."[36]

While leaders in London and Washington worked to end tension in the Dominican Republic, the Cazneaus were drawn to Nicaragua, where Anglo-American rivalry had led to the shelling of Greytown. Frederick Chatfield, the British consul to the Central American states of Costa Rica, Nicaragua, Honduras, San Salvador, and Guatemala was determined to prevent the United States from gaining access to a canal route in Central America. In 1849, he announced to then Foreign Secretary Palmerston that it would be "necessary to take a high hand with the Americans if we are to hold our ground." He wanted a protectorate over all Central America. He had extended the protectorate over the Mosquito Indians from Honduras into Nicaragua and to the left bank of the San Juan River, where he established Greytown, named for Lord Grey, secretary of the colonies.[37]

In July 1854, British authorities at Greytown, which the Americans called San Juan del Norte, attempted to collect port duties from one of Vanderbilt's ships entering the San Juan River, fired on the steamer, then destroyed the buildings and property of Vanderbilt's Accessory Transit Company. Mobs tore down the United States flag and United States minister to Nicaragua Solon Boreland was injured. Joseph Fabens, for whom Jane Cazneau had written, was Vanderbilt's depot agent and U.S. commercial agent at San Juan del Norte. When Capt. George Hollins of the USS *Cyane* bombarded British facilities at Greytown, the British accused the United States of overreacting. The Pierce cabinet supported Hollins, and the governor-general of Jamaica recalled the Greytown officers. After the Greytown incident backfired, Chatfield backed Costa Rica's claim that the border with Nicaragua was the right bank of the San Juan River, which included Vanderbilt's ports of San Juan del Norte and San Juan del Sur on the Pacific. Nicaraguans divided into the republican pro-United States Red Party with its capital at Granada and the pro-European White Party based at León. Granada was on the United States transit route while León was on the proposed trans-isthmus railway planned by the Liverpool Chamber of Commerce.[38]

Britain and her French and Spanish allies were united in their goal of preventing further inroads of United States trade and commerce in Central America. Jane Cazneau was drawn to such a conflict because she was determined to further the goals of the United States in expanding its trade and commerce and founding colonies for slaveholders and free blacks. H. L. Kinney, the founder of Corpus Christi for whom William Cazneau had once led wagon trains into Mexico, had purchased a large grant of land in the western territory of the Mosquito Kingdom from Georgia speculators. He formed the Nicaraguan Land and Mining Company in the area between Lake Nicaragua and Honduras. By March 1855, Fabens worked as Kinney's agent.[39]

Initially, Attorney General Caleb Cushing of Boston supported Kinney, but after he challenged Vanderbilt's monopoly, Cushing had Kinney arrested for violating the neutrality laws as he left New York with colonists. Kinney was backed by twenty-one company directors from New York, Philadelphia, and Washington plus Sen. Thomas J. Rusk of Texas; former Pennsylvania senator James Cooper; Pierce's private secretary, Sidney Webster; and Daniel Webster's son and surveyor of the Port of Boston, Fletcher Webster, who was also the son-in-law of former New York Whig governor Hamilton Fish. George M. Dallas, vice president under James K. Polk and James Buchanan's replacement as Minister to the Court of St. James, was Kinney's attorney. Jane Cazneau promoted Kinney's venture to her Texas friends. Kinney thought William Walker and the administration were his allies, but Pierce administration rivals representing steamer, sailing, and railroad interests failed to achieve any unity of purpose in domestic or foreign affairs.[40]

In May 1855, as the Cazneaus returned to Washington from the Dominican Republic, William Walker (1824–1860) had traveled from San Francisco to Nicaragua with fifty-eight men to protect the equipment, freight, and passengers of Vanderbilt's transit company from British-armed Costa Ricans. Walker, a native of Tennessee whose father owned an insurance company, had trained as a physician in Paris and a lawyer in New Orleans before he worked on newspapers in New Orleans and San Francisco during the Mexican War. In 1853 and 1854, Walker had led similar groups into Western Mexico, but failed to remove the French who had taken over the silver mines of Northern Mexico.[41]

Matters in Nicaragua were further complicated when Vanderbilt's San Francisco and New York shipping agents, C. K. Garrison and Charles Morgan, challenged Vanderbilt for control of the Accessory Transit Company. In late 1855, Walker sided with Morgan and Garrison. Vanderbilt then hired an agent who worked with Costa Rican troops to oust Walker. Vanderbilt diverted his ocean steamers from Nicaragua to Panama, and soon Morgan and Garrison abandoned Walker. Walker survived with recruits and supplies from the United States where the Cazneaus, along with Stephen A. Douglas, Robert J. Walker, James Buchanan, and other expansionists, promoted his efforts as a war based on the Monroe Doctrine.[42]

Many of Walker's supporters, including the Cazneaus, invested in Nicaraguan ventures. Jane Cazneau owned part of the Chontales Silver Mining venture as did Col. John Heiss, Walker's agent in Washington, and Fabens, who switched to Walker after Kinney's failures. Robert Walker, Stephen A. Douglas, and others had made sizable investments in Nicaragua. In April 1856, Jane Cazneau, always expecting to find the magic pot of gold under the rainbow, or to create interest and find commercial backing, wrote to Beach about a strike that could "open a furor for silver mining only second to the California gold fever." In April 1856, Pierce recognized the Patricio Rivas Red Party government of Nicaragua with whom Walker was fighting to maintain the transit route. Pierce hoped for support from southerners at the Democratic convention, but the war for the Monroe Doctrine became one of allied Central American republics against Yankee intruders. The Rivas government withdrew its support of Walker, and Pierce withdrew recognition of the Rivas government.[43]

In May 1856, William Cazneau endorsed Walker's stand against the European forces in Central America in a public meeting in New York. At the end of May, Jane Cazneau arranged for Elizabeth Pellet, a women's historian and wife of Columbia University professor William Henry Pellet, to have her lectures on Nicaragua advertised in the New York *Sun*. In June, Pierre Soulé and John Quitman had Walker's efforts endorsed by the Democratic convention in Cincinnati. By this time, Walker, who some claimed Cazneau was the first to call "the grey-eyed man of destiny," was said to have been the most talked about person in the United States. James Buchanan received the nomination for president and ran on a platform of ascendancy in the Caribbean and Central America. The Cazneaus did not attend the convention because of "a severe disposition" in the family. William Cazneau was then in Washington and the Cincinnati *Daily Enquirer* published his letters, which catalogued British, French, and Spanish activities in Cuba, the Dominican Republic, and Nicaragua designed to control the sea-lanes and commercial traffic of the United States.[44]

Jane Cazneau did not usually miss national conventions; therefore, she was ill or had to rescue her son from some dilemma. In 1850, William Storm had married Cora Hayner, a McManus farm worker. Jane Cazneau obtained an appointment for her son in the New York Customs House working under Ann Stephens's husband, George. While at the customs house, Storm registered twelve patents related to the use and safety of steam engines and improvements to revolving and breech-loading firearms, plus a submarine he called a "Nautilus system of coast defense," which was of great interest to both John A. Quitman and Jefferson Davis. His "peculiar mental condition" was symptomatic of manic-depression as he made and squandered fortunes and was in and out of mental institutions. Jane Cazneau had kept her family life private. In 1856, at forty-nine years old and married six years, she had lost little of her spirit of adventure, her patriotism, or her hope of acquiring wealth.[45]

Jane Cazneau's investments, however, including those in Nicaragua, were risky ventures. With Nicaraguan support gone, Walker had himself elected president to legitimize his presence. Jane Cazneau may have attended Walker's inauguration in July 1856. She wrote to Colonel Heiss from Granada three days afterward, and sent a contract for colonists to Heiss, who conveyed the information on to Senator Douglas. Walker needed money, men, and munitions. In September 1856, Walker repealed the Nicaraguan anti-slavery law. In the northern states, public opinion shifted against him, while in the southern states he became a hero. The British believed Walker had created a place for slaveholders to sell their slaves before emancipation took place in the United States.[46]

Jane Cazneau's continued support of Walker after he made Nicaragua a refuge for slaveholders made her appear to be a pro-slavery advocate. Her stance was compatible with her goal of relocating slaves out of the United States, but her motives were more patriotic than humane. The United States was more important to her than the emancipation of an unskilled workforce of millions with economic chaos. After the Ostend fiasco, Cuba was no longer a viable solution. Thus, Nicaragua became a possible outlet for slaveholders unwilling or unable, because of mortgages, to free their slaves. Walker's land and mining concessions also fit her goals for a secure route for United States transportation and trade goods to the Pacific.[47]

By October 1856, Walker was at war with reunited Nicaraguans and the allied republics under Chatfield's direction. Beach canceled the notices of Pellet's lectures in the *Sun*, and Jane Cazneau wrote to him about her disappointment. She alluded to rumors of ill will between them that she would address in person if able to do so. She was ill, she wrote, and unable to sit up but for a brief time, or else she would have come in person.[48]

In November 1856, James Buchanan was elected president over the American party, or Know-Nothing, candidate Millard Fillmore and Republican John C. Frémont. The Cazneaus lived at the posh St. Nicholas Hotel in New York and continued their work on behalf of Walker as the only American presence in Central America. William Cazneau contracted to furnish one thousand colonists for Walker, but made no attempt to embark until December 1856. Each colonist was promised free passage, thirty dollars, 850 acres of land, and provisions. They were to settle along the transit route and help uphold the Monroe Doctrine. The steamer *Tennessee* made it to Norfolk, Virginia, before mechanical failure developed. The colonists were lucky. In Nicaragua, Walker and his few remaining men were under siege, cholera was rampant, and they ate their mules to survive.[49]

In December 1856, Secretary of War Davis requested Jane Cazneau's address from Attorney General Caleb Cushing. In her reply to Davis, she explained that an American Confederation of Central America backed by Britain, France, and Spain would create a barrier to annexation. She pointed out that the Clayton-Bulwer Treaty (1850) guaranteed against the confiscations that had occurred in Nicaragua and Tehuantepec, and while citizens had recourse against England, it did not secure free access of transit for United States shipping. She called Nicaragua, "a monster" that had thrown Central America into the arms of Europe.[50]

In March 1857, Buchanan became president, and it was soon evident that he no longer supported Walker. Political adversaries Jefferson Davis and Stephen A. Douglas deserted Walker, but Jane Cazneau did not. She advised Buchanan that neutral transit routes and free ports could be secured in all of Central America and Mexico through diplomatic pressure and purchase. In April and May 1857, both Jane and William Cazneau wrote to Attorney General Jeremiah H. Black urging his support for Walker's government, which would encourage colonization along the transit route. Black and Buchanan handled Central American affairs instead of the aging Secretary of State Lewis Cass. The Cazneaus urged the passage of the treaty John Wheeler had negotiated during his short service as minister in 1856 when Pierce had recognized Walker's government. The treaty allowed U.S. citizens to own land and work mines in Nicaragua without giving up their U.S. citizenship. In May 1857, Walker and his few remaining men, famished, ill, and without ammunition, returned to the United States. Walker, feeling angry and abandoned, claimed his efforts were sacrificed for "the paltry profits of a railroad company."[51]

Jefferson Davis and the railroad interests in the Pierce cabinet had overcome the steamer interests and abandoned Cuba, the Dominican Republic, and Nicaragua. A proposed southern rail route would pass through Texas and the territory James Gadsden had purchased in December 1853 from Santa Anna during his last return to power. The treaty was ratified in April 1854 and increased sectional animosity in the United States.[52]

In the spring of 1857, Jane Cazneau began writing for A. Dudley Mann and Colonel Heiss, owners of the Washington *Daily States*. As a Young American, Mann had supplied weapons to Europeans for the revolutions of 1848, and he had served as Marcy's assistant secretary of state in the Pierce administration. A Virginian, Mann invested in steam ships and advocated the development of southern trade, commerce, and industry to encourage European immigration into the South. In 1857 and 1858, William Cazneau presented Mann's steamer projects at Southern commercial conventions. Heiss had become Thomas Ritchie's editor at the Washington *Union* during the Polk administration when Jane Cazneau had declined a position and remained at the *Sun*. Heiss had also been with the Nashville *Union*, the New Orleans *Crescent*, the Louisville *Courier*, and the New Orleans *Delta*.[53]

The Cazneaus had invested heavily in Nicaragua, she in a silver mine and he in the A&P Guano Company. Walker recognized both companies' claims, while the Buchanan administration did not. Jane Cazneau did not cease her efforts to change the policy of the Buchanan administration and wrote to Attorney General Black about Nicaragua: "The steam kings of this city think they can win their own way by dint of money and a stubborn will." While she usually promoted diplomatic pressure and purchase, she advised, "The anarchies in possession of the Isthmus routes fear nothing but power—real absolute and tangible *power*—and a man-of-war is the best diplomatist in such cases." She further advised, "our trade and citizens never will be safe and respected until they are taught they *must* be." She did not advocate the annexation of Nicaragua but advised an end to territorial expansion because it had brought "endless cares and complications."[54]

In November 1857, Jane Cazneau suggested that Buchanan use Walker's plans to return to Nicaragua with a military force as a means to intimidate the Nicaraguan government into signing the Wheeler Treaty. "The departure of Walker can thus be connected into an advantage by making all these powers anxious for your protection." In her opinion, these governments "had no right to the protection of a navy created and owned by our people while they refuse justice to our interests." She said of the Cubans, "*Arms and munitions have been sent out* and it is only a question of time and place how they will be employed." She urged Buchanan to take advantage of Spain so that they would feel grateful for anything they could get from "the accursed Yankees." She then promised to call later and talk with him further, as the previous time they had spoken someone was present that she did not trust.[55]

The Buchanan administration recognized the Nicaraguan government and not Walker's. Jane Cazneau was appeased in that the administration appointed Mirabeau B. Lamar minister to Nicaragua and Costa Rica. Lamar was an old friend of William and Jane Cazneau and he had invested in Jane Cazneau's Nicaraguan mining venture. He dedicated *Verse Memorials* (1857) to Mrs. William L. Cazneau (Cora Montgomery) because of her "social virtues—lofty principles and unselfish affections." In January 1858, William Cazneau repacked Lamar's boxes in New York for shipment to Aspinwal, Panama, the only route to Central America then operating from New York. Jane Cazneau suggested that Lamar hire José Debrin as his secretary. The former Dominican minister of justice understood the British tactics, and William Cazneau packed Debrin's passport along with Lamar's belongings.[56]

Jane Cazneau had not given up on plans to make Nicaragua an outlet for slavery. In April she wrote to Lamar from New York that the Nicaraguan government could prevent filibusters by allowing legitimate colonists into Nicaragua. She suggested that their families settle on the volcanic Island of Ompete in Lake Nicaragua and plant coffee plantations. Also, she informed him "White and Company had an agreement with [Erastus] Corning, [Thurlow] Weed, and the rest of the Tribune clique for abolitionizing Nicaragua a la Kansas by organized Emigration Societies." The "New York legislature had subscribed $300,000 for the cause." Nicaragua was not only a battleground between Americans and Europeans for control of the transit route, but a source of further division in the United States. Former expansionist Whigs and Free-Soilers in the

Republican Party wanted Nicaragua as an outlet for free blacks deported out of the North while conservative Democrats wanted it as a relocation colony for slaveholders.[57]

Lamar found the meticulous and nervous Debrin a bother and fired him. By February 1859, the New York *Times* attacked Lamar and charged that he was in the habit of "allowing important papers to be scattered about on the floor of his office for all to see." The *Times* added, "he was so careless of his personal dignity as to be seen openly lying in a public warehouse, without hat, coat, shoes or stockings." Jane Cazneau defended Lamar in the Washington *Daily States* as a great democrat who mixed with the common people, drank whiskey, and often removed his coat to nap under a tree while president of the Republic of Texas. Privately, she rebuked Lamar. He should pay a closer regard for propriety, she scolded. She assailed his dismissal of Debrin, who would have kept an eye on affairs. The Nicaraguan government had ratified a British treaty of trade and commerce while that of the United States lay untouched. She also heard rumors that Britain was forming a protectorate over Nicaragua. Sir William Gore Ouseley had established a colony in Honduras, and he planned to expand his sphere into Nicaragua.[58]

While working for the Washington *Daily States,* Jane Cazneau explored every effort to affect a secure passage for the United States trade goods to the Pacific. She introduced a Mr. Mata, an associate of Mexican Minister of the Interior Benito Juarez, to President Buchanan. She informed Buchanan that the Juarez faction was willing to sell transit rights across Tehuantepec for a million dollars. This would "open the country to the right class of settlers," meaning slaveholders, as Yucatan had not abolished slavery. Another million would secure the northern frontier with neutral territory down to 28 degrees north latitude—the area that she, Buchanan, Douglas, and Sam Houston had wanted as part of the Treaty of Guadalupe Hidalgo. "Two millions will give us two free highways to the Pacific and put Juarez in the city of Mexico," she declared.[59]

Buchanan pursued the opportunity to benefit from the turmoil in Mexico. Later when Juarez consolidated power and became president, the Mexican liberal government granted William Cazneau land and right-of-way on April 1, 1859, for a wagon road from the Gulf of California to Sonora. In less than a week, Buchanan recognized the revolutionary government of Juarez as the legitimate government of Mexico. By late 1859, Robert McLane and Carlos O'Campo had negotiated a treaty that gave to the United States, in perpetuity, three transit routes across Mexico, with the right to protect those routes without interference. Mexico would receive two million dollars outright and another two million dollars paid in United States claims against Mexico. The United States Congress debated the McLane-O'Campo treaty from January until May 1860 but did not confirm it because of the possible extension of slave territory and the fact that Juarez was not recognized as president by all Mexicans. He represented a liberal faction struggling against pro-European conservative monarchists that for years had tried to establish a monarchy in Mexico.[60]

During her stint with the Washington *Daily States*, Jane Cazneau made a lasting impression on seventeen-year-old Henry Watterson, who has provided the only physical description of her as a Spanish-looking woman. Watterson's father, a Kentucky newspaperman, was serving in Washington, and his mother and Jane Cazneau were friends. Jane Cazneau stayed with them at Willard's Hotel when she was in Washington. Watterson delivered messages for Mann and Heiss while Jane Cazneau taught him the basics of journalism. When he received the Pulitzer Prize for editorial writing in 1918, Watterson claimed that everything he knew he learned from her. In his old age, a confused Watterson idolized her and credited her with perhaps creating every descriptive phrase of that era from labeling Gen. Winfield Scott as "Old Fuss and Feathers" to Walker as the "grey-eyed man of destiny." Watterson thought that her editorials so irked the president that Buchanan sent her to the Dominican Republic to get her out of the country. While Watterson may have known the real story of her departure, Jane Cazneau gave a different version of events in her publications.[61]

The Cazneaus' second Dominican assignment came about after at least two meetings with President Buchanan in the White House in early 1859. Unofficially, William Cazneau's second mission was to settle claims by United States shipping companies against the Dominican Republic and acquire and develop coaling stations through private enterprise. Just as the French had set up a French West Indies Company to thwart the Monroe Doctrine, Cazneau would develop Samana Bay through the use of a private company and thereby absolve the United States government of any involvement. Aside from Spoffard and Tileston Shipping Company, operating out of New York and Boston, Charles Morgan, with branches in New York and New Orleans, planned a steam line to Brazil. Both companies needed coaling and port facilities in the Caribbean. As Jane Cazneau recalled, "I was twice present in the library of the White

House, when the project of a free port at Samana was explained and defended by General Cazneau."[62]

General Cazneau was adamant, and she quoted her husband, "I shall continue . . . until Samana is a free port, or the Dominican Republic is reduced to a Spanish dependency." She claimed that Buchanan and Cass scoffed at the idea that Spain would make such a move, but William Cazneau replied, "Spain has all the cards in hand at this moment, and whether she plays them or not, depends upon how the game is likely to be accepted at Washington." The next day Cass appointed Cazneau as special agent with vague instructions to report on the "state of the Country." Cass and Buchanan hesitated to support Cazneau openly, she wrote, "because of the unsettled domestic situation." Whereas Cazneau had taken no pay during the first mission, this time he drew eight hundred dollars in expenses and eight dollars per diem.[63]

William Cazneau sailed from New York on the British brig *John Butler* because no United States sailing or steam vessels operated near the Dominican Republic. He landed at Puerto Plata on the Atlantic coast approximately 140 miles opposite the capital of Santo Domingo on the Caribbean. Jane Cazneau had arrived the month before on the *Ocean Bird* and visited with former Virginia slaves of the Bethel Church whom, she reported, were still a credit to their Methodist society. While exploring the countryside with an American planter and English mining engineer, she was injured and recovered at the home of the church leader. When William Cazneau arrived, they traveled cross country by mule, the only transportation available, and arrived in the capital city on June 14, 1859.[64]

In his first numbered report, William Cazneau gave the results of their cross-country tour. From Puerto Plata they had climbed steep naturally terraced slopes to the valley of La Vega where tobacco grew and cigars were equal to the quality of Cuba. The valley stretched across the border into Haiti and provided the Haitians an easy means to raid tobacco and sugar warehouses. He compared the resources of the Dominican Republic to those of Mexico and Central America. He explained that mines originally belonged to the sovereign, but when abandoned, reverted to the state. A French company had acquired all mineral rights for gold, silver, and copper deposits, but it was unlikely they would fulfill the contract. Currently, two Americans, identified only as Croswell and Norton, worked the gold mines. The northeast Atlantic coast had tropical rain forests, the southeast savannas had sugar plantations and cattle ranches, the central highlands grew tobacco and cocoa beans, and the southwest quadrant had desert-like conditions ideal for citrus groves with a salt lake below sea level. Each zone had rivers with possible ports. Cazneau proposed a north-south neutral zone between Haiti and the Dominican Republic to end border raids and to provide the United States with a free commerce zone and gates to the Gulf of Mexico and the Caribbean with ports at each end.[65]

Cazneau's reports were numbered and written in triplicate, a tedious, but necessary process because President Buchanan, Secretary Cass, and Attorney General Black all handled foreign affairs. In addition, previous dispatches had disappeared or had been delayed through the British mail service. While four American trading houses once operated in the region, only Collins House of Boston remained and shipped goods by foreign ships. Cazneau wanted to place American trade on the par with that of Europe. In July Cazneau settled the *Charles Hill* claim. The Spofford and Tileston coastal packet had been seized by the anti-American Bonaventura Baez regime that had assumed power for two years while the Cazneaus were away. Although the present government could not pay the claims amounting to more than $275,000, they declared Samana Bay open to American shipping and that compensated Spofford and Tileston, then converting from sail to steam and seeking a coaling and warehouse depot in the area.[66]

On October 10, 1859, Jane Cazneau wrote to Beach at the New York *Sun* about their arrival and reception in the Dominican Republic. The *Sun* had degenerated into little more than an advertising sheet and church newsletter that featured the sermons and writings of Rev. Henry Ward Beecher. She was to write about all that she saw, and the letter published in the *Sun* was similar to one she wrote to President Buchanan a week later. Whereas the letter to Buchanan analyzed the political situation, the one to Beach focused on the former Virginia slaves of the Bethel Church. She began both letters the same, "Our residence here has been little better than an incessant round of sickness and frustration . . . up to this time there has been no day in which I have not been on a sick bed myself or waiting and watching on the side of fever stricken members of my family." Her husband was ill, and Jane Cazneau's son, William, also lived with them. His wife, Cora, died about this time and left an infant daughter, who William and Jane Cazneau reared as Cora Cazneau.[67]

In her guidebook for settlers, *In The Tropics* (1863), Jane Cazneau blamed their fever on getting wet from the drenching showers of August and not changing out of wet clothes. They lived in tents since the only permanent structure remaining at Esmeralda was an outdoor kitchen. She described the fever that began with a lack of appetite, followed by a headache, fever, and chills and compared the malady to the ague [malaria] of the Ohio River basin. Anita Garcia, a neighbor and member of the Santo Domingo Bethel Church, nursed the Cazneau family with a home cure of green limes and hot water. After nine days, Jane Cazneau recovered, and the experience was a turning point in her life. Thereafter, she dedicated her life to the improvement of the black race.[68]

In *Our Winter Eden* (1878), Jane Cazneau admitted, "We are slow to unlearn the deeply ingrained prejudices of birth and education." After fifteen years of observation, she had learned that white men could work in the tropics and the two races of African and European stock could live together in the same country with equal rights before the law. Previously, her efforts to remove blacks from the United States had been to end sectional strife with little concern for the welfare of the individuals.[69]

Jane Cazneau provided Buchanan with a political analysis of the country. The Dominican Republic "was positively at its last gasp as an independent state," she explained. A European party sought reannexation to Spain, while another party was for capitulation to French-dominated Haiti, and yet another hoped for a solution with the United States. Cazneau had assured the Dominicans that the United States did not want to annex the island to extend slavery. "This black phantom is always paraded when the chiefs plan a revolt," she explained. She added that Cazneau had inquired of New York merchants as to the prospects of trade. "Our merchants wanted the free use of the safe harbor of Samana and it is open to them now," she assured. "Our citizens wanted access to the mines and this concession will be made when you authorize a treaty," she advised.[70]

On the same day that Jane Cazneau wrote to Buchanan, her husband dictated a dispatch to Secretary Cass. "The country was under a volcano of revolt led by the pro-European Baéz party," but he had secured a six hundred-dollar payment of the William A. Reed claim for the goods taken when the Spofford and Tileston ship was seized by the former regime. By December, Cazneau had recovered his health and wrote in a shaky hand that the French, British, and Spanish consuls had left the Dominican

Republic. In January 1860, he wrote, "If the United States will take advantage of the present situation, the future of the Dominican Republic would be secured." By February 1860, Cazneau was encouraged. United States citizens were clearing Samana Bay of debris, while others worked the coal mines, and a New York and Baltimore firm was establishing a warehouse. "Only last June, four United States citizens were in business," he observed, and "they wanted to leave." Cazneau expected investments to total a million dollars within the year.[71]

In March 1860, Cazneau's optimism was shattered when the Spanish minister returned and announced that the Dominican Republic was to become a Spanish protectorate. The plan was backed by the military leaders and the European party. Also, Cazneau reported the presence of "a very questionable 'Emigrant Association' from the vicinity of Chesapeake Bay" that represented "a strong order lately organized with reference to an extensive occupation in St. Domingo." He further wrote that they "relied on the rifle as much as the plough for affecting its views." The Knights of the Golden Circle was such a speculative group that planned a slave empire in the American tropics, and publicized their activities in a Baltimore newspaper, *The Cavalier*. Cazneau was upset that U.S. Consul Jonathan Elliot had hosted an organizational meeting.[72]

By the end of July 1860, Cazneau reported that ten thousand Spanish troops bore arms and the army of the Dominican Republic served under Spanish officers. In addition, fifteen hundred Canary Island settlers had arrived and were assigned lands in "a systematic manner." Immigrants included engineers and professional persons. Cazneau assumed the Spanish government sent the settlers "to create a strong link between Cuba and Puerto Rico," both Spanish slaveholding colonies. In September, Cazneau requested commercial agent Jonathan Elliot's removal. The Dominican Minister of Finance, Don Pedro Ricart y Torres, requested that Cazneau reprimand Elliot, who "had become intemperate to a degree that made him unfit for the post." Elliot made "incendiary speeches from his balcony," and tried to incite the colored class to massacre the Canary Islanders. Perhaps Elliot tried to create an incident as an excuse to enslave the blacks, or he was angry that Spain had intervened before his group could consolidate power.[73]

On November 15, 1860, Capt. Richard Kimball of the U.S. schooner *Alice* arrived in Santo Domingo harbor. Cazneau feared that Spain would confiscate the vessel. Kimball was an explorer for unclaimed guano deposits. In October, rivalry over guano had climaxed when Spanish officers sailing a Dominican vessel arrested an American crew loading the natural fertilizer from the rock island of Alta Velo off the Dominican-Haitian border. To Cazneau, it indicated how far Europeans were willing to go to remove United States influence from the Caribbean.[74]

In June 1860, William Cazneau drew eight hundred dollars for Joseph Fabens as an agent for Spofford and Tileston, developers of Samana Bay. In November, Cazneau reported two more payments totaling twenty-two hundred dollars to Fabens. Cazneau warned Cass, "A Spanish officer bragged that the United States would soon be forced to abandon [the] Monroe [Doctrine] and repress United States interests in the Antilles." Earlier in the year, the Dominicans had granted Cazneau land for colonies, permission to build a shipyard, and the right to the coal and other mines. Perhaps the payments were made to Spanish officials who allowed the activities to continue. Spofford and Tileston, through Fabens and Cazneau, had gained title to thirty acres of port frontage on Samana Bay, while Peter J. Sullivan had obtained a concession for a New Orleans steamship line.[75]

In December 1860, Cass resigned as secretary of state and Attorney General Black became the head of the State Department. On January 11, 1861, Cazneau warned that the Spanish protectorate over the Dominicans was to be carried into immediate effect. Cazneau believed that four-fifths of the Dominicans opposed the Spanish and that the country "tottered on the edge of revolt." On March 18, 1861, President Pedro Santana announced the end of the Dominican Republic, and raised the Spanish flag. Cazneau explained that Dominican officials had a choice: sign the agreement or leave the country.[76]

Upon election of Republican Party presidential candidate Abraham Lincoln, the southern states began leaving the Union in December 1860. On November 6, 1860, Jane Cazneau had written to Black about the "treasonable discords of the democratic party" and "narrow-minded senators [that] had cast Cuba and Mexico overboard." William H. Seward, Jane Cazneau's expansionist ally, became secretary of state, and in March 1861, Seward canceled William Cazneau's instructions as special agent, but he hired Jane Cazneau to return to New York. While William Cazneau remained in the former Dominican Republic, Seward paid $750 for Jane Cazneau's travel and office expenses, and an additional $1,300 for her services ending July 1, 1861. No official records explain the fifty-four-year-old woman's assignment, but editorials in the New York *Sun* and the Seward memo, "Thoughts for the President's consideration," reflected her thinking. She and Seward had similar Young American views of trade, commerce, expansion, and dedication to the Union. Seward and the New York merchants and shippers perhaps brought Jane Cazneau to New York to help unite the sections through a national convention.[77]

Although her name does not appear in its columns or masthead, in February 1861, the New York *Sun* again reflected Jane Cazneau's distinctive style. At some point after 1859, Beach had again left the newspaper, and the *Sun* had little more than church news. The paper soon returned to the style and substance it had when Jane Cazneau was political editor in the 1840s. She provided in 1861 what she had advised during the crisis of 1850—a "firm constitutional union praising journal, one not daunted by a monetary class, and that could discern the right through the mist and smoke of sectional prejudice and demagogue sophistry." When states began seceding, a writer in the *Sun* stated that secession was impossible. Other major New York newspapers—the *Times, Evening Post, Tribune, Herald*—recognized the South's right to secede. While some wished the Confederate states well, others considered it good riddance.[78]

Jane Cazneau's presence at the *Sun* was evident on February 15, with "Opinions of the Press," a summary of editorials in the New York press. The next day's editorial praised Abraham Lincoln as a "man of the people" and a cool-headed moderate. She urged that the cabinet should be a unit for the Union and not for the party. By March, she focused on the southern states, reporting the disregard for popular sovereignty and featuring dissent. She warned the southern oligarchy that the people would revolt in time. She also reminded the secession governments that stolen arms and ammunition from Union garrisons, claimed as their share of the government, should be matched with their share of the national debt. She predicted that money would be the great difficulty of the Confederacy. She appealed to the common destiny of a common people:

> No secession ordinance can separate us. We are one people by blood, by interest, and by historic achievements. When the madness of discomfited ambition has ceased to pervert men's minds; when demagogical influences have lost their force, and when reason and patriotism resume their sway, the American people will reunite their interests and their national destinies, and shake hands as brothers in an enduring and glorious peace.[79]

With Jane Cazneau's arrival, the *Sun* began featuring news of the Dominican Republic and its re-colonization by Spain. In early April, Seward approached Lincoln with his plan to create a foreign war and draw the seceded states back into the Union. France and Spain were violating the Monroe Doctrine in Mexico and the Dominican Republic, he argued. When the memo became public, it only created sympathy for the Confederate states in European newspapers. The South Carolinians shelled Fort Sumter on April 12, and Lincoln called for seventy-five thousand volunteers to defend the Union. Seward lodged a formal protest with the Spanish minister, however, about the destruction of the Dominican Republic. Although he had no official capacity, William Cazneau kept Seward informed of developments in the Dominican Republic.[80]

When Fort Sumter fell, the *Sun* declared that in taking the offensive, the traitors had cut themselves off from all honest sympathy and kindled a patriotic rage that enveloped all parties and all classes through the Union states. By May, Jane Cazneau mimicked the New Orleans *Crescent*, which had declared that a line had been drawn between two nationalities.

> If the Southern journals would only tell the truth—if the Southern people were truly informed regarding Northern sentiment, the disastrous rebellion into which they have been so blindly led, would soon be at an end. This is not a war of sections. It is a war of principles, and the line that is drawn is by no means a geographical one. The Union wages no war upon the states, her children, but only upon the traitorous and usurping miscreants.[81]

Jane Cazneau called Jefferson Davis a "Pretended President" surrounded by the peacock aristocracy of the South exalting in the shows and airs of self-appointed rank.[82]

As Lincoln seemed to hesitate and Congress acted bewildered, she prodded the administration gently.

> The freemen of the Union ask nothing of their leaders but to do their duty, and in that they will follow them loyally, with all they possess, to death and beggary, if need be, to save a country for their children. The people will find leaders, and find their way to the heart of this rebellion.[83]

Her object was not to criticize, but "to arouse our rulers to the full measure of their power as the proper leaders of the greatest military force, and the noblest movement for liberty, that ever was embodied and embattled on this globe." She began a regular column called "Spirit of the People," which outlined the formation of volunteer military units, parades, and other patriotic activities. As Confederate raiders began taking their toll on United States merchant ships, in June, a regular feature became reports of seized prizes.[84]

By July, and with New York's newspapers united in a solidarity of purpose and a people determined to defend the United States, Jane Cazneau's duties had ended. By the end of the year, Moses S. Beach was listed as editor of the *Sun*. Cazneau returned to the former Dominican Republic and resumed the responsibilities of caring for her extended family in the war-torn country. William Cazneau wrote to Seward that republicans were carrying out a guerrilla war from the hills.[85]

For fifteen years, Jane Cazneau had been an advocate of territorial and commercial expansion and a steam-powered navy and merchant marine. In 1858, United States merchant ships carried 73.7 percent of foreign trade goods imported into the United States. The shipping fees paid by foreign merchants offset the cost of foreign goods and the trade balance was met by the specie earned by foreign freight carried by American ships. In 1860, the total tonnage of the United States merchant fleet exceeded that of Great Britain by more than five hundred thousand tons. After the war in 1866, the foreign trade carried by United States ships had fallen to 25 percent of imported goods, and the United States had a deficit trade balance with gold draining out of the country to pay for foreign goods and exports carried on foreign ships. By 1870 the total was half a million tons less than Britain, and would fall even more by 1880. The United States would never again reach its antebellum level of commerce on the high seas. Jane Cazneau's life and work up to and after the American Civil War helps explain how that decline in shipping came about.[86]

CHAPTER VIII

"Our Winter Eden," 1861–1878

> I held for many years with a ten-mule power of stupid
> obstinacy to the popular belief, white labor was unsuited
> to the tropics and the two races of African and European
> stock could not live and thrive together in the same
> country on the common basis of equal rights before the
> law.
>
> —*Mrs. William L. Cazneau*[1]

$\mathcal{A}$FTER 1861, WILLIAM CAZNEAU'S CAREER SEEMED TO OVERSHADOW
that of his once more famous wife, Jane, who became responsible for her
son, William Storm, and his daughter, Cora. She was hampered by conditions of war and the Latin culture that confined women to the domestic
sphere. It was not that she was no longer active in her causes, but her progressive loss of eyesight, possibly due to cataracts or glaucoma, hindered
her reading and writing. Nonetheless, between 1863 and 1878, she wrote
four books promoting expansion into the tropics, composed three essays
that Joseph Fabens read before the American Geographical and Statistical
Society, wrote for the New York *Sun,* New York *Herald,* and possibly the
Dominican newspapers, *Courier de Stats Unis* and *Boletin Official.* In addition, she advised President Andrew Johnson, Secretary of State William H.
Seward, and Secretary of the Interior James Harlan on Caribbean affairs.
She took an active role in the drive for the annexation of the Dominican
Republic to the United States and to establish a coaling and naval station
at Samana Bay. In her final years, she lived a relatively quiet life in
Jamaica. She purchased Keith Hall and restored the former plantation

house as a winter resort for tourists. Until her death, she promoted United States commercial expansion into the tropics, where she had extensive, but worthless, investments.[2]

Almost as soon as the American Civil War began, former slaves in union-held territory became an issue for the Union government. Former Whigs and Democrats who had worked for the relocation of blacks before the war continued their efforts. In early April 1862, Joseph W. Fabens delivered an address before the American Geographical and Statistical Society titled "Facts about Santo Domingo, Applicable to the present Crisis." The published speech listed natural resources that would attract investors and settlers and resembled Jane Cazneau's *Texas and Her Presidents* (1845) in both style and format. Earlier in the year, Jane Cazneau had sent Moses S. Beach, editor of the New York *Sun*, the first group of "country narratives of what was best for a new beginner to do in every month of the year." All the scenes and the people were true, she explained, only the names were changed. Because the first group had been lost at sea, she would send copies by a Baltimore ship due in ten days. "I want the Weekly Sun very much and will let you know how to send it." As an afterthought she added, "This country is open to both [races] . . . but the Haitian Republic is likely to be the most agreeable to the colored man." In a few months she wrote to Beach that "St. Domingo" was the "happy solution to the great problem of races." She declared that the tropics would not be given up exclusively to the blacks, and added, "while the South makes money, the North makes *men*," and men made "money without an establishment of brute drudgery." She anticipated a "large emigration from the ruined cotton states."[3]

Before she left New York, Jane Cazneau had editorialized in the *Sun* about New York lawyer Ben F. Butler's use of the Supreme Court's Dred Scott decision that declared slaves property. As property, Butler reasoned, they could be declared contraband of war. He partially solved the dilemma of what to do with the slaves that fled their masters, or were abandoned in areas under Union control. By July 1861, contrabands were used as dock workers in New York where they were maintained by the government and their children schooled while twenty thousand white New Yorkers lived in cellars and ten thousand women worked as prostitutes. Because of the loss of shipping and trade and non-payment of debts by the South, by the end of 1861, almost ten thousand New York businesses had failed and 11,500 New Yorkers were on public assistance. As conditions worsened, the unemployed took out their frustration on the contrabands. New York mobs attacked blacks in August 1862. As Lincoln stated to a black delegation that month, "Your race suffers greatly . . . by living among us, while ours suffers from your presence." Lincoln proposed assistance to those who would emigrate. Frederick Douglass was one of those who advised emigration to the Dominican Republic because he had no hope of blacks overcoming the prejudice of the white race in the United States.[4]

In 1862, Jane Cazneau promoted emigration to the former Dominican Republic rather than Haiti because that country sought to remain exclusively black, whereas the Dominicans had "perfect equality of rights to all lineages." It had been an "accepted condition for half a century and works," she added. Furthermore, she claimed, "The black has been found to be thrifty, industrious and progressive," because he is not "left to luxuriate in wanton vagabondage simply because he is black." She saw "no danger of war between races," but warned, "one is now hatching in the United States that will shock the world by its ferocity." She implored, "Nobody in the United States will believe me . . . anymore than you would believe me when I kept telling you that the south was organizing to quit the union if this government passed into the hands of the republicans."[5]

By July, Jane Cazneau had sent more chapters of the guidebook to Beach. In the accompanying letter, she wrote that blacks "should remain in the country of their birth" but added, "you and I know what an unequal struggle it will be if they expect to strive for social equality with the rich sons of the founders." While she wrote that Haiti was "determined to keep the races restricted," she did not see it in "the best interests of the American African family." She emphasized, "I see all races, and every shade and mix here working well and in harmony."[6]

About the time Union and Confederate forces met at Antietam in September 1862, Jane Cazneau complained to Beach, "I have exhausted every bit of paper I could find in this old ranch, the site of the life in St. Domingo." She suggested "How We Live in San Domingo" as a title for the immigrant guide. She added, "My friends in the border states will learn a few things about the tropics," but disclosed, "they have their eyes on British Honduras." Feeling isolated, she complained, "We are always the same—a stray secesh or a rampant abolitionist occasionally breaks upon us." She was dismayed at the war news of "the thousands of slaughters." Believing the South was driven out of the Union by Free-Soilers and abolitionists she commented, "We are perhaps near the truth as regarding the confederate position than any others." She had no respect for Confederate President Jefferson Davis, however, and concluded, "enough of this grievous civil war unless you want Jeff's sayings and doings too after the fact."[7]

Lincoln's September 1862 preliminary Emancipation Proclamation became effective on January 1, 1863. Fabens, an agent for Spoffard and Tileston Steamship Company, traveled to New York in October 1862 and organized the American West Indies Company in anticipation of black emigration to Santo Domingo. As trustees, the Wall Street investors would oversee the operation. President Hiram Ketchum and Vice President Richard Kimball were members of the 1850 New York Union Committee, a coalition of New York businessmen that formed again in 1860 to coordinate Union sentiment in the face of southern boycotts, urged conciliation until Fort Sumter, then formed the Union Defense Committee and helped arm and equip volunteer regiments dispatched to the front. Other company officers were treasurer George F. Dunning, who supervised the U.S. Assay Office, while Samuel L. Barlow was an attorney specializing in Mexican claims. Joseph W. Currier was assistant treasurer, and Fabens served as secretary. The prospectus listed assets at one million dollars—the amount of investment Cazneau anticipated in 1860 before Spain reclaimed its former colony. In 1862, Spain welcomed the former slaves because they could grow cotton, then in high demand because of the Union blockade of Confederate ports. The company built cabins in Santo Domingo City as temporary shelter until the laborers could be settled permanently in the neutral zone along the border.[8]

On December 12, 1862, Congress abolished slavery in Washington, D.C., and appropriated $100,000 to aid in the colonization of former slaves. The American West Indies Company was only one such project. With $600,000, the Chiriqui Improvement Company formed to establish the Colony of Linconia in Panama, but Britain would not allow former American slaves in any areas they controlled. Bernard Kock arranged for 450 freed slaves to be resettled on the Haitian island of Île à Vache, which ended in disaster and scandal.[9]

By the end of 1862, Jane Cazneau thanked Beach for "the god send" of the *Sun* and other reading materials. Because Beach had not received the last manuscript sent via St. Thomas, she sent rough draft copies of the last three chapters written on odd sheets of paper. She explained that Fabens would deliver the last by hand, and call for any packages, *Suns*, etc. She requested "two or three chapter handbooks for notebooks on our trips." In addition, he should send "a ream of ruled paper with the lines marked distinctly on account of my feeble sight." She confessed, "I wrote at this moment without difficulty, but there is a whole week in which ordinary lines are invisible to me." At fifty-five years of age, her poor eyesight was growing increasingly worse.[10]

Unfortunately, racial violence came to New York as Jane Cazneau had predicted. In August 1862, the New York Empire Brigade, hot and thirsty after a morning of drill for one dollar per month, had raided a hotel bar and a drunken riot took three hours to quell. In November more riots occurred as prices for food, clothing, coal, and shelter soared as winter approached. A lack of food, medicine, clothing, and overdue militia pay were common complaints. After the casualties at Antietam and Lincoln's Emancipation Proclamation, military volunteers dwindled. On March 3, 1863, the draft began with a three-hundred-dollar exemption fee for those who could hire a substitute. The war became one fought by the poor to free the slaves, who were often used as strikebreakers. On July 11, 1863, a riot by dockworkers displaced by machine loaders spread to one against the draft and blacks. Black men, women, children, and babies were killed on the streets, or dragged from their homes and tortured. The Negro Orphan Asylum on Fifth Avenue was burned and the New York *Tribune* and homes of abolitionists were attacked. It took police and federal troops three days to restore order. Government officials advocated colonization as a solution to ease the racial prejudice and to curb the increasing violence against blacks.[11]

In all, five editions of Jane Cazneau's guidebook, *In The Tropics: By a Settler in Santo Domingo* (1863), were published anonymously in New York and London. Richard Kimball, the guano discoverer and vice president of the American West Indies Company, wrote the introduction, but did not identify the author. Fabens perhaps took credit for the manuscript that he had delivered to its New York publisher, or perhaps his speeches about Santo Domingo allowed readers to infer his authorship. In Jane Cazneau's next publication, *The Prince of Kashna* (1866), Kimball clearly identified the author of both books as "C. M." (Cora Montgomery). Jane Cazneau's books contrasted sharply with publications by New York racist and ultra-conservative editor of the New York *Day Book*, Dr. John H. Van Evrie. *Negroes and Negro "Slavery": The First an Inferior Race: The Latter Its Normal Condition* (1863) was a continuation of the pro-slave literature Van Evrie had promoted since 1853 in *DeBow's Review*. Van Evrie claimed that blacks would not work unless enslaved and had promoted a Caribbean slave empire.[12]

Jane Cazneau's book was a self-help guide for blacks with tips for building homes, growing food, and producing cash crops each month of the year. Her son resembled the story's protagonist, a New York clerk whose mental stability benefited by the physical labor of building his own house and growing his own fruits and vegetables. The clerk farmed a forty-acre estate by scientific farming methods and held demonstrations for neighbors. He sold his produce to the captain of a sloop whose main cargo was timber cut from the nearby mountain forest and transported to Santo Domingo City. With the clearing of the underbrush, abandoned orchards and a view of the sea emerged. From Buena Vista, as Esmeralda was named in the book, an old road led to a beach for sea bathing. On the coast road, Yankee Charles, a former steward, ran the Stranger's Rest and provided customers with chowder and the *Weekly Herald, Sun, and Dispatch* salvaged from the trash of the British, French, and Spanish consulates in Santo Domingo City. Rev. Jacob James and his Bethel Church congregation of former Virginia slaves still considered themselves Americans after thirty years and were characters in the book.[13]

In The Tropics, like *Eagle Pass* (1852), was an example of Jane Cazneau's writing featuring people who made a choice not to be trapped by their environment and gained control over their lives. Neighbors were Dominicans, black settlers, and planters who had fled Cuba. During 1863, the Cazneaus settled about forty families along the Haitian border. The settlers did not experience the ideal conditions Jane Cazneau portrayed, but encountered hardship, disease, and civil war.[14]

Shortly after Union victories at Gettysburg and Vicksburg sealed the fate of the Confederacy, Santo Domingo erupted into full-scale civil war. In September 1863, José Salcedo, general of the guerilla forces, announced the independence of the Dominican Republic, and by October, Spanish troops were in control only of the area around the capital. Spanish officials accused the Cazneaus of inciting and aiding the revolt and burned their home at San Cristobal, a structure of lathe and plaster with a thatch roof some fifteen miles west of the capital. The Cazneaus fled with their settlers to the British consulate for protection. Cazneau lodged a protest with the U.S. Consul William G. Jaeger and filed a claim for ten thousand dollars against the Spanish government. The Spanish government then awarded Cazneau's salt mine concession to Davis Hatch, an American representing the former New York customs inspector and speculator Augustus Schell.[15]

The Cazneaus escaped to Jamaica with their settlers and leased a thousand-acre bankrupt plantation in the mountains of St. Catherine Parish. At Bog Walk, the English version of Boca d'Agua, meaning the water's mouth, Keith Hall Plantation was seven miles up the Rio Cobre from Spanish Town. Jane Cazneau possibly selected the site because Linstead, three miles away, was a Jamaican produce and market center.[16]

Jane Cazneau's eyesight improved, or she obtained stronger eyeglasses, for her handwriting became smaller and clearer. Always a voracious reader, she read every book in the decaying plantation house, including the handwritten journal of the former tenant. The result was *The Prince of Kashna: A West Indian Story* (1866). The book was possibly meant for former slaves as beginning readers because it was told through the first-person voice in simple language about life in Africa and the middle passage and had a moral about the rewards of honesty, loyalty, hard work, and education. In the introduction, Richard Kimball informed readers that the Prince of Kashna was no fictitious character, but as late as 1828 travelers recalled seeing the real prince, Sidi Mahmadee, at Keith Hall. With the end of slavery in Jamaica and his master's death, the prince converted Keith Hall into a residence hotel for tourists who took day trips to visit the grotto of Bog Walk. After the prince's death, Keith Hall had fallen into disrepair until the Cazneaus leased it.[17]

In the Dominican Republic, fighting grew more intense, and in March 1865, the pro-American President José Salcedo was assassinated and the pro-European Gen. Pedro Pimental took his place. With the end of the American Civil War, Secretary Seward warned Spain against their challenge to the Monroe Doctrine, and Spain, holding only the capital city and fearful of the largest military force in the world and a naval force of four hundred ships, withdrew in July 1865. Great Britain became conciliatory and proposed that the United States and Britain declare Samana Bay neutral territory, but Seward declined. By August, the pro-European president was forced from office by Gen. José Cabral, a man Cazneau described as, "a warm friend of the Americans." While William Cazneau resumed his work at Samana Bay and the salt mines, in August 1865, Jane Cazneau was in New York, where she arranged the publication of *The Prince of Kashna* (1866). She encouraged the New York Cubans, who had not lost their zeal for independence, but had assumed control of their own destiny rather than depend on the United States.[18]

The physical work and tropical climate helped Jane Cazneau's son, who changed his name to William Mont-Storm, perhaps to escape his past, and lived in Harlem, a fashionable New York suburb. Between June 1865 and October 1877, he registered thirteen additional patents for a variety of items such as improved railroad spikes, a gas engine, a steamroller, a felting hat machine, a safe for ships, a clothes wringer, and others related to liquor—a proof meter and a refining and aging process. During this time, the forty-something-year-old Mont-Storm married Annie Eliza Hasbrouck, a woman nearer his mother's age than his own. Her family always wondered "why she married him."[19]

With the slavery issue settled and the war over, Jane Cazneau experienced a resurgence of energy. She, like Secretary of State Seward, expected territorial expansion to resume. "I handled the preliminaries of the Texas Annexation movement and the Sun not only had the press on that subject but ran up its own circulation at the same time," she wrote Beach. "I would like to do the same with the new affair of the Antilles now looming up." She warned, "I can have other papers, I have in fact been interested and urged to do it but no papers have such claims as the Sun abroad." She wanted to repay an old debt to the Beach family, "If you are inclined to look at the Cuba and St. Domingo affairs and allow me to work it up, draft me a line." She could be reached through J. W. Fabens, 29 Wall Street, who would forward her mail.[20]

From New York in September 1865, Jane Cazneau wrote to Secretary of the Interior James Harlan. She outlined William Cazneau's project for a neutral zone with free ports populated by immigrants of all nations friendly to Haiti and the Dominican Republic. She suggested that Harlan read Cazneau's despatches from 1859 and 1860 and asked that he forward her letter to Secretary Seward. She also wished the matter laid before President Johnson. Harlan, a Kentucky native whose family was involved in the steamboat business, contacted Seward, who wanted a coaling station in the Caribbean. Former slaves, then under the care of the Freedmen's Bureau, would help increase an American presence in the Dominican Republic and populate the neutral zone.[21]

While in New York, Jane Cazneau arranged for her nephew by marriage, S. F. Storm, to rent a shop in the Sun Building to sell resort wear. The younger Beach was in poor health. On December 1, 1865, Jane Cazneau suggested that Beach visit Keith Hall in Jamaica, "It was but eight or nine days from New York to Kingston, then by rail, and then by carriage to Keith Hall." He could take the route preferred by their mutual friend Ann Stephens, who traveled through Cuba to Jamaica to visit her old friend.[22]

At the last Johnson cabinet meeting of December 1865, Seward announced he would tour the Caribbean "for a much needed rest." Seward, his son Frederick, who served as assistant secretary of state, the secretary's wife, Frances, and her sister visited the Danish Virgin Islands before they arrived in Santo Domingo City. William Cazneau met them and took Seward to a private reception with President Buenaventura Baéz. Jane Cazneau was hostess and interpreter at informal meetings held with Seward and Dominican officials. Seward, although a Whig, shared many of Jane Cazneau's ideas about expansion. They both had urged the conversion of the navy and merchant marine to steam. Seward predicted that the "civilization of the West . . . will circle the world." After the Civil War, Seward set out to reclaim the Monroe Doctrine and pursue his vision of Manifest Destiny. He saw the United States stretching out through colonies and trade. Jane Cazneau preferred to use the term, "American System" or a "great circle of republics." At the time, Seward was negotiating for the purchase of the Virgin Islands, Alaska, Puerto Rico, Hawaii, Midway, and Guam as coaling stations.[23]

In Washington, on January 30, 1866, President Johnson urged recognition of the Dominican Republic and recommended that William Cazneau be named consul-general. H. E. Peck and Sir Spencer St. John, the United States and British consuls at Haiti, protested that General Cazneau would work for annexation. The British commercial interests did not want the United States in the Caribbean, and racists and isolationists did not want the racial mixtures as part of the United States. In April, Seward and the Cazneaus exchanged letters in which William Cazneau defended himself against charges that he had defamed the character of Jonathan Elliot, the former commercial agent noted for his drunken sprees. Also, Davis Hatch, who took over Cazneau's salt mine concession under the Spanish and lost it when they left, wrote to Sen. Charles Sumner, chairman of the Senate Foreign Relations Committee, that Cazneau was a bitter Confederate from Texas who had him falsely imprisoned when the Spanish departed. Hatch also claimed that Cazneau had prevented Seward from having contact with other Americans while he was in the Dominican Republic. Jane and William Cazneau both wrote to Seward that General Cazneau had intervened to spare Hatch's life when he had been sentenced to death because of his failure to help the Dominicans oust the Spanish. President Johnson appointed Cazneau minister in residence—a position that did not require Senate confirmation.[24]

During the controversy about William Cazneau's appointment, his father grew ill in San Francisco. Minister Cazneau went to his father's bedside, and on July 17, 1866, the ninety-seven-year-old shipmaster died. Capt. W. L. Cazneau had spent his declining years in the San Francisco-Australian trade and had established warehouses in Australia. William Cazneau's brother, Thomas, was now an officer in the California State Militia and in the Marine Department of the State Investment and Insurance Company of California.[25]

In August 1866, the Johnson administration appointed J. Somers Smith as commercial agent to the Dominican Republic and on September 17, 1866, recognized the government of the Dominican Republic. In November, Smith began negotiations for the lease of Samana Bay for a loan of one or two million dollars, but the government would accept as partial payment arms and a steam packet to use for protection against Haitian raids. In exchange, the United States had the use of the coal mines at Samana for a coal and naval depot.[26]

Assistant Secretary Frederick Seward and Rear Adm. David Porter traveled to the Dominican Republic in January 1867 to arrange the sale or lease of Samana Bay. The Cazneaus served as interpreters at the negotiations. The Cabral regime wanted a loan of two million dollars, but Seward would only consider a lease or sale of the bay. While negotiations lagged, United States business penetrated the formerly exclusive European trade zone. C. K. Garrison, Vanderbilt's rebel agent and one-time ally of William Walker, owned the International Steamship Company with a mail contract to South America. Garrison paid the first year's lease of $100,000 for Samana Bay and paid a royalty to the Dominican government on the mines in the bay. With the collapse of the American West Indies Company to relocate former slaves, Cazneau reorganized the Santo Domingo Cotton Company, but that, too, failed with the 1868 death of Thaddeus Stevens, the chief proponent of providing freed slaves with land, farm implements, and supplies either in the United States or at some other location.[27]

By March 1868, General Baéz, whose loyalty reflected his opportunities, came to power for the fourth time and asked that his republic become a United States territory. Fabens, the agent for Spoffard and Tileston Shipping Company, with wharves and warehouses at Samana, met with Congressman N. P. Banks in Boston at the home of the former abolitionist Dr. Samuel Gridley Howe and gained the reformer's endorsement. In September 1868, Secretary of State Seward also advocated annexation when he became president of the Isthmus Canal Company at an annual salary of twenty thousand dollars while still in office. President-elect U. S. Grant also favored annexation of the Dominican Republic to advance his program of naval expansion and the rebuilding of the United States merchant marine, trade, and commerce to prevent the gold drain and help reverse the trade imbalance.[28]

In President Johnson's fourth annual message, he proposed "annexation of the two republics of the island of St. Domingo." Annexation of both countries would end the European financing of warlords. In the United States, congressional supporters expected payments so Fabens and Garrison arranged with Ben Butler to fund the votes. In January 1869, Gen. N. P. Banks, chairman of the House Committee on Foreign Affairs, led the annexation effort in Congress. Isolationists, radicals, and railroad interests organized against entangling alliances and external protection. The committee tabled the resolution without discussion, 126 to 36.[29]

According to historians and others who have written about the Cazneaus, Jane promoted the annexation of the Dominican Republic in the *Sun* and in the *Herald*. In their books, *To The American Press* (1870) and *Our Winter Eden* (1878), however, the Cazneaus promoted Samana Bay as a free port and opposed annexation. On January 9, 1869, the *Herald* published a letter by Jane Cazneau advocating Samana Bay as a free port. In March 1869, Fabens formed the United States Geological and Mineralogy Survey Company with investors William L. Halsey, Ben Halladay, S. L. M. Barlow, Cyrus McCormick, and John Young, Richard Kimball's brother-in-law. The investors wanted annexation to stabilize the government. Because of Senate objections to foreign bases, investors saw annexation as a means to gain support in Congress for the coal and naval depot. On December 22, 1869, the *Herald* published the text of a paper that Fabens read before the American Geographical and Statistical Society of New York. *Resources of Santo Domingo* (1869), with the exception of the concluding paragraph, was identical to *Facts about Santo Domingo Applicable to the Present Crisis* (1862), which he read and published in April 1862. With the exception of the final paragraph, no doubt Jane Cazneau had written both publications with the same type of promotional material that she had produced for years with sub-headings on history, geography, topographical, climate, soil and productions, forests, agricultural products, fruits and vegetables, animals, mineral resources, politics, and inducements for colonization.[30]

In March 1869, newly inaugurated President Ulysses S. Grant saw annexation as a step in making "America for the Americans." He understood the strategic value of a coaling station and a naval port at Samana Bay. During the Civil War, Confederate ships operating out of Havana had devastated Union shipping. During the war, Britain had converted its merchant marine to iron and propeller-driven steamships, built Confederate raiders that destroyed U.S. merchant shipping, and, as a neutral power, purchased a large percentage of American-owned ships and shipping companies. Few American deepwater shippers survived the Civil War. In addition to the 105,000 tons of shipping seized or destroyed by Confederate raiders, 800,000 tons were absorbed by neutral foreign flags. Not only had foreign trade carried by American bottoms dropped from 73.7 percent to 25 percent during the war, Britain had established direct trade with Southern ports and bypassed New York merchants and shippers. Samana Bay would assist in developing alternate trade and commerce with the West Indies and South America.[31]

In May 1869, Secretary of State Hamilton Fish informed the British foreign minister that certain persons in high positions would not allow the United States to buy Samana Bay or annex the Dominican Republic. Fish, former Whig governor of New York, was concerned about editorials in the *Herald* and the *Sun* praising the republic at a time he wanted to negotiate the losses incurred by Union maritime shipping by the British-built Confederate raiders. Also, he feared "the incorporation of these people of the Latin race would be but the beginning of years of conflict." Secretary of the Navy Gideon Welles shared Fish's views. He was disposing of the naval vessels that depended on coal and coaling stations and was in the process of reducing the navy from five hundred to twenty-nine ships, only seven more than in 1829 and seventeen less than in 1853, when the challenge for the tropical trade began. Furthermore, in May 1869 the Union and Pacific railroads met in Utah and completed intercontinental rail transport.[32]

President Grant, however, sent naval vessels to Santo Domingo to investigate finances, commerce, and the attitude of the Dominicans toward the United States. The mercantile house of Spoffard, Tileston, and Co., which remained under the U.S. flag, was struggling to overcome losses resulting from the war and to regain its former business as the largest deepwater shipping firm in the United States. The firm obtained a concession for a steamship line from New York to Samana Bay, and in June 1869 began regular service with the steamer *Typee*. On July 4, 1869, Fabens,

William Cazneau, Paul Spoffard, Thomas Tileston, Edward Prime, and Edward P. Hollister obtained a charter for the National Bank of Santo Domingo to stabilize the Dominican currency.[33]

Grant also sent his personal aide and engineer, Gen. Orville Babcock, to examine Samana Bay. Jane Cazneau wrote about the meeting in a *Herald* article published on August 13, 1869. The Cazneaus served as hosts and interpreters for a party of about thirty Dominican and U.S. officials who met with President Baéz at their rebuilt cottage and at the Baéz home at Azula. Business people and those interested in the Panama Canal and trade with the western coast of South America attended the meeting.[34]

The Santo Domingo situation was complicated by Fish's agenda to reopen talks with Britain about restitution of damages by Confederate raiders and by President Grant's support of the Cuban war for independence. The Republicans had refused a treaty Seward negotiated with Britain over the Confederate raiders because of partisan differences with the Johnson administration. The Cubans declared independence and freed their slaves in September 1868, and former master and slave fought the Spanish troops with the slogan "Cuba for the Cubans." Grant wanted to recognize the Cubans, but Fish convinced Grant he had two choices, war with Spain over Cuba or the annexation of the Dominican Republic. Grant chose Samana Bay, the "Gibraltar of the Antilles."[35]

In November 1869, General Babcock returned to the Dominican Republic with a treaty for the lease of Samana Bay and another for the annexation of the republic. Again, the Cazneaus served as interpreters at meetings where Maj. R. H. Perry, the new commercial agent, signed the treaties as United States representative. President Grant paid the next $100,000 for the annual lease of Samana Bay with secret service funds. The United States flag was raised over Samana Bay, and Grant ordered the USS *Nantasket* stationed in the bay to prevent Haitian interference.[36]

It appeared that the Cazneaus' plans were to be realized. Then, Davis Hatch, the disgruntled salt mine operator, wrote to his Connecticut senator in February 1870, claiming that he was imprisoned again to prevent his working against annexation. In April 1870, William Cazneau published *To the American Press: The Dominican Negotiations from 1850 to 1870*. He explained, "I do not propose to discuss the political expediency of annexation—of that every American will judge for himself." Cazneau claimed that from 1850 to 1870, cabinets, statesman, naval officers, and patriots, understood "the importance and feasibility of acquiring a superior naval station in these seas." He outlined the three stages of negotiations for Samana Bay as a lease in the Pierce administration, a free port during the Buchanan and Lincoln administrations, and the current annexation phase that came about because it was seen as the only way to get confirmation by Congress and to end the raids from Haiti sponsored by Europeans. As William Cazneau wrote, it was not the "inevitable destiny" that "territorial fruits" would gravitate to the United States because Europeans were working to confederate the West Indies and keep it out of the American trade system.[37]

On May 27, 1870, Perry, the commercial agent, handed Secretary Fish a "bundle of papers," which, according to Fish's diary entry, "present no specific fact." Nonetheless, the evidence helped destroy the annexation movement. Fish had Perry contact Sen. Orris S. Ferry of Connecticut, who had the Hatch letters. Hatch's letters and Perry's claims did irrevocable damage to the Cazneaus' reputations and linked their names with the "Samana Bay Treaty Ring," the twenty who would make a 20 percent profit—the first scandal of the Grant administration.[38]

Four days after Perry's meeting with Fish, Grant demanded that Congress approve the annexation treaty. He said that the bay would lead to "a coast-wise commerce of immense magnitude, which will go far toward restoring to us our lost merchant marine." Grant saw annexation as a matter of national security—the United States needed to rebuild its deepwater merchant marine and help reduce the gold drain from the treasury. During the Senate debate on annexation, on June 8, 1870, Senator Ferry of Connecticut rose "flourishing a bundle of documents which purported to show how foully Hatch had been treated by Cazneau," and he demanded an investigation. A special investigating committee was appointed with Sen. James Nye as chairman.[39]

The Nye Committee hearings opened with a letter Perry had since written to Fish detailing how Fabens, Cazneau, Baéz, and Babcock would benefit at the expense of the U.S. Treasury. Perry then testified that Cazneau was "running the whole thing down there," and he too claimed that Cazneau was a Confederate from Texas. During the Civil War, Perry had shot his commanding officer during a mutiny, but charges were dismissed. He was transferred to New Orleans, where he was charged with mule theft, bank swindling, and rape. Although he faced a court-martial, he resigned, went to Mexico, and fought against Maximilian. Perry was accepted into the U.S. Army during Reconstruction and was police chief of Galveston when appointed commercial agent to the Dominican Republic. The nephew of Commodore Oliver H. Perry had wanted the U.S. marshal job in western Texas, and as he told Fabens, he wanted fame and not money. In the course of the hearings, Perry's background became public along with the knowledge that he had returned to the states at the request of the Dominican government. His "contempt for the colored citizens" was evident. The government complained that he had slapped a black plaintiff's face in court, then retired to his office and claimed diplomatic immunity.[40]

The most damaging testimony against William Cazneau was that of Davis Hatch. Hatch had come to the Dominican Republic in 1862 as an agent for August Schell and conservative New York investors. Dominican republicans arrested Hatch in 1866 for aiding Spain during the war, and again in 1868 for trying to overthrow the Baéz government that urged annexation. Hatch claimed that he was imprisoned for writing letters against Cazneau's appointment as U. S. consul in 1866 and to prevent him from opposing annexation. During the hearings, Cazneau remained in charge of operations in the Dominican Republic and only sent a deposition. Fabens and Babcock gave testimony favorable to themselves. Fabens, who had shown no loyalty in the past, portrayed Cazneau as the manipulator of events and himself merely as an agent following orders. Babcock defended William Cazneau as being loyal to the Union but with sympathy for the Southern dilemma of slavery.[41]

The majority report of the Nye Committee exonerated William Cazneau of any wrongdoing, affirmed Hatch's guilt in trying to overthrow the Baez government, and questioned Perry's credibility. The minority report, however, written by Sen. Carl Schurz of Missouri, took issue with every point. While Grant stood behind Cazneau, two thousand copies of Schurz's report maligned Cazneau. Schurz represented Central and Union Pacific railroad interests who faced freight competition from the merchant marine and had yet to show a profit after a year's operation. Guilty of distributing spoils and hoping to make a profit from twenty years on the front lines of the trade and commerce war, the Cazneaus became scapegoats while their financial backers, the Wall Street bankers, businessmen, and corrupt politicians escaped notice.[42]

In June 1870, the Senate voted against the annexation of the Dominican Republic, but Grant did not give up on obtaining a naval base at Samana Bay. He appointed a commission to investigate. The special commission was headed by Dr. Andrew White, a respected reformer, and included Frederick Douglass, Dr. Samuel Gridley Howe, and Speaker of the House Ben Wade. Beginning in January 1871, the commissioners traveled through the Dominican Republic and Haiti for twenty-two days. They urged annexation. Douglass, discouraged by what he saw in Haiti, wrote, "If this is the outcome of self-government by my race, Heaven help Us!" White agreed, writing, "The great hope of the masses was that annexation would bring them peace and security." The committee published its report in April but it did nothing to change the votes in Congress. Howe remained at Samana, started a mission school, and President Grant appointed him governor of Samana. With Senate rejection of a coaling and naval station on June 16, 1871, Grant had no alternative or secret funds to pay for another year's lease of the bay. He revoked the Navy orders and the Stars and Stripes came down at Samana Bay. After another survey, Panama investors realized a canal would cost more than they were willing to invest, and withdrew support for the coaling and naval station.[43]

Dr. Howe and his wife, Julia, composer of the "Battle Hymn of the Republic," remained at the Samana mission until 1874. That year, the Dominican Republic erupted into war as pro-American "Reds" fought the "Blues," European-backed liberals supplied from Haiti. The British consul directed Haitian operations and vowed to make peace if the United States left Samana and let Haiti have the mountains along the border. The European-backed Gen. Ignacio Gonzales overthrew Baéz and abrogated the treaty with the United States for the ninety-nine-year lease of Samana Bay. Britain loaned Gonzales several million dollars at no interest and with no payment schedule. Spoffard and Tileston closed their wharves, warehouses, and coal depot, and went bankrupt. It would be two years before Richard Henry Dana, the crusading editor of *Sun*, revealed how railroad interests had corrupted Congress.[44]

For seventeen years, William and Jane Cazneau had invested their lives, their fortunes, and their reputations to extend United States trade, commerce, and republican ideals into the Caribbean and Central America. While William Cazneau tried to salvage investments in the Dominican Republic, Jane Cazneau returned to Jamaica. On October 15, 1872, William Leslie Cazneau and his wife, Jane Montgomery Cazneau, purchased the bankrupt Keith Hall Plantation from James Derbyshire and Alexander Turnbull. Cazneau mulled his failures and complained to his Texas brother-in-law, R. O. W. McManus, "Fish . . . and his son-in-law

Webster know what they received for their services, but this golden market will soon be closed upon them." Sidney Webster was Spain's Washington agent. Cazneau called the Samana Bay controversy "an astounding chapter of infamy," but he was optimistic and predicted "the whole story will see the light someday."[45]

Jane Cazneau, undaunted by the failure, restored Keith Hall as a residential hotel for tourists. She described Keith Hall as an "old fashioned place among the wildly romantic hills of St. Catherine." The house had been built by the governor of Jamaica, Sir Basil Keith, at the time of the American Revolution. Day trips took tourists from the British capital of Kingston with its ruins of Port Royal by railway along the Rio Cobre and across the sugarcane fields of the Liguanea Plain stretched between the Blue Mountains and the sea. From Spanish Town, the old Spanish capital of St. Jago de La Vega with narrow, winding streets, tourists traveled by buggies beside the Rio Cobre to Bog Walk, lunched at Keith Hall, then went to Linstead across the mountains to Port Marie on the north shore, where steamers waited for tourists to continue their cruise.[46]

Keith Hall was Jane Cazneau's winter eden and resort. The place had long been a tourist attraction. In the early part of the century, Lady Nugent concluded the excursion from Spanish Town to Keith Hall was "the most romantic, beautiful, and picturesque road she ever saw." She described the path that wound upward along the side of a mountain and at places was excavated into the rock so that the mountain hung over the road almost touching the horses' heads. At the bottom of the precipice was a beautiful and rapid river. The mountains were perpendicular, with trees growing as if out of rock. The inclined road "wound between huge boulders that lay about with trees and shrubs still growing on them." Upon leaving the gorge, whose mists rose above the rim of the cliffs, she ate lunch at the manor house.[47]

In 1891, Stuart Villers, a South America and the West Indies traveler, wrote that Bog Walk was the most impressive site he had visited in South America and the West Indies. The view of the deep blue-green mountains above and the purple plain below had not changed since Lady Nugent's visit. At the edge of the cliff Villers described a magnificent garden of flowering shrubs, trailing, creeping, and climbing plants at a picturesque little hotel as the perfect "hiatus for artists and lovers of nature." He did not name the park designed and created by Jane Cazneau's Garden School, but Cazneau Park was located on Jamaican maps until the 1950s. While she supervised the Cazneau School and reared granddaughter Cora, Jane Cazneau entertained guests and swapped reminiscences with visitors and old friends at Keith Hall. Ann Stephens may have come each winter and listened to stories that inspired her serials. William Cazneau found Keith Hall too remote from which to conduct business in Kingston with the U.S. Consul J. K. Roberts, son of shipping tycoon Marshall Roberts.[48]

J. K. Roberts was involved in the Cuban War of Independence (1868–1878), and it seems impossible that the Cazneaus were not supportive in some way. In 1865, Jane had claimed, "By an odd set of coincidences I have been better informed than the state department itself." She urged Beach, "I think we can and ought to encourage the Cubans of all colors without ruining the country." In 1866, the New York Cubans issued a pamphlet, *Voice of America*, possibly written by Jane Cazneau. As the rebellion spread throughout Cuba, Spain increased its military forces from 14,000 to 110,000 soldiers, but the 26,000 Cubans and their 40,000 freed slaves fought a guerrilla war partly supplied out of Kingston on ships owned by J. K. Roberts.[49]

Cuban rebels were supplied out of Jamaica by the *Virginius*, a side-wheel steamer originally built as a Confederate blockade-runner and at that time owned by Marshall Roberts and his son. In late October 1873, a Spanish gunboat captured the *Virginius*, heavily loaded with arms and supplies, and officials shot Capt. Joseph Fry, seven Americans, sixteen British volunteers, and twenty-eight Cubans before British officials stopped the executions. With Spanish losses at eighty thousand men, Spain wanted peace, but the Cubans fought on for independence. While the *Virginius* was being returned to the United States, Spanish officials claimed she was lost at sea.[50]

By 1874, the sixty-seven-year-old Cazneaus could offer the Cubans little more than moral support. They had little money, Jane Cazneau was almost blind, and William Cazneau had a lingering case of malaria. Their only wealth was in undeveloped land in the war-torn Dominican Republic and unrecorded land deeds in Texas. The Cazneaus had deeds to one-half of the Rivas Grant amounting to 55,350 acres and a city lot in Eagle Pass, where Cazneau's store and warehouse had stood near an additional 100 acres. Mrs. Cazneau had 1,000 acres on the Rio Grande at Kingsbury's Falls and still claimed the eleven leagues purchased in 1833. The Cazneaus made plans to return to Texas and recover their Eagle Pass property, which was then in the possession of a foreign-owned cattle syndicate managed out of San Antonio.[51]

In June 1875, William Cazneau wrote to R. O. W. McManus that he was negotiating the sale of their Jamaican property and would proceed to Texas. William and Jane Cazneau sent McManus their powers of attorney and deeds to record. Cazneau's family estate was settled after his brother's recent death, and he gave what claims he had on the Pacific Coast to his brother's sons. All else he settled on his wife, "For my great object is to secure her happiness and that I feel she is most likely to find in the sympathies of her own kindred." Jane Cazneau feared that the Texas land situation was similar to a case in western New York that after twenty years and great outlay brought no return. Cazneau was more concerned with the land and mining interests in Santo Domingo, which were "far too large to be lightly sacrificed." He was torn whether to go first to Santo Domingo or directly to Texas.[52]

As Cazneau explained to McManus, when he left Eagle Pass for Washington in 1853 to file his claim for loss of goods in Mexico, he expected to return to Texas. When he received the deeds, McManus recorded them in Eagle Pass, the county seat of Maverick County. County Clerk Albert Turpe informed him that William Stone, a store clerk when Cazneau was in Eagle Pass, had obtained a tax deed on part of the property. Turpe offered to take possession of a place called by the local Mexicans "El ranchero del general," where one wall of the adobe house still remained. Turpe soon advised McManus to get a good attorney for there were more claimants than land and the case would go to court. McManus then hired S. Rhodes Fisher, an Austin attorney, who as an infant had lived in the same room with Jane McManus at Cazneau and Grasmeyer's store in Matagorda, and whose sister left the memoirs of the Cazneaus' romance before the Texas Revolution. Turpe next wrote that he could do no more without putting myself out of office or in trouble. He located Deisderio de Luna, Cazneau's shepherd, who said Stone and Enoch Jones of San Antonio had taken the Cazneau herd of sheep and goats back in 1853 for merchandise they claimed Cazneau lost in Mexico.[53]

William Cazneau never returned to Texas, for he died on January 8, 1876, from complications of his lingering fever. His burial place in Jamaica is unknown, but it is possibly at St. Thomas-in-the-Vale Church Cemetery at Bog Walk. His obituary appeared in the San Antonio *Herald* on March 22, 1876, and stated, "He leaves a wife, now old and blind, who with her pen did more for Texas in her days of trial, than any other person." It also stated that in 1833 Jane Cazneau translated into German a sketch of the advantages Texas offered the emigrant. The appeal to Germans was perhaps meant to help in her legal battle against the foreign-owned cattle syndicate.[54]

From Jamaica, Jane Cazneau sent her brother irrevocable power of attorney to enter into and take possession of any and all real estate in the state of Texas. The U. S. consul in Coahuila, Mexico, A. G. Carothers, checked on matters in Eagle Pass while traveling to his post in Mexico. In 1876, no mails passed between San Antonio and Eagle Pass because a Mexican revolution spilled across the border. Carothers obtained the abstracts of those who had filed claims against Cazneau's land. By May 1877, Turpe decided to return to his father's farm in Medina County and wrote to McManus that his job paid nothing and the rowdies had run all potential buyers away. He advised McManus to secure a local attorney, A. N. Oliphant, as he had a hard fight ahead with heavy capital against him. Others had established tax titles and possession bonds to the extent that the twenty-five-league Rivas grant had twenty-eight leagues of claims filed against it, not counting the Cazneau claim of twelve leagues. Carothers contacted judges Richard S. Walker and Alexander W. Terrell, who agreed to help McManus fight the foreign syndicate in court.[55]

By early 1877, Jane Cazneau returned to New York, perhaps with her friend Ann S. Stephens and Stephens's daughter. On January 27, 1877, the seventy-year-old Cazneau made a will and bequeathed all her property to Ann Stephens and her daughter, Ann Sophia, to use for the support of Cazneau's son. At his death, her property was to go to Ann and her daughter. She did not mention Cora, who had married John D. Hutchins, an engineer and resident of Jamaica, at fourteen or fifteen years of age and moved to New York. Jane Cazneau listed an impressive schedule of property in Texas, Santo Domingo, and Jamaica, but bequeathed her brother only one-half of the eleven-league Perfecto Valdez grant they still claimed.[56]

Jane Cazneau returned to Jamaica and on November 21, 1877, deeded 983 acres of Keith Hall to Rev. Charles A. Winn of the Wesleyan Society for a note of eight hundred pounds. She reserved the 187 acres of orchards and gardens bordering Bog Walk for the Cazneau Park and School. She rented a cottage in Kingston and had few possessions. She received five pounds interest per annum from a dividend she held from the bankrupt estate of Nunes and Brothers. In 1878, Jane Cazneau returned to New York and published *Our Winter Eden: Pen Pictures of the Tropics* (1878). The loosely organized sketches of people and places were written in the Dominican

Republic years before. She defended William Cazneau's efforts to make Samana Bay a free port and condemned Seward's attempts to annex the Dominican Republic that had ended in failure.[57]

Jane Cazneau visited her aunt Britannia Sherman in Brookfield, Connecticut, and perhaps on her advice, made another will. It is possible that Ann Stephens discovered that Jane Cazneau's property claims were entangled in legalities and worthless. Lemuel Hawley Baldwin, the nephew of Britannia Sherman's deceased husband, Lemuel Hawley Sherman, agreed to be executor of her estate for the ten thousand-dollar claim against the Spanish government. Baldwin, a New York attorney, would provide for Jane's son and supervise Cora's estate. Jane Cazneau made no provision for her brother, who had worked for years to recover their Texas land. In her second will dated November 21, 1878, Cazneau was adamant that Rev. Thomas Lea was to be trustee of her Jamaica lands and mortgages due for use of the Cazneau Garden School. Second, she bequeathed all the Dominican property to her son and his wife for their use during their natural lives, then held in trust for Cora's children. Whether she feared Cora had her father's character defects, or she was concerned that Cora's husband, J. D. Hutchins, would squander her inheritance, is unknown. Cazneau willed the Texas lands to Cora, during her natural life, subject to the power of executor Baldwin.[58]

With her legal affairs in more order than ever in her life, the following Sunday, Jane Cazneau attended church services at the Plymouth Church of the Pilgrims in Brooklyn, New York. She was impressed by the sermon given by the former abolitionist, Henry Ward Beecher (1813–1887), and later called at his residence. Beecher espoused such causes as the biological theory of evolution, the scientific and historical study of biblical texts, women's rights and suffrage, and Cuban independence. Cazneau informed Beecher of her transformation after her illness and care given her by Anita Garcia, to whom she owed her life. She was determined to repay the debt by helping educate the black children in Samana and Jamaica. Cazneau informed Beecher, "Fifteen years ago, . . . I would have deemed it doing service to God to put a bullet through your head!" She had considered him "a fearful agitator—an enemy of the Nation." In her view, abolitionists set back emancipation and drove southerners out of the Union.[59]

Jane Cazneau and her daughter-in-law, Annie Storm, booked passage from New York to Jamaica for Sunday, December 8, 1878. Cazneau was to file her will in Samana and Jamaica and return with her husband's remains for burial in the United States. After inquiring about the safety of the ship from its former master, Jane Cazneau booked passage for Annie Storm and herself on the *Emily B. Souder*, a brigantine-rigged cargo steamer bound for Turk's Island with stops at Puerto Plata and Samana in the Dominican Republic. They did not have first-class accommodations, but shared adjoining cabins above deck. The ship sailed on time with nine paying passengers—three women and a baby, and six men, who were traveling on business or who owned sugar plantations in the Dominican Republic. The *Souder* had a crew of twenty-seven from six different countries, an Irish stewardess, and a German captain, a veteran of the Hamburg Line, the Peninsular and Oriental Line, and for the last three years, a captain for the Clyde Line of Philadelphia.[60]

According to pilots in New York harbor, the *Emily B. Souder* was "a rattletrap," but she was no worse than others of her age that made up the U.S. merchant fleet. She was built in Philadelphia for the New York-Charleston coastal trade. After the end of the war, she made a few trips to the Windward Islands before she was sent around the Horn to San Francisco, where she remained about two years. In 1867, her owners sold her to Chilean capitalists for $200,000 with half the cash down, but upon arrival, her condition was so unseaworthy for guano that they forfeited the down payment. W. F. Weld and Co. of Boston rebuilt the vessel, and in 1872 the ship began the New York to New Orleans run until authorities thought the ship had brought yellow fever to New Orleans. In the summer of 1877, W. P. Clyde and J. K. Roberts purchased the *Souder* for $32,000. Clyde said the ship was overhauled in Philadelphia when the *Tybee*, purchased from Spoffard and Tileston, was retired. The *Souder* made one trip to the West Indies and, as proof of his confidence in the ship, R. S. Burgess, superintendent of Clyde's West Indies Department, took passage.[61]

The *Souder* at 203 feet long and 31.5 feet wide had a wooden propeller and, like most ships of its type built during the Civil War, was built with unseasoned timber and ten-penny nails. It was not a strong ship, but it had lifeboats, rafts, and cork life preservers for the passengers and the crew. According to Clyde, the ship was valued at $35,000 and fully insured. According to Roberts, the ship was valued at $75,000 with little insurance. The insurance brokers would not say how much insurance the ship carried. During the last general inspection, Clyde claimed the *Souder* had a rating of 1.5 for four years, the highest for vessels of its age. Lloyds of London had a circle with a dot in the center beside the name of the ship as a symbol designating it had not been inspected in over a year. Only thirty-four of the eight hundred steamships they carried had such a mark. Harbor pilots said, "the old ship was safe in fair weather, but if she encountered a storm, the gingerbread," as they called the hull, "would come apart and it was a fifty-fifty chance whether she would sink or float." The ship was to be retired after this voyage. In twenty-five years, the Clyde Line had never lost a ship. The *Souder* was an example, however, of the type of ship operating in the U.S. Merchant Marine Service.[62]

New York harbor pilots speculated that on December 10, 1878, the *Souder* was about 400 miles south of New York and about 100 to 150 miles off the coast of Cape Hatteras headed for the Bermuda sea-lanes. The surviving crewmembers explained that the wind rose and the sea began to roll. The relatively shallow Hatteras Banks off North Carolina are a little over a half-mile in depth and extend outward for 180 miles until the sea bottom abruptly drops down a cliff for three and one-half miles to the Hatteras Abyssmal Plain. On December 10, 1878, a westerly front created gale force winds from Boston to Panama, damaging ships and wharves. The United States Signal Service reported winds of forty-eight miles per hour at New York, Baltimore, and Charleston. In New York, the barometric pressure reading fell to 28.81 inches of mercury, the lowest on record. It was the largest storm to hit the coast of the United States since record keeping began.[63]

In New York, nothing was heard of the *Emily B. Souder* until December 28, when the London *Evening Telegram* wired its sister paper the New York *Evening Telegram* the following message: "FOUNDERED AT SEA. Only Two Men Saved. They are landed at Kingston, Jamaica." On December 28, 1878, the *Evening Telegram*, the New York *Sun*, the New York *Tribune*, and the New York *Times* carried the news of the disaster at sea. No details were given, only that two crewmen had survived when they were picked up by a passing sailing vessel, the *Abbot Devereaux*, bound out of Boston for Jamaica. Newspapers gave the description of the lost vessel, her general condition, the cargo, and passengers and crew. Jane Cazneau was identified as a passenger from New York and the widow of General Cazneau, late United States agent of San Domingo City and an eminent Texan. Jane Cazneau's age was given as fifty-five, although she was closer to seventy-two years old. Whether she had given the wrong age, or if she actually looked younger can not be known, but her daughter-in-law's age was listed as sixty, while she was actually sixty-five years old.[64]

The next day the New York papers carried additional information about the ship and crew. On December 31, with no new information, the *Tribune* publicized its most famous passenger as front page news, "A SKETCH OF MRS. CAZNEAU THE REMARKABLE CAREER OF ONE OF THE PASSENGERS OF THE SOUDER." Although the sketch was said to have been written by "one who was acquainted with her for many years," it contained many errors and has since been the source of fallacies perpetuated about Jane Cazneau. The most glaring error was that her "Texan residence led to her ownership in slave property and her advocating the divine right of slavery." Rev. Henry Ward Beecher likely wrote the sketch because it had extensive quotes and references to his last meeting with her and about her change in attitude about the black race as if Beecher were responsible. In closing, the *Tribune* article offered a tribute to Jane Cazneau: "Few women leave a record more desirable," she was "Never a 'woman's rights woman' in any sense," but "always eager to do the duty which lay next to her." Furthermore, "Her character was a marked one, and commanded the admiration of all who knew her."[65]

On January 9, 1879, the surviving crewmen arrived in New York, and on January 10, newspapers carried the stories of their ordeal at sea. The men described the ship's going down, their ten hours of suspense, and their rescue. Clyde claimed that his company only leased the ship from Roberts and denied that the ship was overloaded and unfit. Upon their arrival in port, quartermaster Theodore Steinert of Germany and seaman Alfred Anderson of Sweden told their story to reporters: On December 9, the *Souder* encountered a small northeaster. The next morning at daybreak, the captain discovered the ship was leaking. The engineer sounded the well and found five feet of water. The steam pumps were set in motion, but they could not hold their own against the leak. The captain ordered the whole port watch into the afterhold where he supposed the leak was located. An effort was made to move part of the cargo to look at the keelsons. By this time, the sea was running high under a gale from the southeast. The other watch was called on deck and all hands were set to work heaving off the deck a load of lumber, boxes, and the heavy iron sugar pans, but they could not be budged, even with the help of the male passengers, who helped lessen the load in the blowing gale.[66]

An effort was made to get some of the cargo out of the hold, but it was thrown hither and yon by the rolling of the ship. The captain ordered the foremast cut away. Until 4:30 in the afternoon the ship obeyed her helm. At that time the water reached the fires in the engine room. The male passengers went back to the women in the cabins, and all strapped on cork jackets and ascended to the deck, where they were made fast to the rigging to await the loosening of the lifeboats. The fires went out and the engine stopped.[67]

The sails on the main mast were insufficient and the ship was soon drifting broadside in the tremendous seaway that was running high. Several times she rolled her bulwarks under and had she not been well loaded, she would have gone over on her beam ends. The sea made a clean breach over her and occasionally an enormous wave struck the windward side of the vessel and swept from her decks everything that was not fastened down. At about 5 P.M. an effort was made to launch a boat from the leeward side of the ship, and while the boat was hanging on the davits the first officer, three passengers, and two of the crew boarded, and it was let down into the sea. It was instantly swamped and its ten inmates drifted far to the leeward. As the men were launching the second boat, Steinert saw a tall, elderly woman clinging to the boat ropes. "It is really useless to get into this boat," she said, "It will undoubtedly be overturned as the other." The speaker was reported to have been Jane Cazneau, but the description of a tall, dark-complexioned woman well past middle age was that of her daughter-in-law, Annie Storm. Jane Cazneau was only five feet, three inches tall. The woman got into the lifeboat as did five of the crew and two other passengers. Purser Doty, an engineer, three of the crew, and several passengers made up the third boat. The fourth boat had been stove in when they left port.[68]

After the boats pushed off, there were ten persons left on board. The cylinders of the life raft were rusted and full of holes large enough a man could thrust in his hand, so Captain Kuehl, Engineer Tice, Second Mate Thompson, and Mr. Crosby made a raft from the lumber on deck, as Steinert, Anderson and another seaman lashed themselves to the forward hatch. A passenger they could not help, most likely the blind Jane Cazneau, plus one of the cooks and a cabin boy were clinging to the rigging aft, just as Jane Cazneau had described in *The Camel Hunt* (1851) when she and William Cazneau were in a similar storm and she wrote: "Where shall the lover of the 'fierce, beautiful and free,' find anything comparable with a storm at sea." At about 5:30, the after part of the ship sank out of sight and within five minutes the ship was gone. The forward hatch rose to the surface. Nothing could be seen of those who had been clinging to the rigging.[69]

Anderson and Steinert lashed themselves to the life raft that floated by. The ship's cargo floated all about them, but they saw no sign of the passengers or the rest of the crew. The storm passed, and two days later crewmembers on the Jamaica-bound *Abbot Devereaux* rescued them. The ship had lost her main gaff in the storm, and in repairing the sail, had headed off course when the lookout spotted the drifting seamen. The *Sun* reported that the Clyde Line officials expected that others would be rescued by passing ships. They never were.[70]

Conclusion

❧

Few women leave a record more desirable than has Mrs. Cazneau. Never a 'woman's rights woman' in any sense, she was always eager to do the duty which lay next to her—to do it without ostentation, but thoroughly and completely. Her character was a marked one, and commanded the admiration of all who knew her.

—*New York* Tribune *(1878)*[1]

*J*ANE McMANUS STORM CAZNEAU DIED THE WAY SHE LIVED—AT THE center of a storm of controversy. She seldom took the easy path and reached with reckless abandon for that which always seemed to lie beyond her grasp, but not beyond her vision or her ambition. She was a complex person who lived during an era of national confusion and sectional animosity, but she adapted to her surroundings and grew spiritually and intellectually until her death. As a journalist she admitted her mistakes, consoled the oppressed, offended the comfortable, lectured politicians, and commended statesmen. As a visionary, she foresaw a nation with equal rights for all in a world where representative government was the norm rather than the exception. Like most visionaries, her messages were not appreciated in her time by isolationists, racists, or reactionaries. As an advisor to government officials and as a publicist for republican causes, she helped form United States domestic and foreign policy from the mid-1840s into the 1870s.[2]

In many ways, Jane Cazneau's biography provides an alternative view to the dichotomy of North-South, abolitionist-secessionist, Democratic-Republican histories of the antebellum era. Her colleagues were the nationalists of all sections and political parties who sought a conciliatory path to carry the nation forward through what she termed the "mist and smoke of sectional prejudice." They sought to resolve the slavery issue through the colonization of free blacks and slaveholders in the tropics. They would then use these colonies to expand trade, commerce, and political ideals into a worldwide circle of republics.[3]

Cazneau's experiences in Mexico and the American tropics help illustrate the intensity of the undeclared Anglo-American war of trade, commerce, and political ideals in the years before, during, and immediately after the American Civil War. Within three years of her death, the United States began to rebuild its navy, and after 1890, United States commerce in Latin America bypassed that of the United Kingdom. In 1895, Sen. Carl Schurz of Missouri, who had written the minority Nye Committee Report that smeared the Cazneaus' reputations, promoted the "new Manifest Destiny of commerce." That year, John L. O'Sullivan died and his obituary mentioned neither the *United States Magazine and Democratic Review* nor Manifest Destiny. Cazneau's words echoed in 1895, but she was forgotten except by her protégé, who claimed that she taught him everything he knew about journalism. Like Cazneau, Henry Watterson, Pulitzer Prize-winning editor of the Louisville *Courier,* was noted for his work in bringing the North and South together and for his short descriptive phrases.[4]

Jane Cazneau's public life contributes to a better understanding of the role professional women played in the mid-nineteenth century. As a journalist, editor, and organizer of the Associated Press, she was accepted by most of her editor colleagues in the male-dominated-world of politics and journalism. Through superior intellect and hard work, she earned their respect. Cazneau was not a "woman's rights woman" who agitated for suffrage, but she publicized the harsh living and working conditions of women at home and abroad. She exposed the oppression of women in factories, in the needle and hat trades, on Indian reservations, in Mexico, and in the Caribbean. She advised women to educate themselves and improve their skills, and urged vocational schooling for Native Americans, freed slaves, and unskilled immigrants. At the end of her public life, she established a vocational school in Jamaica.[5]

Cazneau had an inquisitive nature and an insatiable hunger for knowledge. As an international traveler, she spent hours at sea and in isolation and therefore did not feel subject to the laws of conformity. In addition, her adventure-seeking personality contributed to her advanced thinking. She experienced the Mexican War as she passed through the lines of combat, and to her, war was not romantic or heroic, but blood, death, and destruction—a reality that did not come to many of her generation until the Civil War. She understood that territorial expansion had its limits because of competition from abroad and prejudice at home, but she realized that commercial infiltration and free trade could accomplish the same republican goals.[6]

She published extensively, observed the public workings of government from the House and Senate galleries, attended receptions, and at home and abroad sat in the smoke-filled back rooms and parlors where the inner workings of the governments took place. Her position of power as a journalist allowed her to expose or ignore, exalt or condemn. She admonished partisan politicians to follow the republican ideals of an earlier generation and to keep in mind the common good of the commonwealth.[7]

As a writer, journalist, and editor, Cazneau held positions of legitimate power. Her influence was apparent when editors, political leaders, and foreign dignitaries singled her out for favors or criticism. Her knowledge and analytical skills made her a valuable ally and a formidable foe. She advised presidents, cabinet members, and members of Congress for more than thirty years, but they did not always appreciate or follow her advice. Her most unique contribution to the times, however, was her description of the United States' territorial and commercial expansion as a holy mission of republicanism—one she described as "Manifest Destiny." The phrase justified the nation's need for self-assurance at a time when it was reaching for natural geographical boundaries, penetrating commercial markets abroad, and examining the nature of democracy at home. When she died the United States was no longer an experiment, but a model, which had achieved a national greatness beyond the slavery issue.[8]

Although it appeared that all she attempted seemed to fail, many of the policies Jane Cazneau advocated eventually succeeded. She promoted the need for a steam navy and merchant marine fifty years before Alfred T. Mahan. She wrote about the problems of the working class sixty years before it became a Progressive crusade, advocated agrarian reform fifty years before Populists took up the cause, and assisted republicans in the Western Hemisphere a century before the United States government recognized the needs of the common people of her sister republics.[9]

As the years drifted by, Jane Cazneau's friends, family, and associates who knew the facts of her remarkable career as Cora Montgomery died. Any papers that she had went down with the *Emily B. Souder* or were lost somewhere between Jamaica, New York, or Eagle Pass. Her letters, books, columns, and articles, leave little more than a hint of her intelligence and conversational wit. They give a mere suggestion of her sexuality and explosive temper, a bare glimpse of her courage and spirituality, and a slight trace of her humor seen in the sparkle of violet eyes beneath raven hair and a dark complexion. Some things are known with certainty about Jane Cazneau—she was dedicated to the expansion of liberty and republican government. She had a special place in her heart for the abandoned and neglected, and she had a deep and abiding love for her country and faith in its people and in its future.[10]

Appendix A

❧

Newspaper Articles by Montgomery [Jane Cazneau]

Published	Written	Place	Topic
[Austin] *Texas State Gazette*			
Sept. 7, 1850	Aug. 12, 1850	Eagle Pass	Texas Duty
[New Orleans] *Daily Delta*			
Dec. 12, 1851	November 1851	Eagle Pass	National Highways
Dec. 14, 1851	Nov. 16, 1851	Eagle Pass	Border Policy
[New York] *Herald*			
May 15, 1847			
May 19, 1847			
May 22, 1847			
May 8, 1848			
June 24, 1853			Hostility to Cuba
June 27, 1853			Cuban Annexation
Jan. 9, 1869	Dec. 19, 1868	St. Domingo	Samana Free Port
Aug. 13, 1869	Aug. 2, 1869	St. Domingo	Host Meeting
Dec. 22, 1869	Dec. 21, 1869	Washington	St. Domingo
Dec. 28, 1878			Obituary
[New York] *La Verdad*			
Jan. 9, 1848		New York	Prospectus
Feb. 13, 1848		New York	*Eco de Europa*

PUBLISHED	WRITTEN	PLACE	TOPIC
[New York]			
La Verdad			
Feb. 26, 1848		New York	Cuba's status
Mar. 12, 1848		New York	Hemispheric unity
Mar. 26, 1848		New York	Europe
Apr. 9, 1848		New York	England's designs
Apr. 27, 1848		New York	Annexation of Cuba
May 28, 1848		New York	Cuban rebellion
June 17, 1848		New York	Eur. revolution
[New York] *Sun*			
		Washington	Slidell-Van Ness
Dec. 12, 1845	Dec. 10, 1845	Washington	Benton-Calhoun
Dec. 15, 1845	Dec. 13, 1845	Washington	Buchanan Plan
Dec. 17, 1845	Dec. 15, 1845	Washington	War panic-makers
Dec. 18, 1845	Dec. 16, 1845	Washington	Fort-building
Dec. 19, 1845	Dec. 17, 1845	Washington	Pres. aspirants
Dec. 23, 1845	Dec. 21, 1845	Washington	California
Dec. 24, 1845	Dec. 22, 1845	(unknown)	Texian Navy
Feb. 28, 1846	Feb. 24, 1846	Washington	Slidell
Mar. 2, 1846	Feb. 22, 1846	Washington	Downplays war
Mar. 3, 1846	Feb. 27, 1846	Washington	Yucatan
Mar. 14, 1846	Mar. 12, 1846	Washington	Colquitt
Mar. 15, 1846	Mar. 12, 1846	Washington	Ambitious politicians
Mar. 30, 1846	Mar. 26, 1846	Washington	Anti-standing army
Apr. 3, 1846	Mar. 31, 1846	Washington	Oregon
Apr. 4, 1846	Apr. 1, 1846	Washington	Oregon
Apr. 7, 1846	Apr. 4, 1846	Washington	Polk's war
June 4, 1846	June 2, 1846	Washington	Mail steamers
June 13, 1846	June 11, 1846	Washington	Rio Grande border
June 23, 1846	*1	Washington	Rep. of Rio Grande
July 7, 1846		Washington	Slavery vs. peonage
July 16, 1846		Washington	Rep. of Rio Grande
July 17, 1846		Washington	Peace terms
Aug. 10, 1846		Washington	Wilmot Proviso
Aug. 17, 1846		Washington	War costs
Sept. 1, 1846		Charleston (TS 1)	Steam travel
Dec. 11, 1846	Dec. 1, 1846	Charleston (TS 2)	Charleston
Dec. 25, 1846	Dec. 2, 1846	Charleston (TS 3)	Margaret Fuller
Jan. 8, 1847	Dec. 3, 1846	Havana (TS 5)	Havana
Jan. 12, 1847	Dec. 19, 1846	Havana (TS 6)	Harbor
Jan. 13, 1847	Dec. 22, 1846	Havana (TS 7)	Anti-monarchy
Jan. 14, 1847	December[2]	Regla (TS 8)	Money article

PUBLISHED	WRITTEN	PLACE	TOPIC
[New York] *Sun*			
Jan. 15, 1847	Dec. 23, 1846	Regla (TS 8)	Money article
Jan. 16, 1847	December 1846	Matanzas (TS 4)	Yo Mori Valley
Jan. 16, 1847	December 1846	Matanzas (TS 9)	Cubans
Jan. 25, 1847	Jan. 9, 1847	Havana	Mexico
Jan. 30, 1847	Dec. 26, 1846	Havana (TS 10)	Censorship
Feb. 12, 1847	Jan. 13, 1847	Vera Cruz	Mexico
Feb. 13, 1847	December 1846	Havana (TS 11)	Gunabaco
Feb. 27, 1847	Dec. 30, 1846	Havana (TS 12)	Naval reform
Mar. 13, 1847	Dec. 31, 1846	Havana (TS 13)	Charities
Mar. 25, 1847	Jan. 1, 1847	Havana (TS 14)	Cuban life
Mar. 26, 1847	Jan. 2, 1847	Havana (TS 15)	Superstition
Apr. 15, 1847	Mar. 8, 1847	Mexico City	Fall of government
Apr. 16, 1847	Mar. 23, 1847	Vera Cruz	Mexico
Apr. 19, 1847	Mar. 29, 1847	Vera Cruz	La Playa
Apr. 24, 1847	Mar. 30, 1847	Vera Cruz	Benton bribe
Apr. 27, 1847	Apr. 5, 1847	Vera Cruz	General Scott
May 1, 1847			*Weekly Sun* recap
May 3, 1847	Mar. 28, 1847	Vera Cruz	Yankees
May 6, 1847	Mar. 31, 1847	Vera Cruz	Annexation
May 7, 1847	March 1847	Vera Cruz	Mexicans
May 8, 1847			*Weekly Sun* recap
May 13, 1847	Apr. 16, 1847	Vera Cruz	San Juan
May 13, 1847	Apr. 16, 1847	Vera Cruz	Independence
May 14, 1847	Apr. 12, 1847	Vera Cruz	Troops
May 15, 1847			*Weekly Sun* recap
May 20, 1847	Apr. 13, 1847	Vera Cruz	San Juan
May 21, 1847	Apr. 13, 1847	Near Vera Cruz	Robin Hood
May 21, 1847	Apr. 13, 1847	Vera Cruz	Jalapa
May 22, 1847	Apr. 16, 1847	Vera Cruz	Tariff
May 24, 1847	Apr. 20, 1847	Vera Cruz	Cerro Gordo
May 29, 1847			*Weekly Sun* recap
July 19, 1847	June 20, 1847	*3	No. 1 Cuba
July 22, 1847	June 22, 1847	Havana	No. 2 Cuba
July 23, 1847	June 24, 1847	Havana	Cuba
July 30, 1847	June 29, 1847	Havana	No. 4 Texas Guide
Aug. 9, 1847	June 24, 1847	Havana	No. 3 Slavers
Aug. 20, 1847	July 1, 1847	Havana	No. 5 Censors
Aug. 25, 1847	July 4, 1847	Havana	No. 6 Annexation
Aug. 31, 1847	Aug. 7, 1847	Havana	Junta
Oct. 18, 1847	Sept. 1, 1847	Havana	Cuban slaves
Nov. 25, 1847	Oct. 26, 1847	Havana	Slave trading
Jan. 10, 1848	Jan. 7, 1847	Washington	Candidates

PUBLISHED	WRITTEN	PLACE	TOPIC
[New York] *Sun*			
Mar. 28, 1848		Washington	Revolution
Apr. 15, 1848	Mar. 31, 1848	Washington	Veterans
May 4, 1848	May 1, 1848	Washington	Candidates
Jan. 2, 1879			Obituary
[New York] *Tribune*			
Jan. 14, 1847	Dec. 16, 1847	Cuba	Flogged
Apr. 9, 1847			
Apr. 20, 1847	Mar. 29, 1847	Vera Cruz	Benton bribe
Apr. 30, 1847	Apr. 8, 1847	Vera Cruz	La Playa
May 19, 1847			
May 22, 1847			
May 27, 1847			
July 15, 1850	May. 21, 1850	Eagle Pass	Peonage
Mar. 8, 1850	Feb. 1, 1850	Eagle Pass	Slavery
Oct. 17, 1850	Sept. 12, 1850	Eagle Pass	Peonage
Dec. 11, 1850	Oct. 24, 1850	Eagle Pass	Peonage
Dec. 13, 1850	Nov. 1, 1850	Eagle Pass	Defense
Feb. 1, 1851	Dec. 14, 1850	Eagle Pass	Politics
Feb. 1, 1851	Dec. 14, 1850	Eagle Pass	Manuel Rios
Mar. 6, 1851	Jan. 8, 1851	Eagle Pass	Partisans
Mar. 6, 1851	Jan. 28, 1851	Eagle Pass	Victor Espeta
Mar. 8, 1851	Feb. 1, 1851	Eagle Pass	Morality
Aug. 2, 1851	July 8, 1851	Eagle Pass	Melon sugar
Dec. 9, 1853			Dominicans
Dec. 31, 1878			Obituary

---

[1] Those with no date collected by Susan Knight. See Susan R. Knight, "The Life and Ideas of Cora Montgomery and the Journalism of Expansion" (Senior thesis, University of Texas at Austin, n.d.).

[2] No date given.

[3] No location given.

Appendix B

Table A: Textual Analysis

Grammatik[1]	O'Sullivan[2]	Percent Similar	Anon.[3]	Cazneau[4]	Percent Similar
First 300 words	291		300	301	
Words per sentence	29	78	37	37	100
Short sentences	9	44	4	2	50
Long sentences	2	100	2	6	33
Simple sentences	2	50	3	2	66
Big words	37	80	46	41	89
Sentences per paragraph	5	36	14	10	71
Grade level	13	81	16	16	100
Passive voice	5	36	14	10	71
Complex sentences	68	83	82	77	94
Complex vocabulary	12	55	22	25	88
Grammar flags	22	79	28	27	96
Punctuation	1	25	4	2	50
Noun phrase	0	0	2	2	100
Object-verb	0	0	1	4	25
Run-on	0	0	1	1	100
Prepositional phrases	0	0	3	3	100
Pronoun	1	0	0	0	100
Jargon	1	0	0	0	100

O'Sullivan   41.5

Cazneau   79.6

[1] "Statistics," Grammatik, WordPerfect 6.1 for Windows, very strict.

[2] John L. O'Sullivan, "Seeing a Friend Off in a Packet," *United States Magazine and Democratic Review*, 16 (July-Aug., 1845), 23–24.

[3] Anon., "Annexation," *United States Magazine and Democratic Review*, 16 (July–Aug., 1845), 5–10.

[4] C. Montgomery, "The Presidents of Texas," *United States Magazine and Democratic Review*, 16 (Mar., 1845), 282–91.

Selected Bibliography

❧

PRIMARY MANUSCRIPTS:

George Bancroft. Papers. Massachusetts Historical Society, Boston, Mass.
Bexar Archives. San Antonio, Tex.
Biographies of Leading Texans (Obituaries). Texas State Library. Austin, Tex.
Jeremiah S. Black. Papers. Library of Congress. Washington, D.C.
John Henry Brown. Annals of Travis County. Austin Public Library Archives. Austin, Tex.
James Buchanan. Papers. Historical Society of Pennsylvania. Philadelphia, Pa.
Aaron Burr. Papers of Aaron Burr, 1756–1836. New York Historical Society Library. New York, N.Y.
Connecticut Valley Historical Museum. Wallingford Scrapbook Collection. Springfield, Conn.
Early American Imprints. American Antiquarian Society. Worchester, Mass.
Jane McManus Storm Cazneau. Papers. New York Historical Society Library. New York, N.Y.
Jane McManus Storm Cazneau. Vertical File. Center for American History. University of Texas at Austin. Austin, Tex.
William Leslie Cazneau. Papers. New York Historical Society Archives. New York, N.Y.
Anthony Dey. Galveston Bay and Texas Land Company Records. Western Americana Collection. Beinecke Rare Book and Manuscript Library. Yale University, New Haven, Conn.
Stephen A. Douglas. Papers. Special Collections. University of Chicago Library. Chicago, Ill.

Amos Eaton. Papers. Manuscript Section. New York State Library. Albany, N.Y.

Duff Green. Papers. Library of Congress. Washington, D.C.

Valentín Goméz Farías. Papers. Garcia Collection. Nettie Lee Benson Latin American Collection. University of Texas at Austin. Austin, Tex.

Edward Hanrick. Papers, 1833–1859. Center for American History. University of Texas at Austin. Austin, Tex.

Sam Houston. Letters. Private Collection. Madge Roberts. San Antonio, Tex.

Sam Houston. Papers. Catholic Archives of Texas. Austin, Tex.

John Herndon James. Papers, 1812–1938. The Daughters of the Republic of Texas Library at the Alamo. San Antonio, Tex.

Eliza Jumel. Papers. New York Historical Society Library. New York, N.Y.

Mirabeau Buonaparte Lamar. Papers. Records and Archives Division. Texas State Library. Austin, Tex.

William McManus. William McManus Account Book, 1810–1816. Manuscripts Division. New York State Library. Albany, N.Y.

William Marcy. Papers. Library of Congress. Washington, D.C.

James Morgan. Papers. Galveston and Texas History Center, Rosenberg Library, Galveston, Tex.

Robert Owen. Papers. Co-operative Union, Ltd., Holyoake House. Manchester, England.

James K. Polk, 1845–1848. Public Papers of the Presidents of the United States. Office of the Federal Register. National Archives and Records Services. Washington, D.C.

Thomas J. Rusk. Papers. Center for American History. University of Texas at Austin. Austin, Tex.

William Henry Seward. Papers. Rush Rhees Library of Rare Books and Special Collections. University of Rochester. Rochester, N.Y.

Spanish Collection. Spanish and Mexican Land Grants. Texas General Land Office. Austin, Tex.

Thomas W. Streeter. Collection of Documents on Texas History. Western Americana Collection. Beineke Rare Book and Manuscript Library. Yale University. New Haven, Conn.

Nicholas P. Trist. Papers. Library of Congress, Washington, D.C.

Nicholas P. Trist. Papers. Southern Historical Collection. University of North Carolina at Chapel Hill. Chapel Hill, N.C.

Robert J. Walker. Papers. New York Historical Society Library. New York, N.Y.

Thurlow Weed. Papers. Rush Rhees Library of Rare Books and Special Collections. University of Rochester. Rochester, N.Y.

Emma Willard College. Archives of Troy Female Seminary. Troy, N.Y.

Samuel May Williams. Papers. Galveston and Texas History Center. Rosenberg Library. Galveston, Tex.

UNPUBLISHED DOCUMENTS:

(Jamaica). Saint Catherine's Parish. Deed Records. Jamaica Archives. Spanish Town, Jamaica.

(Republic of Texas). Passenger Lists. Quarterly Returns for the Republic of Texas. Records and Archives Division. Texas State Library, Austin, Tex.

(Republic of Texas). Thomas Johnson. "Report of Commission appointed to check into the conditions of the Records and Archives of the General Land Office." 9th Congress. Republic of Texas, 1844 Tex.

(Texas). Matagorda County. Deed Records. Matagorda County Court House, Bay City, Tex.

(United States). Department of Commerce. Record Group 36, Passenger Lists. Vessels Arriving at New Orleans, 1820–1902, National Archives. Washington, D.C.

(United States). Department of State. Record Group 59. Diplomatic Instructions, Special Missions, Consular Despatches, National Archives and Records Services. Washington, D.C.

(United States). Department of War. Records Office of the Chief Engineer, Letters Received from the Secretary of War, Record Group 77, National Archives, Library of Congress. Washington, D.C.

PUBLISHED DOCUMENTS:

(Jamaica). *Blue Book, Island of Jamaica.* Jamaica: Governor's Printing Office, 1880–1900.

(New Jersey). New Jersey State Senate. *Report of the Committee Appointed to Investigate The Affairs of the Plainfield Bank.* Trenton: Sherman and Harron (Printers to the Legislature), 1847.

(Texas). *Abstract of Title to Antonio Rivas Grant in Maverick County, Texas.* San Antonio: Texas Title Guaranty, 1938.

(Texas). *Constitution of the Proprietors of the Town of Matagorda Including Town Minutes.* Bay City: Matagorda County Historical Survey Society, 1963.

(United States). Congress. *The New American State Papers*. Vol. 7, "Transportation." Wilmington: Scholarly Resources, 1972.

(United States). Congress. Senate. Senate Executive Document 31. Mexican Claims, 1876. 44th Cong., 2nd sess., ser. 1720.

(United States). Congress. Executive Document. No. 51. Report of the Secretary of War, communicating . . . the report of Capt. Thomas J. Cram, November 1856 . . . on the oceanic routes to California. Feb. 16, 1857. 34th Cong., 3rd sess., ser. 1720.

(United States). Congress. Special Reports. No. 53. 31st Cong., 1st sess., vol. 1. Advise to refund duty paid on goods. Claim of William L. Cazneau. Sen. Moses Norris. Feb. 15, 1850, ser. 1720.

(United States). Congress. Senate Executive Document 72. Messages of the U.S. President in Response of the Senate calling for the Correspondence between the Government of the United States and Mexico, respecting a Right of Way across the Isthmus of Tehuantepec. Referred to Committee of Foreign Relations, July 28, 1852. 32nd Cong., 2nd sess. (Letters to and from California and Oregon via Chagres and Panama), ser. 1621

(United States). Congress. Senate Executive Documents 97. Messages of the U.S. President in Response of the Senate calling for the Correspondence between the Government of the United States and Mexico, respecting a Right of Way across the Isthmus of Tehuantepec. Referred to Committee of Foreign Relations, July 28, 1852. 32nd Cong., 2nd sess., ser. 1621.

(United States). Congress. Senate Report No. 234. Report of the U.S. Senate Select Committee on the Memorial of Davis Hatch. June 25, 1870. 41st Cong., 2nd sess., ser. 1409.

(United States). J. D. B. DeBow, ed. *Statistical View of the United States . . . Being a Compendium of the Seventh Census*. Washington D.C.: Beverley Tucker, Senate Printer, 1854.

(United States). Navy Oceanographer Office. Publication no. 9 (1958). Beaufort Scale.

(United States). *The War of the Rebellion: A Compilation of the Official Records of the Union and Confederate Armies*. 70 vols. Washington, D.C.: United States War Department, 1880–1901. Comp. by the late Lt. Robert M. Scott under Secretary of War Alexander Ramsey.

NEWSPAPERS:

(Austin) *Texas State Gazette* (1850)
London *Evening Telegram* (1878)
(London) *Times* (1851)
(Macon) *The Georgia Telegraph* (1845)
Matagorda *Bulletin* (1838)
New Orleans *Delta* (1851)
New York *American Sun* (1847)
New York *Daily Tribune* (1847–1878)
New York *Evening Telegram* (1878–1879)
New York *Herald* (1853, 1869, 1878)
(New York) *La Verdad* (1848–1853)
New York *Morning News* (1845)
New York *Sun* (1843–1878)
New York *Times* (1878)
(New York) *The Workingman's Advocate* (1845)
San Antonio *Daily Herald* (1851–1877)
San Francisco *Chronicle* (1904)
(San Francisco) *Daily Alta Californian* (1866)
Troy *Budget and City Register* (1826–1835)
Troy *Daily Press* (1879, 1891)
Troy *Daily Whig* (1838)
Troy *Sentinel* (1824)
(Washington) *Congressional Globe* (1844)
Washington *Daily States* (1857)

PUBLISHED PRIMARY SOURCES:

Abstract of Original Titles of Record in the General Land Office. Austin: Pemberton Press, 1964.
[Anon.]. "The Late William Ladd: The Apostle of Peace." *United States Magazine and Democratic Review,* 10 (Mar., 1842), 209–23.
Armstrong, James. *Some Facts on the Eleven-League Controversy.* Austin: Southern Intelligencer, 1859.
Bass, Ferris A., Jr., and B. R. Brunson, eds. *Fragile Empires: The Texas Correspondence of Samuel Swartwout and James Morgan, 1836–1856.* Austin: Shoal Creek Publishers, 1978.

Beach, Moses Y. *The Wealth and Biography of the Wealthy Citizens of the City of New York.* 10th ed. New York: Sun Office, 1848.

Benton, Thomas Hart. *Thirty Years' View; or a History of the Working of the American Government for Thirty Years, from 1820 to 1850.* 2 vols. New York: D. Appleton, 1854–1856. Reprint, New York: Greenwood Press, 1968.

Bollaert, William. *William Bollaert's Texas.* Eds. W. Eugene Hollon and Ruth Lapham Butler. Norman: University of Oklahoma Press, 1956.

Brown, Francis H. "Cazneau Quick Step March." New York: J. L Hewitt, 1842.

Brownson, Orestes A. "Political Portraits with Pen and Pencil." *United States Magazine and Democratic Review,* 11 (Nov., 1842), 502–7.

Buchanan, James. *The Works of James Buchanan.* Ed. John Basset Moore. 12 vols. Philadelphia: J. B. Lippincott, 1908–1911. Reprint, New York: Antiquarian Press, 1960.

Calhoun, John C. *The Papers of John C. Calhoun.* 23 vols. Eds. Clyde N. Wilson and W. Edwin Hamphill. Columbia: University of South Carolina Press, 1977.

Cazneau, Jane McManus Storm by year of publication. [Name under which published in brackets.] See Appendix A for signed newspaper articles.

_____. [Anon.] "The Course of Civilization," *United States Magazine and Democratic Review,* 4 (Sept., 1839), 208–17.

_____. _____. "The Great Nation of Futurity." *United States Magazine and Democratic Review,* 6 (Nov., 1839), 426–30.

_____. _____. "Free Trade." *United States Magazine and Democratic Review,* 9 (Oct., 1841), 329–42.

_____. _____. "Hurrah for a War with England." *United States Magazine and Democratic Review,* 9 (Nov., 1841), 411–15.

_____. _____. "The Home League." *United States Magazine and Democratic Review,* 9 (Dec., 1841), 539–53.

_____. _____. "The Gypsies." *United States Magazine and Democratic Review,* 10 (July, 1842), 58–68.

_____. _____. "The Coup-De-Grace." *United States Magazine and Democratic Review,* 11 (Nov., 1842), 542–44.

_____. _____. "Rambles in Yucatan." *United States Magazine and Democratic Review,* 11 (Nov., 1842), 529–39.

_____. _____. "Oregon." *United States Magazine and Democratic Review,* 12 (Apr., 1843), 339–59.

_____. _____. "The Texas Question." *United States Magazine and Democratic Review*, 14 (Apr., 1844), 423–30.

_____. _____. "Lady Hester Stanhope." *United States Magazine and Democratic Review*, 13 (Nov., 1843), 536–41.

_____. _____. "The Legal Wrongs of Women." *United States Magazine and Democratic Review*, 14 (May, 1844), 477–83.

_____. [C. Montgomery]. "The Presidents of Texas." *United States Magazine and Democratic Review*, 16 (Mar., 1845), 282–91.

_____. [Anon.]. "The Mexican Question." *United States Magazine and Democratic Review*, 16 (May, 1845), 419–25.

_____. [Anon.]. "Annexation." *United States Magazine and Democratic Review*, 16 (July-Aug., 1845), 5–10.

_____. [Corinne Montgomery]. *Texas and Her Presidents with a Glance at Her Climate and Agricultural Capabilities.* New York: E. Winchester, New World Press, 1845.

_____. [Anon.]. "Principles, Not Men." *United States Magazine and Democratic Review*, 23 (July, 1848), 3–12.

_____. _____. "The Mosquito King and the British Queen." *United States Magazine and Democratic Review*, 25 (Nov., 1849), 405–16.

_____. _____. "The Mosquito King and the British Queen, concluded." *United States Magazine and Democratic Review*, 25 (Dec., 1849), 529–38.

_____. _____. "The King of Rivers." *United States Magazine and Democratic Review*, 25 (Dec., 1849), 506–15.

_____. [Cora Montgomery]. "The Union of the Seas." *The Merchant's Magazine*, 22 (Feb., 1850), 145–54.

_____. _____. *The King of Rivers.* New York: Charles Wood, 1850.

_____. _____. *The Queen of the Islands.* New York: Charles Wood, 1850.

_____. _____. *The Queen of Islands and the King of Rivers.* New York: Charles Wood, 1850.

_____. [Anon.]. "British Aggression in Central America." *United States Magazine and Democratic Review*, 29 (Jan., 1851), 3–14.

_____. [Joseph W. Fabens]. *The Camel Hunt; a Narrative of Personal Adventure.* Boston: James Munroe and Co., 1851.

_____. [Anon.]. "Narcisso [sic] Lopez and His Companions," *United States Magazine and Democratic Review*, 29 (Oct., 1851), 292–301.

_____. _____. "Soulouque and the Dominicans," *United States Magazine and Democratic Review*, 31 (Feb., 1852), 137–49.

_____. _____. "Soulouque and the Dominicans, contd.," *United States Magazine and Democratic Review*, 31 (Mar., 1852), 234–39.

_____. [Cora Montgomery]. *Eagle Pass; or Life on the Border.* New York: George P. Putnam, 1852.

_____. [Mrs. William Leslie Cazneau]. *Eagle Pass; or Life on the Border.* New York: George P. Putnam, 1852. Reprint, edited and with an introduction by Robert Crawford Cotner, Austin: The Pemberton Press, 1966.

_____. [Cora Montgomery, ed.]. *Our Times: A Monthly Review of Politics, Literature, & Etc.*, 1 (Oct., 1852), 97–192.

[Anon.]. "On the Rumored Occupation of San Domingo by the Emperor of France," *United States Magazine and Democratic Review*, 32 (Feb., 1853), 173–92.

_____. [Joseph W. Fabens]. *A Story of Life on the Isthmus.* New York: George P. Putnam, 1853.

_____. [Cora Montgomery]. *Eagle Pass; or Life on the Border.* 2nd ed. New York: George P. Putnam & Co., 1853; published with [Joseph W. Fabens]. *Life on the Isthmus.* (New York: George P. Putnam & Co., 1853).

_____. [Joseph W. Fabens]. *Facts about Santo Domingo.* New York: George P. Putnam, 1862.

_____. [Anon.]. *In the Tropics: By a Settler in Santo Domingo.* New York: Carleton Publishers, 1863; London: Bentley Publishing, 1863.

_____. [Joseph W. Fabens]. *The Uses of the Camel: Considered with a view to his Introduction into our Western States and Territories. A Paper read before the American Geographical and Statistical Society, March 2, 1865.* New York: Carleton, 1865; Washington: F. Taylor, 1865.

_____. [Anon.]. *The Prince of Kashna: A West Indian Story.* New York: Carleton Publishers, 1866.

_____. [Joseph W. Fabens]. *Resources of Santo Domingo.* New York: Carleton, 1863; Washington: Majors & Knapp, 1869; Washington: F. Taylor, 1871.

_____. _____. *Life in Santo Domingo.* New York: Majors & Knapp, 1873.

_____. [Mrs. William Leslie Cazneau]. *Our Winter Eden: Pen Pictures of the Tropics.* New York: Author's Publishing, 1878.

Cazneau, William L. *To the American Press: The Dominican Negotiations.* Santo Domingo: Impre de Garcia Hermanos, 1870.

Child, David Lee. *The Taking of Naboth's Vineyard, or History of the Texas Conspiracy.* New York: S. W. Benedict, 1845.

Cooper, James Fenimore. *The Last of the Mohicans*, with an introduction by Richard Slotkin. New York: 1826. Reprint, New York: Penguin Classics, 1986.

Davis, Jefferson. *The Papers of Jefferson Davis.* Ed. Lynda Crist. 9 vols. Baton Rouge: Louisiana State University Press, 1985.

Davis, Robert E., ed. *The Diary of William Barret Travis, August 30, 1833 to June 26, 1834.* Waco: Texian Press, 1966.

Douglass, Frederick. *Frederick Douglass Papers.* Series One: Speeches, Debates, and Interviews. Vol. 4: 1864–1880. Eds. John W. Blassingame and John R. McKenny. New Haven: Yale University Press, 1991.

Emory, William H. *Report on the United States and Mexican Boundary Survey, Made under the Direction of the Secretary of the Interior by William H. Emory.* 3 vols. Austin: Texas State Historical Association, 1987.

Franklin, Ethel Mary, ed. "Memoirs of Mrs. Annie P. Harris." *Southwestern Historical Quarterly,* 40 (Jan., 1937), 231–46.

Fuller, Margaret. *The Letters of Margaret Fuller.* Ed. Robert N. Hudspeth. 4 vols. Ithaca: Cornell University Press, 1987.

Garrison, William Lloyd, ed. *Lectures of George Thompson: History of His Connection with the Anti-Slavery Cause in England.* Boston: Isaac Knapp, 1836.

Helm, Mary S. *Scraps from Texas History, 1828–1843.* Austin: By author, 1884.

Holley, Mary Austin. *Texas.* Lexington: J. Clarke and Co., 1836. Reprint, Austin: Texas State Historical Association, 1985.

Houston, Sam. *The Writings of Sam Houston.* Eds. Amelia Williams and Eugene C. Barker. 8 vols. Austin: The University of Texas Press, 1938–1943.

Jenkins, John H., gen. ed. *The Papers of the Texas Revolution, 1835–1836.* 10 vols. Austin: Presidial Press, 1973.

Kenley, John R. *Memories of a Maryland Volunteer.* Philadelphia: J. B. Lippincott & Co., 1873.

Lamar, Mirabeau B. *Papers of Mirabeau Buonaparte Lamar.* Ed. Harriet Smither. 6 vols. Austin: Texas State Library, 1927. Reprint, New York: AMS Press, 1973.

MacDonald, William, comp and ed. *Documentary Source Book of American History, 1606–1926.* New York: Macmillan, 1926.

McLean, Malcolm, comp. and ed. *The Papers Concerning Robertson's Colony in Texas.* 19 vols. Arlington: University of Texas at Arlington, vols. 1–4, 1974–1978. Fort Worth: Texas Christian University Press, vols. 5–19, 1978–1993.

Manning, William R., ed. *Diplomatic Correspondence of the United States Inter-American Affairs, 1831–1860.* 12 vols. Washington, D.C.: Carnegie Endowment, 1932–1939.

Mauro, Garry, comp. *Guide to Spanish and Mexican Land Grants in South Texas.* Austin: Texas General Land Office, 1988.

New Orleans City Directory, 1846–1850. The Historic New Orleans Collection, Kemper and Leila Williams Foundation Research Center, New Orleans, La.

Olmsted, Frederick Law. *Journey Through Texas or a Saddle-Trip on the Southern Frontier.* New York: Dix, Edward, 1857. Reprint, Austin: University of Texas Press, 1978.

O'Sullivan, John L. "Poor Esther, the Jewess—a Reminiscence of Morocco." *United States Magazine and Democratic Review,* 15 (Jan., 1845), 319–20.

_____. "Seeing a Friend off in a Packet." *United States Magazine and Democratic Review,* 16 (July-Aug., 1845), 23–24.

Owen, Robert Dale. "Rights of Women." *The Free Enquirer,* 1 (Dec. 10, 1828), 54–55.

Polk, James K. *James K. Polk. The Diary of a President.* Ed. Allan Nevins. New York: Longman, Green and Co., 1929.

_____. *The Diary of James K. Polk during His Presidency, 1845–1849.* Ed. Milo M. Quaife. 4 vols. Chicago: University of Chicago Press, 1910.

Ratterman, Elleanore Callaghan. "With Walker in Nicaragua. The Reminiscences of Elleanore (Callaghan) Ratterman." *Tennessee Magazine of History,* 7 (1915), 315–30.

Roberts, Madge Thornall. *Star of Destiny: The Private Life of Sam and Margaret Houston.* Denton: University of North Texas Press, 1993.

Ruffin, Edmund. *The Diary of Edmund Ruffin.* Ed. William Kauffman Scarborough. Foreword by Avery Craven. 2 vols. Baton Rouge: Louisiana State University Press, 1972.

Smith, George Winston, and Charles Judah, eds. *Chronicles of the Gringos: The U.S. Army in the Mexican War, 1846–1848.* Albuquerque: University of New Mexico Press, 1968.

Smither, Harriet, ed. "The Diary of Adolphus Sterne," *Southwestern Historical Quarterly,* 38 (July, 1934), 57–155.

Stephens, Ann S. *The Heiress: An Autobiography.* Philadelphia: T. B. Peterson and Brothers, 1859.

_____. "A Woman of Genius." *The Hesperian,* 3 (Aug., 1839), 29–31.

Stowe, Harriet Beecher. *Uncle Tom's Cabin.* Boston: John P. Jewitt, & Co., 1852. Reprint, New York: Harper Classics, 1965.

Viele, Teresa Griffin. *Following the Drum.* Foreword by Sandra L. Myres. Lincoln: University of Nebraska Press, 1984.

Villers, Stuart. *Adventures Amidst the Equilateral Forests and Rivers of South America; Also West Indies and the Wilds of Florida* to which is added "Jamaica Revisited." London: John Murray, 1891.

Walker, Robert J. *Letter of Mr. Walker, of Mississippi Relative to the Annexation of Texas: in Reply to the Call of the People of Carroll County, Kentucky, to Communicate His Views on that Subject.* Washington: Globe Office, 1844.

Walker, Gen. William. *The War in Nicaragua.* Mobile: Goetzel, 1860.

Wallace, Ernest, and David M. Vigness, eds. *Documents of Texas History.* Lubbock: Texas Technological College, 1960.

Watterson, Henry. *"Marse Henry": An Autobiography.* New York: George H. Doran, 1919.

White, Gifford, ed. and with a foreword by James M. Day. *The 1840 Census of the Republic of Texas.* Austin: Pemberton Press, 1966.

Williams, Villamae, ed. *Stephen F. Austin's Register of Families.* Baltimore: Genealogical Publishing, 1984.

Wright, Philip, ed. *Lady Nugent's Journal of Her Residence in Jamaica from 1801 to 1805.* Kingston: Institute of Jamaica, 1966.

SECONDARY SOURCES:

Books:

Abernethy, Thomas Perkins. *The Burr Conspiracy.* Gloucester, Mass.: Peter Smith, 1968.

Abrahams, Peter. *Jamaica, an Island Mosaic.* London: Her Majesty's Stationary Office, 1957.

Adams, F. Q. *New York Panorama.* New York: Random House, 1938.

Addison, C. G. *The Knights Templar History.* New York: Arno Press, 1978.

Awbrey, Betty Dooley, and Claude Dooley. *Why Stop? A Guide to Texas Historical Markers.* 3rd ed. Houston: Gulf Printing, 1992.

Bancroft, Frederick. *The Life of William H. Seward.* 2 vols. New York: Harper & Bros., 1900.

Barker, Eugene C. *The Life of Stephen Fuller Austin, 1793–1836.* Austin: Texas State Historical Association, 1925, 1949.

Barrientos, Francisco. *When Francisco Madero Came to the Border.* Laredo: Border Studies Center, 1995.

Bate, W. N. *General Sidney Sherman.* Waco: Texian Press, 1974.

Bauer, K. Jack. *The Mexican War, 1846–1848.* New York: Macmillan, 1974.

_____. *A Maritime History of the United States.* Columbia: University of South Carolina Press, 1988.

_____. *Zachary Taylor.* Baton Rouge: Louisiana State University Press, 1985.

Baughman, James P. *Charles Morgan and the Development of Southern Transportation.* Nashville: Vanderbilt University Press, 1968.

Bell, Ian. *The Dominican Republic.* Boulder: Western Press, 1981.

Benjamin, Gilbert Giddings. *Germans in Texas.* Philadelphia: Report of German American Annuals, 1909.

Biggers, Don H. *German Pioneers in Texas.* Fredericksburg: Fredericksburg Publishing Co., 1925.

Biographical Directory of U.S. Congress, 1774–1989. Washington, D.C.: Government Printing Office, 1989.

Bleyer, Willard G. *Main Currents in the History of American Journalism.* New York: DeCapo Press, 1973.

Bliven, Rachel, et. al. *A Resourceful People: A Pictorial History of Rensselaer County, New York.* Troy, N.Y.: Rensselaer County Historical Society, 1987.

Bradford, Richard. *The Virginius Affair.* Boulder: Colorado Associated University Press, 1980.

Broderick, Warren F., ed., *Brunswick . . . A Pictorial History.* Brunswick, N.Y.: Brunswick Historical Society, 1978.

Brooks, Elizabeth. *Prominent Women of Texas.* Akron: Werner Publishing, 1896.

Brown, Charles H. *Agents of Manifest Destiny: The Lives and Times of the Filibusters.* Chapel Hill: University of North Carolina Press, 1980.

Brown, John Henry. *Indian Wars and Pioneers of Texas.* Austin: L. E. Daniel, 1880. Reprint, Greenville: Southern Historical Press, 1978.

Brunson, B. R. *The Adventures of Samuel Swartwout in the Age of Jefferson and Jackson.* Lewistown, Maine: Edwin Mellon University Press, 1989.

Cafruny, Alan W. *Ruling the Waves: The Political Economy of International Shipping.* Berkeley: University of California Press, 1987.

Caiger, Stephen L. *British Honduras Past and Present.* London: George Allen, 1951.

Caldwell, Robert Granville. *The López Expeditions to Cuba, 1848–1851.* Princeton: Princeton University Press, 1915.

Callahan, James Morton. *Cuba and International Relations: A Historical Study in American Diplomacy.* Baltimore: John Hopkins Press, 1899.

Campbell, Randolph B. *An Empire for Slavery: The Peculiar Institution in Texas, 1821–1865.* Baton Rouge: Louisiana State University Press, 1989.

_____. *Sam Houston and the American Southwest*. New York: HarperCollins, 1993.

Cantrell, Gregg. *Stephen F. Austin: Empresario of Texas*. New Haven: Yale University Press, 1999.

Carmen, Carl. L. *The Hudson*. New York: Farrar & Rinehart, 1939.

Chaffin, Tom. *Fatal Glory: Narciso López and the First Clandestine U.S. War against Cuba*. Charlottesville: University Press of Virginia, 1996.

Champagne, Duane, ed. *Chronology of North American History*. Detroit: Gale Research, 1994.

Chapman, Charles E. *A History of the Cuban Republic*. New York: Macmillan, 1927.

Chipman, Donald E. *Spanish Texas, 1519–1821*. Austin: University of Texas Press, 1992.

Cole, Donald B. *Martin Van Buren and the American Political System*. Princeton: Princeton University Press, 1984.

Connor, Seymour V. *Adventure in Glory*. Austin: Steck-Vaughn, 1965.

Connor, Seymour V., and Odie B. Faulk, eds. and comps. *North America Divided: The Mexican War, 1846–1848*. New York: Oxford University Press, 1971.

Coons, William Solyman, comp. *Koon and Coons Families of Eastern New York*. Rutland, Vt.: Tuttle, 1937.

Crouthamel, James L. *James Watson Webb: A Biography*. Middleton, Conn.: Weslayan University Press, 1969.

Cundall, Frank. *Historic Jamaica*. London: Institute of Jamaica, 1915.

Davis, H. P. *Black Democracy*. New York: Biblo & Tannen, 1967.

Davis, Mary B., ed. *Native America in the 20th Century*. New York: Garland Publishing Co., 1994.

Davis, William C. *Three Roads to the Alamo: The Lives and Fortunes of David Crockett, James Bowie, and William Barret Travis*. New York: HarperCollins, 1998.

Dicken-Garcia, Hazel. *Journalistic Standards in Nineteenth-Century America*. Madison: University of Wisconsin Press, 1989.

Dillon, Merton. L. *Benjamin Lundy and the Struggle for Negro Freedom*. Urbana: University of Illinois Press, 1966.

Downes, Robert B. and Jane B. Downes. *Journalists of the United States*. Jefferson, N.C: McFarland Publishing, 1991.

Dozier, Craig L. *Nicaragua's Mosquito Shore: The Years of British and American Presence*. University: University of Alabama Press, 1985.

Duncan, William Cary. *The Amazing Madame Jumel.* New York: Frederick A. Stokes, 1935.

Dunn, Shirley W. *The Mohicans and Their Land, 1609–1730.* Fleischmanns, N.Y.: Purple Mountain Press, 1994.

Dyer, Brained. *Zachary Taylor.* New York: Barnes and Noble, 1946.

Elliot, Charles Winslow. *Winfield Scott: The Soldier and the Man.* New York: Macmillan, 1937.

Engle, Eloise, and Arnold S. Lott. *America's Maritime Heritage.* Annapolis: United States Naval Institute, 1975.

Englefield, Dermot, Janet Seaton, and Isabel White, comps. *Facts about the British Prime Ministers.* New York: H. H. Wilson, 1995.

Fagg, John Edwin. *Cuba, Haiti, and the Dominican Republic.* Englewood Cliffs, N.J.: Prentice-Hall, 1965.

Faulk, Odie. *Too Far North . . . Too Far South.* Los Angeles: Westernlore Press, 1967.

Fayle, C. Ernest. *A Short History of the World's Shipping Industry.* London: George Allen, 1933.

Flick, Alexander C., ed. *History of the State of New York.* 10 vols. New York: Columbia University Press, 1933.

Foner, Eric. *Free Soil, Free Labor, Free Men: The Ideology of the Republican Party before the Civil War.* New York: Oxford University Press, 1970.

Foner, Philip S. *Business and Slavery: The New York Merchants and the Irrepressible Conflict.* Chapel Hill: University of North Carolina Press, 1941.

Freehling, William H. *The Reintegration of American History: Slavery and the Civil War.* New York: Oxford University Press, 1994.

Frederickson, George M. *The Black Image in the White Mind: The Debate on Afro-American Character and Destiny, 1817–1914.* Middleton, Conn.: Wesleyan University Press, 1971.

Fried, Albert. *John Brown's Journey: Notes and Reflections on His America and Mine.* Garden City, N.Y.: Anchor Press, 1978.

Fuller, John D. P. *The Movement for the Acquisition of All Mexico, 1846–1848.* Baltimore: Johns Hopkins Press, 1936.

Gallardo, Alexander. *Britain and the First Carlist War, 1833–1839.* Norwood, Pa.: Norwood, 1978.

Gallay, Allan, ed. *Colonial Wars of North America, 1512–1763.* New York: Garland Publishing, 1996.

Gara, Larry. *The Presidency of Franklin Pierce.* Lawrence: University Press of Kansas, 1991.

Garber, Paul Neff. *The Gadsden Treaty*. Philadelphia: University of Pennsylvania Press, 1924.

Goetzmann, William H. *Army Exploration in the American West, 1803–1863*. New Haven: Yale University Press, 1959. Reprint, Austin: Texas State Historical Association, 1991.

_____. *When the Eagle Screamed: The Romantic Horizon in American Diplomacy, 1800–1860*. New York: John Wiley & Sons, 1966.

Goldsmith, Barbara. *Other Powers: The Age of Suffrage, Spiritualism, and the Scandalous Victoria Woodhull*. New York: Alfred A. Knopf, 1998.

Graebner, Norman A. *Empire on the Pacific: A Study in American Continental Expansion*. New York: Ronald Press, 1955.

Graham, Philip. *The Life and Poems of Mirabeau B. Lamar*. Chapel Hill: University of North Carolina Press, 1938.

Grayson, Benson Lee. *The Unknown President: The Administration of President Millard Fillmore*. Washington: University Press of America, 1981.

Greer, Germaine. *The Change: Women, Aging and the Menopause*. New York: Fawcett Books, 1991.

Guthrie, Keith. *Texas Forgotten Ports*. 3 vols. Austin: Eakin Press, 1995.

Hagan, Kenneth. *The People's Navy: The Making of American Sea Power*. New York: Free Press, 1991.

Haggerty, Richard A., ed. *Dominican Republic and Haiti*. Washington, D.C.: Library of Congress, 1989.

Hamilton, Holman. *Zachary Taylor*. New York: Bobbs-Merrill, 1951.

Hammell, A. B. J. *The Empresario Don Martin De Leon*. Waco: Texian Press, 1973.

Hansen, William P. and Fred L. Israel, eds. *The American Indian and the United States: A Documentary History*. 4 vols. New York: Random House, 1973.

Hasbrouck, Kenneth E., comp. *The Hasbrouck Family in America, with European Background*. 3 vols. New Paltz, N.Y.: Hasbrouck Family Association, 1961, 1987.

Hassard, John R. G. *Life of the Most Reverend John Hughes, D.D.* New York: D. Appleton, 1866.

Hatcher, Mattie Austin. *The Opening of Texas to Foreign Settlement, 1801–1821*. Austin: University of Texas Press, 1927. Reprint, Philadelphia: Porcupine Press, 1976.

Hawley, Emily C. *Annals of Brookfield County Connecticut*. Brookfield: Hawley, 1929.

Henson, Margaret Swett and Deolece Parmelee. *The Cartwrights of San Augustine: Three Generations of Agrarian Entrepreneurs in Nineteenth-Century Texas.* Austin: Texas State Historical Association, 1993.

Henson, Margaret Swett. *Juan Davis Bradburn: A Reappraisal of the Mexican Commander of Anahuac.* College Station: Texas A&M University Press, 1982.

_____. *Lorenzo de Zavala: The Pragmatic Idealist.* Fort Worth: Texas Christian University Press, 1996.

_____. *Samuel May Williams: Early Texas Entrepreneur.* College Station: Texas A&M University Press, 1976.

Herr, Pamela. *Jessie Benton Frémont: A Biography.* New York: Franklin Watts, 1987.

Herrick, Walter R., Jr. *The American Naval Revolution.* Baton Rouge: Louisiana State University Press, 1966.

Heyl, Erik. *Early American Steamers.* 3 vols. Buffalo, N.Y.: By author, 1953.

Hillman, Jos. *The History of Methodism in Troy, N.Y.* Troy, N.Y.: n.p., 1888.

Hodge, Frederick Webb, ed. *Handbook of American Indians North of Mexico.* Bureau of American Ethnology Bulletin 30. 2 vols. Washington, D.C.: Smithsonian, 1907–1910, 1912. Reprint, Totowa, N.Y.: Rowman & Littlefield, 1975.

Holt, Michael F. *Political Parties and American Political Development: From the Age of Jackson to the Age of Lincoln.* Baton Rouge: Louisiana State University Press, 1992.

Holt, William S. *Treaties Defeated by the Senate.* Baltimore: John Hopkins Press, 1933.

Horgan, Paul. *The Great River: The Rio Grande in North American History.* 2 vols. New York: Rinehart, 1954.

Hunt, Alfred N. *Haiti's Influence on Antebellum America: Slumbering Volcano in the Caribbean.* Baton Rouge: Louisiana State University Press, 1988.

James, Edward T., ed. *Notable American Women, 1607–1950.* 3 vols. Cambridge, Mass.: The Belknap Press of Harvard University Press, 1971.

Jenkins, John H. and Kenneth Kesselus. *Edward Burleson: Texas Frontier Leader.* Austin: Jenkins Press, 1990.

Jeter, Lorraine Bruce. *Matagorda: Early History.* Baltimore: Gateway Press, 1974.

Johannsen, Robert W. *Stephen A. Douglas.* New York: Oxford University Press, 1973.

_____. *To the Halls of the Montezumas: The Mexican War in the American Imagination.* New York: Oxford University Press, 1985.

Johnson, Allen, and Dumas Malone, eds. *Dictionary of American Biography.* 10 vols. plus supplements. New York: Charles Scribner's Sons, 1964.

Johnson, Willis Fletcher. *The History of Cuba.* 5 vols. New York: B. F. Buck, 1920.

Katz, Frederick. *The Secret War in Mexico.* Chicago: University of Chicago Press, 1981.

Kelley, Pat. *River of Lost Dreams: Navigation on the Rio Grande.* Lincoln: University of Nebraska Press, 1984.

Kemble, John H. *The Panama Route, 1848–1869.* New York: DeCapo Press, 1972.

Kenedy, Paul M. *The Rise and Fall of the British Naval Mastery.* New York: Charles Scribner's Sons, 1976.

Kingston, Mike, ed. *Texas Almanac, 1986–1987.* Dallas: Dallas *Morning News,* 1986–1987.

Knight, Melvin K. *The Americans in Santo Domingo.* New York: Vanguard Press, 1928.

Kryzanek, Michael J., and Howard J. Wiarda. *The Politics of External Influence in the Dominican Republic.* New York: Pragere, 1988.

Lack, Paul D. *The Texas Revolutionary Experience.* College Station: Texas A&M University Press, 1992.

Lavender, David. *The Great West.* New York: Houghton Mifflin, 1965. Reprint, New York: American Heritage, 1987.

LePoer, Barbara A. *A Concise Dictionary of Indian Tribes of North America,* ed. Kendall T. LePoer. Algonac, Mich.: Reference Publications, 1979.

Lester, Richard I. *Confederate Finance and Purchasing in Great Britain.* Charlottesville, University Press of Virginia, 1975.

Levernier, James, and Hennig Cohen, eds. *The Indians and Their Captives.* Westport, Conn.: Greenwood Press, 1977.

Livezey, *Mahan on Sea Power.* Norman: University of Oklahoma Press, 1954.

Lombardi, Cathryn and John V. *Latin American History: A Teaching Atlas.* Madison: University of Wisconsin Press, 1983.

Long, David F. *Nothing Too Daring: A Biography of Commodore David Porter, 1780–1843.* Annapolis: U.S. Naval Institute, 1970.

McCormac, Eugene Irving. *James K. Polk: A Political Biography.* Berkeley: University of California Press, 1922.

McDonald, Archie P. *Travis.* Austin: Jenkins Publishing, 1976.

McFeely, William S. *Grant: A Biography.* New York: W. W. Norton, 1981.

McKerns, Joseph P., ed. *Biographical Dictionary of American Journalism.* New York: Greenwood Press, 1989.

McManus, Edgar J. *A History of Negro Slavery in New York.* Syracuse: Syracuse University Press, 1966.

McPherson, James M. *The Struggle for Equality: Abolitionists and the Negro in the Civil War and Reconstruction.* Princeton: Princeton University Press, 1964.

Macoy, Robert, comp. *Dictionary of Freemasonry.* New York: Masonic Publishing Co., 1895. Reprint, New York: Bell Publishing, 1989.

Magner, James A. *Men of Mexico.* Freeport, N.Y.: Books for Library Press, 1968.

Mainiero, Lina, ed. *American Women Writers.* 4 vols. New York: Frederick Ungar Publishing, 1979.

Malsch, Brownson. *Indianola, the Mother of Western Texas.* Austin: Statesmen Press, 1988.

Marcosson, Isaac F. *"Marse Henry": A Biography of Henry Watterson.* New York: Dodd, Mead, & Co., 1951.

Mardock, Robert Winston. *The Reformers and the American Indian.* Columbia: University of Missouri Press, 1971.

Matagorda County Historical Commission. *Historic Matagorda County.* 3 vols. Houston: D. Armstrong Publishing, 1986.

Matthews, Jean V. *Woman's Struggle for Equality: The First Phase, 1828–1876.* Chicago: Ivan R. Dee, 1997.

May, Robert E. "'Plenipotentiary in Petticoats': Jane M. Cazneau and American Foreign Policy in the Mid-Nineteenth Century." In Edward L. Crapol, ed. *Women and American Foreign Policy.* 2nd ed. Wilmington: Scholarly Resources, Inc., 1992.

_____. *The Southern Dream of a Caribbean Empire, 1854–1861.* Baton Rouge: Louisiana State University Press, 1973.

Meditz, Sandra W., ed. *Islands of the Commonwealth Caribbean: A Regional History.* Washington, D.C.: Library of Congress, 1989.

Meltzer, Milton. *Bound for the Rio Grande: The American Struggle, 1845–1850.* New York: Alfred A. Knopf, 1974.

Merk, Frederick. *Manifest Destiny and Mission in American History: A Reinterpretation.* New York: Vintage Press, 1963.

_____. *Slavery and the Annexation of Texas.* New York: Alfred A. Knopf, 1972.

Miller, Floyd J. *The Search for a Black Nationality: Black Emigration and Colonization, 1787–1863.* Urbana: University of Chicago Press, 1975.

Miller, Perry. *The Raven and the Whale: The War of Words and Wits in the Era of Poe and Melville.* New York: Harcourt, Brace, and Company, 1956.

Miller, Ray. *Texas Forts: A History and Guide.* Houston: Cordovan Press, 1985.

Mott, Frank Luther. *A History of American Magazines, 1741–1850.* 5 vols. Cambridge, Mass.: Harvard University Press, 1930–1968.

Mowat, R. B. *The Diplomatic Relations of Great Britain and the United States.* London: Edward Arnold Press, 1925.

Muir, Andrew Forest. *Texas in 1837.* Austin: University of Texas Press, 1958.

Mulroy. Kevin. *Freedom on the Border: The Seminole Maroons in Florida, the Indian Territory, Coahuila, and Texas.* Lubbock: Texas Tech University Press, 1993.

Myers, Gustavus. *The History of Tammany Hall.* New York: Born & Leveright, 1917.

Myerson, Joel, gen. ed. *Dictionary of Literary Biography.* 183 vols. Detroit: Gale Research, 1979.

National Cyclopedia of American Biography. 10 vols. New York: James T. White & Co., 1897.

Naylor, Robert A. *Penny Ante Imperialism: The Mosquito Shore and the Bay of Honduras, 1600–1914: A Case Study in British Informal Empire.* Rutherford, N.J.: Fairleigh Dickinson University Press, 1989.

Nelson, Anna Kasten. "President Polk and the War." In Robert E. Burke and Frank Freidel, eds. *Secret Agents: President Polk and the Search for Peace with Mexico.* New York: Garland Publishing, 1988.

———. "Moses Y. Beach: Special Agent." In Robert E. Burke and Frank Freidel, eds. *Secret Agents: President Polk and the Search for Peace with Mexico.* New York: Garland Publishing, 1988.

Nelson, William Javier. *Almost a Territory: America's Attempt to Annex the Dominican Republic.* Newark: University of Delaware Press, 1990.

Nevins, Allan. *The American Press Opinion: Washington to Coolidge: A Documentary Record of Editorial Leadership and Criticism, 1785–1927.* 2 vols. Boston: M. A. Heath, 1928. Reprint, Port Washington, N.Y.: Kennikat Press, 1969.

———. *Hamilton Fish: The Inner History of the Grant Administration.* 2 vols. New York: Frederick Ungar Publishing, 1936.

———. *Ordeal of the Union.* Vol. I. *Fruits of Manifest Destiny, 1847–1852.* New York: Charles Scribner's Sons, 1947.

_____. *Ordeal of the Union.* Vol. II. *A House Dividing, 1852–1857.* New York: Charles Scribner's Sons, 1947.

Nichols, Roy Franklin. *Franklin Pierce: Young Hickory of the Granite Hills.* 2nd ed. Philadelphia: University of Pennsylvania Press, 1969.

O'Brien, Frank M. *The Story of the Sun.* New York: D. Appleton, 1928.

Olliff, Donathan C. *Reforma Mexico and the United States: A Search for Alternatives to Annexation, 1854–1861.* University: University of Alabama Press, 1981.

One Hundred Influential Books Printed before 1900. New York: Grolier, 1947.

Paneth, Donald, ed. and comp. *The Encyclopedia of Journalism.* New York: Facts on File, 1983.

Paolino, Ernest N. *The Foundations of the American Empire: William Henry Seward and U.S. Foreign Policy.* Ithaca: Cornell University Press, 1973.

Payne, George Henry. *History of Journalism in the United States.* New York: D. Appleton and Co., 1920. Reprint, Westport, Conn.: Greenwood Press, 1970.

Peterson, Merrill D. *The Great Triumvirate: Webster, Clay, and Calhoun.* New York: Oxford University Press, 1987.

Pratt, Julius W. *A History of United States Foreign Policy.* New York: Prentice Hill, 1955.

Rauch, Basil. *American Interest in Cuba: 1848–1855.* New York: Columbia University Press, 1948.

Reichstein, Andreas V. *Rise of the Lone Star: The Making of Texas.* College Station: Texas A&M University Press, 1989.

Rezneck, Samuel. *Profiles out of the Past of Troy, New York, Since 1789.* Troy, N.Y.: n.p., 1970.

Rippy, J. Fred. *The Caribbean Danger Zone.* New York: G. P. Putnam's Sons, 1940.

_____. *Rivalry of the United States and Great Britain over Latin America, 1808–1830.* Baltimore: John Hopkins Press, 1929.

_____. *The United States and Mexico.* New York: Alfred A. Knopf, 1926.

Robertson, William Spence. *Hispanic-American Relations with the United States.* New York: Oxford University Press, 1923.

Rodman, Seldon. *Quisqueya: A History of the Dominican Republic.* Seattle: University of Washington Press, 1964.

Rodriguez, Mario. *A Palmerston Diplomat in Central America.* Tucson: University of Arizona Press, 1964.

Rossi, Alice S. *The Feminist Papers.* Boston: Northeastern University Press, 1973.

Santoni, Pedro. *Mexicans at Arms: Puro Federalists and the Politics of War, 1845–1848.* Fort Worth: Texas Christian University Press, 1996.

Schoenhals, Kai. *Dominican Republic.* World Bibliography Series. London: Oxford University Press, 1990.

Schwartz, Rosalie. *Across the Rio to Freedom: U.S. Negroes in Mexico.* El Paso: Texas Western University Press, 1975.

Scisco, Louis Dow. *Political Nativism in New York State.* New York: Columbia University Press, 1901.

Scott, Anne Firor. *Women in American Life.* New York: Houghton Mifflin, 1970.

Schroeder, John H. *Shaping a Maritime Empire: The Commercial and Diplomatic Role of the American Navy, 1829–1861.* Westport, Conn.: Greenwood Press, 1985.

Scroggs, William O. *Filibusters and Financiers: The Story of William Walker and His Associates.* New York: Macmillan, 1916.

Seigel, Stanley. *A Political History of the Texas Republic, 1836–1845.* Austin: University of Texas Press, 1956.

Sherlock, Philip. *This is Jamaica.* London: Hodden & Stoughton, 1968.

Sheridan, Doris. *The McManus Family Revised.* New York: By author, 1993.

Slaudenraus, P. J. *The African Colonization Movement, 1816–1865.* New York: Columbia University Press, 1961.

Smith, Justin H. *The War with Mexico.* 1919. Reprint, Gloucester, Mass.: Peter Smith, 1963.

Speer, William S., comp. *Encyclopedia of the New West.* Texas vol. Marshall, Tex.: The United States Biographical Publishing Co., 1881.

Spellman, Paul N. *Forgotten Texas Leader: Hugh McLeod and the Texan Santa Fe Expedition.* College Station: Texas A&M University Press, 1999.

Stephens, A. Ray, and William M. Holmes. *Historical Atlas of Texas.* Norman: University of Oklahoma Press, 1989.

Stern, Madeline B. *Books and Book People in Nineteenth-Century America.* New York: R. R. Boucher Press, 1978.

———. *We the Women: Career Firsts of Nineteenth-Century America.* New York: Artemis Press, 1962.

Stevens, John D. *Sensationalism and the New York Press.* New York: Columbia University Press, 1991.

Stoutenburgh, John L., Jr. *Dictionary of the American Indian.* New York: Philosophical Library, 1960.

Streeter, Thomas W., comp. and ed. *Bibliography of Texas, 1795–1845, Index.* 5 vols. Cambridge, Mass.: Harvard University Press, 1955–1960.

Stuart, Graham H. *Latin America and the United States.* New York: D. Appleton-Century, 1938.

Sturtevant, William C., ed. *Handbook of North American Indians.* 20 vols. Washington: Smithsonian Institution, 1978.

Summer, Jane, comp. *Some Early Travis County, Texas Records.* Easly, S.C.: Southern Historical Press, 1979.

Swanton, John R. *The Indian Tribes of North America.* Bureau of American Ethnology Bulletin 145. Washington, D.C.: Smithsonian, 1952.

Swift, Roy L., and Leavett Corning. *Three Roads to Chihuahua: The Great Wagon Roads of the Southwest.* Austin: Eakin Press, 1988.

Tansill, Charles Callan. *The United States and Santo Domingo, 1798–1873.* Baltimore: John Hopkins Press, 1938.

Taylor, George Rogers. *The Transportation Revolution, 1815–1860.* Armont, N.Y.: M. E. Sharpe, 1951.

Taylor, John M. *William Henry Seward: Lincoln's Right Hand.* New York: HarperCollins, 1991.

Tebbel, John. *A History of Book Publishing in the United States.* New York: R. R. Bowker, 1972.

Tebbel, John, and Sarah Watts. *The Press and the Presidency.* New York: Oxford University Press, 1985.

Tijerina, Andrés. *Tejanos and Texas under the Mexican Flag, 1821–1836.* College Station: Texas A&M University Press, 1994.

Tinling, Marion, comp. *Women Remembered: A Guide to Landmarks of Women's History in the United States.* New York: Greenwood Press, 1986.

Tischendorf, Alfred. *Great Britain and Mexico in the Era of Porforio Diaz.* Durham, N.C.: Duke University Press, 1961.

Todd, Charles Burr. *General History of the Burr Family: With a Genealogical Record from 1193 to 1891.* 2nd ed. New York: By author, 1891.

Trelease, Allen W. *Indian Affairs in Colonial New York: The Seventeenth Century.* Ithaca: Cornell University Press, 1960.

Tyler, Ron, Douglas E. Barnett, Roy R. Barkley, Penelope C. Anderson, and Mark F. Odintz, eds. *The New Handbook of Texas.* 6 vols. Austin: Texas State Historical Association, 1996.

Van Alstyne, Richard W. *The Rising American Empire.* New York: Oxford University Press, 1960.

Van Deusen, Glyndon G. *The Jacksonian Era, 1828–1848.* New York: Harper & Row, 1959.

_____. *William Henry Seward.* New York: Oxford University Press, 1967.

Vidal, Gore. *Burr: A Novel.* New York: Random House, 1973.

VonMehren, Joan. *Minerva and the Muse: A Life of Margaret Fuller.* Amherst: University of Massachusetts Press, 1994.

Waldman, Carl. *Atlas of the North American Indian.* New York: Facts on File, 1985.

Wall, Joseph Fraizer. *Henry Watterson: Reconstructed Rebel.* New York: Oxford University Press, 1956.

Wallace, Edward S. *Destiny and Glory.* New York: Coward-McCann, 1957.

_____. *General William Jennings Worth: Monterrey's Forgotten Hero.* Dallas: Southern Methodist University Press, 1953.

Wallace, Patricia Ward. *Waco: Texas Crossroads.* Woodland Hills, Calif.: Windsor, 1983.

Walker, Mack. *Germany and the Emigration, 1816–1885.* Cambridge, Mass.: Harvard University Press, 1964.

Weddle, Robert S. *San Juan Bautista: Gateway to Spanish Texas.* Austin: University of Texas Press, 1968.

Weise, Arthur James. *Troy's One Hundred Years, 1789–1889.* Troy, N.Y.: W. H. Young, 1891.

Welles, Sumner. *Naboth's Vineyard: The Dominican Republic, 1844–1924.* 2 vols. New York: Payson & Clarke, 1928.

Werner, M. R. *Tammany Hall.* New York: Greenwood Press, 1968.

White, Gifford, comp. *First Settlers of Matagorda County, Texas.* Austin: Gifford White, 1986.

Wilentz, Sean. "Society, Politics, and the Market Revolution, 1815–1848." In Eric Foner, ed. *The New American History.* Philadelphia: Temple University Press, 1990.

Williams, Elgin. *The Animating Pursuits of Speculation: Land Traffic in the Annexation of Texas.* New York: Columbia University Press, 1949.

Wright, Lyle H. *American Fiction, 1774–1850, a Contribution toward a Bibliography.* 2nd rev. ed. San Marino, Calif.: Huntington Library, 1969.

Wright, William C. *The Secession Movement in the Middle Atlantic States.* Rutherford, N.J.: Farleigh Dickinson University Press, 1973.

JOURNAL ARTICLES:

Allen, Margaret V. "The Political and Social Criticism of Margaret Fuller." *South Atlantic Quarterly,* 72, no. 4 (1973), 560–72.

Angel, William D. "Vantage on the Bay: Galveston and the Railroads." *East Texas Historical Journal*, 22 (Spring, 1984), 3–18.

Barker, Eugene C. "Land Speculators as a Cause of the Texas Revolution." *Southwestern Historical Quarterly*, 10 (July, 1906), 77–95.

Beach, M. S. "Origin of the Treaty of Guadalupe Hidalgo." *Scribner's Monthly Century Magazine*, 17 (Nov., 1878), 299–300.

_____. "A Secret Mission to Mexico." *Scribner's Monthly Century Magazine*, 18 (May, 1879), 136–40.

Brent, Robert H. "Nicholas P. Trist and the Treaty of Guadalupe Hidalgo." *Southwestern Historical Quarterly*, 57 (Jan., 1954), 454–74.

Brister, Louis E. "Johann Von Racknitz: German Empresario and Soldier of Fortune in Texas and Mexico, 1832–1848." *Southwestern Historical Quarterly*, 99 (July, 1995), 49–80.

Costeloe, Michael P. "The Mexican Church and the Rebellion of the Polkos." *Hispanic American Historical Review*, 46 (May, 1966), 170–78.

Cox, James A. "Ordeal by Water." *True: The Man's Magazine*, 22 (July, 1959), 37–38, 66–72.

Curti, Merle E. "Young America." *American Historical Review*, 32 (July, 1927), 34–55.

Davenport, Harbert. "General Jose Maria Jesus Carabajal [sic]." *Southwestern Historical Quarterly*, 55 (Apr., 1952), 475–83.

"Descendants of Paix Cazneau." *New England Historical and Genealogical Register*, 142 (Apr., 1988), 127–48.

Dolch, O. L., Jr. "The Last Frontier." *Naylor's Epic Century Magazine*, 4 (Feb., 1938), 22–23.

Field, William T. "Fort Duncan and Old Eagle Pass." *Texas Military History*, 6 (Summer, 1967), 160–71.

Graf, LeRoy P. "Colonizing Projects in Texas South of the Nueces, 1820–1845." *Southwestern Historical Quarterly*, 50 (Apr., 1947), 431–47.

Greaser, Galen D. and Jesús F. de la Teja, "Quieting Title to Spanish and Mexican Land Grants in the Trans–Nueces: The Bourland and Miller Commission, 1850–1852," *Southwestern Historical Quarterly*, 95 (Apr., 1992), 445–64.

Hamilton, Holman. "Texas Bonds and Northern Profits: A Study in Compromise, Investment, and Lobby Influence." *Mississippi Valley Historical Review*, 43 (Mar., 1957), 579–94.

Hardin, Stephen L. "'A Hard Lot': Texas Women in the Runaway Scrape." *East Texas Historical Journal,* 29 (Spring, 1991), 41–45.

Hooks, Michael Q. and Jesús F. de la Teja. "The Texas General Land Office: Preserving East Texas Land Records." *East Texas Historical Journal* (Spring, 1989), 55–62.

Hudson, Linda. "Antonio Martinez, the Problems of Administering Texas during the Last Years of Spanish Control." *Touchstone,* 6 (1987), 4–16.

Kerrigan, William T. "Race, Expansion, and Slavery in Eagle Pass, Texas, 1852." *Southwestern Historical Quarterly,* 101 (Jan., 1998), 275–301.

Kinkade, Patricia. "Jane McManus Storms Cazneau: Journalist and Expansionist." In *Essays in History: The E. C. Barksdale Student Lectures,* 10 (1987–1988), 7–34.

Levermore, C. H. "Rise of Metropolitan Journalism." *American Historical Review,* 6 (Apr., 1901), 446–65.

Lofton, Williston. "Northern Labor and the Negro during the Civil War." *Journal of Negro History,* 34 (July, 1949), 251–73.

Mathis, Robert Neil. "Gazaway Bugg Lamar: A Southern Businessman and Confidant in New York City." *New York History,* 56 (July, 1975), 298–313.

McArthur, Judith. "Myth, Reality, and Anomaly: The Complex World of Rebecca Hagerty." *East Texas Historical Journal,* 24 (Fall, 1986), 18–32.

May, Robert E. "Lobbyists for Commercial Empire: Jane Cazneau, William Cazneau, and U.S. Caribbean Policy, 1846–1878." *Pacific Historical Review,* 48 (1979), 383–90.

Merk, Frederick. "A Safety Valve Thesis and Texas Annexation." *Mississippi Valley Historical Review,* 49 (Dec., 1964), 413–36.

Morrison, Michael A. "Martin Van Buren, the Democracy, and the Partisan Politics of Texas Annexation." *Journal of Southern History,* 61 (Nov., 1995), 695–724.

Narrett. David E. "A Choice of Destiny." *Southwestern Historical Quarterly,* 100 (Jan., 1997), 271–302.

Nelson, Anna Kasten. "Jane Storms Cazneau: Disciple of Manifest Destiny." *Prologue: The Journal of the National Archives,* 17 (Spring, 1986), 25–40.

_____. "Mission to Mexico—Moses Y. Beach, Secret Agent." *New York Historical Society Quarterly,* 59 (July, 1975), 227–45.

Pessen, Edward. "Moses Beach Revisited: A Critical Examination of His Wealthy Citizens Pamphlets." *Journal of American History,* 58 (Sept., 1971), 415–26.

Pitre, Merline. "Frederick Douglass and the Annexation of Santo Domingo." *Journal of Negro History*, 62 (Oct., 1977), 390–400.

Porter, Kenneth Wiggins. "The Seminole Negro-Indian Scouts." *Southwestern Historical Quarterly*, 55 (Jan., 1952), 358–60.

Poyo, Gerald E. "Evolution of Cuban Separatist Thought in the Emigré Communities of the United States, 1848–1895." *Hispanic American Review*, 66 (Aug., 1986), 485–507.

Pratt, Julius W. "The Origin of 'Manifest Destiny.'" *American Historical Review*, 32 (July, 1927), 795–98.

Reilly, Tom. "Jane McManus Storms: Letters from the Mexican War, 1846–1848." *Southwestern Historical Quarterly*, 85 (July, 1981), 21–44.

Rippy, J. Fred. "Border Troubles along the Rio Grande." *Southwestern Historical Quarterly*, 23 (Oct., 1919), 91–96.

Rippy, James Fred. "Diplomacy Regarding the Isthmus of Tehuantepec, 1848–1860." *Mississippi Valley Historical Review*, 4 (1919–1920), 513–21.

St. John, Robert P. "Jemima Wilkinson." *Quarterly Journal of the New York State Historical Association*, 11 (Apr., 1930), 158–75.

Saxon, Gerald D. "Anthony Butler: A Flawed Diplomat." *East Texas Historical Journal*, 24 (Spring, 1986), 3–14.

Sears, Louis Martin. "Nicholas P. Trist, a Diplomat with Ideals." *Mississippi Valley Historical Review*, 11 (June, 1924), 85–98.

_____. "Some Correspondence of Robert Dale Owen." *Mississippi Valley Historical Review*, 10 (Dec., 1923), 306–24.

Scholnick, Joshua David. "Democrats Abroad: Continental Literature and the American Bard in the *United States and Democratic Review.*" *American Periodicals*, 3 (1993), 75–99.

Shearer, Ernest C. "The Carvajal Disturbances." *Southwestern Historical Quarterly*, 55 (Oct., 1951), 204–30.

Sonnichsen, C. L. Review. *Eagle Pass; or Life on the Border.* By Mrs. William L. Cazneau [Cora Montgomery]. In *Southwestern Historical Quarterly*, 70 (Oct., 1966), 343–45.

Stern, Madeline B. "The House of the Expanding Doors." *New York History*, 23 (Jan., 1942), 43–50.

Tyler, Ronnie C. "The Callahan Expedition of 1855: Indians or Negroes?" *Southwestern Historical Quarterly*, 70 (Apr., 1967), 574–85.

Van Alstyne, Richard W. "British Diplomacy and the Clayton-Bulwer Treaty." *Journal of Modern History*, 11 (Mar., 1939), 151–62.

Wesley, Charles S. "Lincoln's Plan for Colonizing the Emancipated Negro." *Journal of Negro History,* 4 (Jan., 1919), 7–13.

Wilson, H. L. "President Buchanan's Proposed Intervention in Mexico." *American Historical Review,* 5 (1900), 687–701.

Wilson, Major L. "The Repressible Conflict: Seward's Concept of Progress and the Free Soil Movement." *Journal of Southern History,* 37 (Nov., 1971), 533–48.

THESES AND DISSERTATIONS:

Cashion, Peggy M. "Women in the Mexican War." M.A. thesis, University of Texas at Arlington, 1990.

Eastman, James A. "Ann Sophia Stephens." M.A. thesis, Columbia University, 1952.

Fuller, Landon Edward. "*United States Magazine and Democratic Review,* 1837–1859: A Study in its History, Contents, and Significance." Ph.D. diss., University of North Carolina, 1948.

Geary, Susan Elizabeth. "Scribbling Women: Essays on Literary History and Popular Literature in the 1850s." Ph.D. diss., Brown University, 1976.

Harrison, James C. "The Failure of Spain in East Texas: The Occupation and Abandonment of Nacogdoches, 1779–1821." Ph.D. diss., University of Nebraska, 1980.

Knight, Susan R. "The Life and Ideas of Cora Montgomery and the Journalism of Expansion." Senior thesis, University of Texas at Austin, n.d.

Lee, Basil Leo. "Discontent in New York City, 1861–1865." Ph.D. diss., Catholic University of America, 1943.

Mishler, Doug A. "Manifestos, Filibusters, and the Follies of Young America: Foreign Policy Dynamics in the Pierce Administration, 1853–1857." M.A. thesis, University of Nevada, Reno, 1988.

Sampson, Robert Dean. "'Under the Banner of the Democratic Principle': John Louis O'Sullivan, the Democracy, and the *Democratic Review.*" Ph.D. diss., University of Illinois, Urbana, 1995.

Stansifer, Charles Lee. "The Central-American Career of E. George Squier." Ph.D. diss., Tulane University, 1959.

Notes

⋄⋎⋄

INTRODUCTION

1. Henry Watterson, editor, Louisville *Courier*, quoted in Edward S. Wallace, *Destiny and Glory* (New York: Coward-McCann, 1957), 251.

2. Joseph Frasier Wall, *Henry Watterson: Reconstructed Rebel* (New York: Oxford University Press, 1956), 25; Storm to Bancroft, July 23, 1846, George Bancroft Papers (Massachusetts Historical Society, Boston, Mass.).

3. Most authors use "Storms," one of her pen names, rather than her married name, "Storm." See Tom Reilly, "Jane McManus Storms: Letters from the Mexican War, 1846–1848," *Southwestern Historical Quarterly*, 85 (July, 1975), 230–45; Patricia Kinkade, "Jane McManus Storms Cazneau," in *Essays in History: The E. C. Barksdale Student Lectures* (Arlington: University of Texas–Arlington, 1987–1988), 7–32; Anna Kasten Nelson, "Jane Storms Cazneau: Disciple of Manifest Destiny," *Prologue: The Journal of the National Archives*, 17 (Spring, 1986), 25–40; Robert E. May, "'Plenipotentiary in Petticoats': Jane M. Cazneau and American Foreign Policy in the Mid-Nineteenth Century," in Edward L. Crapol (ed.), *Women and American Foreign Policy* (2nd ed.; Wilmington: Scholarly Resources, Inc., 1992), 19–44; Robert E. May, "Lobbyists for Commercial Empire: Jane Cazneau, William Cazneau, and U.S. Caribbean Policy, 1846–1878," *Pacific Historical Review*, 48, no. 3 (1979), 383–90; Gore Vidal, *Burr: A Novel* (New York: Random House, 1973); William W. Freehling, *The Reintegration of American History: Slavery and the Civil War* (New York: Oxford University Press, 1994),138–57. An obstacle in researching Jane Cazneau's life has been her many names. Although she was separated from Allen Storm, she used her maiden name in Texas, then used Storm again after the Burr scandal. She published anonymously, as Josephine, an American lady, as Storms, J. M. Storms, Montgomery, C. Montgomery, and Corinne Montgomery before settling on Cora Montgomery. After her second marriage, she published as Cora Montgomery, Joseph W. Fabens, Schoolmaster, and anonymously. As a widow, she published as Mrs. William L. Cazneau. She signed letters as J. M. Storm, J. M. S., J. M. Cazneau, Jane Montgomery Cazneau, and J. M. C. See bibliography for published works by Jane McManus Storm Cazneau by year of publication and pseudonym; Appendix A for signed newspaper articles; Appendix B for a grammatical analysis of anonymous publications.

4. "Sketch of Mrs. Cazneau," New York *Tribune*, Dec. 31, 1878; "Lost off Cape Hatteras," New York *Tribune*, Dec. 28, 1878; "The Emily B. Souder Lost," New York *Tribune*, Dec. 30, 1878; Allan Nevins, *Ordeal of the Union*, vol. I, *Fruits of Manifest Destiny, 1847–1852* (New York: Charles Scribner's Sons, 1947), 148–49.

5. "Sketch of Mrs. Cazneau"; "Lost off Cape Hatteras"; "The Emily B. Souder Lost." The ship carried cargo for nineteen small commission houses in New York that consisted of dry goods, agricultural implements, woodenware, paints, paper, cartridges, guns, drugs, sewing machines, and more than fifty kegs of beer; "Last Will and Testament of Jane McManus Cazneau," Nov. 21, 1878, box 3, fols. 53–66, John Herndon James Papers, 1812–1938 (Daughters of the Republic of Texas Library at the Alamo, San Antonio, Texas).

6. "Bad News of the Souder," New York *Sun*, Dec. 29, 1878; "The Lost Emily B. Souder," New York *Sun*, Dec. 30, 1878; "Disasters on the Columbian Coast," New York *Tribune*, Dec. 30, 1878; "Foundered," New York *Evening Telegram*, Dec. 28, 1878; "THE LOST EMILY B. SOUDER, HER GOING DOWN DESCRIBED BY THE ONLY KNOWN SURVIVORS," New York *Sun*, Jan. 10, 1879; U.S. Navy Oceanographer Office, Publication, No. 9 (1958), *Beaufort Scale*, No. 7, MODERATE GALE, wind 36 mph, sea heaps up and white foam from breaking waves begins to be blown in streaks along the direction of the wind, with wave heights from 13 to 20 feet; No. 8, FRESH GALE, wind 44 mph, moderate waves of greater length; edges of crests break into spindrift (spray), with wave heights 13 to 20 feet; No. 9 STRONG GALE wind 48 mph, high waves; dense streaks of foam; sea begins to roll; spray affects visibility, waves of 13 to 20 feet. Joseph W. Fabens [Jane Cazneau], *The Camel Hunt*, (Boston: John Munroe & Co., 1851), 38.

7. "Catalogue of the Members of Troy Female Seminary, 1824–1825," Broadside (Emma Willard College Archives, Troy, N.Y.); Doris Sheridan (comp.), *William McManus Account Book, 1810–1819* (Troy, N.Y.: By author, 1992), 1–74; Doris Sheridan, *The McManus Family Revised* (Troy, N.Y.: By author, 1993), 1–5.

8. May, "Lobbyists for Commercial Empire," 383–412; May, "'Plenipotentiary in Petticoats,'" 19, 39; Reilly, "Jane McManus Storms," 21–44; Peggy M. Cashion, "Women in the Mexican War" (M.A. thesis, University of Texas at Arlington, 1990); Kinkade, "Jane McManus Storms Cazneau," 7–34.

9. "Sketch of Mrs. Cazneau"; *La Verdad* (New York), Jan. 8–June 26, 1848; "Meeting of Female Industry Association," *Workingman's Advocate* (New York), Mar. 22, 1845; "The Female Industrial Association," New York *Sun*, Mar. 6, 10, 14, May 1, 1845; R. D. Owen to Nicholas P. Trist, July 4, 1846, Papers of Nicholas P. Trist (Library of Congress, Washington, D.C.); William L. Marcy to Prosper M. Wetmore, Feb. 9, 1848, Papers of William L. Marcy (Library of Congress, Washington, D.C.); Col. J. W. Webb to William H. Seward, Mar. 12, 1849, Papers of William Henry Seward, Department of Rare Books and Special Collections (Rush Rhees Library, University of Rochester, Rochester, N.Y.); J. M. Storm to George Bancroft, June 20, 1848, Bancroft Papers; Mrs. William L. Cazneau (Cora Montgomery), *Eagle Pass; or Life on the Border* (New York: George P. Putnam, 1852; reprint, edited and with an introduction by Robert Crawford Cotner, Austin: The Pemberton Press, 1966), 59.

10. Seymour V. Connor and Odie B. Faulk (eds.), *North America Divided: The Mexican War, 1846–1848* (New York: Oxford University Press, 1971), 156–57 (first quotation); Nelson, "Jane Storms Cazneau," 28; May, "Lobbyists for Commercial Empire," 411–12; Wallace, *Destiny and Glory*, 275; J. M. Storm to James Buchanan, Feb. 18, 1848, James Buchanan Papers (Historical Society of Pennsylvania, Philadelphia, Pa.).

CHAPTER I

1. Anon. [Jane Cazneau], *In The Tropics: By a Settler in Santo Domingo* (New York: Carleton Publishing, 1863; London: Bently, Ltd., 1863), 13.

2. William Solymon Coons (comp.), *Koon and Coons Families of Eastern New York* (Rutland, Vt.: Tuttle Publishing, 1937), xxi–x; Sheridan, *McManus Family Revised,* 1–5.

3. Coons (comp.), *Koon and Coons Families,* 4, 188, 198, 200; Alexander C. Flick (ed.), *History of the State of New York* (10 vols.; New York: Columbia University Press, 1933), I, 63, III, 53, 63; II, 273–77; Coons (comp.), *Koon and Coons Families,* xxi–xxii; Carl L. Carmen, *The Hudson* (New York: Farrar & Rinehart, 1939), 70, 76; F. Q. Adams, *New York Panorama* (New York: Random House, 1938), 97–98; "Mahican," in Barbara Leitch LePoer, *A Concise Dictionary of Indian Tribes of North America,* ed. Kendall T. LePoer (Algonac, Mich.: Reference Publications, 1979), 248; "Mahican," in John L. Stoutenburgh Jr. (comp.), *Dictionary of the American Indian* (New York: Philosophical Library, 1960), 226; Mary B. Davis (ed.), *Native America in the 20th Century* (New York: Garland, 1994), 80; "Mahican," in Bruce G. Trigger (ed.), *Northeast,* vol. 15 of William C. Sturtevant (ed.), *Handbook of North American Indians* (20 vols.; Washington: Smithsonian Institute, 1978), 206; Alan Gallay (ed.), *Colonial Wars of North America, 1512–1763* (New York: Garland Publishing, 1996), 410; Rachel Bliven, et al., *A Resourceful People: A Pictorial History of Rensselaer County, New York* (Troy, N.Y.: Rensselaer County Historical Society, 1987), 80–82, 88, 90; Allen W. Trelease, *Indian Affairs in Colonial New York: The Seventeenth Century* (Ithaca: Cornell University Press, 1960), 40, 330, 338; Duane Champagne (ed.), *Chronology of North American History* (Detroit: Gale Research, 1994), 55, 61, 67, 72; James Fenimore Cooper, *The Last of the Mohicans,* with an introduction by Richard Slotkin, (1826; reprint, New York: Penguin Classics, 1986); Carl Waldman (ed.), *Atlas of the North American Indian* (New York: Facts on File, 1985), 100; Shirley W. Dunn, *The Mahicans and Their Land, 1609–1730* (Fleischmanns, N.Y.: Purple Mountain Press, 1994), 78, 128, 245. While most of the original Indians moved to western New York or to Ohio with Moravian missionaries, a few migrated to Connecticut and formed the Stockbridge tribe.

4. Coons (comp.), *Koon and Coons Families,* 4, 188, 198, 200.

5. Sheridan, *McManus Family,* 1–5; Warren F. Broderick (ed.), *Brunswick . . . A Pictorial History* (Brunswick: Brunswick Historical Society, 1978), 49–51.

6. John R. Swanton, *The Indian Tribes of North America,* Bureau of American Ethnology Bulletin 145 (Washington, D.C.: Smithsonian, 1952), 41–42; Flick (ed.), *History of New York,* IV, 27–28, 203; James Levernier and Hennig Cohen (eds.), *The Indians and Their Captives* (Westport, Conn.: Greenwood Press, 1977), 231; Gallay, *Colonial Wars of North America,* 149, 410; Holcombd E. Vaughn (ed.), *History of Indian-White Relations,* vol. 4 of Sturtevant (ed.), *Handbook of North American Indians,* 287, 432–36; Bliven, *A Resourceful People,* 28, 32; M. R. Werner, *Tammany Hall* (New York: Greenwood Press, 1968), 11.

7. Sheridan, *McManus Family Revised,* 1–5; Doris Sheridan (comp.), *William McManus Account Book, 1810–1819* (Troy, N.Y.: By author, 1992).

8. Sheridan (comp.), *Account Book,* 3, 10, 66, 36–41; Trelease, *Indian Affairs in Colonial New York,* 338; Charles Burr Todd, *General History of the Burr Family* (2nd ed.; New York: By author, 1891), 110; Dunn, *The Mahicans and Their Land,* 245.

9. Sheridan (comp.), *Account Book,* 3, 10, 66, 36–41; Trelease, *Indian Affairs in Colonial New York,* 8, 230–38; Gallay (ed.), *Colonial Wars of North America,* 149, 410; "Mahican," in Trigger

(ed.), *Northeast,* vol. 15 of Sturtevant (ed.), *Handbook of North American Indians,* 203–9; William P. Hansen and Fred L. Isreal (eds.), *The American Indian and the United States: A Documentary History* (4 vols.; New York: Random House, 1973), IV, 2292–94; Frederick Webb Hodge (ed.), *Handbook of American Indians North of Mexico,* Bureau of American Ethnology Bulletin 30 (2 vols.; Washington: U.S. Government Printing Office, 1907; reprint, Totowa, N.Y.: Rowan & Littlefield, 1975), I, 786.

10. Sheridan, *McManus Family,* 2, 4–6; Sheridan (comp.), *Account Book,* 1–74; Hodge, *Handbook of American Indians North of Mexico,* I, 786.

11. Robert Winston Mardock, *The Reformers and the American Indian* (Columbia: University of Missouri Press, 1971), 16–17; Cora Montgomery, *King of the Rivers* (New York: Charles Wood, 1850), 4–5; Cora Montgomery, *Eagle Pass; or Life on the Border* (New York: George R. Putnam, 1852), 41, 59, 95, 109; Mrs. William Leslie Cazneau, *Our Winter Eden: Pen Portraits of the Tropics* (New York: Author's Publishing, 1878), 29; Anon. [Jane Cazneau], *The Prince of Kashna: A West Indies Story* (New York: Carleton, 1865), 153. Cazneau wrote about Indians in Cuba, Wisconsin, Mexico, Texas, Jamaica, and the Dominican Republic; J. M. Storm to Robert Owen, Jan. 12, 1846, Papers of Robert Owen, copy provided by Holyoake House, Manchester, England; Isaac F. Marcosson, *"Marse Henry," a Biography of Henry Watterson: Reconstructed Rebel* (New York: Dodd, Mead, & Co., 1951), 46–47; Republic of Texas, quarterly returns, passenger list, fol. 7 (Archives, Texas State Library, Austin, Tex.); "The Lost Emily B. Souder," New York *Tribune,* Jan. 10, 1879; Levernier and Cohen (eds.), *The Indians and Their Captives,* 232; Cooper, *The Last of the Mohicans,* iv, xvii, xxv.

12. Sheridan (comp.), *Account Book,* 38, 61, 78, 96, 60, 101; Madeline B. Stern, "Ann Sophia Stevens," in James (ed.), *Notable American Women,* 360; Swanton, *Indian Tribes,* 41; "Mahican," in Vaughn (ed.), *History of Indian-White Relations,* 287, 432; James A. Eastman, "Ann Sophia Stephens" (M.A. thesis, Columbia University, 1952), 4; *Antebellum Writers in New York and the South,* vol. 43 of Joel Myerson (ed.), *Dictionary of Literary Biography,* (183 vols.; Detroit: Gale Research, 1979), 318.

13. Sheridan (comp.), *Account Book,* 37, 42, 45, 78; Samuel Rezneck, *Profiles out of the Past of Troy, New York, Since 1789* (Troy, N.Y.: n.p., 1970), 25–29.

14. Sheridan (comp.), *Account Book,* 37, 42, 45, 78; Broderick (ed.), *Brunswick . . . A Pictorial History,* 142; Blivin, *A Resourceful People,* 30.

15. Sheridan (comp.), *Account Book,* 51–72, 91; Sheridan, *McManus Family,* 2–19; Jos. Hillman, *The History of Methodism in Troy, N.Y.* (Troy, N.Y.: n.p., 1888), 199; Arthur James Weise, *Troy's One Hundred Years, 1789–1889* (Troy, N.Y.: W. H. Young, 1891), 91; Robert P. St. John, "Jemima Wilkinson," *Quarterly Journal of the New York State Historical Association,* 11 (Apr., 1930), 158, 169.

16. Montgomery, *Eagle Pass,* dedication page; Sheridan (comp.), *Account Book;* Todd, *Burr Family,* 236. Aaron Burr's grandfather, Rev. Jonathan Edwards, ministered to the Stockbridge Indians before he became president of Princeton University. The Edwards, Wheeler, Todd, and Burr families were intermarried several times over, and insanity ran in the family.

17. J. E. B. DeBow (ed.), *Statistical View of the United States . . . Being a Compendium of the Seventh Census . . .* (Washington: Beverley Tucker, Senate Printer, 1854), 82; Edgar J. McManus, *A History of Negro Slavery in New York* (Syracuse: Syracuse University Press, 1966), 162, 174–75; Sheridan, *McManus Family,* 3, 13; Adams, *New York Panorama,* 134; Albert Fried, *John Brown's Journey: Notes and Reflections on His America and Mine* (Garden City, N.Y.: Anchor Press, 1978), 186–93.

18. Weise, *Troy's One Hundred Years*, 244, 338; Sheridan, *McManus Family*, 4–6, 23–24; Sheridan (comp.), *Account Book*, 64; "Lawyers of the Day," Troy *Daily Times*, Nov. 18, 1880.

19. Rezneck, *Profiles out of the Past of Troy*, 110; "Emma Willard," in James (ed.), *Notable American Women*, III, 610–13.

20. "Catalogue of the Members of Troy Female Seminary, 1824–1825," Broadside, Emma Willard College Archives; Sheridan, *McManus Family*, 14; "Emma Willard," in James (ed.), *Notable American Women*, III, 610–13; Anne Firor Scott, *Women in American Life* (New York: Houghton Mifflin, 1970), 46; Sean Wilentz, "Society, Politics, and the Market Revolution, 1815–1848," in Eric Foner (ed.), *The New American History* (Philadelphia: Temple University Press, 1990), 59.

21. Rezneck, *Profiles out of the Past of Troy*, 60–61; Sheridan, *McManus Family*, 20; Bliven, *A Resourceful People*, 36–39.

22. "Convention of the People at Sandlake," Troy *Sentinel*, Oct. 19, 1824; "People's Ticket," Troy *Sentinel*, Oct. 29, 1824; Rezneck, *Profiles out of the Past of Troy*, 15; Bliven, *A Resourceful People*, 29–32; "Mr. McManus," Troy *Budget and City Register*, Jan. 10, 1826; *Biographical Directory of the U.S. Congress, 1774–1989* (Washington, D.C., U.S. Government Printing Office, 1989), 1480; John C. Calhoun, *The Papers of John C. Calhoun*, eds. Clyde N. Wilson and W. Edwin Hemphill (23 vols.; Columbia: University of South Carolina Press, 1977), X, 73.

23. Sheridan, *McManus Family*, 14; "Married," Troy *Sentinel*, Aug. 23, 1825; Amos Eaton, "Account Book, 1834–1844," Amos Eaton Papers, drawer 10685, box 3, Manuscript Section (New York State Library, Albany, N.Y.).

24. Anon.[Jane Cazneau], "A Gauntlet for the Men," Washington *Daily States*, Apr. 21, 1857; "DIED," Troy *Budget*, Dec. 4, 1838.

25. Eliza Burr vs. Aaron Burr, box 1, fol. 13, affidavits, no. 43–44, Eliza Jumel Papers (New York Historical Society Library, New York, N.Y.); Sheridan, *McManus Family*, 13–14; Aaron Burr to James Workman, Nov. 16, 1832, Papers of Aaron Burr (New York Historical Society Library, New York, N.Y.); William Cary Duncan, *The Amazing Madame Jumel* (New York: Frederick A. Stokes, 1935), 258; Gore Vidal, *Burr*, 63, 68.

26. David B. Gracy II, "Moses Austin," in Ron Tyler, Douglas E. Barnett, Roy R. Barkley, Penelope C. Anderson, and Mark F. Odintz (eds.), *The New Handbook of Texas* (6 vols.; Austin: Texas State Historical Association, 1996), I, 293; Linda Hudson, "Antonio Martinez, the Problems of Administering Texas during the Last Years of Spanish Control," *Touchstone*, 6 (1987), 11; Gregg Cantrell, *Stephen F. Austin: Empresario of Texas* (New Haven: Yale University Press, 1999), 94, 110–27.

27. Andreas Reichstein, "Galveston Bay and Texas Land Company," in Tyler, et al. (eds.), *New Handbook of Texas*, III, 53–54.

28. Anthony Dey Galveston Bay and Texas Land Company Records, box 2, fol. 28, box 4, fols. 80–82, 88, 90, Western Americana Collection (Beinecke Rare Book and Manuscript Library, Yale University, New Haven, Conn.).

29. Depositions, box 1, fol. 1, Jumel Papers; Todd, *Burr Family*, 97, 110; "Biographies of Leading Texans," I, 138–39, typescript (Archives, Texas State Library, Austin, Tex.); Galveston Bay and Texas Land Company, box 4, fols. 88, 90, Dey Records; Gustavus Myers, *The History of Tammany Hall* (New York: Born & Leveright, 1917), 53.

30. Sheridan, *McManus Family*, 2; *Las Siete Partidas*, vol. 17 (Bexar Archives, San Antonio, Texas), 1; Burr to McManus, Nov. 17, 1832, Burr Papers; St. John, "Jemima Wilkinson," 169.

31. Aaron Burr to Judge Workman, Nov. 16, 1832, Burr Papers; Thomas Perkins Abernethy, *The Burr Conspiracy* (Glouchester, Mass.: Peter Smith, 1968), 16–25, 73–74, 167–68, 240, 268.

32. Burr to Workman, Nov. 16, 1832, Burr Papers.

Chapter II

1. Jane M. McManus to Joseph D. Beers, Oct. 29, 1835, Samuel May Williams Papers (Galveston and Texas History Center, Rosenberg Library, Galveston, Texas).

2. Margaret Swett Henson, *Samuel May Williams: Early Texas Entrepreneur* (College Station: Texas A&M University Press, 1976), 3; Archie P. McDonald, *Travis* (Austin: Jenkins Press, 1976), 51–53.

3. Corinne Montgomery, *Texas and Her Presidents with a Glance at Her Climate and Agricultural Capabilities* (New York: E. Winchester, New World Press, 1845), 16; Margaret Swett Henson, *Juan Davis Bradburn: A Reappraisal of the Mexican Commander of Anahuac* (College Station: Texas A&M University Press, 1982), 77, 114; Henson, *Samuel May Williams*, 32–36; Margaret Swett Henson, "Anahuac Disturbances," in Tyler, et al. (eds.), *The New Handbook of Texas*, I, 159–60; Cantrell, *Stephen F. Austin*, 215–61; Randolph B. Campbell, *An Empire For Slavery: The Peculiar Institution in Texas, 1821–1865* (Louisiana State University Press, 1989), 24; Mrs. Mary S. Helm, *Scraps From Texas History, 1828–1843* (Austin: By author, 1884), 143. Mrs. Helm's husband, Elias R. Wightman, founded Matagorda. She listed the following colonies as they were then known: Austin, DeWitt, Milam, Lovell [McMullen and McGloin], League [Nashville Assn.], Burnet, Thorne, Wavell, Barzel, Woodbury, and the Mexican Mining Company.

4. Henson, *Samuel May Williams*, 9–13, 24–25, 31; A. Ray Stephens and William M. Holmes, *Historical Atlas of Texas* (Norman: University of Oklahoma Press, 1989), Map 22, "Empresario Grants."

5. Henson, *Samuel May Williams*, 46, 53–54; Malcolm D. McLean (comp. and ed.), *Papers Concerning Robertson's Colony in Texas* (19 vols.; Arlington: University of Texas at Arlington, vols. 1–4, 1974–1978; Fort Worth: Texas Christian University Press, vols. 5–19, 1978–1993), VII, 27, 49; Judith N. McArthur, "Myth, Reality, and Anomaly: The Complex World of Rebecca Hagerty," *East Texas Historical Journal*, 24 (Fall, 1986), 23, says that Houston was investigating Indian migration into Texas.

6. McLean (comp. and ed.), *Robertson's Colony*, VII, 30; Charles D. Sayre to S. M. Williams, Jan. 22, Feb. 3, 1833, Williams Papers; Henson, *Juan Davis Bradburn*, 83; Craig H. Roell, "Charles D. Sayre," in Tyler, et al. (eds.), *New Handbook of Texas*, V, 907.

7. Henson, *Samuel May Williams*, 25, 16–17, 23; J. M. Storm to M. B. Lamar, Oct. 1845, no. 2195, Papers of Mirabeau Buonaparte Lamar, Archives and Records Division (Texas State Library, Austin, Tex.); Montgomery, *Eagle Pass*, 15.

8. Spanish Collection, box 23, fol. 23, Archives Division (Texas General Land Office, Austin, Tex.); Andreas V. Reichstein, *Rise of the Lone Star: The Making of Texas* (College Station: Texas A&M University Press, 1989), 109. Sawyer represented the Arkansas and Texas, the Rio Grande and Texas, and the Colorado and Red River land companies, plus

those of James Grant and John Charles Beales on the Rio Grande. Robert E. Davis (ed.), *The Diary of William Barret Travis, August 30, 1833 to June 26, 1834* (Waco: Texian Press, 1966), 36.

9. Jane Cazneau file (Center for American History, University of Texas at Austin, Austin, Tex.); Austin to Williams, May 8, 1832, Williamson to Hoxey, Apr. 15, 1833, in McLean (comp. and ed.), *Robertson's Colony*, VII, 44–49; Robert M. Williamson to Asa Hoxey, Nov. 1, 1832, Edward Hanrick Papers (Center for American History, University of Texas at Austin, Austin, Tex.); Michael Q. Hooks and Jesús F. de la Teja, "The Texas General Land Office: Preserving East Texas Land Records," *East Texas Historical Journal* (Spring, 1989), 55–62.

10. Spanish Collection, box 23, fol. 23; LeRoy P. Graf, "Colonizing Projects in Texas South of the Nueces, 1820–1845," *Southwestern Historical Quarterly*, 50 (Apr., 1947), 440; Merton L. Dillon, *Benjamin Lundy and the Struggle for Negro Freedom* (Urbana: University of Illinois Press, 1966), 224–25; Reichstein, *Rise of the Lone Star*, 107; Joseph Milton Nance, "Samuel Bangs" and Marilyn M. Sibley, "Benjamin Lundy," in Tyler, et al. (eds.), *New Handbook of Texas*, I, 367, IV, 338; McLean (comp. and ed.), *Robertson's Colony*, VII, 47, 49.

11. James Armstrong, *Some Facts on the Eleven-League Controversy* (Austin: Southern Intelligencer, 1859), 5, 11, 13; Ray Miller, *Texas Forts: A History and Guide* (Houston: Cordovan Press, 1985), 208; McLean (comp. and ed.), *Robertson's Colony*, VII, 355; Betty Dooley Awbrey and Claude Dooley, *Why Stop? A Guide to Texas Historical Markers* (3rd ed.; Houston: Gulf Printing, 1992), 295, 299; Patricia Ward Wallace, *Waco: Texas Crossroads* (Woodland Hills, Calif.: Windsor Press, 1983), 15; John Henry Brown, *Indian Wars and Pioneers of Texas* (Austin: L. E. Daniel, 1880; reprint, Greenville: Southern Historical Press, 1978), 12, 25, 121. The Cherokee mixed-bloods and their associated tribes, the Creek, Kichai, Shawnee, Delaware, Kickapoo, Choctaw, Caddo, Seminole, Biloxi, Alabama, and Coushatta, settled along the Red, Neches, and Sabine Rivers. Aaron Burr to Jane McManus, Nov. 17, 1832, Burr Papers; "Jemima Wilkinson," in Allen Johnson and Dumas Malone (eds.), *Dictionary of American Biography* (10 vols. plus supplements; New York: Charles Scribner's Sons, 1936), X, 226–27.

12. Spanish Collection, box 23, fol. 23; Henson, *Juan Davis Bradburn*, 83; Samuel Sawyer to John Austin, July 14, 1833, Williams Papers; Anthony Dey Galveston Bay and Texas Land Company Records, series 4, box 6, fol. 93, "Account Book, 1828–1834," 258–59.

13. McLean (comp. and ed.), *Papers Concerning Robertson's Colony*, VIII, 155–59; *Abstract of the Original Titles of Record in the General Land Office* (Austin: Pemberton Press, 1964). Two women were widows, 21 percent had Hispanic surnames. Sixteen different empresarios had women listed: Austin, 46; Robertson and Vehlein, 22 each; Powers and Hewetson, 14; DeLeon, 11; de Zavala, 10; DeWitt, Burnet, and McMullen and McGloin, 8 each; Taylor, 7; Madero, Milam, and Nacogdoches, 4 each; Smythe, 3. See *Las Siete Partidas*, vol. 17, 1–6, 145–46, (Bexar Archives, San Antonio, Tex.); Mary Austin Holley, *Texas* (Lexington: J. Clarke & Co., 1836; reprint, Austin: Texas State Historical Association, 1985), 145–46.

14. Account Book, box 4, fol. 85, box 6, fol. 93, Dey Records; David E. Narrett, "A Choice of Destiny," *Southwestern Historical Quarterly*, 100 (Jan., 1997), 278–79; Henson, *Samuel May Williams*, 47–48; McLean (comp. and ed.), *Robertson's Colony*, VII, 513; Stephen F. Austin to Samuel May Williams, May 31, 1833, Williams Papers.

15. Edward Hanrick to S. M. Williams, Aug. 22, 1833, Williams Papers; Henson, *Samuel May Williams*, 48.

16. Sawyer to John Austin, July 14, 1833; Bill for surveying, Aug. 31, 1833, Williams Papers; R. O. W. McManus to S. Rhodes Fisher, June 22, 1885, James Papers; Henson, *Samuel May Williams*, 47–48, 54.

17. Valdez Grant, box 1, fol. 1, Spanish Collection; Mack Walker, *Germany and the Emigration 1816–1885* (Cambridge: Harvard University Press, 1964), 42–50, 58–68.

18. Mattie Austin Hatcher, *The Opening of Texas to Foreign Settlement, 1801–1821* (Austin: University of Texas Press, 1927; reprint, Philadelphia: Porcupine Press, 1976), 273–74; Don H. Biggers, *German Pioneers in Texas* (Fredericksburg: Fredericksburg Publishing Co., 1925), 6–12; Walker, *Germany and the Emigration*, 42–50, 58, 62–67; Louis Brister, "Johann von Racknitz: German Empresario and Soldier of Fortune in Texas and Mexico, 1832–1848," *Southwestern Historical Quarterly*, 99 (July, 1995), 56–61.

19. William Cary Duncan, *The Amazing Madame Jumel* (New York: Frederick A. Stokes, 1935), 4, 258–67; box 1, fol. 1, Jumel Papers.

20. J. McManus to Col. Burr, no date, Jumel Papers; Jane McManus to Justus Morton, $250, Oct. 2, 1833, deed records, Matagorda County Court House, Bay City, Tex., book A, 92–93; C. G. Addison, *The Knights Templar History* (New York: Arno Press, 1978), 33; J. Maria McManus to Sam Houston, Apr. 20, 1840, Sam Houston Papers (Catholic Archives of Texas, Austin, Tex.); Robert Macoy (comp.), *Dictionary of Freemasonry* (New York: Masonic Publishing Co., 1895; reprint, New York: Bell Publishing, 1989), 239.

21. Matagorda County Historical Commission, *Historic Matagorda County* (3 vols.; Houston: D. Armstrong, 1986), I, 33; June Zimmerman, et al., "Logan Vandeveer," in Tyler, et al. (eds.), *New Handbook of Texas*, VI, 700; Brown, *Pioneers of Texas*, 23–25; Gilbert Giddings Benjamin, *Germans in Texas* (Philadelphia: German American Annuals, 1909), 15–22. The identity of the German indentures is unknown, but George Erath and the Biegel, Dietrich, and Ehllinger families came in 1833 and give scant particulars of their arrival, while the Kleberg and von Roeder families recorded their trek from Germany in great detail.

22. R. O. W. McManus to S. Rhodes Fisher, June 22, 1885, James Papers; Ethel Mary Franklin (ed.), "Memoirs of Mrs. Annie P. Harris," *Southwestern Historical Quarterly*, 40 (Jan., 1937), 231–34, 239; Lorraine Bruce Jeter, *Matagorda: Early History* (Baltimore: Gateway Press, 1974), 18; William Goetzmann, *Army Exploration in the American West, 1803–1863* (New Haven: Yale University Press, 1959; reprint, Austin: Texas State Historical Association, 1991), 236; *Constitution of the Proprietors of the Town of Matagorda Including Town Minutes* (Bay City: Matagorda County Historical Society, 1963), "Minutes," Aug. 1, 1832, p. 19.

23. Franklin (ed.), "Memoirs of Mrs. Annie Harris," 239; Roy A. Clifford, "Josiah Pugh Wilbarger," in Tyler, et al. (eds.), *New Handbook of Texas*, VI, 965; Henson, *Samuel May Williams*, 57–60; Eugene C. Barker, *The Life of Stephen F. Austin, 1793–1836* (Austin: Texas State Historical Association, 1949), 296–320.

24. Sheridan, *McManus Family Revised*, 35–36; A. B. J. Hammell, *The Empresario: Don Martin DeLeon* (Waco: Texian Press, 1973), 163; Reichstein, *Rise of the Lone Star*, 107–9; Keith Guthrie, *Texas Forgotten Ports*, (3 vols.; Austin: Eakin Press, 1995), III, 41–44; Odie B. Faulk, "John R. Bartlett," Marilyn M. Sibley, "Nicholas Clopper," and Margaret Swett Henson, "New Washington Association," in Tyler, et al. (eds.), *New Handbook of Texas*, I, 400, II, 164, IV, 1005–6; box 4, fol. 85, Dey Records; *Constitution and Minutes of the Town of Matagorda*, "Minutes," Mar. 26, 1834, p. 32; "Passenger Lists of Vessels Arriving at New Orleans, 1820–1902," RG 36, Aug. 5, 1833–May 1835 (National Archives, Washington, D.C.).

25. J. E. B. DeBow (ed.), *Statistical View of the United States . . . Being a Compendium of the Seventh Census . . .*, IV, ix; William Lloyd Garrison (ed.), *Lectures of George Thompson: History of His Connection with the Anti-Slavery Cause in England* (Boston: Isaac Knapp, 1836), xix, xxvi, 179–80; Petition of G. L. Thompson, Sept. 5, 1829, Duff Green Papers (Library of Congress, National Archives, Washington, D.C.); Franklin (ed.), "Memoirs of Mrs. Annie Harris," 238, 245; Goetzmann, *Army Exploration*, 168.

26. Sheridan, *McManus Family Revised*, 35–36; Duncan, *The Amazing Madame Jumel*, 4, 258–67; Mrs. Stephens quoted in Wallace, *Destiny and Glory*, 257.

27. Louis Dow Scisco, *Political Nativism in New York State* (New York: Columbia University Press, 1901), 23, 31, 35; Vidal, *Burr*, 272.

28. Valdez grant, box 23, fol. 23, Spanish Collection; Jane M. McManus to S. M. Williams, July 29, 1834, Williams Papers; Sheridan, *McManus Family Revised*, 5.

29. Margaret Swett Henson, *Lorenzo de Zavala: The Pragmatic Idealist* (Fort Worth: Texas Christian University Press, 1996), 72–75; Gerald D. Saxon, "Anthony Butler: A Flawed Diplomat," *East Texas Historical Journal*, 24 (Spring, 1986), 5–8.

30. Villamae Williams (ed.), *Stephen F. Austin's Register of Families* (Baltimore: Genealogical Publishing Co., 1984), Appendix, R-2. Mar. 17, 1835, no. 2 and 3, Carancahua E. side, 1 League No. 6 deeded to Newell, 1 League No. 5, Kellers Bayou, 1 League No. 29 Prairy Creek, 1 League No. 22 Trespalacios, 1 League No. 20 Trespalacios, 1 Next west to Gulf, 1 League, No. 25 if not deeded for No. 6; Jane McManus to S. M. Williams, June 19, 1835, Williams Papers.

31. Henson, *Lorenzo de Zavala*, 75; Henson, *Samuel May Williams*, 62–70; Andrés Tijerina, *Tejanos and Texans under the Mexican Flag, 1821–1836* (College Station: Texas A&M University Press, 1994), 136; "Passenger Lists," June 1, 1835–Apr. 31, 1836, RG 36 (National Archives, Washington, D.C.), Schooner *Mary*, July 23, 1835. "Miss Jane McManus, age 25, f, US, traveler."

32. Eugene C. Barker, "Stephen Fuller Austin" and Stephen L. Hardin, "Battle of Gonzales," in Tyler, et al. (eds.), *New Handbook of Texas*, I, 294–97, III, 228–29; Stephen L. Hardin, "'A Hard Lot': Texas Women in the Runaway Scrape," *East Texas Historical Journal*, 29 (Spring, 1991), 35; Margaret Swett Henson and Deolece Parmelee, *The Cartwrights of San Augustine* (Austin: Texas State Historical Association, 1993), 92; Henson, *Samuel May Williams*, 76; *Abstract/Indices of Spanish and Mexican Land Grants*, Spanish Collection.

33. McLean (comp. and ed.), *Papers Concerning Robertson's Colony*, VII, 49; Samuel M. Williams to Francis W. Johnson, Dec. 1, 1832, Williams Papers; Robert M. Williamson to Asa Hoxey, Feb. 2, Apr. 13, Apr. 15, Aug. 26, 1833, Asa Hoxey to Edward Hanrick, Nov. 6, 27, 1833, Hanrick Papers; Tijerina, *Tejanos and Texans*, 56; Armstrong, *Eleven-League Controversy*, 11, 13.

34. Jane M. McManus to Joseph D. Beers, Oct. 29, 1835, Williams Papers; Henson, *Samuel May Williams*, 82; Franklin (ed.), "Memoirs of Mrs. Annie Harris," 244.

35. Duncan, *The Amazing Madame Jumel*, 129, 131, 257, 266.

36. Jane McManus to Samuel M. Williams, Jan. 3, 1836, Williams Papers.

37. William S. Speer (ed.), *Encyclopedia of the New West*, Texas vol. (Marshall, Tex.: United States Biographical Publishing, 1881), 241–42; W. N. Bate, *General Sidney Sherman: Solider, Statesman, and Builder* (Waco: Texian Press, 1974), 133–35; proofs, June 6, 1836, indictment,

June 16, 1836, decree, July 8, 1836, reports, Sept. 14, 1836, insufficient evidence, Feb. 6, 1837, jury finds, Mar. 5, 1837, box 1, fol. 13, Jumel Papers.

38. Narrett, "A Choice of Destiny," 285, 290–91; Garrison, *Lectures of George Thompson*, iii, xix; xxvi; Republic of Texas Constitution, General Provisions, Section 10; indicies, Galveston Bay and Texas Land Company, Spanish Collection.

39. Jane M. McManus to James Morgan, Sept. 20, 1837, deed records, Matagorda County, bk. B, 245, Bay City. The area is now in Jackson County at the head of Carancahua Bay on FM 2280; Ferris A. Bass Jr. and B. R. Brunson (eds.), *Fragile Empires: The Texas Correspondence of Samuel Swartwout and James Morgan, 1836–1856* (Austin: Shoal Creek Publishers, 1978), 79.

40. Passenger Lists, quarterly returns for the Republic of Texas, fol. 7, Archives and Records Division (Texas State Library, Austin, Tex.); John H. Jenkins (gen. ed.), *The Papers of the Texas Revolution, 1835–1836* (10 vols.; Austin: Presidial Press, 1973), IV, 1971. Thomas Stewart was a purser on the *William Robbins* and helped W. L. Cazneau recapture the vessel from the Mexican Navy.

41. Board of Land Commissioners, Matagorda County, Jan. 1–Mar. 1, 1838, in Gifford White (comp.), *First Settlers of Matagorda County, Texas* (Austin: Gifford White, 1986), 16, 20, 28; Jane M. McManus, eleven-league claim, filed and recorded, June 5, 1838, deed records, Matagorda County, bk. A, 128, Bay City, Tex.; Sheridan, *McManus Family*, 20, 23–24.

42. Jane Cazneau file; Brown, *Indian Wars and Pioneers of Texas*, 172–78; Jeter, *Matagorda Early History*, 25–27; Jane McManus to William Selkirt, Oc. 20, 1837, bk. A, 92–93, bk. B, 157, deed records, Matagorda County, Bay City, Tex.

43. Malcolm D. McLean, "Robertson's Colony," and Gilbert M. Cuthbertson, "Regulator-Moderator War," in Tyler, et al. (eds.), *New Handbook of Texas*, V, 623–24, 517; Eugene C. Barker, "Land Speculators as a Cause of the Texas Revolution," *Southwestern Historical Quarterly*, 10 (July, 1906), 77–95; Armstrong, *Eleven-League Controversy*, 1–12, 17.

44. Henson, *Samuel May Williams*, 3; William C. Davis, *Three Roads to The Alamo: The Lives and Fortunes of David Crockett, James Bowie, and William Barret Travis* (New York: HarperCollins, 1998), 196–203; Randolph B. Campbell, *Sam Houston and the American Southwest* (New York: HarperCollins, 1993), 27–35; McLean (comp. and ed.), *Papers Concerning Robertson's Colony*, VII, 27; Aaron Burr to Judge Workman, Nov. 16, 1832, Aaron Burr Papers (New York Historical Society Library, New York, N.Y.); William Bollaert, *William Bollaert's Texas*, eds. W. Eugene Hollon and Ruth Lapham Butler (Norman: University of Oklahoma Press, 1956), 105; Jane Cazneau file; L. W. Kemp, "Volney Erskine Howard," in Tyler, et al. (eds.), *New Handbook of Texas*, III, 746; Paul N. Spellman, *Forgotten Texas Leader: Hugh McLeod and the Texan Santa Fe Expedition* (College Station: Texas A&M Press, 1999), 8. Volney Howard lived intermittently in Texas and in the 1849 and 1851 elections defeated Texas Speaker of the House Hugh McLeod for U.S. Representative of the Western District.

45. Andrew Forest Muir, *Texas in 1837* (Austin: University of Texas Press, 1958), 123; William Ransom Hogan, "Rampant Individualism in the Republic of Texas," *Southwestern Historical Quarterly*, 44 (Apr., 1941), 454–80; Jane McManus to J. T. Belknap, Dec. 31, 1838, book B, 347, deed records, Matagorda County.

46. Williams (comp.), *Register of Families*, claims, R-2; Jeter, *Matagorda Early History*, 26–27; "George Morse Collinsworth," "Volney Erskine Howard," "John D. Newell," and Julia L. Vivian, "Dugald MacFarlane," in Tyler, et al. (eds.), *New Handbook of Texas*, II, 200, III, 746, IV, 991, 400.

47. Marion Tinling (comp.), *Women Remembered: A Guide to Landmarks of Women's History in the United States* (New York: Greenwood Press, 1986), 273. The first marker described her life as "A comedy of grandiose plans and bungled opportunities," but has since been replaced by a more respectful citation. Gifford White (ed.), *The 1840 Census of the Republic of Texas* (Austin: Pemberton, 1966), 103; Galveston *Semi-Weekly Journal*, Feb. 2, 1852; R. O. W. McManus, General Land Office, Records and Archives, claims fols. 1-000231 09; 1-000297 10; 1-001397 01; B-000195 08; B-001600 01; C-005593 00. He is buried in the Texas State Cemetery, Austin.

48. James Morgan to Samuel Swartwout, Feb. 1, 1838, Swartwout to Morgan, May 6, 1838, Morgan to Swartwout, June 10, 1838, in Bass and Brunson (eds.), *Fragile Empires*, 66, 78; B. R. Brunson, *The Adventures of Samuel Swartwout in the Age of Jefferson and Jackson* (Lewistown, Maine: Edwin Mellon University Press, 1989), 75.

49. "A Gauntlet for the Men," Washington *Daily States*, Apr. 21, 1857; Ann S. Stephens, "A Woman of Genius," *The Hesperian*, 3 (Aug.,1839), 29–31; Eastman, "Ann Sophia Stephens," 5; Troy *Daily Whig*, Nov. 27, 1838; Fanny Fern quoted in Pamela Herr, *Jessie Benton Frémont: A Biography* (New York: Franklin Watts, 1987), 101.

50. Sheridan, *McManus Family Revised*, 34; Bass and Brunson (eds.), *Fragile Empires*, 78, 204; "Pupils," *Catalogue of the Members of Troy Female Seminary*, Aug. 1, 1825 (Emma Willard College Archives); David F. Long, *Nothing Too Daring: A Biography of Commodore David Porter, 1780–1843* (Annapolis: U.S. Navy, 1970), 300; "Santa Anna's Grant to Porter," New York *Herald*, May 9. 1853; "Cornelius Van Ness," and "George Van Ness," in Tyler, et al. (eds.), *New Handbook of Texas*, VI, 705, 706; J. M. Storm to George Bancroft, July 1846, Bancroft Papers.

51. "The Ups and Downs of an Eccentric Inventor," Troy *Daily Press*, Jan. 26, 1891; "Estate of Jane M. Cazneau, Probate Proceedings," in *Abstract of Title to Antonio Rivas Grant in Maverick County, Texas* (San Antonio: Texas Title Guaranty, 1938), 15; Kenneth E. Hasbrouck (comp.), *The Hasbrouck Family in America, with European Background* (3 vols.; New Paltz, N.Y.: Hasbrouck Family Association, 1961), I, 221.

52. Willard G. Bleyer, *Main Currents in the History of American Journalism* (New York: DeCapo Press, 1973), 211–12; Anon. [Jane Cazneau], "Lady Hester Stanhope," *United States Magazine and Democratic Review*, 13 (Nov., 1843), 540–41; "Aleppo," *Our Times: A Monthly Review of Politics, Literature, &c*, ed. Cora Montgomery, 1 (Oct., 1852), 114, 168; Macoy (comp.) *Dictionary of Freemasonry*, 211.

53. J. Maria McManus to Sam Houston, Apr. 20, 1840, Houston Papers.

54. Asa P. Ufford to Edward Hanrick, Oct. 25, 1854, Hanrick Papers; Armstrong, *Eleven-League Controversy*, 13–16. The Alabama planters went bankrupt in 1837. Hoxey's land reverted to Hanrick, who was imprisoned for debt in Baltimore, and the land reverted to the Bank of the United States, from which Asa and Joseph Ufford made their purchase. The Uffords sued for possession in Williamson County courts, where Williams's fraud was discovered. R. O. W. McManus continued until his death with his attempt to recover land or payment. After the Civil War his attorney was S. Rhodes Fisher, who had lived with the McManus family at Cazneau's store in Matagorda as a baby. R. O. W. McManus to S. Rhodes Fisher, June 1885, James Papers.

CHAPTER III

1. J. M. Storms to M. B. Lamar, Oct. 1845, no. 2195, Lamar Papers.

2. Sheridan, *McManus Family Revised*, 6; James Morgan to Samuel Swartwout, Feb. 10, 1843, in Bass and Brunson (eds.), *Fragile Empires*, 204; Macoy (comp.), *A Dictionary of Freemasonry*, 143.

3. Robert Dean Sampson, "'Under the Banner of the Democratic Principle': John Louis O'Sullivan, the Democracy and the *Democratic Review*" (Ph.D. diss., University of Illinois, Urbana, 1995), 121–29; Anon. [Jane Storm], "The Course of Civilization," *United States Magazine and Democratic Review*, 4 (Sept.,1839), 208–17; Anon. [Jane Storm], "The Great Nation of Futurity," *United States Magazine and Democratic Review*, 4 (Nov., 1839), 426–30; William L. Marcy to Prosper M. Wetmore, Feb. 9, 1848, Marcy Papers; J. M. Storms to George Bancroft, July 23, 1846, Bancroft Papers.

4. Sampson, "'Under the Banner of the Democratic Principle,'" 123–24; [Storm], "The Great Nation of Futurity," 426–30.

5. Landon Edward Fuller, "*United States Magazine and Democratic Review, 1837–1859*: A Study in its History, Contents, and Significance" (Ph.D. diss., University of North Carolina, 1948), 12, 53–56.

6. Anon. [Jane Storm], "Free Trade," *United States Magazine and Democratic Review*, 9 (Oct., 1841), 329–42; Anon. [Jane Storm], "Hurrah for a War with England," *United States Magazine and Democratic Review*, 9 (Nov., 1841), 411–15; Anon. [Jane Storm], "The Home League," *United States Magazine and Democratic Review*, 9 (Dec., 1841), 539–53.

7. Susan Elizabeth Geary, "Scribbling Women: Essays on Literary History and Popular Literature in the 1850s" (Ph.D. diss., Brown University, 1976), 61; John Tebbel, *A History of Book Publishing in the United States* (New York: R. R. Bowker, 1972), 246–50; "Jane McManus Cazneau," "Ann Stephens," "Mrs. E. D. E. N. Southworth," "Elizabeth Ellet," and "Lydia Sigourney," in Edward T. James (ed.), *Notable American Women, 1607–1950* (3 vols.; Cambridge, Mass.: The Belknap Press of Harvard University Press, 1971), I, 315, 569, III, 288, 327, 360; *One Hundred Influential Books Printed before 1900* (New York: Grolier Publishing, 1947), 12; Madeline B. Stern, *Books and Book People in the Nineteenth Century* (New York: R. R. Boucher, 1978), 162–64; Frank Luther Mott, *A History of American Magazines, 1741–1850* (5 vols.; Cambridge, Mass.: Harvard University Press, 1930–1968), I, 549; C. Montgomery, "The Presidents of Texas," *United States Magazine and Democratic Review*, 16 (Mar., 1845), 282–91; Fuller, "*United States Magazine and Democratic Review*," 12.

8. Rose Kavo, "Jane Maria McManus Cazneau," in Lina Mainiero (ed.), *American Women Writers: A Critical Reference Guide from Colonial Times to the Present* (4 vols.; New York: Frederick Ungar, 1979–1982), I, 328; Reilly, "Jane McManus Storms," 25.

9. Fuller, "*United States Magazine and Democratic Review*," 1–3, 16, 24, 56–64; O. [O'Sullivan], "Seeing a Friend off in a Packet," *United States Magazine and Democratic Review*, 16 (July-Aug., 1845), 23–24; [O'Sullivan], "Poor Esther, the Jewess—a Reminiscence of Morocco," *United States Magazine and Democratic Review*, 15 (Jan., 1845), 319; Sampson, "'Under the Banner of the Democratic Principle,'" 132–37, 253–54.

10. Sheridan, *McManus Family Revised*, 13, 24; Coons (comp.), *Koon and Coons Families*, 199; James Morgan to Samuel Swartwout, Feb. 10, 1843, in Bass and Brunson (eds.), *Fragile Empires*, 204.

11. Sampson, "'Under the Banner of the Democratic Principle,'" 4, 141, 172, 187–204, 240, 253.

12. Anon. [Orestes A. Brownson]. "Political Portraits with Pen and Pencil," *United States Magazine and Democratic Review*, 11 (Nov.,1842), 502; Fuller, "*United States Magazine and Democratic Review*," 49–50; John L. O'Sullivan to James K. Polk, Feb. 15, 1845, Papers of James K. Polk, Presidential Papers (National Archives, Washington, D.C.).

13. Anon. [Jane Storm], "The Coup-De-Grace," *United States Magazine and Democratic Review*, 11 (Nov., 1842), 542–44; Fuller, "*United States Magazine and Democratic Review*," 64; Sampson, "'Under the Banner of the Democratic Principle,'" 221–30. For a comparison of Storm's and O'Sullivan's handwriting see: (hers) O'Sullivan to Polk, Feb. 15, 1845, Sept. 20, 1845, (his) O'Sullivan to Polk, July 8, 1844, Polk Papers; Joan von Mehren, *Minerva and the Muse: A Life of Margaret Fuller* (Amherst: University of Massachusetts Press, 1994), 217.

14. Hazel Dicken-Garcia, *Journalistic Standards in Nineteenth-Century America* (Madison: University of Wisconsin Press, 1989), 68, 118; Fuller, "*United States Magazine and Democratic Review*," 12, 25–27.

15. Mott, *American Magazines*, 505; "Meeting of the Female Industry Association," [New York] *Workingman's Advocate*, Mar. 8, 1845.

16. Glyndon G. Van Deusen, *The Jacksonian Era, 1828–1848* (New York: Harper & Row, 1959), 95; Alice S. Rossi (ed.), *The Feminist Papers* (Boston: Northeastern University Press, 1973), 86–99; "People's Ticket," Troy *Sentinel*, Oct. 29, 1824; Robert Dale Owen, "Rights of Women," *The Free Enquirer*, Dec. 10, 1828, 54–55; "Fanny Wright," Troy *Daily Whig*, Oct. 1, 1838, Nov. 19, 1838.

17. Anon. [Jane Storm], "Oregon," *United States Magazine and Democratic Review*, 12 (Apr., 1843), 343–56; David Lavender, *The Great West* (New York: Houghton-Mifflin, 1965; reprint, New York: American Heritage, 1987), 186–97, 230–33.

18. [Storm], "Oregon," 344–48, 356; Norman A. Graebner, *Empire on the Pacific: A Study in American Continental Expansion* (New York: Ronald Press, 1955), 3–8, 34.

19. Elgin Williams, *The Animating Pursuits of Speculation: Land Trafficking in the Annexation of Texas* (New York: Columbia University Press, 1949), 147; Amelia Williams and Eugene C. Barker (eds.), *The Writings of Sam Houston* (8 vols.; Austin: University of Texas Press, 1938–1943), IV, 265–66; Storms to Lamar, Oct. 1845, Lamar Papers.

20. James Morgan to Mrs. J. M. Storms, Jan. 25, 1844, James Morgan Papers, Galveston and Texas History Center (Rosenberg Library, Galveston, Tex.); Morgan to Swartwout, Feb. 10, 1843, in Bass and Brunson (eds.), *Fragile Empires*, 204; Frank Wagner, "William Leslie Cazneau," Thomas W. Cutrer, "Hugh McLeod," W. W. White, "Duff Green," and Robert Bruce Blake, "Thomas Jefferson Green," in Tyler, et al. (eds.), *The New Handbook of Texas*, I, 1053, IV, 434, III, 312, 317; Jane Summer (comp.), *Some Early Travis County Texas Records* (Easly, S.C.: Southern Historical Press, 1979), 18, 106, 107, 153; John Henry Brown, "Annals of Travis County," typescript, 33 vols. (Austin Public Library Archives, Austin, Tex.), IV, 20, XI, 32, XV, 18; Thomas W. Streeter (comp. and ed.), *Bibliography of Texas, 1795–1845* (5 vols.; Cambridge: Harvard University Press, 1960), II, no. 527, no. 620, no. 621; Stanley Siegel, *A Political History of the Texas Republic, 1836–1845* (Austin: University of Texas Press, 1956), 188–237.

21. Swartwout to Morgan, Feb. 10, Mar. 20, 1843, in Bass and Brunson (eds.), *Fragile Empires*, 204, 206; James Morgan to Mrs. J. M. Storms Jan. 26, 1844, Morgan Papers.

22. Anon. [Jane Storm], "The Texas Question," *United States Magazine and Democratic Review*, 14 (Apr., 1844), 423–27; Robert J. Walker, *Letter of Mr. Walker . . .* (Washington:

Globe Office, 1844), 9, 1; Frederick Merk, "A Safety Valve Thesis and Texas Annexation," *Mississippi Valley Historical Review*, 49 (Dec., 1962), 413–36.

23. [Storm], "The Texas Question," 423–27; Philip S. Foner, *Business and Slavery: The New York Merchants and the Irrepressible Conflict* (Chapel Hill: University of North Carolina Press, 1941,), vii, 2, 19; Fried, *John Brown's Journey*, 176; Dr. Alexander Duncan of Ohio quoted in Merk, "A Safety Valve Thesis," 420.

24. [Storm], "The Texas Question," 430; Graebner, *Empire on the Pacific*, 17, 79; Siegel, *A Political History of the Texas Republic*, 123; Thomas W. Cutrer, "Bernard Elliott Bee Sr.," in Tyler, et al. (eds.), *New Handbook of Texas*, I, 457; Alfred Tischendorf, *Great Britain and Mexico in the Era of Porforio Diaz* (Durham: Duke University Press, 1961), 5–7.

25. Morgan to Swartwout, Mar. 25, May 16, 1844, in Bass and Brunson (eds.), *Fragile Empires*, 233, 239; B. R. Brunson, "Samuel Swartwout," in Tyler, et al. (eds.), *New Handbook of Texas*, VI, 165–66; Holman Hamilton, "Texas Bonds and Northern Profits: A Study in Compromise, Investment, and Lobby Influence," *Mississippi Valley Historical Review*, 43 (Mar., 1957), 580–87; "Mrs. J. M. Storms, F, 34," *Ship's Registry Index*, July 1844, New York Port of Entry Records (New York Public Library Archives, New York, N.Y.).

26. Moses Y. Beach in "Cabinet Maker of Olden Days," "Former Cabinet Maker of Valley Turned Newspaper Publisher," and "Century-Old Sun Owes Birth to Springfield," in "Springfield Scrapbooks," (18 vols.; Connecticut Valley Historical Museum, Springfield, Conn.), XIV, 15, XVII, 9; Anna Kasten Nelson, "Mission to Mexico—Moses Y. Beach, Secret Agent," *New York Historical Society Quarterly*, 59 (July, 1975), 228–29.

27. Moses Y. Beach (ed.), *The Wealth and Biography of the Wealthy Citizens of the City of New York*. (10th ed.; New York: Sun Office, 1848), 2; Edward Pessen, "Moses Beach Revisited: A Critical Examination of His Wealthy Citizens Pamphlets," *Journal of American History*, 58 (Sept.,1971), 415, 419, 421, 426.

28. Frank M. O'Brien, *The Story of the Sun* (New York: D. Appleton, 1928), 60, 107; John D. Stevens, *Sensationalism and the New York Press* (New York: Columbia University Press, 1991), 20–22, 27–28.

29. New York *Sun*, Oct. 17, 19, 22, 1844, Mar. 3, 1845.

30.Van Deusen, *Jacksonian Era*, 95; "Locofoco," New York *Tribune*, Jan. 14, 1847; Michael F. Holt, *Political Parties from the Age of Jackson to the Age of Lincoln* (Baton Rouge: Louisiana State University Press, 1992), 64; "A day of fearful significance," New York *Sun*, Aug. 14, 1846. For anti-annexation pamphlets see George Allen, *The Complaint of Mexico, and Conspiracy of Liberty* (1843), no. 1484, James Freeman Clarke, "The Annexation of Texas. A Sermon," (1844), no. 1451, *The Texas Revolution* (1843), in Streeter (comp. and ed.), *Bibliography of Texas*.

31. James Morgan to Mrs. J. M. Storms, Oct. 26, 1844, Morgan Papers.

32. Phinehas Johnson to R. J. Walker, Feb. 2, 1844; Lewis Cass to R. J. Walker, May 12, 1844; George Bancroft to R. J. Walker, June 19, 1844, Robert J. Walker Papers (New York Historical Society Library, New York, N.Y.); M. B. Lamar to Moses Beach, [Macon] *The Georgia Telegraph*, Feb. 11, 1845; Jane M. Cazneau to M. S. Beach, Dec. 27, 1849, Aug. 25, 1865, Jane Cazneau Papers (New York Historical Society Library, New York, N.Y.). These Cazneau papers are copies of originals owned by Brewster Y. Beach of Greenwich, Conn. Eugene Irving McCormac, *James K. Polk: A Political Biography* (Berkeley: University of California Press, 1922), 308; J. W. Webb to W. H. Seward, Mar. 12, 1849, J. M. Storms to

W. H. Seward, Mar. 18, 1849, Seward Papers; Horace Greeley, "Peon Slavery on the Rio Grande," New York *Tribune*, July 15, 1850.

33. Montgomery, "The Presidents of Texas," 282–91.

34. Ibid., 283–91; Philip Graham, *The Life and Poems of Mirabeau B. Lamar* (Chapel Hill: University of North Carolina Press, 1938), 69–72; Storm to Lamar, Oct. 1845, Lamar Papers; J. Maria McManus to Sam Houston, Apr. 20, 1840, Houston Papers.

35. Robert Neil Mathis, "Gazaway Bugg Lamar: A Southern Businessman and Confident in New York City," *New York History*, 56 (July, 1975), 302; J. M. Storms to M. B. Lamar, Feb. 2, 1845, Lamar Papers.

36. Jean V. Matthews, *Women's Struggle for Equality: The First Phase, 1828–1876* (Chicago: Ivan R. Dee, 1997), 92–93. Reformers were women who felt they had been unjustly denied opportunities for growth. "The Female Industrial Association," New York *Sun*, Mar. 6, 10, 14, May 1, 1845; "Meeting of Female Industry Association," [New York] *Workingman's Advocate*, Mar. 8, 22, 1845; "Women of the Nineteenth Century," New York *Sun*, July 29, 1845.

37. "Female Industrial Association," New York *Sun*, May 1, 1845.

38. Anon. [Jane Storm], "The Legal Wrongs of Women," *United States Magazine and Democratic Review*, 14 (May, 1844), 483.

39. "Ann Stephens," "Carolyn Sawyer," and "Mrs. E. D. E. N. Southworth," in James (ed.), *Notable American Women*, III, 236, 327, 360; Graham, *The Life and Poems of Mirabeau B. Lamar*, 69–72; Tebbel, *A History of Book Publishing*, 245; Margaret Fuller to James Nathan, June 12, 1845, in *The Letters of Margaret Fuller*, ed. Robert N. Hudspeth (4 vols.; Ithaca: Cornell University Press, 1987), IV, 118.

40. Madeline B. Stern, "The House of the Expanding Doors," *New York History*, 23 (Jan., 1942), 43–46, 50; Storm to Lamar, Oct. 1845, Lamar Papers; Margaret V. Allen, "The Political and Social Criticism of Margaret Fuller," *South Atlantic Quarterly*, 72, no. 4 (1973), 560–72; Cashion, "Women in the Mexican War," 76–83; Wallace, *Destiny and Glory*, 247.

41. David Lee Child, *The Taking of Naboth's Vineyard, or History of the Texas Conspiracy . . .* (New York: S. W. Benedict, 1845).

42. Anon. [Storm], "Annexation," 5.

43. Ibid, 5, 8–9; Frederick Merk, *Slavery and the Annexation of Texas* (New York: Alfred A. Knopf, 1972), 98–100.

44. Julius Pratt, "The Origin of 'Manifest Destiny,'" *American Historical Review*, 32 (July, 1927), 795–98; "Speech of Mr. R. W. Winthrop of Mass. in H. R., 3 January 1846," *Congressional Globe*, 29th Cong., 1st sess., appendix, 99; Wall, *Henry Watterson*, 25; Sampson, "'Under the Banner of the Democratic Principle,'" 3.

45. Statistics, "Grammatik," Word Perfect, v. 6.1, Novell, Inc., Orem, Utah; O'Sullivan, "Seeing a Friend off in a Packet," 23; Anon. [Storm], "Annexation," 8; Montgomery, "The Presidents of Texas," 282; Sampson, "'Under the Banner of the Democratic Principle,'" 159.

46. Joshua David Scholnick, "Democrats Abroad: Continental Literature and the American Bard in the *United States and Democratic Review*," *American Periodicals*, 3 (1993), 76–79; O'Sullivan, "Seeing a Friend off in a Packet," 23–24; J. L. O'Sullivan to My Dear Sir, Sept. 20, 1845, Feb. 15, 1845, Jane M. Storm to James K. Polk, Feb. 8, 1848 (same handwriting, but different style), Polk Papers; Sampson, "'Under the Banner of the Democratic Principle,'" 375–79; Perry Miller, *The Raven and the Whale: The War of Words and Wits in the Era of Poe and*

Melville (New York: Harcourt, Brace and Company, 1956), 109–10; "Editorials," New York *Morning News,* Nov. 15, 20, 1845.

47. Montgomery, "The Presidents of Texas," 283–88; Montgomery, *Texas and Her Presidents; DeBow's Commercial Review,* 1 (Jan., 1846), 95; Sam Houston to Margaret Houston, Nov. 10, 1845, private collection, copy furnished by Madge T. Roberts, San Antonio, Tex.; Elizabeth Brooks (comp.), *Prominent Women of Texas* (Akron: Werner Publishing, 1896), vii.

48. Montgomery, "Correspondence," New York *Sun,* Apr. 3, July 11, 22, Aug. 5, 22, 26, 1845; Cathryn L. and John V. Lombardi, *Latin American History: A Teaching Atlas* (Madison: University of Wisconsin Press, 1983), 53; William A. Goetzmann, *When the Eagle Screamed: The Romantic Horizon in American Diplomacy, 1800–1860* (New York: John Wiley & Sons, 1966), 55–56.

49. Anon. [Jane Storm], "The Mexican Question," *United States Magazine and Democratic Review,* 16 (May, 1845), 419–28.

50. Storm to Lamar, Oct. 1845, Lamar Papers; J. M. Cazneau to William H. Seward, June 18, 1850, Seward Papers; Graham, *The Life and Poems of Mirabeau B. Lamar,* 71; Montgomery, "Correspondence," New York *Sun,* June 23, 1846.

51. Montgomery, "Correspondence," New York *Sun,* Dec. 15, 1845; J. M. Cazneau to M. Y. Beach, Dec. 27, 1850, Jane Cazneau Papers; Wall, *Henry Watterson,* 25; Joseph P. McKerns (ed.), *Biographical Dictionary of American Journalism* (New York: Greenwood Press, 1989), 23–33; George Henry Payne, *History of Journalism in the United States* (New York: Holt, Rinehart and Winston, 1965), 249, 253; "Editorials," New York *Morning News,* Dec. 27, 1845, Jan. 5, 1846.

52. Sampson, "'Under the Banner of the Democratic Principle,'" 371–91.

53. Montgomery, "Correspondence," New York *Sun,* Mar. 11, 1845, Dec. 12, 15, 23, 1845.

54. Montgomery, "Correspondence," New York *Sun,* Dec. 17, 18, 19, 24, 1845.

55. Montgomery, "Correspondence," New York *Sun,* Dec. 12, 15, 17, 19, 23, 24, 1845; Storm to Lamar, Oct. 1845, Lamar Papers; K. Jack Bauer, "Zachary Taylor," and David M. Vigness, "Pedro de Ampudia," in Tyler, et al. (eds.), *New Handbook of Texas,* VI, 222, I, 157.

56. Montgomery, "Correspondence," New York *Sun,* Mar. 2, 3, 1846; Storm to Lamar, Mar. 27, 1846, Lamar Papers.

57. Montgomery, "Correspondence," New York *Sun,* Mar. 2, 3, 17, 30, 1846.

57. Montgomery, "Correspondence," New York *Sun,* Dec. 12, 15, 17, 18, 19, 23, 24, 1845, Feb. 28 Mar. 2, 3, 14, 15, 30, Apr. 3, 1846; K. Jack Bauer, *Zachary Taylor* (Baton Rouge: Louisiana State University Press, 1985), 35–47.

57. Bauer, *Zachary Taylor,* 36–47; K. Jack Bauer, *The Mexican War, 1846–1848* (New York: Macmillan, 1974), 36–50.

58. Montgomery, "Correspondence," New York *Sun,* Mar. 2, 3, 17, 30, Apr. 3, 4, 17, May 13, 1846; Goetzmann, *When the Eagle Screamed,* 55–57; Art Leatherwood, "Battle of Resaca de la Palma," and Joseph P. Sanchez, "Battle of Palo Alto," in Tyler, et al. (eds.), *New Handbook of Texas,* V, 550, 26–27; Wall, *Henry Watterson,* 25; "William Leslie Cazneau," San Antonio *Daily Herald,* Mar. 22, 1876, in "Biographies of Leading Texans," typescript, 4 vols. (Texas State Library, Austin, Tex.), I, 138–39.

59. Meron L. Dillon, "Jane Cazneau," in James (ed.), *Notable American Women,* I, 315; May, "Lobbyists for Commercial Empire," 386; Payne, *History of Journalism,* 249, 253; C. H.

Levermore, "Rise of Metropolitan Journalism," *American Historical Review*, 6 (Apr., 1901), 458; Allen Nevins, *The American Press Opinion: Washington to Coolidge: A Documentary Record of Editorial Leadership and Criticism, 1785–1927*, (2 vols.; Boston: M. A. Heath, 1928; reprint, Port Washington, N.Y.: Kennikat Press, 1969), I, 3; Col. J. W. Webb to William H. Seward, Mar. 12, 1849, J. M. Storms to W. H. Seward, Mar. 18, 1849, Seward Papers; Reilly, "Jane McManus Storms," 25.

CHAPTER IV

1. Thomas Hart Benton, *Thirty Years' View; or a History of the Working of the American Government for Thirty Years, from 1820 to 1850* (2 vols.; New York: D. Appleton, 1854–1856; reprint, New York: Greenwood Press, 1968), II, 704.

2. M. S. Beach, "A Secret Mission to Mexico," *Scribner's Monthly Century Magazine*, 18 (May, 1879), 136–40; Justin H. Smith, *The War With Mexico* (New York: Macmillan, 1919), 11–13; Wallace, *Destiny and Glory*, 245–75; Frederick Merk, *Manifest Destiny and Mission in American History: A Reinterpretation* (New York: Knopf, 1963; reprint, New York: Vintage Books, 1966), 132–34, 167, 200n–201n; Seymour V. Connor, *Adventure in Glory* (Austin: Steck-Vaughn, 1965), 89; Goetzmann, *When the Eagle Screamed*, 68–71; Seymour V. Connor and Odie B. Faulk (eds. and comps.), *North America Divided: The Mexican War, 1846–1848* (New York: Oxford University Press, 1971), 156–57; Anna Kasten Nelson, "Mission to Mexico," 227–45; Nelson, "Jane Storms Cazneau," 25–40; Anna Kasten Nelson, "Moses Y. Beach: Special Agent," in Robert E. Burke and Frank Freidel (eds.), *Secret Agents: President Polk and the Search for Peace with Mexico* (New York: Garland, 1988), 72–96; May, "Lobbyists for Commercial Empire," 386–87; May, "'Plenipotentiary in Petticoats,'" 19–44; Reilly, "Jane McManus Storms," 21–44; Kinkade, "Jane McManus Storms Cazneau," 7–34; Cashion, "Women in the Mexican War," 75–80; Montgomery, "Correspondence," New York *Sun*, Dec. 1, 1846 to May 29, 1847; Cora Montgomery, *La Verdad*, Jan. 9–June 17, 1848; J. M. Storm to James K. Polk, Aug. 26, 1847–Feb. 8, 1848, Polk Papers; J. M. Storm to William L. Marcy, June 1847, Marcy Papers; J. M. Storm to George Bancroft, July 1846–Oct. 20, 1848, Bancroft Papers; J. M. Storm to James Buchanan, June 1846–Dec. 12, 1847, Buchanan Papers.

3. Montgomery, "Correspondence," *The Weekly Sun*, Apr. 24, 1847, *The American Sun*, May 6, 1847; Merrill D. Peterson, *The Great Triumvirate: Webster, Clay, and Calhoun* (New York: Oxford University Press, 1987), 346–47, 419, 424; Michael A. Morrison, "Martin Van Buren, the Democracy, and the Partisan Politics of Texas Annexation," *Journal of Southern History*, 61 (Nov., 1995), 716; John D. P. Fuller, *The Movement for the Acquisition of All Mexico, 1846–1848* (Baltimore: John Hopkins Press, 1936), 35–37, 65, 130; Charles H. Brown, *Agents of Manifest Destiny: The Lives and Times of the Filibusters* (Chapel Hill: University of North Carolina Press, 1980), 109, 264, 350, 462; William O. Scroggs, *Filibusters and Financiers; The Story of William Walker and His Associates* (New York: Macmillan, 1916), 5, 367; Benton, *Thirty Year's View*, II, 705; Aaron Burr quoted in Tom Chaffin, *Fatal Glory: Narciso López and the First Clandestine U.S. War against Cuba* (Charlottesville: University Press of Virginia, 1996), 8.

4. Fuller, *All Mexico*, 35–37, 65, 86, 101, 119; Montgomery, "Correspondence," New York *Sun*, Mar. 2, 3, Apr. 4, 19, May 6, 7, 13, 29, June 4, 23, July, 7, 17, Aug. 10, Sept. 1, 1846.

5. J. M. Storm to Robert Owen, Jan. 12, 1846, Owen Papers.

6. Bauer, *Zachary Taylor*, 36–47; Bauer, *The Mexican War*, 36–50.

7. Lombardi and Lombardi, *Latin American History: A Teaching Atlas*, 53 (Map 2); Montgomery, "Correspondence," New York *Sun*, Mar. 15, 30, Apr. 3, 4, 1846; Robert W. Johannsen, *To the Halls of the Montezumas: The Mexican War in the American Imagination* (New York: Oxford University Press, 1985), 25; Cora Montgomery, *La Verdad*, Mar. 12, Apr. 9, 1848; Cora Montgomery, *Our Times* (Oct., 1852), 190; J. M. Storm to George Bancroft, July 1846, Bancroft Papers.

8. Nelson, "Mission to Mexico," 232; M. S. Beach, "Origin of the Treaty of Guadalupe Hidalgo," *Scribner's Century Magazine*, 17 (Nov., 1878), 300; J. M. Storm to Lamar, Mar. 27, 1846, in Harriet Smither (ed.), *Papers of Mirabeau Buonaparte Lamar* (6 vols.; Austin: Texas State Library, 1927; reprint, New York: AMS Press, 1973), IV, 55; Frank Wagner, "William L. Cazneau," and Herbert Gambrell, "Mirabeau B. Lamar," in Tyler, et al. (eds.), *The New Handbook of Texas*, I, 1053, IV, 37–39; John R. G. Hassard, *Life of the Most Reverend John Hughes, D.D.* (New York: D. Appleton, 1866), 286–87, 329.

9. Hassard, *Life of Hughes*, 287; Scisco, *Political Nativism in New York State*, 36, 45; Bauer, *The Mexican War*, 46–48; Milo M. Quaife (ed.), *The Diary of James K. Polk during his Presidency, 1845–1849* (4 vols.; Chicago: University of Chicago Press, 1910), I, 408–9.

10. Milton Meltzer, *Bound for the Rio Grande: The Mexican Struggle, 1845–1850* (New York: Alfred A. Knopf, 1974), 266; Bauer, *Zachary Taylor*, 172; Montgomery, "Correspondence," New York *Sun*, June 4, 23, 1846.

11. Montgomery, "Correspondence," New York *Sun*, Mar. 15, 1846; Thomas W. Cutrer, "Hugh McLeod," and David M. Vigness, "Republic of the Rio Grande," in Tyler, et al. (eds.), *New Handbook of Texas*, IV, 434, V, 537; Connor and Faulk (eds. and comps.), *North America Divided*, 186–87; J. M. Storm to James Buchanan, June 1846, Buchanan Papers; Wallace, *Destiny and Glory*, 266.

12. James Morgan to J. M. Storm, Oct. 26, 1844, Morgan Papers; "Transactions of The Right Worshipful Grande Lodge of Free and Accepted Masons of the Republic of Texas (1845)," in Streeter (comp.), *Bibliography of Texas*, nos. 527, 620, 621 in microfilm edition of Thomas W. Streeter Collection of Documents on Texas History, Western Americana Collection (Beineke Rare Books and Manuscripts Library, Yale University, New Haven, Conn.); Smither (ed.), *Lamar Papers*, IV, 37, 135.

13. Cornelia J. Randolph to Virginia Trist, June 29, 1846, Nicholas Trist Papers, Southern Historical Collection (University of North Carolina, Chapel Hill, N.C.).

14. J. M. Storm to Robert Owen, June 29, 1845, Owen Papers.

15. R. D. Owen to Nicholas P. Trist, July 4, 1846, Nicholas P. Trist Papers (Library of Congress); Louis Martin Sears, "Nicholas P. Trist, a Diplomat with Ideals," *Mississippi Valley Historical Review*, 11 (June, 1924), 191; Louis Martin Sears, "Some Correspondence of Robert Dale Owen," *Mississippi Valley Historical Review*, 10 (Dec., 1923), 321; William Leslie Cazneau, Sale by Sheriff, Feb. 2, 1847, five Matagorda city lots sold, Matagorda County Deed Records (Matagorda County Courthouse, Bay City, Tex.).

16. Bauer, *Zachary Taylor*, 172; Montgomery, "Correspondence," New York *Sun*, July 7, 16, 17, 1846.

17. Storm to Bancroft, July 23, 1846, Bancroft Papers; "George Bancroft," in James Grant Wilson and John Fiske (eds.), *National Cyclopedia of American Biography* (39 vols.; New York:

D. Appleton and Co., 1888; reprint, Detroit: Gale Research Co., 1968), I, 154; Montgomery, "Tropical Sketches," New York *Sun*, Dec. 11, 1846; *La Verdad*, Apr. 27, June 17, 1848.

18. Anna Kasten Nelson, "President Polk and the War," in Burke and Freidel (eds.), *Secret Agents*, 28–29; Montgomery, "Correspondence," New York *Sun*, Aug. 10, 1846.

19. Montgomery, "Correspondence," New York *Sun*, Aug. 17, 1846; David Wilmot quoted in Fried, *John Brown's Journey*, 174.

20. Montgomery, "Correspondence," New York *Sun*, Sept. 1, 1846; J. M. Storm to Nicholas P. Trist, Sept. 21, 1846, Trist Papers (Library of Congress).

21. Meltzer, *Bound for the Rio Grande*, 266; William R. Manning, (ed.), *Diplomatic Correspondence of the United States Inter-American Affairs, 1831–1860* (12 vols.; Washington, D.C.: Carnegie Endowment, 1932–1939), IX, 195–96.

22. Pedro Santoni, *Mexicans at Arms: Puro Federalists and the Politics of War, 1845–1848* (Fort Worth: Texas Christian University Press, 1996), 4, 5, 18; Beach, "A Secret Mission to Mexico," 137; Reilly, "Jane McManus Storms," 21; Nelson, "President Polk and the War," 25; J. M. Storm to George Bancroft, July 1846, Bancroft Papers.

23. Beach, "A Secret Mission to Mexico," 136–40; Merk, *Manifest Destiny*, 131–36; Fuller, *All Mexico*, 95; U.S. Congress, Senate Executive Document No. 97, "Message of U.S. President in Answer of Responses of the Senate calling for the correspondence between the government of the United States and Mexico, respecting a right of way across the Isthmus of Tehuantepec, July 28, 1852. Refer to Committee of Foreign Relations," 32nd Cong., 2nd sess. (National Archives, Washington, D.C.).

24. John Basset Moore (ed.), *The Works of James Buchanan* (12 vols.; Philadelphia: J. B. Lippincott, 1908–1911; reprint, New York: Antiquarian Press, 1960), VII, 119–21; Alan Nevins (ed.), *James K. Polk: A Diary of a President, 1845–1849* (New York: Longmans, Green, and Co., 1929), 217–18; Foner, *Business and Slavery*, 2; N. P. Trist to J. M. Storm, Nov. 24, 1846, in Beach, "A Secret Mission to Mexico," 138.

25. John Tebbel and Sarah Watts, *The Press and the Presidency* (New York: Oxford University Press, 1985), 125; Montgomery, "Tropical Sketches," New York *Sun*, Dec. 11, 25, 1846, Jan. 2, 12, 13, 14, 15, 16, 30, Feb. 13, 27, Mar. 13, 25, 1847; Montgomery, *The Sun Weekly*, Jan. 9, 16, 23, Feb. 6, 13, 27, Mar. 13, 26, 1847.

26. Montgomery, "Tropical Sketches," New York *Sun*, Dec. 11, 25, 1846, Jan. 2, 12, 13, 14, 15, 16, 30, Feb. 13, 27, Mar. 13, 25, 1847. Also see in *The Sun Weekly*, Jan. 9, 16, 23, Feb. 6, 13, 27, Mar. 13, 26, 1847.

27. Buenaventura Aroujo to Valentín G. Farías, Jan. 9, 1847, Valentín Gómez Farías Papers, Garcia Collection (Nettie Lee Benson Latin American Collection, University of Texas at Austin, Austin, Tex.); [Anon.], "The Late William Ladd, The Apostle of Peace," *United States Magazine and Democratic Review*, 10 (Mar., 1842), 209–23. Ladd, an international figure in world peace, proposed a Congress of Nations to settle disputes.

28. Nelson, "Mission to Mexico," 237, n23. British consul records "lost" per Public Record Office letter, Apr. 19, 1971; Beach, "Origins of the Treaty of Guadalupe Hidalgo," 299; Moses Y. Beach to James Buchanan, June 4, 1847, in Manning (ed.), *Diplomatic Correspondence*, VIII, 906–7.

29. Montgomery, "Correspondence," New York *Sun*, June 13, 1846, Feb. 12, 1847; John H. Schroeder, *Shaping a Maritime Empire: The Commercial and Diplomatic Role of the American Navy*,

1829–1861 (Westport, Conn.: Greenwood Press, 1985), 80–87; Beach, "A Secret Mission to Mexico," 138; Nelson, "Moses Y. Beach," 80–82; John Black to James Buchanan, Jan. 28, 1847, consul dispatches, Mexico City, RG 59, Department of State (National Archives, Washington, D.C.).

30. Beach, "A Secret Mission to Mexico," 138; Montgomery, "Near Vera Cruz," New York *Sun*, May 21, 1847.

31. Beach, "A Secret Mission to Mexico," 136–37; May, "'Plenipotentiary in Petticoats,'" 22.

32. Beach, "A Secret Mission to Mexico," 138–39; Moses Y. Beach to V. P. V. Gómez Farías, Feb. 4, 1847, "Acto para Establecer el Banco Nacional de Mejico," Feb. 6, 1847, Gómez Farías Papers; Nelson, "Moses Y. Beach," 82; Merk, *Manifest Destiny and Mission*, 134; John Black to James Buchanan, Jan. 28, 1847, consul dispatches, Mexico City, RG 59, Department of State (National Archives, Washington, D.C.).

33. Beach, "A Secret Mission to Mexico," 139; Reilly, "Jane McManus Storms," 34; Nelson, "Mission to Mexico," 240; Michael P. Costeloe, "The Mexican Church and the Rebellion of the Polkos," *Hispanic American Historical Review*, 46 (May, 1966), 174–77; Montgomery, "City of Mexico," New York *Sun*, Apr. 15, 1847.

34. Costeloe, "The Rebellion of the Polkos," 171–77, Montgomery, "Latest from Mexico," New York *Sun*, Apr. 15, 1847; Reilly, "Jane McManus Storms," 31; Nelson, "Moses Y. Beach," 81.

35. Beach, "A Secret Mission to Mexico," 139.

36. Wallace, *Destiny and Glory*, 245; Montgomery, "Vera Cruz," New York *Sun*, Apr. 19, 1847; John R. Kenley, *Memories of a Maryland Volunteer* (Philadelphia: J. B. Lippincott & Co., 1873), 253–54; Charles Winslow Elliott, *Winfield Scott: The Soldier and the Man* (New York: Macmillan, 1937), 455.

37. Montgomery, "Vera Cruz," New York *Sun*, Apr. 16, May 3, 1847.

38. Beach, "A Secret Mission to Mexico," 139–40; Montgomery, "Vera Cruz," New York *Sun*, May 3, 1847.

39. Sears, "Nicholas P. Trist," 93; Tebbel and Watts, *The Press and the Presidency*, 127, 129.

40. Costeloe, "The Rebellion of the Polkos," 172–73; Nelson, "Moses Y. Beach," 83; D. B. B. [Drusilla Beach], "Mexico," New York *Sun*, Apr. 24, 1847; B. [Moses Y. Beach], "Mexico," *New York Sun*, Apr. 24, 1847.

41. Montgomery, "Vera Cruz," New York *Sun*, Apr. 19, May 6, Extra *Sun*, May 8, 1847.

42. Montgomery, "Vera Cruz," New York *Sun*, May 6, 1847.

43. Montgomery, "Prospects and Plans in Mexico," New York *Tribune*, Apr. 30, 1847.

44. Beach, "A Secret Mission to Mexico," 140; Marcosson, *"Marse Henry,"* 47; Montgomery, "Vera Cruz," New York *Sun*, Apr. 27, 1847; Kenley, *Memories of a Maryland Volunteer*, 254–65.

45. Montgomery, "Near Vera Cruz," *Weekly Sun*, May 22, 1847; George Winston Smith and Charles Judah (eds.), *Chronicles of the Gringos: The U.S. Army in the Mexican War, 1846–1848* (Albuquerque: University of New Mexico Press, 1968), 229–31; Johannsen, *To the Halls of the Montezumas*, 298–99; Kenley, *Memories of a Maryland Volunteer*, 370.

46. M. Y. B. [Moses Y. Beach], "Correspondence," *New York Sun*, May 8, 1847; Beach, "A Secret Mission to Mexico," 140; New Jersey, Senate, *Report of the Committee Appointed to Investigate the Affairs of the Plainfield Bank* (Trenton: Sherman and Harron, 1847), 5–18;

Editorial, "An Offer," New York *Sun*, Jan. 18, 1848; "Newspaper Enterprising and Hoaxes," New York *Herald,* June 14, 1848.

47. Montgomery, "Vera Cruz," New York *Sun*, May 13, 22, 1847.

48. Montgomery, "Vera Cruz," New York *Sun*, May 24, 1847.

49. Ibid.

50. Beach, "A Secret Mission to Mexico," 139–40; Nevins (ed.), *Polk Diary*, I, 216; Sears, "Nicholas P. Trist," 191.

51. Nelson, "Jane Storms Cazneau," 32; Nevins (ed.), *Polk Diary*, 216–17, 230. Nevins omitted reference to Storm's visit. Beach, "A Secret Mission to Mexico," 140; Manning (ed.), *Diplomatic Correspondence*, IX, 195–96, 906–7; Quaife (ed.), *Diary of James K. Polk*, III, 22–24.

52. "Our Position on Mexico," New York *Sun*, May 17, 1847; "What are we to do with Mexico," New York *Sun*, May 22, 1847; "Correspondence," New York *Sun*, May 29, 1847; D. B. B. [Drusilla Beach], "Extract from our private correspondence," New York *Sun*, EXTRA, Apr. 24, 1847.

53. "The Sun and the Administration," New York *Sun*, May 27, 1847; J. M. Cazneau to Moses Y. Beach, Dec. 27, 1849, Jane Cazneau Papers. Those unaware that Beach and his daughter wrote the "All Mexico" letters that were printed in the *Weekly Sun* without bylines has led to the erroneous conclusion that Jane Storm advocated All Mexico.

54. J. M. Storms to James Buchanan, [May 1847], Buchanan Papers; Hamilton Holman, "Texas Bonds and Northern Profits," 580.

55. "Seeing the Elephant," New York *Sun*, May 1, 1847; Johannsen, *To the Halls of the Montezumas*, 87; J. M. Storm to James Buchanan, n.d. May, July 19, 1847, Buchanan Papers; J. M. Storm to W. L. Marcy, June 4, 14, 1847; W. L. Marcy to J. M. Storm, June 11, 14, 1847, Marcy Papers.

56. J. M. Storm to James Buchanan, June 14, July 8, 19, Aug. 24, 1847, Buchanan Papers; Moses Y. Beach to James K. Polk, June 26, July 17, 1847, Polk Papers; Montgomery, "Letters from Cuba, Nos. 1–6," New York *Sun*, July 19, 22, 30, Aug. 9, 20, 25, 31, Oct. 18, Nov. 25, 1847; J. M. Storm to James K. Polk, Aug. 26, 1847, Polk Papers; Montgomery, *La Verdad*, Feb. 13, 1848.

57. Benton, *Thirty Years' View*, II, 705; J. M. Storm to James Buchanan, Nov. 1847, Dec. 12, 1847, Buchanan Papers; Cora Montgomery, "Letters from Cuba," New York *Sun*, Sept. 1, Oct. 25, 26, Nov. 25, 1847.

58. Robert H. Brent, "Nicholas P. Trist and the Treaty of Guadalupe Hidalgo," *Southwestern Historical Quarterly*, 57 (Jan., 1954), 464–66; Fuller, *All Mexico*, 158–59; Benton, *Thirty Years' View*, II, 704; Storm to Buchanan, Dec. 12, 1847, Buchanan Papers; W. L. Cazneau to R. O. W. McManus, June 2, 1875, James Papers; Cora Montgomery, "The Mosquito King," *La Verdad*, Mar. 12, 1848; Charles Lee Stansifer, "The Central-American Career of E. George Squier" (Ph. D. diss., Tulane University, 1959), 43.

59. Cora Montgomery, *La Verdad*, Jan. 9, Feb. 13, 26, Mar. 12, 26, Apr. 9, 27, May 28, June 17, 1848.

60. Jane Storm and M. S. Beach corresponded from Feb. 20, 1849, to Dec. 1, 1865, Jane Cazneau Papers; Montgomery, "Correspondence," New York *Sun*, Jan. 10, 1848.

61. Montgomery, "Correspondence," *La Verdad*, Jan. 9, 1848.

62. J. M. Storm to James K. Polk, Feb. 8, 1848, Polk Papers; J. M. Storm to George Bancroft, July 23, 1848, Bancroft Papers.

63. Cora Montgomery, *La Verdad*, Feb. 26, 1848; Storm to Polk, Feb. 8, 1848, Polk Papers.

64. J. M. Storm to George Bancroft, Feb. 1848, Bancroft Papers.

65. "Correspondence," *La Verdad*, Mar. 28, 1848. An examination of the library stacks of sources on the Mexican War do not mention corruption.

66. "Ireland," *La Verdad*, Feb. 13, 1848; "News From Europe," *La Verdad*, Feb. 26, 1848; "The Temple of Freedom," *La Verdad*, Mar. 12, 26, 28, Apr. 9, 1848; "Political Revolutions," *La Verdad*, May 28, 1848; Montgomery quoted in Merk, *Manifest Destiny*, 200n.

67. Montgomery, "Correspondence," New York *Sun*, Apr. 15, 1848.

68. Montgomery, "England . . . Yucatan," *La Verdad*, June 17, 1848.

CHAPTER V

1. Cora Montgomery [Jane Cazneau], *The Queen of Islands* (New York: Charles Wood, 1850), 3. The pamphlet began as a declaration: "Borne down by foreign soldiers, for whose support she is taxed, until almost the necessities of life are doubled in price; deprived of freedom of speech, of press, and of conscience; forbid to discuss or even petition for relief, and overwhelmed by importations of slaves from Africa, whose presence she does not desire, but who are held upon her disarmed citizens in perpetual threat, Cuba has reached that point of suffering in which it becomes suicide and crime to remain passive."

2. Montgomery, "Correspondence," New York *Sun*, Dec. 24, 1845; Montgomery, "Tropical Sketches," nos. 1–15, New York *Sun*, Dec. 11, 1846 to Mar. 25, 1847.

3. Montgomery, "Tropical Sketches," nos. 1–15, New York *Sun*, Dec. 11, 25, 1846, Jan. 2, 12, 13, 14, 15, 30, Feb. 13, 27, Mar. 13, 25, 1847. See also *The Sun Weekly*, Jan. 9, 16, 23, Feb. 6, 13, 27, Mar. 13, 26, 1847; Nelson, "Jane Storms Cazneau," 25–27, 32, 35; May, "Lobbyists for Commercial Empire," 386; Basil Rauch, *American Interest in Cuba: 1848–1855* (New York: Columbia University Press, 1948), 192.

4. Chaffin, *Fatal Glory*, 7–10, 29.

5. J. M. Storm to M. S. Beach, Feb. 20, 1849, Jan. 8, 1850, Jane Cazneau Papers; Cora Montgomery (ed.), *La Verdad*, Jan. 9 to June 17, 1848; Anon. [Jane Storm], "The King of Rivers," *United States Magazine and Democratic Review*, 25 (Dec., 1849), 506–15; Cora Montgomery, *The King of Rivers* (New York: Charles Wood, 1850); Montgomery, *The Queen of Islands*; Cora Montgomery, *The Queen of Islands and the King of Rivers* (New York: Charles Wood, 1850); J. M. Storm to James K. Polk, Aug. 26, 1847, Jan. 4, 1849, Polk Papers; J. M. Storm to George Bancroft, n.d. Jan., June 20, Oct. 20, 1848, Bancroft Papers; J. M. Storm to James Buchanan, Aug. 24, n.d. Nov., Dec. 12, 1847, Feb. 18, July 24, 1848, Jan. 18, 1853, Nov. 14, 1857, June 5, 1858, Buchanan Papers.

6. Montgomery, *The Queen of Islands and the King of Rivers*, 6–8; Rauch, *American Interest in Cuba*, 11, 15–17, 183–85.

7. Richard W. Van Alstyne, *The Rising American Empire* (New York: Oxford University Press, 1960), 88, 148; Rauch, *American Interest in Cuba*, 17; Charles E. Chapman, *A History of the Cuban Republic* (New York: Macmillian, 1927), 56; Gerald E. Poyo, "Evolution of Cuban

Separatist Thought in the Emigré Communities of the United States, 1848–1895," *Hispanic American Review*, 66 (Aug., 1986), 485–89.

8. Robert Granville Caldwell, *The López Expedition to Cuba, 1848–1851* (Princeton: Princeton University Press, 1915), 37n, 117; Van Alstyne, *The Rising American Empire*, 149, 154; Rauch, *American Interest in Cuba*, 28, 31–36; Willis Fletcher Johnson, *The History of Cuba* (5 vols.; New York: B. F. Buck, 1920), III, 10; William Spence Robertson, *Hispanic-American Relations with the United States* (New York: Oxford University Press, 1923), Appendix, Tables I–VI, Cuba, Imports-Exports, 1830–1860.

9. "In a naive point of view," [London] *Times*, Sept. 9, 1850; Johnson, *The History of Cuba*, III, 3; Rauch; *American Interest in Cuba*, 22; Caldwell, *López Expedition to Cuba*, 117; Lombardi and Lombardi, *Latin American History: A Teaching Atlas*, 75.

10. Van Alstyne, *The Rising American Empire*, 100, 132, 146; Rauch, *American Interest in Cuba*, 20–23, 42.

11. Montgomery, "Tropical Sketches," New York *Sun*, Jan. 12, 13, 15, 16, 1847; Rauch, *American Interest in Cuba*, 54.

12. Montgomery, "Outrage on American Flag in Cuba," New York *Tribune*, Jan. 14, 1847; Montgomery, "Tropical Sketches," New York *Sun*, Jan. 12, 1847; "Margaret Fuller," in Joel Myerson (ed.), *Dictionary of Literary Biography* (183 vols.; Detroit: Gale Research, 1979), LXXIII, 112.

13. Montgomery, "Tropical Sketches," New York *Sun*, Jan. 12, 14, 15, Feb. 13, 1847.

14. Nelson, "Jane Storms Cazneau," 35; M. Y. B. [Moses Y. Beach], "Correspondence, New Orleans," New York *Sun*, May 8, 1847; Montgomery, "Cuba Under the United States Flag," New York *Sun*, July 23, 1847; Rauch, *American Interest in Cuba*, 38, 51–58. Unaware of Storm's role, Rauch credited Beach with the press campaign that was the basis of Cuban policy for the Polk, Pierce, and Buchanan administrations. He called O'Sullivan a "brilliant journalist," and identified "Montgomery" as Beach's daughter. J. M. Storm to James Buchanan, July 8, 1847, Buchanan Papers.

15. J. M. Storm to James Buchanan, July 8, 1847, Buchanan Papers; Montgomery, "Letters From Cuba," New York *Sun*, July 2, 19, 30, Aug. 9, 20, 25, 1847; Montgomery, "Cuba Under the Flag of the United States," New York *Sun*, July 23, 1847.

16. Montgomery, "Letters From Cuba," New York *Sun*, July 30, Aug. 9, 25, 1847; Rauch, *American Interest in Cuba*, 25, 35–37, 42–44; Buenaventura Aroujo to Valentín Gómez Farías, Jan. 9, 1847, Gómez Farías Papers.

17. Montgomery, "Havana," New York *Sun*, July 30, Aug. 9, 25, 31, Oct. 18, Nov. 25, 1847; Rauch, *American Interest in Cuba*, 25, 35–37, 42–44.

18. Montgomery, "Havana," New York *Sun*, Aug. 25, 1847; Rauch, *American Interest in Cuba*, 21, 31.

19. Montgomery, "Havana," New York *Sun*, Aug. 31, 1847; Rauch, *American Interest in Cuba*, 35–43.

20. Merk, *Manifest Destiny and Mission*, 116–25, 132–34, 167, 200; J. M. Storm to Buchanan, Aug. 24, 1847; Buchanan Papers; Van Alstyne, *The Rising American Empire*, 149, 154–55; J. M. Storm to James K. Polk, Aug. 26, 1847, Polk Papers; Johnson, *The History of Cuba*, III, 10; Rauch, *American Interest in Cuba*, 36, 53, 58–64; Alexander Gallardo, *Britain and the First Carlist War, 1833–1839* (Norwood, Pa.: Norwood, 1978), 3, 30, 115, 230. The

Quadruple Alliance of Britain, France, Portugal, and the pro-British Isabella II fought against Prince Carlos, who was backed by the Northern Powers of Prussia, Austria, and Russia. Britain's trade with the former Spanish colonies was at stake. M. Y. Beach, "Correspondence," New York *Sun*, June 26, 1847.

21. Rauch, *American Interest in Cuba*, 62, 64–65.

22. Cora Montgomery (ed.), *La Verdad*, Jan. 9, Feb. 13, 26, Mar. 12, 26, Apr. 9, 27, May 28, June 17, 1848; Rauch, *American Interest in Cuba*, 55, 61–65, 109.

23. Montgomery, "Correspondence," *La Verdad*, Jan. 9, 1848; Montgomery, "Monarchy in Mexico," *La Verdad*, Feb. 13, 1848; Montgomery, "Disinherited," *La Verdad*, Feb. 26, 1848; Montgomery, "Designs," *La Verdad*, Apr. 9, 1848; Montgomery, "Stowaway Copies," *La Verdad*, June 17, Feb. 26, 1848; Montgomery, "Correspondence," New York *Sun*, Jan. 10, 1848; William H. Marcy to Prosper M. Wetmore, Feb. 9, 1848, Marcy Papers; Rauch, *American Interest in Cuba*, 26; Storm to Bancroft, n.d. Feb., June 20, 1848, Bancroft Papers.

24. Storm to Buchanan, Feb. 18, 1848, Buchanan Papers; Macoy (comp.), *A Dictionary of Freemasonry*, 386, 690.

25. Rauch, *American Interest in Cuba*, 54–65, 71–83; Edward S. Wallace, *General William Jennings Worth: Monterrey's Forgotten Hero* (Dallas: Southern Methodist University Press, 1953), 169, 185.

26. Johnson, *The History of Cuba*, III, 31–37; Rauch, *American Interest in Cuba*, 79–80.

27. Rauch, *American Interest in Cuba*, 62, 67, 76–84, 90.

28. Ibid., 64, 166, 109.

29. Storm to Buchanan, July 24, 1848, Jan. 18, 1853, Buchanan Papers.

30. "Newspaper Enterprizes and Hoaxes," New York *Herald*, June 14, 1848; Levermore, "The Rise of Metropolitan Journalism," 459; *Report of the Committee Appointed to Investigate the Affairs of the Plainfield Bank*, 16.

31. "The Island of Cuba its Destiny," New York *Herald*, June 22, 1848; Alfred N. Hunt, *Haiti's Influence on Antebellum America: Slumbering Volcano in the Caribbean* (Baton Rouge: Louisiana State University Press, 1988), 20–23.

32. New York *Herald*, June 22, 1848; J. M. Cazneau to Moses Y. Beach, Dec. 27, 1849, Jan. 8, 1850, J. M. Cazneau to Mr. Wood, Nov. 1, 1850, Jane Cazneau Papers; Wallingford, Connecticut, Historical Society Scrapbook Collection, vol. 17, p. 9, vol. 14, p. 15. Beach moved to Wallingford, built an elegant mansion, and lived until 1868.

33. J. M. Storm to George Bancroft, June 20, Oct. 20, 1848, Bancroft Papers; McCormac, *James K. Polk: A Political Biography*, 633, 643.

34. Quaife (ed.), *Diary of James K. Polk*, III, 480; Anon. [Jane Storm], "Principles, Not Men," *United States Magazine and Democratic Review*, 23 (July, 1848), 3–12.

35. Rauch, *American Interest in Cuba*, 80, 92–94, 104, 108–9; Wallace, *William Jennings Worth*, 185; J. M. Storm to D. S. Dickinson, Jan. 4, 1849, Polk Papers.

36. J. M. Storm to M. S. Beach, Feb. 20, 1849, Jane Cazneau Papers; J. M. McManus to James Morgan, Sept. 20, 1837, deed records (Matagorda County Courthouse, Bay City, Tex.), book B, p. 245; James Morgan to Mary [Swartwout] Livingston, Jan. 9, 1849, deed records, Matagorda County, book G, p. 367; R. O. W. McManus to S. Rhodes Fisher, n.d. June 1885, box 3, fols, 58, 62, James Papers.

37. Rauch, *American Interest in Cuba*, 216, 252; J. M. Storm to James Buchanan, Dec. 12, 1847, Jan. 18, 1853, Buchanan Papers; J. M. Storm to Col. J. W. Webb, Mar. 10, 1849, enclosed with Col. J. W. Webb to William H. Seward, Mar. 12, 1849, J. M. Storm to William H. Seward, Mar. 18, 1849, Seward Papers; James L. Crouthamel, *James Watson Webb: A Biography* (Middleton, Conn.: Wesleyan University Press, 1969), 91.

38. Montgomery, *The Queen of Islands and the King of Rivers*, frontispiece; Montgomery, *Eagle Pass*, 48; Patrick L. Cazneau, family genealogist, to Linda S. Hudson, Dec. 8, 1995, letter; Ben E. Pingenot, "Eagle Pass," Frank Wagner, "William Leslie Cazneau," and Erma Baker, "John Twohig," in Tyler, et al. (eds.), *New Handbook of Texas*, II, 751–52, I, 1053, VI, 606.

39. Montgomery, "King of Rivers," 506–15; Montgomery, *King of Rivers*, frontispiece, 3–7; Freehling, *The Reintegration of American History*, 18, 142–43, 165. Freehling says that slaveholders believed that colonization would end slavery in twenty-five years.

40. Montgomery, *King of Rivers*, 5; Robert W. Johannsen, *Stephen A. Douglas* (New York: Oxford University Press, 1973), 209; Goetzmann, *Army Exploration*, 352.

41. Montgomery, "King of Rivers," esp. 514–15; Montgomery, *King of Rivers*, 3–6, 10, 14, 19.

42. Montgomery, *King of Rivers*, 3, 7; Montgomery, *The Queen of Islands*, 6–8; Allan Nevins, *Ordeal of the Union*, vol. 1, 511–15; J. D. B. DeBow (ed.), *Statistical View of the United States . . . Being a Compendium of the Seventh Census* (Washington, D.C.: Beverley Tucker, Senate Printer, 1854), Table 71, "Slave Population of the United States," Table 18, "White Population of the United States." The Seventh Census (1850) confirms that ten northern states had reported slaves in 1840, but had none in 1850. The transition states of Delaware, Maryland, and the District of Columbia had a decrease in the slave population. Overall, the slave population increased by 22 percent while the white population of the free labor states grew by 39.42 percent.

43. J. M. Storm to George Bancroft, June 20, 1848, Bancroft Papers; Freehling, *The Reintegration of American History*, 18, 28, 142–45; Foner, *Business and Slavery*, 25, 37, 42, 55–56, 66–69, 138.

44. Montgomery, *The Queen of Islands and the King of Rivers*, 7–25, 40; Rauch, *American Interest in Cuba*, 110–19, 245–47.

45. Montgomery, *The Queen of Islands and the King of Rivers*, 7–16, 22–25, 40.

46. Rauch, *American Interest in Cuba*, 118, 245.

47. Ibid., 122–25; Caldwell, *López Expedition to Cuba*, 78.

48. J. M. Cazneau to Mr. Wood, Nov. 1, 1850, Jane Cazneau Papers; J. M. Storm to William H. Seward, Sept. 27, 1849, J. M. Cazneau to William H. Seward, Dec. 10, 1849, Seward Papers.

49. *Baldwin, et al. vs. Max Goldfrank, et al.*, Vicente Garza Deeds, Bexar County, Tex., Maverick County, Tex., 1848–1876, box 3, fol. 58, James Papers.

50. Fabens [Cazneau], *The Camel Hunt*, 5–16, 28–48; Joseph W. Fabens [Jane Cazneau], *A Story of Life on the Isthmus* (New York: George P. Putnam, 1853); Wallace, *Destiny and Glory*, 267–68. Wallace wrote that Jane accompanied her husband to Morocco and Panama in late 1849, and that Fabens and William Cazneau met through Henry Kinney. In several bibliographies, Fabens is shown as the author of books known to have been written by Cazneau, such as: *In The Tropics, Life in Santo Domingo* (New York: Carleton, 1863), *The Prince of Kashna*, and *The Uses of the Camel: Considered with a view to his Introduction into our Western States and Territories. A paper read before the American Geographical and Statistical Society, March 2, 1865* (New

York: Carleton, 1865; Washington: F. Taylor, 1865); *Facts about Santo Domingo,* . . . (New York: George P. Putnam, 1862); *Resources of Santo Domingo* (New York: Carleton, 1863; Washington: Major & Knapp, 1869; Washington, F. Taylor, 1871). See Lyle H. Wright, *American Fiction, 1851–1875, a Contribution toward a Bibliography* (San Marino: Huntington Library, 1957), 67, listed Fabens as author of Jane Cazneau's books on the tropics. Fabens was born in Salem, Massachusetts, and entered Harvard in 1838 but dropped out. He claimed to have toured Europe to regain his health, but his college song, "The Last Cigar," hints as to why he left Andover Theological Seminary. He was a colonel in the Republic of Texas Army. In 1843, Fabens became United States consul at Cayenne, French Guiana, where he tended his father's business interests. See "Joseph Warren Fabens," in *National Cyclopedia of American Biography* (10 vols.; New York: James T. White, 1897), VII, 178.

51. Fabens [Cazneau], *The Camel Hunt,* 28–48.

52. Jane M. Cazneau to M. Y. Beach, Dec. 27, 1849, Jane Cazneau Papers.

53. J. M. Cazneau to M. Y. Beach, Jan. 8, 1850, Jane Cazneau Papers; Claim of William L. Cazneau, Sen. Moses Norris, sponsor, Feb. 15, 1850, Special Senate Reports, No. 53, 31st Cong., 1st sess., Washington, D.C., vol. 1, advise to refund duty paid on goods.

54. Cazneau to Beach, Jan. 8, 1850, Jane Cazneau Papers.

55. Cora Montgomery, "The Union of the Seas," *The Merchant's Magazine,* 22 (Feb., 1850), 154.

56. Merle E. Curti, "Young America," *American Historical Review,* 32 (July, 1927), 34–55; Goetzmann, *When the Eagle Screamed,* 82; Nevins, *Ordeal of the Union,* 544, 556; Rauch, *American Interest in Cuba,* 220; Foner, *Business and Slavery,* 55.

57. J. M. Cazneau to Mr. Wood, Nov. 1, 1850, Jane Cazneau; Montgomery, *The Queen of Islands and the King of Rivers,* 7, 15; Montgomery, "Union of the Seas,"154; Ketchum quoted in Foner, *Business and Slavery,* 55; Rauch, *American Interest in Cuba,* 109, 122, 149, 207; DeBow quoted in Rauch, *American Interest in Cuba,* 187–90.

58. "A Gauntlet for the Men," Washington *Daily States,* Apr. 21, 1857; Montgomery, *Eagle Pass,* 22; J. M. Cazneau to James Buchanan, Jan. 8, 1853, Buchanan Papers.

CHAPTER VI

1. Cazneau [Montgomery], *Eagle Pass,* 123–24.

2. J. M. Cazneau to Mr. Wood, Nov. 1, 1850, Jane Cazneau Papers; Fabens [Cazneau], *The Camel Hunt,* 7. Because of Fabens's name being identified with the style of the *Camel Hunt* and its sequel, *Life on the Isthmus* (New York: George P. Putnam, 1853), bibliographers have identified Fabens as the author of other anonymous works by Cazneau. See Wright, *American Fiction, 1851–1875,* 67. Wright lists Fabens as author of *The Prince of Kashna, In The Tropics,* also published as *Life in Santo Domingo, by a Settler.* See also "Joseph Warren Fabens," in *The National Cyclopedia of American Biography,* VII, 178.

3. Cazneau, *Eagle Pass,* frontispiece, dedication; "George P. Putnam," in Myerson (gen. ed.), *Dictionary of Literary Biography,* XLIX, 374; Brooks (comp.), *Prominent Women of Texas,* vii; C. L. Sonnichsen, review of *Eagle Pass; or Life on the Border* by Mrs. William L. Cazneau [Cora Montgomery] edited, with an introduction by Robert Crawford Cotner, *Southwestern Historical Quarterly,* 70 (Oct., 1966), 343–45; Jane Cazneau file.

4. Harriet Beecher Stowe, *Uncle Tom's Cabin* (Boston: John P. Jewitt and Co., 1852; reprint, New York: Harper Classics, 1965), xx–xxi; Review of *Eagle Pass; or Life on the Border* by Cora Montgomery in *DeBow's Commercial Review*, 13 (Dec., 1852), 642; Teresa Griffin Viele, *Following the Drum*, foreword by Sandra L. Myres, (Lincoln: University of Nebraska Press, 1984), 4–10; Cazneau, *Eagle Pass*, preface, passim; William T. Kerrigan, "Race, Expansion, and Slavery in Eagle Pass, Texas, 1852," *Southwestern Historical Quarterly*, 101 (Jan., 1998), 299.

5. Cazneau, *Eagle Pass*, 11-12; Fabens [Cazneau], *The Camel Hunt*, 5.

6. Cazneau, *Eagle Pass*, 15–23; J. M. Storm to M. B. Lamar, Oct. 1845, in Smither (ed.), *Papers of Mirabeau Buonaparte Lamar*, IV, pt. 1, 108; Archie P. McDonald, *Travis* (Austin: Jenkins Publishing, 1976), 84–85; Brownson Malsch, *Indianola, the Mother of Western Texas* (Austin: Statesmen Press, 1988), 36.

7. Cazneau, *Eagle Pass*, 19–31.

8. Ibid., 95–97; "A Sketch of Mrs. Cazneau," New York *Tribune*, Dec. 30, 1878.

9. Cazneau, *Eagle Pass*, 26–31; Malsch, *Indianola*, 20; "San Antonio San Diego Mail Line," in Stephens and Holmes, *Historical Atlas of Texas*, no. 37.

10. Cazneau, *Eagle Pass*, 40–41.

11. Ibid., 40–41; Mardock, *The Reformer and the American Indian*, 9–10, 15–16. Cazneau's views reflected those of Minnesota's Episcopalian Bishop Henry Benjamin Whipple.

12. Cazneau, *Eagle Pass*, 40–41; Fabens [Cazneau], *The Camel Hunt*, 217.

13. Cazneau, *Eagle Pass*, 32–34, 44; "George Van Ness," in Tyler, et al. (eds.), *New Handbook of Texas*, VI, 706; Odie Faulk, *Too Far North . . . Too Far South* (Los Angeles: Westernlore Press, 1967), 143.

14. Cazneau, *Eagle Pass*, 32–46; Carl Coke Rister, "Beales's Rio Grande Colony," in Tyler, et al. (eds.), *New Handbook of Texas*, I, 435–36; "Federal Military Posts before the Civil War," in Stephens and Holmes, *Historical Atlas of Texas*, no. 35.

15. Cazneau, *Eagle Pass*, 48–57.

16. "Fort Duncan," Ben E. Pingenot, "Eagle Pass," Martin Donell Kohout, "Coons' Rancho," in Tyler, et al. (eds.), *New Handbook of Texas*, II, 1098–99, 751–52, 312–13; Jane Cazneau file.

17. May, "Lobbyists for Commercial Empire," 386, 389, 390–92; "Transactions of The Right Worshipful Grand Lodge of Free and Accepted Masons of the Republic of Texas, 1845," in Streeter (comp.), *The Bibliography of Texas, Index*, no. 620, 621; "The Many Friends of Gen. Thomas N. Cazneau," New York *Times*, Dec. 17, 1871; "Descendants of Paix Cazneau," *New England Historical and Genealogical Register*, 142 (Apr., 1988), 139; James and William Cazneau (1753–1801) (Firm), "Corn Hill, Boston, Imported from London and Bristol, Wholesale & Retail goods in brass, copper, steel, and iron," Early American Imprints Collection., 1st ser., no. 42073 (American Antiquarian Society, Worchester, Mass.); "Capt. W. L. Cazneau," San Francisco *Daily Alta Californian*, July 14, 1866; James A. Cox, "Ordeal by Water," *True: The Man's Magazine*, 22 (July, 1959), 37–38, 66–72; "Gen. T. N. Cazneau," *California Mail Bag*, 3 (July-Aug., 1873), 77; Francis H. Brown, "Cazneau Quick Step March," (New York: J. L. Hewitt, 1842); *New Orleans City Directory, 1846–1850*, The Historic New Orleans Collection (Kemper and Leila Williams Foundation Research Center, New Orleans, La.); John Henry Brown, "Annals of Travis County," typescript, vol. 12, p. 8 (Austin Public Library Archives, Austin, Tex.). Cazneau's sister, father, and mother came to see the Texans

off to Santa Fe. Wallace, *Destiny and Glory*, 266; Paul D. Lack, *The Texas Revolutionary Experience* (College Station: Texas A&M University Press, 1992), 219; John H. Jenkins and Kenneth Kesselus, *Edward Burleson: Texas Frontier Leader* (Austin: Jenkins Press, 1990), 347.

18. J. M. Storm to George Bancroft, n.d. Feb. 1848, Bancroft Papers; Roy L. Swift and Leavett Corning, *Three Roads to Chihuahua: The Great Wagon Roads of the Southwest* (Austin: Eakin Press, 1988), 78; William MacDonald (ed.), "Treaty of Guadalupe Hidalgo," in *Documentary Source Book of American History, 1606–1926* (New York: Macmillian, 1926), 382; Robertson, *Hispanic-American Relations with the United States*, 257.

19. *Lemuel H. Baldwin, et al. vs. Max Goldfrank, et al.*: Vicente Garza Deeds, Bexar County, Maverick County, 1848–1876, William L. Cazneau to Robert O. W. McManus, June 2, 1875, box 3, fols. 58–66, James Papers; Tischendorf, *Great Britain and Mexico in the Era of Porforio Diaz*, 5–7; Claim of William L. Cazneau, Sen. Moses Norris, Feb. 15, 1850, Special Senate Reports, no. 53, 31st Cong., 1st sess., vol. 1, advise to refund duty paid on goods; J. Fred Rippy, "Border Troubles along the Rio Grande," *Southwestern Historical Quarterly*, 23 (Oct., 1919), 91–96; MacDonald (ed.), *Documentary Source Book*, 382; Paul Horgan, *The Great River: The Rio Grande in North American History*, (2 vols.; New York: Rinehart, 1954), II, 788–91; Frank Wagner, "Levi Jones," in Tyler, et al. (eds.), *New Handbook of Texas*, III, 987; J. M. Cazneau to Mr. Wood, Nov. 1, 1850, Jane Cazneau Papers.

20. Cazneau, *Eagle Pass*, 50, 67–69; Mike Kingston (ed.), *Texas Almanac, 1986–1987* (Dallas: Dallas Morning News, 1986–1987), 328. Quemado now has sixteen thousand acres of truck farms and orchards. Maverick County has 105 miles of irrigated farms along the river.

21. Cazneau, *Eagle Pass*, 64–65.

22. Ibid., 65–67; Fabens [Cazneau], *The Camel Hunt*, preface.

23. Cazneau, *Eagle Pass*, 72–77; Seventh Census of the United States, 1850, schedule I (free inhabitants) Texas, Bexar County. Twenty-seven of the soldiers were musicians. Rosalie Schwartz, *Across the Rio to Freedom: U.S. Negroes in Mexico* (El Paso: Texas Western University Press, 1975), 39; Kenneth Wiggins Porter, "The Seminole Negro-Indian Scouts," *Southwestern Historical Quarterly*, 55 (Jan., 1952), 358–60.

24. Cazneau, *Eagle Pass*, 69–80; J. M. Cazneau to Moses Y. Beach, Dec. 27, 1849, Jane Cazneau Papers; Cora Montgomery, "Peon Slavery on the Rio Grande, Eagle Pass, May 21, 1850," New York *Tribune*, July 15, 1850.

25. J. M. Cazneau to Hon. Wm. H. Seward, June 18, 1850, Jan. 16, 1851, Seward Papers.

26. Cora Montgomery, New York *Tribune*, July 15, Oct. 17, Dec. 11, 1850, Feb. 1, Mar. 6, 8, Aug. 2, 1851; Myerson (ed.), *Dictionary of Literary Biography*, LIX, 142, LXXIII, 112, CLXXXIII, 126. On July 19, 1850, Fuller, her lover, and their child drowned when their ship wrecked in sight of Long Island. Ralph Waldo Emerson published her collected letters, books, and columns.

27. J. M. Cazneau to William H. Seward, Dec. 30, 1850, Seward Papers; Cora Montgomery, "Peon Slavery on the Rio Grande—Letter from the Border, Eagle Pass, May 21, 1850," New York *Tribune*, July 15, 1850.

28. Cora Montgomery, "Texas and Her Duty," [Austin] *Texas State Gazette*, Sept. 7, 1850; Hamilton, "Texas Bonds and Northern Profits," 580.

29. J. M. Cazneau to M. S. Beach, (lined through, Mr. Wood above), Sept. 30, 1850, Jane Cazneau Papers.

30. *Abstract of the Title to Antonio Rivas Grant*, Garry Mauro (comp.), *Guide to Spanish and Mexican Land Grants in South Texas* (Austin: Texas General Land Office, 1988), 255; William L. Cazneau, General Land Office Records, Bexar file 1–1237, no. 742, vol. 18, Austin, Tex.; William L. Cazneau, patent, Oct. 24, 1849, Bexar County deed records, book H, p. 14; Galen D. Greaser and Jesús F. de la Teja, "Quieting Title to Spanish and Mexican Land Grants in the Trans–Nueces: The Bourland and Miller Commission, 1850–1852," *Southwestern Historical Quarterly*, 95 (Apr., 1992), 445–64; J. M. Cazneau to William H. Seward, June 3, 1851, Seward Papers. Jane Cazneau requested that Seward, a patent lawyer, send William Cazneau the Patent Office report because his copy had disappeared in the mining districts of Mexico.

31. William H. Emory, *Report on the United States and Mexican Boundary Survey, Made under the Direction of the Secretary of the Interior by William H. Emory* (3 vols.; Austin: Texas State Historical Association, 1987), I, Pt. 1, 79, "View of Fort Duncan, near Eagle Pass (1852)," in the collections of the Center for American History, University of Texas at Austin; also see in Kerrigan, "Race, Expansion, and Slavery," 284.

32. U.S. Census (1850), "Bexar County, Eagle Pass," 285.

33. Ibid., 285; Cazneau, *Eagle Pass*, 94–95, 153–67; Thomas W. Cutrer, "Ludovic Colquhoun," in Tyler, et al. (eds.), *New Handbook of Texas*, II, 231–32; Albert Turpe, district clerk, Maverick County, to R. O. W. McManus, Apr. 5, Dec. 21, 1875, James Papers; Bollaert, *William Bollaert's Texas*, 352.

34. Cazneau, *Eagle Pass*, 66–99; Donald E. Chipman, *Spanish Texas, 1519–1821* (Austin: University of Texas, 1992), 105–115.

35. Pat Kelley, *River of Lost Dreams: Navigation on the Rio Grande* (Lincoln: University of Nebraska Press, 1984), 34–55; Cazneau, *Eagle Pass*, 170.

36. Kelley, *River of Lost Dreams*, 34, 43–55; Horgan, *The Great River*, II, 788–92; Goetzmann, *Army Exploration*, 183, 237–38; John Mason Hart, "Charles Stillman," Caleb Coker, "William Warren Chapman," and Caleb Coker, "Helen Ellsworth Blair Chapman," in Tyler, et al. (eds.), *New Handbook of Texas*, VI, 102, II, 45–46, 45.

37. Cazneau, *Eagle Pass*, 143–47; Kelley, *River of Lost Dreams*, 8; Horgan, *The Great River*, II, 792; Rippy, "Border Troubles," 91, 94–100; "José María Jesús Carbajal," and David M. Vigness, "Republic of the Rio Grande," in Tyler, et al. (eds.), *New Handbook of Texas*, I, 971, V, 537; Bauer, *The Mexican War*, 37; Ernest C. Shearer, "The Carvajal Disturbances," *Southwestern Historical Quarterly*, 55 (Oct., 1951), 204–17. Seventy discharged troops from Fort Duncan served under Capt. James Todd, Cols. John Ford, Robert Wheat, and a Captain Cabasco; Majors Gonzales, McMicken, Everitt, and Andrew Walker; and Captains Norton, Howell, Edmonson, Brown, and Garcia.

38. James Fred Rippy, "Diplomacy Regarding the Isthmus of Tehuantepec, 1848–1860," *Mississippi Valley Historical Review*, 4 (1919–1920), 513–21; James Fred Rippy, *The United States and Mexico* (New York: Alfred A. Knopf, 1926), 74; Mexican Border Commission of 1873, report, House of Representatives Document no. 13, 44th Cong., 2nd sess., 137–45, 179–80; John H. Kemble, *The Panama Route, 1848–1869* (New York: DaCapo Press, 1972), 14, 79–80.

39. Malsch, *Indianola*, 312; H. Bailey Carroll, "Texan Santa Fe Expedition," in Tyler, et al. (eds.), *New Handbook of Texas*, VI, 270–71; Mexican Claims, United States, Senate Executive Document no. 31, 44th Cong., 2nd sess., 24–25, 113, 131.

40. J. M. Cazneau to Mr. Wood, Nov. 1, 1850, Jane Cazneau Papers.

41. J. M. Cazneau to William H. Seward, Jan. 16, 1851, Seward Papers; Fabens [Cazneau], *The Camel Hunt*, 10–11; Cazneau, *Eagle Pass*, 50–51, 100–1, 125; Awbrey and Dooley, *Why Stop?*, 147. In 1885, Eagle Pass had Texas's largest coal mine.

42. Cazneau, *Eagle Pass*, 41, 143–54; Kevin Mulroy, *Freedom on the Border: The Seminole Maroons in Florida, the Indian Territory, Coahuila, and Texas* (Lubbock: Texas Tech University Press, 1993), 68–70; Fabens [Cazneau], *A Story of Life on the Isthmus*, 201. She watches through her lorgnette.

43. Rippy, "Border Troubles," 91–100; Cazneau, *Eagle Pass*, 73–77, 95, 137–39, 148–49, 186–88; Anita, 130–35; Barbara, 71–72, 78–80; Carlos 154–158; Victor 110–16; Pablito, 122–23; Dona Refugia, 135; Domingo, 60, 124; Fabiano, 52, 61–64; Francesca, 52–55; Jesus, 104, 106; Josepha, 36–39; Marco, 108; Marcos, 37–39; Margarita, 132–34; Pablito, 120, 123, 126–27; Placida, 106–9; Servero Valdez, 34–39; and Manuel Rios, 82–87, 110. Patrick Foley, "Jean Marie Odin," in Tyler, et al. (eds.), *New Handbook of Texas*, IV, 1111–12.

44. Cazneau, *Eagle Pass*, 139; James C. Harrison, "The Failure of Spain in East Texas: The Occupation and Abandonment of Nacogdoches, 1779–1821" (Ph.D. diss., University of Nebraska, 1980), 156. Racial mixing was recognized and Spanish-whites were mestizos, Negro-Spanish were mulattos, and Indian-Negros were zambos.

45. Cazneau, *Eagle Pass*, 37–39, 82–87, 110–17; J. M. Cazneau to W. H. Seward, Eagle Pass, Dec. 30, 1850, Eagle Pass, Jan. 16, 1851, Washington, June 3, 1851, Seward Papers; Cora Montgomery, "American Citizens Enslaved, December 14, 1850," New York *Tribune*, Feb. 1, 1851; Cora Montgomery, "A New Class of Slave States, January 18, 1851," and Cora Montgomery, "Enslaving American Citizens in Mexico, January 28, 1851," New York *Tribune*, Mar. 6, 1851; Cora Montgomery, "Three Forms of Servitude on the Border, February 1, 1851," New York *Tribune*, Mar. 8, 1851.

46. Cazneau, *Eagle Pass*, 82–87, 109–18; William L. Marcy to Alfred Conklin, May 5, 1853, in Manning (ed.), *Diplomatic Correspondence of the United States*, IX, 130–31.

47. Cazneau, *Eagle Pass*, 109–16; Cora Montgomery, "A New Class of Slave States, January 18, 1851," New York *Tribune*, Mar. 6, 1851.

48. Cazneau to Wood, Nov. 1, 1850, Jane Cazneau Papers; Rauch, *American Interest in Cuba*, 121–23, 129, 148–49, 156, 159.

49. Caldwell, *The López Expeditions to Cuba*, 54–85, 102–3; Chapman, *History of the Cuban Republic*, 36–38; Brained Dyer, *Zachary Taylor* (New York: Barnes and Noble, 1946), 348; Holman Hamilton, *Zachary Taylor* (New York: Bobbs-Merrill, 1951), 368–69, 370; Cazneau, *Eagle Pass*, 51.

50. Jane Cazneau file; Anon., [Cazneau], "Narcisso (sic) Lopez and His Companions," *United States Magazine and Democratic Review*, 29 (Oct., 1851), 292–301; Seymour V. Connor, "James B. Shaw," in Tyler, et al. (eds.), *New Handbook of Texas*, V, 999; Harriet Smither (ed.), "The Diary of Adolphus Sterne," *Southwestern Historical Quarterly*, 38 (July 1934), 58, 149, 153.

51. Montgomery, "The National Highways," New Orleans *Delta*, Dec. 12, 1851; Montgomery, "The Immediate Requirements of Our Border Policy," New Orleans *Delta*, Dec. 14, 1851; J. M. Cazneau to Wm. H. Seward, Dec. 30, 1851, Seward Papers; Cazneau, *Eagle Pass*, 58; Ronnie C. Tyler, "The Callahan Expedition of 1855: Indians or Negroes?" *Southwestern Historical Quarterly*, 70 (Apr., 1967), 574, 583.

52. Cazneau, *Eagle Pass*, 57–58, 167–68.

53. Ibid., 77–78.

54. Cazneau, *Eagle Pass*, 153–67; Fabens [Cazneau], *The Camel Hunt*, 27; Cazneau, review, "Lazarus on *Love and Marriage* (New York: Fowler & Wells, 1852)," *Our Times*, 1 (Oct., 1852), 153. Moritz Lazarus (1824–1903) founded comparative psychology.

55. *Lemuel H. Baldwin, et al. vs. Max Goldfrank, et al.*: Vicente Garza deeds, Bexar County, Maverick County, 1848–1876, box 3, fols. 58–66, James Papers; Robert S. Weddle, *San Juan Bautista: Gateway to Spanish Texas* (Austin: University of Texas Press, 1968), 286–87.

56. J. M. Cazneau to James Buchanan, Jan. 18, 1853, Buchanan Papers.

57. Donald B. Cole, *Martin Van Buren and the American Political System* (Princeton: Princeton University Press, 1984), 419; Holt, *Political Parties and American Political Development*, 64–73, 218, 222, 234; J. M. Storm to Moses Y. Beach, Dec. 27, 1849, Jane Cazneau Papers; Rauch, *American Interest in Cuba*, 193–94.

58. Johannsen, *Stephen A. Douglas*, 348–49; Rauch, *American Interest in Cuba*, 64, 92, 191–94, 212–15, 232, 227; Montgomery, *The Queen of Islands and the King of Rivers*; Montgomery, "The Union of the Seas," 154; Frederick Katz, *The Secret War in Mexico* (Chicago: University of Chicago Press, 1981), 112, 120. Bacon and Pierce operated sixteen cotton ships to Galveston. By 1852, Pierce owned stock in the Buffalo Bayou, Brazos, and Colorado Railway. Brown, *Agents of Manifest Destiny*, 113. Belmont, birth name Schoenberg, was the nephew by marriage of John Slidell, Buchanan's political adviser.

59. J. M. Cazneau to Thomas J. Rusk, July 7, 1852, Thomas J. Rusk Papers (Center for American History, University of Texas at Austin, Austin, Tex.); J. M. Cazneau to Stephen A. Douglas, July 13, 1852, Papers of Stephen A. Douglas (University of Chicago Library Archives, Chicago, Ill.).

60. United States, Senate, Senate Executive Documents, 97, 72; "Messages of U.S. President in Response of the Senate calling for the Correspondence between the Government of the United States and Mexico, respecting a Right of Way across the Isthmus of Tehuantepec." Referred to Committee of Foreign Relations, July 28, 1852, 32nd Cong., 3rd sess. (Library of Congress, Washington, D.C.); Rauch, *American Interest in Cuba*, 192–93.

61. Robert A. Naylor, *Penny Ante Imperialism: The Mosquito Shore and the Bay of Honduras, 1600–1914, a Case Study in British Informal Empire* (Rutherford, N.J.: Fairleigh Dickinson University Press, 1989), 179–82; Craig L. Dozier, *Nicaragua's Mosquito Shore: The Years of British and American Presence* (University: University of Alabama Press, 1985), 79, 83, 91; Scroggs, *Filibusters and Financiers*, 77.

62. Cora Montgomery (ed.), *Our Times*, 1 (Oct., 1852), 99–192.

63. J. M. Cazneau to James Buchanan, Jan. 18, 1853, Buchanan Papers; "Phoebe Jane Cazneau," San Francisco *Chronicle*, June 6, 1904, p. 12; Rauch, *American Interest in Cuba*, 182.

64. Robert E. May, *The Southern Dream of a Caribbean Empire* (Baton Rouge: Louisiana State University Press, 1973), 147; Rippy, *The United States. and Mexico*, 91–93; Tischendorf, *Great Britain and Mexico in the Era of Porforio Diaz*, 5; Shearer, "The Carvajal Disturbances," 228; W. L. Cazneau to R. O. W. McManus, June 24, 1875, James Papers.

65. J. M. Cazneau to Stephen A. Douglas, Mar. 29, 1853, Douglas Papers.

66. Albert Turpe to R. O. W. McManus, Dec. 21, 1875, A. G. Carruthers to R. O. W. McManus, Oct. 29, 1876, box 3, fol. 60–63, James Papers; "W. L. Cazneau," U.S. Senate Executive Document 1720, Mexican claims, 120; U.S. Senate Executive Document 31, 44th

Cong., 2nd sess., claim denied. Brown, *Indian Wars and Pioneers of Texas*, 587–88, 220; Rippy, "Border Troubles," 91, 94–100; S. W. Pease, "Enoch Jones," in Tyler, et al. (eds.), *New Handbook of Texas*, III, 980.

67. Horgan, *The Great River*, 788–92; Frederick Law Olmsted, *Journey Through Texas or a Saddle-Trip on the Southern Frontier* (New York: Dix, Edward, 1857; reprint, Austin: University of Texas Press, 1978), 334.

68. Cazneau, *Eagle Pass*, 186–88; Harbert Davenport, "General Jose Maria Jesus Carabajal (sic)," *Southwestern Historical Quarterly*, 55 (Apr., 1952), 482; Francisco Barrientos, *When Francisco Madero Came to the Border* (Laredo: Border Studies Center, 1995), 3–8; Donathan C. Olliff, *Reforma Mexico and the United States: A Search for Alternatives to Annexation, 1854–1861* (University: University of Alabama Press, 1981), 98–101. In April 1859, Benito Juarez granted William Leslie Cazneau rights for a wagon road across Northern Mexico. See *Abstract to Title of Rivas Grant*. In 1873, McManus filed the Cazneau deeds. A cattle syndicate then filed deeds and created El Indio Ranch in 1880. Others had claims of tax liens and liens of debt against Cazneau. Heirs only received a settlement on the Kingsbury Falls deed. Her son's attorney and granddaughter pursued the Rivas claim. In 1902, Max Goldfrank opened the land for settlement and Dolch and Dobroski began irrigation. In 1906, Goldfrank deeded additional land to the El Indio Cattle Company. See the James Papers.

Chapter VII

1. J. M. Cazneau to James Buchanan, Nov. 14, 1857, Buchanan Papers.

2. Fabens [Cazneau], *The Camel Hunt*; Joseph Fabens [Jane Cazneau], *Life on the Isthmus* (New York: George P. Putnam, 1853), published with Cora Montgomery, *Eagle Pass; or Life on the Border* (2nd ed.; New York: George P. Putnam & Co., 1853); Kai Schoenhals, *Dominican Republic*, World Bibliography Series (London: Oxford University Press, 1990), 69; "Joseph W. Fabens," in Wright, *American Fiction*, 67.

3. William L. Marcy to Alfred Conkling, May 5, 1853, in Manning (ed.), *Diplomatic Correspondence of the United States*, IX, 130–31; Charles Callan Tansill, *The United States and Santo Domingo, 1798–1873* (Baltimore: John Hopkins Press, 1938), 172–76; Rauch, *American Interest in Cuba*, 214–15; Montgomery, New York *Sun*, Dec. 24, 1845; Montgomery, "The Black Banner," *Our Times*, 1 (Oct., 1852), 115–18; Montgomery, "Soulouque and the Dominicans," *United States Magazine and Democratic Review*, 29 (Feb., 1852), 137–149; Montgomery, "Soulouque and the Dominicans, contd.," *United States Magazine and Democratic Review*, 30 (Mar., 1852), 234–39; Anon., "On the Rumored Occupation of San Domingo by the Emperor of France," *United States Magazine and Democratic Review*, 32 (Feb., 1853), 173–92.

4. Montgomery, "The Black Banner," 115–16; Montgomery, "The Mosquito King and the British Queen," *United States Magazine and Democratic Review*, 25 (Nov., 1849), 405–16; Anon., "British Aggression in Central America," *United States Magazine and Democratic Review*, 29 (Jan., 1851), 3–14; Montgomery, "Soulouque and the Dominicans," 137–149; Montgomery, "Soulouque and the Dominicans, contd.," 234; Cazneau, *Eagle Pass*, 57; Montgomery, "On the Rumored Occupation of San Domingo," 173–92; May, "'Plenipotentiary in Petticoats,'" 19.

5. J. Fred Rippy, *Rivalry of the United States and Great Britain over Latin America, 1808–1830* (Baltimore: John Hopkins Press, 1929), 308–10; Sir Walter Raleigh quoted in Alan W.

Cafruny, *Ruling the Waves: The Political Economy of International Shipping* (Berkeley: University of California Press, 1987), 38.

6. K. Jack Bauer, *A Maritime History of the United States* (Columbia: University of South Carolina Press, 1988), 62–65.

7. Roy Franklin Nichols, *Franklin Pierce: Young Hickory of the Granite Hills* (2nd ed.; Philadelphia: University of Pennsylvania Press, 1969), 396; Rauch, *American Interest in Cuba*, 159; Doug A. Mishler, "Manifestos, Filibusters, and the Follies of Young America: Foreign Policy Dynamics in the Pierce Administration, 1853–1857" (M. A. thesis, University of Nevada, Reno, 1988), 5–7; "In a naive point of view," *Times* (London), Sept. 9, 1851.

8. Tansill, *The United States and Santo Domingo*, 172–75; Rauch, *American Interest in Cuba*, 182; Schroeder, *Shaping a Maritime Empire*, 118–23; Cafruny, *Ruling the Waves*, 50; Paul M. Kenedy, *The Rise and Fall of the British Naval Mastery* (New York: Charles Scribner's Sons, 1976), 149–55; C. Ernest Fayle, *A Short History of the World's Shipping Industry* (London: George Allen, 1933), 239; George Rogers Taylor, *The Transportation Revolution, 1815–1860* (Armont, N.Y.: M. E. Sharpe, 1951), 448.

9. Rauch, *American Interest in Cuba*, 232; Rippy, *Rivalry over Latin America*, 308–10; William Javier Nelson, *Almost a Territory: America's Attempt to Annex the Dominican Republic* (Newark: University of Delaware Press, 1990), 46–47.

10. Tansill, *The United States and Santo Domingo*, 172–73; J. Fred Rippy, *The Caribbean Danger Zone* (New York: G. P. Putnam's Sons, 1940), 118; John Edwin Fagg, *Cuba, Haiti, and the Dominican Republic* (Englewood Cliffs, N.J.: Prentice-Hall, 1965), 144–46.

11. Sandra W. Meditz (ed.), *Islands of the Commonwealth Caribbean* (Washington, D.C.: Library of Congress, 1989), Figure 21, "Caribbean Sea-Lanes"; Michael J. Kryzanek and Howard J. Wiarda, *The Politics of External Influence in the Dominican Republic* (New York: Pragere, 1988), 5, 153, 167n; Cazneau, "The Black Banner," 115–16; Bauer, *Maritime History of the United States*, 84–87.

12. Benson Lee Grayson, *The Unknown President: The Administration of President Millard Fillmore* (Washington: University Press of America, 1981), 120; Foner, *Business and Slavery*, 82; James Morton Callahan, *Cuba in International Relations* (Baltimore: John Hopkins Press, 1899), 259; Geary, "Scribbling Women," 131; [Jane Cazneau], "Tehuantepec," *New York Herald*, May 1, 9, 27, June 27, 1853; Rauch, *American Interest in Cuba*, 212; Paul Neff Garber, *The Gadsden Treaty* (Philadelphia: University of Pennsylvania Press, 1924), 45.

13. W. L. Marcy to W. L. Cazneau, Nov. 2, 1853, Records of U.S. Department of State, Record Group 59, Special Missions, M37 (National Archives, Washington, D.C.); Mishler, "Manifestos, Filibusters, and the Follies of Young America," 10; Rauch, *American Interest in Cuba*, 193, 217; May, "Lobbyists for Commercial Empire," 392.

14. W. L. Marcy to Gen. P. M. Wetmore, Feb. 9, 1848, quoted in Nelson, "Jane Storms Cazneau," 35; James Gadsden to Jefferson Davis, July 19, 1854, in Lynda Crist (ed.), *The Papers of Jefferson Davis* (9 vols.; Baton Rouge: Louisiana State University Press, 1985), V, 80; Robert Dean Sampson, "'Under the Banner of the Democratic Principle,'" 375–76; Allan Nevins, *Hamilton Fish: The Inner History of the Grant Administration* (New York: Dodd, Mead, and Co., 1936), 254; Sumner Welles, *Naboth's Vineyard: The Dominican Republic, 1844–1924* (2 vols.; New York: Payson & Clarke, 1928), I, 136–37, 313; May, "Lobbyists for Commercial Empire," 393; Julius W. Pratt, *A History of United States Foreign Policy* (New York: Prentice Hill, 1955), 324; United States Senate, "Report of the U.S. Senate Select Committee on the

Memorial of David Hatch, 25 June 1870," Senate Report No. 234, 41st Cong., 2nd sess. Two thousand copies of the minority report were printed with the testimony of R. H. Perry, who shot his commanding officer, received a dishonorable discharge for mule theft and rape in New Orleans, then served as Reconstruction police chief in Galveston before he was assigned to the Dominican Republic. Tansill, *The United States and Santo Domingo*, 176–79, 372–77, 395–403, 410–18.

15. W. L. Cazneau, Despatches, nos. 561–1097, Department of State, RG 59, Special Missions, M37; J. M. Cazneau to M. S. Beach, Dec. 27, 1854, Jane Cazneau Papers; Ian Bell, *The Dominican Republic*, (Boulder: Western Press, 1981), 27; "Transactions of The Right Worshipful Grande Lodge of Free and Accepted Masons of the Republic of Texas, Grand Royal Chapter of the Republic of Texas," No. 3 in Streeter (comp.), *Bibliography of Texas*, nos. 620–621.

16. Cazneau, *Our Winter Eden*, 6–11; Bauer, *Maritime History of the United States*, 103; Kryzanek and Wiarda, *The Politics of External Influence*, 5, 153, n167. During the Reagan administration, Adm. Harry D. Train, commander of the U.S. Atlantic Fleet, began talks with the Dominican Republic to lease Samana Bay. Eloise Engle and Arnold S. Lott, *America's Maritime Heritage* (Annapolis: United States Naval Institute, 1975), 153; Cox, "Ordeal By Water," 39, 72; Nelson, *Almost A Territory*, 47; "Capt. W. L. Cazneau," San Francisco *Daily Alta Californian*, July 17, 1866; "Gen. T. N. Cazneau," *California Mail Bag*, 3 (July-Aug., 1873), 77.

17. Marcy to Cazneau, Dec. 2, 1853, W. L. Cazneau to W. L. Marcy, Jan. 23, 1854, Special Missions, M37.

18. Cazneau to Marcy, Jan. 23, Feb. 12, 1854, Special Missions, M37.

19. Cazneau to Marcy, Feb. 12, 1854, Special Missions, M37; H. P. Davis, *Black Democracy* (New York: Biblo & Tannen, 1967), 129; J. M. Cazneau to W. L. Marcy, Feb. 7, 1854, Department of State, Miscellaneous Letters, RG 59.

20. J. M. Cazneau to M. S. Beach, Washington, May 30, 1854, Jane Cazneau Papers; W. L. Cazneau to R. O. W. McManus, June 24, 1875, box 3, fol. 59, James Papers; Floyd J. Miller, *The Search for a Black Nationality: Black Emigration and Colonization, 1787–1863* (Urbana: University of Chicago Press, 1975), 101, 113–14, 166–68, 239; P. J. Slaudenraus, *The African Colonization Movement, 1816–1865* (New York: Columbia University Press, 1961), 9–10, 115, 120–21, 187–89; Fried, *John Brown's Journey*, 187, 196–99; Rauch, *American Interest in Cuba*, 246–47, 264–99; Tansill, *The United States and Santo Domingo*, 178–81.

21. W. L. Cazneau to W. L. Marcy, July 24, Aug. 18, 19, Sept. 23, 1854, Special Missions, M37; "Thomas Tileston," in Johnson and Malone (eds.), *Dictionary of American Biography*, IX, 541; Tansill, *The United States and Santo Domingo*, 186–89.

22. Gadsden to Davis, July 19, 1854, Crist (ed.), *Davis Papers*, V, 78–82.

23. W. L. Cazneau to W. L. Marcy, July 24, Aug. 18, 19, Sept. 23, 1854, Special Missions, M37; Schomburgk quoted in Tansill, *The United States and Santo Domingo*, 189; Bell, *The Dominican Republic*, 39.

24. W. L. Cazneau to W. L. Marcy, Nov. 17, 23, 1854, Special Missions, M37; Schomburgk to Clarendon, Nov. 22, 1854, in Tansill, *The United States and Santo Domingo*, 195–96, 202.

25. Marcy and Crampton quoted in Tansill, *The United States and Santo Domingo*, 192–93; *Encyclopedia Britannica* (30 vols.; Micropedia, 15th ed.; Chicago: Encyclopedia Britannica,

1983), II, 965. In *La Verdad*, Feb. 13, Mar. 12, 28, Apr. 9, 1854, Cora Montgomery announced, "Ireland. They will be free!" and "it is our destiny to assist in the upraising the hallowed edifice of freedom."

26. "Further Details," New York *Tribune*, Dec. 30, 1878; "Ups and Downs of an eccentric Trojan Inventor . . . career of mother," Troy *Daily Press*, Jan. 26, 1891; Mishler, "Manifestos, Filibusters, and the Follies of Young America," 35–36.

27. Crampton to Clarendon, Oct. 9, 1854, in Tansill, *The United States and Santo Domingo*, 193, 204; R. B. Mowat, *The Diplomatic Relations of Great Britain and the United States* (London: Edward Arnold Press, 1925), 155.

28. Cazneau to Marcy, Oct. 9, Nov. 16, 17, 18, 23, Dec. 4, 1854; Jonathan Elliot to W. L. Cazneau, Nov. 16, 1854, Special Missions, M37; Schomburgk to Lord Clarendon, Sept. 20, 1854, in Tansill, *The United States and Santo Domingo*, 189–90.

29. Cazneau to Marcy, Nov. 16, 17, 18, 23, Dec. 5, 6, 16, 1854, Special Missions, M37; Tansill, *The United States and Santo Domingo*, 197.

30. Cazneau to Marcy, Nov. 23, 1854, Special Missions, M37; Scroggs, *Filibusters and Financiers*, 72–76, 95–98. Joseph W. Fabens had asked Capt. George Hollins of the USS *Cyane* to remove the British and Hollins shelled Greytown, creating an international incident. Schomburgk to Clarendon, Dec. 18, 21, 1854, in Tansill, *The United States and Santo Domingo*, 199; Dermot Englefield, Janet Seaton, and Isabel White (comps.), *Facts about the British Prime Ministers* (New York: H. H. Wilson, 1995), 182. Lord Palmerston declared "Civis Rommanus Sun" a British citizen would be protected anywhere under the sun.

31. José Debrin to General Cazneau, Dec. 16, 1854, Felix Delmonte to General Cazneau, Dec. 14, 1854, Alfonso A. Gundi to General Cazneau, Dec. 28, 1854, W. L. Cazneau to W. L. Marcy, Dec. 26, 1854, Special Missions, M37; Tansill, *The United States and Santo Domingo*, 193–96.

32. J. M. Cazneau to M. S. Beach, Dec. 27, 1854, Jane Cazneau Papers.

33. Tansill, *The United States and Santo Domingo*, 201–3; W. L. Cazneau to W. L. Marcy, June 9, 1855, Special Missions, M37.

34. Rauch, *American Interest in Cuba*, 264–99.

35. J. M. Cazneau to M. S. Beach, June 20, 25, 1855, Jane Cazneau Papers.

36. J. M. Cazneau to M. S. Beach, Sept. 11, 1855, Jane Cazneau Papers.

37. Mario Rodriguez, *A Palmerston Diplomat in Central America* (Tucson: University of Arizona Press, 1964), 327; Scroggs, *Filibusters and Financiers*, 72–76, 95–98; Van Alstyne, *The Rising American Empire*, 158–60; Richard W. Van Alstyne, "British Diplomacy and the Clayton-Bulwer Treaty," *Journal of Modern History*, 11 (Mar., 1939), 151–53, 162.

38. "Information Concerning Nicaragua Transit," in Smither (ed.), *The Papers of Mirabeau Buonaparte Lamar*, IV, 137; "Report of the Secretary of War, communicating, . . . the report of Captain Thomas J. Cram . . . on the oceanic routes to California," in United States Congress, *The New American State Papers*, vol. 7 "Transportation," (Wilmington: Scholarly Resources, 1972), 605–18.

39. May, *The Southern Dream of a Caribbean Empire*, 89; Brown, *Agents of Manifest Destiny*, 155, 222.

40. Scroggs, *Filibusters and Financiers*, 101–30; Nichols, *Franklin Pierce*, 397–98; Larry Gara, *The Presidency of Franklin Pierce* (Lawrence: University Press of Kansas, 1991), 144.

41. May, *The Southern Dream of a Caribbean Empire*, 90; Gara, *The Presidency of Franklin Pierce*, 130; Elleanore Callaghan Ratterman, "With Walker in Nicaragua. The Reminiscences of Elleanore (Callaghan) Ratterman," *Tennessee Magazine of History*, 7 (1915), 315.

42. Gen. William Walker, *The War in Nicaragua* (Mobile: Goetzel, 1860), 387, 408, 421; May, *The Southern Dream of a Caribbean Empire*, 94; Scroggs, *Filibusters and Financiers*, 101, 146; Brown, *Agents of Manifest Destiny*, 350.

43. J. M. Cazneau to M. S. Beach, Apr. 14, 1856, Jane Cazneau Papers; May, *The Southern Dream of a Caribbean Empire*, 101-104, 132-133; Scroggs, *Filibusters and Financiers*, 171–74.

44. May, "Lobbyists for Commercial Empire," 396–97; May, "'Plenipotentiary in Petticoats,'" 30; J. M. Cazneau to M. S. Beach, May 31, 1856, Jane Cazneau Papers; "Elizabeth Pellet," in Joel Myerson (gen. ed.), *Dictionary of Literary Biography*, vol. 30 "American Historians" (Detroit: Gale Research Publications, 1979), 84; Wall, *Henry Watterson*, 25.

45. Sheridan, *McManus Family Revised*, 22–24; Jane Cazneau, "Last Will and Testament," box. 3, fol. 60, James Papers; J. A. Quitman, Chairman Military Committee, H.R. to Jefferson Davis, Sec. of War, Feb. 5, 1857; Engineering Department to Jefferson Davis, Feb. 13, 1857; Ordinance Office to Jefferson Davis, Feb. 14, 1857; Jefferson Davis to J. A. Quitman, Feb. 16, 1857, Records Office of the Chief of Engineers, Letters Received from the Secretary of War, RG 77, file no. SW-1595 (National Archives, Washington, D.C.); Scroggs, *Filibusters and Financiers*, 335; Johannsen, *Stephen A. Douglas*, 515–23.

46. May, *The Southern Dream of a Caribbean Empire*, 113; May, "'Plenipotentiary in Petticoats,'" 30; Stephen L. Caiger, *British Honduras Past and Present* (London: George Allen, 1951), 117.

47. Welles, *Naboth's Vineyard*, I, 313; Crouthamel, *James Watson Webb*, 24, 125; Fried, *John Brown's Journey*, 187–88, 193–94, 196–201; Eric Foner, *Free Soil, Free Labor, Free Men: The Ideology of the Republican Party before the Civil War* (New York: Oxford University Press, 1970), 268–69; May, "'Plenipotentiary in Petticoats,'" 30–32.

48. J. M. Cazneau to M. S. Beach, Oct. 6, 1856, Jane Cazneau Papers.

49. "Filibusters for Walker," New York *Times*, Dec. 25, 1856; "A Letter from William Leslie Cazneau to John McKeon, D.A.," New York *Times*, Dec. 27, 1856; Ratterman, "With Walker," 320.

50. Jefferson Davis to Caleb Cushing, Dec. 9, 1856, J. M. Cazneau to Jefferson Davis, n.d. Dec. 1856, in Crist (ed.), *Davis Papers*, V, 519, 526.

51. Scroggs, *Filibusters and Financiers*, 335–52; May, "'Plenipotentiary in Petticoats,'" 31; W. L. Cazneau to Jeremiah S. Black, "Memorandum of Costa Rican Assaults on the Nicaraguan Transit and British violations of the Clayton-Bulwer Treaty," Mar. 18, Apr. 3, 1857; J. M. C. to Dear Sir, May 4, 1857, the Papers of Jeremiah S. Black (Library of Congress, Washington, D.C.); Walker, *The War in Nicaragua*, 278; J. M. Cazneau to James Buchanan, Apr. 3, Nov. 14, 1857, Buchanan Papers.

52. Goetzmann, *Army Exploration*, 296–303.

53. J. M. Storm to M. B. Lamar, Oct. 1846, Apr. 2, 1858 in Smither (ed.), *Lamar Papers*, IV, 101, 129–30; Rauch, *American Interest in Cuba*, 257; Tebbel and Watts, *The Press and the Presidency*, 129; May, "Lobbyists for Commercial Empire," 401; Wall, *Henry Watterson*, 25; W. L. Cazneau to Dear General, July 24, 1857, W. L. Cazneau to Hon. A. Dudley Mann, Aug. 3, 1857, William Leslie Cazneau Papers (New York Historical Society Archives, New York, N.Y.);

Edmund Ruffin, *The Diary of Edmund Ruffin*, ed. William Kauffman Scarborough, foreword by Avery Craven (2 vols.; Baton Rouge: Louisiana State University Press, 1972), I, 177; Freehling, *The Reintegration of American History*, 145.

54. May, "Lobbyists for Commercial Empire," 399–403; May, "'Plenipotentiary in Petticoats,'" 32; J. M. Cazneau to M. S. Beach, Dec. 27, 1854, Jane Cazneau Papers; J. M. Cazneau to J. S. Black, Sept. 10, 1857, Black Papers.

55. J. M. Cazneau to James Buchanan, Nov. 14, 1857, Buchanan Papers; May, *The Southern Dream of a Caribbean Empire*, 164.

56. Scroggs, *Filibusters and Financiers*, 358–60; M. B. Lamar to J. M. Cazneau, Oct. 4, 1857, W. L. Cazneau to M. B. Lamar, Jan. 3, 1858, in Smither (ed.), *Lamar Papers*, VI, 345, IV, 73; José Debrin to General Cazneau, Dec. 16, 1854, Special Missions, M37.

57. J. M. Cazneau to M. B. Lamar, Apr. 2, 1858, in Smither (ed.), *Lamar Papers*, IV, 129, 135–36; Fried, *John Brown's Journey*, 199.

58. "Our Minister in Nicaragua," New York *Times*, Feb. 8, 1859; "Minister Lamar," Washington *Daily States*, Feb. 8, 1859; J. M. Cazneau to M. B. Lamar, Feb. 9, 1859, in Smither (ed.), *Lamar Papers*, IV, 203, 206–7; Van Alstyne, "British Diplomacy and the Clayton-Bulwer Treaty," 162.

59. J. M. Cazneau to James Buchanan, June 5, 1858, Buchanan Papers; May, *The Southern Dream of a Caribbean Empire*, 140–45; James A. Magner, *Men of Mexico* (Freeport, N.Y.: Books for Library Press, 1968), 371–77.

60. H. L. Wilson, "President Buchanan's Proposed Intervention in Mexico," *American Historical Review*, 5 (1900), 698–701; William S. Holt, *Treaties Defeated by the Senate* (Baltimore: John Hopkins University Press, 1933), 58, 91–96; Olliff, *Reforma Mexico*, 98–101; Callahan, *Cuba in International Relations*, 299.

61. Marcosson, *"Marse Henry,"* 46–47; Wall, *Henry Watterson*, 24–25. Watterson credited Jane Cazneau with writing the Treaty of Guadalupe Hidalgo. Watterson had the ability to strike a short phrase that could deflate the most exalted politician. His favorite target was Theodore Roosevelt. Johannsen, *Stephen Douglas*, 692; May, *The Southern Dream of a Caribbean Empire*, 158.

62. William L. Cazneau, *To the American Press: The Dominican Negotiations* (Santo Domingo: Impre de Garcia Hermanos), 1870), 7; Cazneau, *Our Winter Eden*, 118–20.

63. Cazneau, *To the American Press*, 7; Cazneau, *Our Winter Eden*, 121.

64. W. L. Cazneau to Lewis Cass, June 19, 1859, Special Missions, M37; "The Dominican Republic, October 10, 1859," New York *Sun*, Nov. 5, 1859.

65. Cazneau to Cass, June 19, 1859, Special Missions, M37.

66. Cazneau to Cass, July 14, 19, 23, 30, 1859, Special Missions, M37.

67. "The Dominican Republic," New York *Sun*, Nov. 5, 1859; J. M. Cazneau to James Buchanan, Oct. 17, 1859, Buchanan Papers.

68. [Cazneau], *In the Tropics*, 189–214.

69. Cazneau, *Our Winter Eden*, 107–8.

70. J. M. Cazneau to James Buchanan, Oct. 17, 1859, Buchanan Papers.

71. W. L. Cazneau to Lewis Cass, Oct. 17, Dec. 13, 1859, Jan. 30, Feb. 22, 1860, Special Missions, M37.

72. W. L. Cazneau to Lewis Cass, Mar. 4, 1860, Special Missions, M37; May, *The Southern Dream of a Caribbean Empire*, 123, 149–54.

73. W. L. Cazneau to Lewis Cass, July 25, Mar. 4, Sept. 10, 1860, Special Missions, M37.

74. W. L. Cazneau to Lewis Cass, Oct. 13, 1860, Special Missions, M37.

75. W. L. Cazneau to Lewis Cass, June 30, Oct. 13, Nov. 17, 1860 Special Missions, M37; "Joseph Warren Fabens," in *The National Cyclopaedia of American Biography*, VII, 178; Nevins, *Hamilton Fish*, 255–57; Tansill, *The United States and Santo Domingo*, 345–46.

76. W. L. Cazneau to Lewis Cass, Jan. 17, Feb. 16, 1861, Special Missions, M37; Tansill, *The United States and Santo Domingo*, 212–14.

77. Cazneau to Black, Nov. 6, 1860, Black Papers; Ernest N. Paolina, *The Foundations of the American Empire: William Henry Seward and U.S. Foreign Policy* (Ithaca: Cornell University Press, 1973), xi, 25–28; William H. Seward to W. L. Cazneau, Mar. 11, 1861, J. M. Cazneau, in account with instructions, Apr. 7, 1859, drawn on Department of State, July 1, 1861, $1,300, J. M. Cazneau, July 1, 1861, $752, for office and travel expense, receipt, Aug. 20, 1861, Special Missions, M37.

78. J. M. Cazneau to Moses Y. Beach, Jan. 8, 1850, Jane Cazneau Papers; Glyndon G. Van Duesen, *William Henry Seward* (New York: Oxford University Press, 1967), 280–87; Foner, *Business and Slavery*, 248–76; William C. Wright, *The Secession Movement in the Middle Atlantic States* (Rutherford, N.J.: Farleigh Dickinson University Press, 1973), 167, 178, 198, 219. Those who supported secession until Fort Sumter were the New York *Daily News*, New York *Morning News, Daybook*, New York *Times*, New York *Tribune*, New York *Evening Post*, and New York *Herald*; "The Impossibility of Secession," New York *Sun*, Jan. 2, 1861.

79. "Letter from Dominica," New York *Sun*, Feb. 15, 1861; "Plucking the Fat Geese," New York *Sun*, Feb. 26, 1861; "The struggle for possession of the new president . . .," New York *Sun*, Feb. 27, 1861; "How a Southern Government is Made," New York *Sun*, Mar. 19, 1861; "Discontent in Alabama," New York *Sun*, Mar. 21, 1861; "The Secession Troubles," New York *Sun*, Mar. 26, 1861.

80. W. L. Cazneau to W. H. Seward, Mar. 23, May 13, June 28, 1861 Special Missions, M37; "Important from the West Indies," New York *Sun*, Mar. 30, 1861; "The Civil War," New York *Sun*, Apr. 15, 1861.

81. "The Confederate Traitors," New York *Sun*, Apr. 15, 1861; "The Line is Drawn," New York *Sun*, May 4, 1861.

82. "The Line is Drawn," New York *Sun*, May 4, 1861; "The Object of the Conspiracy," New York *Sun*, June 11, 1861.

83. "We think nothing at present warrant a revolution," New York *Sun*, May 4, 1861.

84. Ibid.; "More Prizes Captured," New York *Sun*, June 8, 1861.

85. "M. S. Beach, Editor and Sole Proprietor of the *Sun* and shall do its duty in quelling the unnatural rebellion," New York *Sun*, Jan. 1, 1862; W. L. Cazneau to W. H. Seward, Aug. 23, 1861, Special Missions, M37.

86. Fayle, *History of the World's Shipping Industry*, 238; Bauer, *Maritime History of the United States*, 103; Taylor, *The Transportation Revolution*, 200, 204, 206. The total tonnage figure represents deep sea, coastal, river, and lake vessels.

CHAPTER VIII

1. Cazneau, *Our Winter Eden*, 107–8.

2. W. L. Cazneau to W. H. Seward, May 13, 1861, United States Department of State, Record Group 59, Special Missions, M37; Fabens [Cazneau], *Facts About Santo Domingo*; [Cazneau], *In the Tropics*; [Cazneau], *The Prince of Kashna*; Fabens [Cazneau], *Uses of the Camel*; Fabens [Cazneau], *Resources of Santo Domingo*; Cazneau, *Our Winter Eden*.; Jane Cazneau, *Hill Homes of Jamaica*, listed in Cazneau, *Our Winter Eden*, but no copies located. See sketch of Keith Hall in Jane Cazneau file; J. M. Cazneau to Dear Sir [Andrew Johnson], Apr. 9, 1866, J. M. Cazneau to Hon. James Harlan, Sept. 6, 1865, Seward Papers.

3. Fabens [Cazneau], *Facts about Santo Domingo*; Montgomery, *Texas and Her Presidents*; J. M. Cazneau to M. S. Beach, private, Apr. 24, June 2, 1862, Jane Cazneau Papers.

4. "Slaves Contraband of War," New York *Sun*, May 28, 1861; Foner, *Business and Slavery*, 160, 200–16, 237; Scisco, *Political Nativism in New York State*, 58, 227; Basil Leo Lee, "Discontent in New York City, 1861–1865" (Ph.D. diss., Catholic University of America, 1943), 103, 137–45, 163–74, 181; Charles S. Wesley, "Lincoln's Plan for Colonizing the Emancipated Negro," *Journal of Negro History*, 4 (Jan., 1919), 7–13; Miller, *The Search for a Black Nationality*, 101, 114, 239, 149–51; Frederick Douglass, *Frederick Douglass Papers*, eds. John W. Blassingame and John R. McKenny, vol. 4: 1864–1880 (New Haven: Yale University Press, 1991), 500.

5. J. M. Cazneau to M. S. Beach, June 6, 1862, Jane Cazneau Papers.

6. J. M. Cazneau to M. S. Beach, July 6, 1862, Jane Cazneau Papers.

7. J. M. Cazneau to M. S. Beach, Sept. 24, Oct. 7, 1862, Jane Cazneau Papers.

8. Tansill, *The United States and Santo Domingo*, 216–19, 225–27; Foner, *Business and Slavery*, 22, 271, 308–11. Ketchum was a former New York judge on the Court of Appeals. William D. Angel Jr., "Vantage on the Bay: Galveston and the Railroads," *East Texas Historical Journal*, 22 (Spring, 1984), 8–9. Kimball was former president of the Galveston, Houston, & Henderson Railroad.

9. Frederick Bancroft, *The Life of William H. Seward* (2 vols.; New York: Harper & Bros., 1900), II, 345–47; P. J. Slaudenraus, *The African Colonization Movement, 1816–1865* (New York: Columbia University Press, 1961), 245–47; Welles, *Naboth's Vineyard*, I, 317; James M. McPherson, *The Struggle for Equality: Abolitionists and the Negro in the Civil War and Reconstruction* (Princeton: Princeton University Press, 1964), 154–56; Wesley, "Lincoln's Plan for Colonization," 7–21; John M. Taylor, *William Henry Seward: Lincoln's Right Hand* (New York: Harper Collins, 1991), 190–91. Kock pocketed the hundred dollars provided for each settler's supplies and tainted the reputations of those in the movement.

10. J. M. Cazneau to My Dear Mr. Beach, n. d., 1862, Jane Cazneau Papers; Germaine Greer, *The Change: Women, Aging and the Menopause* (New York: Fawcett Books, 1991), 20.

11. Lee, "Discontent in New York City," ix, 10, 47, 59, 82–90; McPherson, *The Struggle for Equality*, 231–33; Williston Lofton, "Northern Labor and the Negro during the Civil War," *Journal of Negro History*, 34 (July, 1949), 251–73; Adams, *New York Panorama*, 136–38; Merline Pitre, "Frederick Douglas and the Annexation of Santo Domingo," *Journal of Negro History*, 62 (Oct., 1977), 390–400. See sketch from *Harper's Weekly* of the orphanage fire in Barbara Goldsmith, *Other Powers: The Age of Suffrage, Spiritualism, and the Scandalous Victoria Woodhull* (New York: Alfred A. Knopf, 1998), 78–79.

12. Cazneau, *In The Tropics*; [Cazneau], *Prince of Kashna*, preface; "Richard Kimball," in *National Cyclopedia of American Biography*, X, 32; Tansill, *The United States and Santo Domingo*, 216–19; George M. Frederickson, *The Black Image in the White Mind: The Debate on Afro-American Character and Destiny, 1817–1914* (Middleton, Conn.: Wesleyan University Press, 1971), 92–93, 138–39.

13. Cazneau, *In The Tropics*, 14–15, 69, 296; Tansill, *The United States and Santo Domingo*, 219, 383.

14. Cazneau [Montgomery], *Eagle Pass*.

15. Tansill, *The United States and Santo Domingo*, 219–20; Richard A. Haggerty (ed.), *Dominican Republic and Haiti* (Washington, D.C.: Library of Congress, 1989), 16–17; Protest of William Cazneau, Oct. 15, 1863, with William G. W. Jaeger to William H. Seward, Dec. 27, 1863, despatches from U. S. Consuls in Santo Domingo, T56, Department of State, RG59 (National Archives, Washington, D.C.); J. M. Cazneau to Dear Sir, [Andrew Johnson], Apr. 9, 1866, Seward Papers. Jane Cazneau praised Lincoln's agent, Jaeger, but condemned others.

16. Philip Sherlock, *This is Jamaica* (London: Hodden & Stoughton, 1968), 94; Peter Abrahams, *Jamaica, an Island Mosaic* (London: Her Majesty's Stationary Office, 1957), 95–96.

17. [Cazneau], *The Prince of Kashna*, v, vi.

18. Graham H. Stuart, *Latin America and the United States* (New York: D. Appleton-Century, 1938), 279; Nelson, *Almost a Territory*, 49, n56; Tansill, *The United States and Santo Domingo*, 222–25; Walter R. Herrick Jr., *The American Naval Revolution* (Baton Rouge: Louisiana State University Press, 1966), 13; Gerald E. Poyo, "Evolution of Cuban Separatist Thought," 494–95.

19. Hasbrouck (comp.) *The Hasbrouck Family in America*, I, 221; Last Will and Testament of Jane McManus Cazneau, Jan. 27, 1877, Jane Cazneau file; Last Will and Testament of Jane McManus Cazneau, Nov. 21, 1878, James Papers, 1812–1938, box 3, fols. 58–66.

20. J. M. Cazneau to M. S. Beach, Aug. 25, 1865, Jane Cazneau Papers.

21. J. M. Cazneau to James Harlan (Secretary of Interior), Sept. 6, 1865, Seward Papers; Tansill, *The United States and Santo Domingo*, 225.

22. J. M. Cazneau to M. S. Beach, Aug. 25, 1865, J. M. Cazneau to My Dear Mrs. Beach, Nov. 30, Dec. 1, 1865, Jane Cazneau Papers.

23. Tansill, *The United States and Santo Domingo*, 225–26; Welles, *Naboth's Vineyard*, I, 316–17; Major L. Wilson, "The Repressible Conflict: Seward's Concept of Progress and the Free Soil Movement," *Journal of Southern History*, 37 (Nov., 1971), 533, 541–42, 548; Van Alstyne, *The Rising American Empire*, 100, 146; Rauch, *American Interest in Cuba*, 249; J. M. Cazneau to Dear Sir, [Andrew Johnson], Apr. 9, 1866, Seward Papers.

24. Welles, *Naboth's Vineyard*, I, 319–20; Tansill, *The United States and Santo Domingo*, 228–34; J. M. Cazneau to Dear Sir, [Andrew Johnson], Apr. 9, 1866, Seward Papers.

25. "Capt. W. L. Cazneau dead at 97," San Francisco *Daily Alta Californian*, July 14, 1866. Data furnished by Patrick Cazneau, family historian, Sebastopol, California.

26. Tansill, *The United States and Santo Domingo*, 232–39; J. M. Cazneau to Dear Sir, [Andrew Johnson], Apr. 9, 1866, Seward Papers.

27. Tansill, *The United States and Santo Domingo*, 239–41, 254–55; Nevins, *Hamilton Fish*, I, 255.

28. W. L. Cazneau to W. H. Seward, Dec. 18, 1867, Department of State, RG 59, Santo Domingo Consular Despatches, T56; Melvin K. Knight, *The Americans in Santo Domingo* (New York: Vanguard Press, 1928), 8; Paolino, *The Foundations of the American Empire*, 131–40. Members of the Panama Company were: C. K. Garrison of the International Merchant Marine; Marshall O. Roberts, formerly of the U.S. Mail Steamship Company, president of the New York Newfoundland Telegraph Co., investor in the Louisiana Tehuantepec Transit Co.; William H. Seward Jr.; Richard Schell, who owned most of Lower California; Frederich Conkling, president of ETNA Insurance Company; Robert H. Pruyn, minister to Japan; William H. Vanderbilt; William C. Fargo, founder of the American Express Company; William H. Appleton, New York merchant; William E. Dodge, Sun Mutual Insurance Company; Moses Grinnell, Seward's campaign manager; William M. Evarts, attorney general of the United States; William T. Coleman, president of the New York Chamber of Commerce; Peter Cooper, iron manufacturer; Abram S. Hewitt, financier; Frederick M. Kelley; and Peter J. Sullivan, minister to Columbia.

29. Welles, *Naboth's Vineyard*, I, 354–55; Tansill, *The United States and Santo Domingo*, 275–80.

30. Welles, *Naboth's Vineyard*, I, 236, 345–46, 265–66; Cazneau, *To the American Press*, 17–18, 20; Cazneau, *Our Winter Eden*, 127–30; Nevins, *Hamilton Fish*, I, 255, 260–66. For investors of the Geological Company see: "William L. Halsey," "Ben Holladay," "S. L. M. Barlow," "Cyrus McCormick," and "John Young," in Johnson and Malone (eds.), *Dictionary of American Biography*, I, 613, V, 141, VI, 607, X, 630; "Union Mass Meeting," New York *Times*, Feb. 22, 1860. Halsey was secretary, Barlow specialized in business law and Mexican claims, Cyrus M. McCormick produced farm machinery and was a director of the Union Pacific Railroad, Ben Holladay financed Russell, Majors, and Waddell, had the overland mail route to California with one million dollars a year in subsidies, sold out to Wells, Fargo, and Company, and organized the California, Oregon, and Mexico Steamship Company and Northern Pacific Transportation Company. John Young of Philadelphia was an editor for the Philadelphia *Press*, the New York *Herald*, and established the San Diego *Daily Union*, Washington, D. C. *Chronicle*, and the San Francisco *Chronicle*. He was Richard Kimball's brother-in-law. Prof. William L. Gabb, a paleontologist, surveyed California and published a two hundred-page survey of the minerals of the Dominican Republic. In 1873, he surveyed Costa Rica and died of fever contracted in Costa Rica.

31. Richard I. Lester, *Confederate Finance and Purchasing in Great Britain* (Charlottesville, University of Virginia Press, 1975), 196–99; Bauer, *A Maritime History of the United States*, 78–80, 103.

32. Nevins, *Hamilton Fish*, I, 261–62; Welles, *Naboth's Vineyard*, I, 372–74; Herrick, *The American Naval Revolution*, 13–18.

33. Nevins, *Hamilton Fish*, I, 261–62; Welles, *Naboth's Vineyard*, I, 300; "Thomas Tileston," "Edward Prime," "William Prime," "Sam Prime," and "Edward P. Hollister," in Johnson and Malone (eds.), *Dictionary of American Biography*, V, 141, VIII, 227, IX, 941. Tileston was president of the Phoenix Bank of New York, the Atlantic Insurance Co., and organized the New York Clearinghouse. Prime was a Presbyterian clergyman who had edited the New York *Observer* (1854–1855). He was chaplain to the U.S. minister to Rome in 1860, and by 1869 wrote on worldwide missionary work. Prime's brother, William, edited the New York *Journal of Commerce* and was president of the Associated Press. Another brother, Sam, was editor of the

New York *Observer* (1840) and a contributor to *Harper's Weekly* on religion and philanthropy. Hollister had been minister to Haiti.

34. "St. Domingo," New York *Herald*, Aug. 13, 1869; Nevins, *Hamilton Fish*, I, 265.

35. Nevins, *Hamilton Fish*, I, 270, 275, 335, 362.

36. Tansill, *The United States and Santo Domingo*, I, 372, 386; Nevins, *Hamilton Fish*, I, 277–78.

37. Cazneau, *To the American Press*, 1; Nevins, *Hamilton Fish*, I, 383.

38. United States Senate, Senate Report no. 234, 41st Cong., 2nd sess., "Hatch Report," June 25, 1870 (National Archives, Washington, D.C.). Perry's testimony has led historians to label Cazneau as follows: Tansill, *The United States and Santo Domingo*, 269–80, "few qualms"; Nelson, *Almost a Territory*, 51, "user"; Knight, *The Americans in Santo Domingo*, 7, "shifty"; Welles, *Naboth's Vineyard*, I, 311–12, "tenacious adventurer"; Pratt, *A History of United States Foreign Policy*, "corrupt"; Rippy, *The Caribbean Danger Zone*, 121, "corrupt"; Selden Rodman, *Quisqueya: A History of the Dominican Republic* (Seattle: University of Washington Press, 1964), 74, "unscrupulous"; Nevins, *Hamilton Fish*, I, 252, 256, "rover and speculator," but also says Washington politicians were prejudiced because of Cazneau's French name and Catholic religion.

39. Nevins, *Hamilton Fish*, I, 328–31, 501; Bauer, *Maritime History of the United States*, 241–44; Tansill, *The United States and Santo Domingo*, 395–98.

40. "Hatch Report"; Tansill, *The United States and Santo Domingo*, 372–402, 409; Nevins, *Hamilton Fish*, I, 332–33, 364; Welles, *Naboth's Vineyard*, I, 320.

41. Welles, *Naboth's Vineyard*, I, 136–37; William S. McFeeley, *Grant: A Biography* (New York: W. W. Norton, 1981), 343–51.

42. "Hatch Report"; Tansill, *The United States and Santo Domingo*, 411; Welles, *Naboth's Vineyard*, I, 393–95.

43. Tansill, *The United States and Santo Domingo*, 421, 462; Knight, *The Americans in Santo Domingo*, 16; Rippy, *The Caribbean Danger Zone*, 121–23.

44. "The Samana Bay Company," New York *Tribune*, Apr. 7, 1874; Nevins, *Hamilton Fish*, I, 328–29; Bauer, *Maritime History of the United States*, 252–55. In 1871, it cost Alden B. Stockwell of the Pacific mail $900,000 to get favorable legislation to build two iron and screw propeller-driven ships. By 1875, Pacific Mail received four million dollars each year from Central Pacific and Union Pacific to raise rates. Between 1875 and 1880, railroad barons established Occidental Shipping with British ships and brought Pacific Mail to bankruptcy. Kenneth Hagan, *The People's Navy: The Making of American Sea Power* (New York: Free Press, 1991), 175–77.

45. James Derbyshire and Alexander Turnbull to William Cazneau and his wife Jane Montgomery Cazneau, Oct. 15, 1872, J. M. Cazneau to C. A. Winn, deed records, St. Catherine's Parish, libel 979, fol. 288, 1877 (Jamaica Archives, Spanish Town, Jamaica); William L. Cazneau to R. O. W. McManus, June 2, 24, 1875, box 3, fols. 58–66, James Papers. The Treaty of Washington (May 8, 1871) established arbitration from 1871–1872 and Britain was held liable for $15,500,000 in claims by the *Alabama* and other C.S.A. raiders. Courts sat in 1874–1876 and 1882–1885 to determine distribution.

46. Cazneau to Beach, Dec. 1, 1865, Jane Cazneau Papers; Frank Cundall, *Historic Jamaica* (London: Institute of Jamaica, 1915), 146.

47. Philip Wright (ed.), *Lady Nugent's Journal of Her Residence in Jamaica from 1801 to 1805* (Kingston: Institute of Jamaica, 1966), 61–62. The party traveled in curricles, two-wheeled

carriages with two horses; gigs, two-wheeled open carriages with one horse; and kittareens, the Irish version of the two-wheeled French Cabriolet with two passengers facing forward and two facing backward and pulled by a skewbald horse. Jane M. Cazneau to Mrs. Beach, Dec. 1, 1865, Jane Cazneau Papers.

48. Stuart Villers, *Adventures Amidst the Equilateral Forests and Rivers of South America; Also West Indies and the Wilds of Florida* to which is added "Jamaica Revisited," (London: John Murray, 1891), 173, 205–7. Villers saw only American buggies of hickory. "Keith Hall," postcard, Jane Cazneau file. The postcard was donated by Ann Stephens's nephew.

49. William Cazneau to R. O. W. McManus, Nov. 1, 1874, June 24, 1875, James Papers; *Blue Book, Island of Jamaica* (Jamaica: Governor's Printing Office, 1880–1900), S19, schools; J. M. Cazneau to M. S. Beach, Aug. 25, 1865, Jane Cazneau Papers; Richard Bradford, *The Virginius Affair* (Boulder: Colorado Associated University Press, 1980), 7, 11–13, 25, 31; Johnson, *The History of Cuba*, 155–60, 181–82, 199, 202, 207, 221.

50. Bradford, *The Virginius Affair*, 25, 31; Johnson, *History of Cuba*, 275–99.

51. *Abstract of Title to Antonio Rivas Grant*, Cazneau to McManus, Nov. 1, 1874, June 4, 24, 1875, James Papers.

52. Cazneau to McManus, June 4, 24, 1875, James Papers.

53. Turpe to McManus, Mar. 29, 1876, Apr. 5, May 25, Dec. 21, 1875, Turpe to Simpson and James, Mar. 10, 1877, A. G. Carothers to R. O. W. McManus, Oct. 29, 1876, box 3, fol. 59, 62, James Papers; *Abstract of Title to Rivas Grant*, Crawford's 1854 deed was witnessed by G. P. Devine and F. P. J. Meyer. United States, *The War of the Rebellion: A Compilation of the Official Records of the Union and Confederate Armies* (70 vols.; Washington: U.S. War Department, 1880–1901), ser. 1, vol. 1, 360, 561; Brown, *Indian Wars and Pioneers of Texas*, 587; Cazneau, *Eagle Pass*, 34. The Cazneaus had more powerful adversaries than Stone and Crawford. Goldfrank, Frank, and Co. of San Antonio managed a cattle syndicate that filed deeds for William Cazneau's unrecorded share of the Rivas grant from Garza to Crawford and from Crawford to Devine. Franklin (ed.), "Memoirs of Mrs. Annie P. Harris," 231–46.

54. "William Leslie Cazneau," San Antonio *Daily Herald*, Mar. 22, 1876, in *Biographies of Leading Texans*, part I, 138–39.

55. *Abstract to Title of Rivas Grant*; Carothers to McManus, Oct. 29, 1876, Turpe to McManus, May 1877, power of attorney from Jane Cazneau to R. O. W. McManus, Aug. 15, 1876, box 3, fol. 60, 61, James Papers; "Veteran Claims Allowed Today," Dallas *Herald*, June 6, 1874. District Chairmen were R. O. W. McManus, W. P. Lane, John S. Ford, J. H. Brown, M. S. Munson, F. W. Taylor, Frank White, S. C. Robertson, E. DeMorse, and J. H. Reagan. The Cazneaus were not the only victims of land theft and fraud. By 1883, the Legislature had created the Land Fraud Board to investigate forged titles, destroyed records, and other irregularities. Charles DeMorse, the Cazneaus' old friend from their Matagorda days, served on the board.

56. Jane Maria Cazneau, Last Will and Testament, Jan. 27, 1877, Jane Cazneau file. 1. An estate known as Keith Hall, about eight hundred acres of land; with all the furniture and live stock. 2. The Esmeralda, an estate near San Domingo City in the island of San Domingo, containing about twenty acres. 3. A wharf in the city of San Domingo, and a square of land in the city with four dwelling houses. 4. Certain mining rights, land grants, and contracts, in the name of General Cazneau. 5. A claim for $10,000 against the Spanish government for the

spoilation of Esmeralda while in occupation of Santo Domingo. 6. Forty acres of land at Samana Bay, the papers of which were in the hands of the American consul at Samana Bay. 7. Her half of a land grant of eleven square leagues of land in Waco, Texas, on the Brazos River, half owned by her brother R. O. W. McManus as compensation for his services in defraying the expenses in prosecuting the litigations. 8. About one thousand acres of land at Eagle Pass composing an estate called Eagle Pass. The deed in the possession of R.O.W. McManus, who has been paid for his services by transfer of land on Cane Island in the Brazos River. 9. A tract of land adjoining Eagle Pass, called the Rivas grant. Affidavit of Cora C. Hutchins, July 3, 1891, box 3, fol. 66, James Papers.

57. Cazneau to Winn, Nov. 1877, deed records, St. Catherine's Parish, Jamaica; Inventories, 1B/11/3, vol. 162, fol., 212, Spanish Town (Jamaica Archives). This deed was contested; her last will was not recorded in Jamaica, but the Cazneau school continued until 1893. *Blue Book, Island of Jamaica*, S19, schools. In 1880 the school had fifty-six pupils and in 1893 had thirty-nine. In 1900, the Wesleyans closed all schools. Cundall, *Jamaica*, 144. Keith Hall was destroyed in an earthquake in 1907, but Cazneau Park was marked on old maps until the 1950s when ALCAN, ALCOA, Kaiser, and Reynolds began mining the solid bauxite cliffs of Bog Walk. Cazneau, *Our Winter Eden*, appendix.

58. Jane M. Cazneau, Last Will and Testament, Nov. 21, 1878, box 3, fol. 61, *Baldwin, et al. vs. Goldfrank, et al.*, box 3, fol. 58, McManus to Fisher, June 23, 1884–June 28, 1885, box 3, fol. 63, James Papers. By 1884, Baldwin, the executor for William Storm, and McManus agreed to share any settlement, but the suit outlived both men and several attorneys. In 1892, Cora won a settlement on an undisclosed small tract of land, but had not yet collected on it in 1894 when correspondence in the James Papers ended because Gov. James Hogg appointed James, then Cora's attorney, chief justice of the Fourth Court of Civil Appeals. In 1906, when Simon Lavanburg died, Max Goldfrank, as agent, deeded the property to the El Indio Cattle Company. It is not known if the Cazneau heirs received any restitution for the Rivas grant.

59. "Sketch of Mrs. Cazneau," New York *Tribune*, Dec. 31, 1878; Goldsmith, *Other Powers*, 85, 170, 335, 402–3.

60. "Sketch of Mrs. Cazneau," New York *Tribune*, Dec. 31, 1878; "Lost off Cape Hatteras," New York *Sun*, Dec. 28, 1878; "The Emily B. Souder Lost," New York *Tribune*, Dec. 30, 1878. The ship carried a miscellaneous cargo for nineteen small commission houses in New York. The manifest listed dry goods, groceries, agricultural implements, wooden ware, paints, paper, seventeen cases of cartridges, eight guns, drugs, more than a dozen sewing machines, and fifty-three kegs of beer. The guns and cartridges were likely for the Cubans.

61. Sketch of the *Emily B. Souder* in Erik Heyl, *Early American Steamers* (3 vols.; Buffalo: By author, 1953), I, 139–40.; "Description of the Lost Vessel," New York *Tribune*, Dec. 28, 1878; "The Emily B. Souder Lost," New York *Tribune*, Dec. 30, 1878; "Lost off Cape Hatteras," New York *Sun*, Dec. 28, 1878; "Foundered at Sea," New York *Evening Telegram*, Dec. 28, 1878. Roberts was U. S. consul at Kingston, Jamaica, and had owned the *Virginius*.

62. "Description of the Lost Vessel," New York *Tribune*, Dec. 28. 1878.

63. Livezey, *Mahan on Sea Power* (Norman: University of Oklahoma Press, 1981), 130; "Bad News of the Souder," New York *Sun*, Dec. 29, 1878.

64. "The Lost Emily B. Souder," New York *Sun*, Dec. 30, 1878; "Disasters on the Columbian Coast," New York *Tribune*, Dec. 28, 1878; "Foundered at Sea," New York *Evening*

Telegram, Dec. 28, 1878; "Lost off Cape Hatteras," New York *Sun*, Dec. 28, 1878; "Foundered in Mid-Ocean, New York *Times*, Dec. 28, 1878; "The Emily B. Souder Lost," New York *Tribune*, Dec. 28, 1878.

65. "Bad News of the Souder," New York *Sun*, Dec. 29, 1878; "Sketch of Mrs. Cazneau," New York *Tribune*, Dec. 31, 1878.

66. "THE LOST EMILY B. SOUDER, HER GOING DOWN DESCRIBED BY THE ONLY KNOWN SURVIVORS," New York *Sun*, Jan. 10, 1879; U.S. Navy Oceanographer Office, "Beaufort Scale," publication no. 9 (1958). "No. 7, MODERATE GALE, wind 36 mph, sea heaps up and white foam from breaking waves begins to be blown in streaks along the direction of the wind, with wave heights from 13-20 feet; No. 8, FRESH GALE, wind 44 mph, moderate waves of greater length; edges of crests break into spindrift (spray), with wave heights 13 to 20 feet; No. 9, STRONG GALE wind 48 mph, high waves; dense streaks of foam; sea begins to roll; spray affects visibility, waves of 13 to 20 feet." In 1838, Sir Francis Beaufort standardized a scale from zero to eleven of wind velocity and wave height and description mandatory for all ship's logs in the Royal Navy. Based on the observation of the seamen, the Beaufort Scale explains the sailor's terms.

67. "THE LOST EMILY B. SOUDER," New York *Sun*, Jan. 10, 1879.

68. Ibid.; U.S. Navy Oceanographer Office, "Beaufort Scale." "No. 10 WHOLE GALE, wind 53 mph, very high waves with long overhanging crests; resulting in foam in great places blown in dense white streaks along the direction of the wind; the whole surface of the sea takes on a white appearance; rolling of the sea become heavy; visibility affected, wave height 20–30 feet; No. 11, STORM, wind 61 mph, exceptionally high waves; small and medium ships lost to view for a long while below the waves; sea is covered with white foam; everywhere the edges of the wave crests are blown into foam; visibility is affected, wave height 30–45 feet."

69. "THE LOST EMILY B. SOUDER," New York *Sun*, Jan. 10, 1879; Fabens [Cazneau], *The Camel Hunt*, 38.

70. "THE LOST EMILY B. SOUDER," New York *Sun*, Jan. 10, 1879.

CONCLUSION

1. "A Sketch of Mrs. Cazneau," New York *Tribune*, Dec. 31, 1878.

2. Reilly, "Jane McManus Storms," 230–45; Kinkade, "Jane McManus Storms Cazneau"; Nelson, "Jane Storms Cazneau," 17 (Spring, 1986), 25–40; Nelson, "Mission to Mexico," 227–45; Nelson, "President Polk and the War," 75–90; Cashion, "Women in the Mexican War"; Merton L. Dillon, "Jane McManus Cazneau," in James (ed.), *Notable American Women*, I, 315; Rose F. Kavo, "Jane Maria McManus Cazneau," in Mainiero (ed.), *American Women Writers*, I, 328; Robert E. May, "Jane Maria Eliza McManus Cazneau," in Tyler, et al. (eds.), *New Handbook of Texas*, I, 1052–53; May, "'Plenipotentiary in Petticoats,'" 19–44; May, "Lobbyists for Commercial Empire," 383–90.

3. Published works by Jane McManus Storm Cazneau by year of publication and pseudonym. See Appendix A for signed newspaper articles; Appendix B for textual analysis. Anon., "The Great Nation of Futurity," 426–30; Anon., "Free Trade," 329–42; Anon., "Hurrah for a War with England," 411–15; Anon., "The Home League," 539–53; Anon., "The Gypsies," *United States Magazine and Democratic Review*, 10 (July, 1842), 58–68; Anon., "The Coup-De-

Grace," 542–44; Anon., "Rambles in Yucatan," *United States Magazine and Democratic Review,* 11 (Nov., 1842), 529–39; Anon., "Oregon," 339–59; Anon., "The Texas Question," 423–30; Anon., "The Legal Wrongs of Women," 477–83; Montgomery, "The Presidents of Texas," 282–91; Anon., "The Mexican Question," 419–25; Anon., "Annexation," 5–10; Montgomery, *Texas and Her Presidents;* Anon., "Principles, Not Men," 3–12; Anon., "The Mosquito King and the British Queen," 405–16; Anon., "The Mosquito King and the British Queen, concluded," *United States Magazine and Democratic Review,* 25 (Dec., 1849), 529–38; Anon., "The King of Rivers," 506–15; Montgomery, "The Union of the Seas," 145–54; Montgomery, *The King of Rivers;* Montgomery, *The Queen of the Islands;* Montgomery, *The Queen of Islands and the King of Rivers;* Anon., "British Aggression in Central America," 3–14; Fabens [Cazneau], *The Camel Hunt;* Anon., "Soulouque and the Dominicans," 137–49; Anon., "Soulouque and the Dominicans, contd.," 234–39; Montgomery, *Eagle Pass;* Cora Montgomery (ed.), *Our Times,* 97–192; Anon., "On the Rumored Occupation of San Domingo," 173–92; Fabens [Cazneau], *A Story of Life on the Isthmus;* Montgomery, *Eagle Pass,* published with Fabens [Cazneau], *Life on the Isthmus;* Fabens [Cazneau], *Facts about Santo Domingo;* Anon., *In the Tropics;* Fabens [Cazneau], *Uses of the Camel;* Anon., *The Prince of Kashna;* Fabens [Cazneau], *Resources of Santo Domingo;* Cazneau, *Our Winter Eden.*

4. Henry Watterson, *"Marse Henry": An Autobiography* (2 vols.; New York: George H. Doran, 1919), I, 56–58; Rippy, *Rivalry of the United States and Great Britain over Latin America,* 313; Pratt, *A History of U.S. Foreign Policy* , 324; Goetzmann, *When the Eagle Screamed,* xv–xvii, 50; Brown, *Agents of Manifest Destiny,* 464; Wall, *Henry Watterson,* 25; "Obituary," New York *Tribune,* Mar. 26, 1895.

5. "Sketch of Mrs. Cazneau," New York *Tribune,* Dec. 31, 1878; *La Verdad,* Jan. 8–June 26, 1848; Montgomery, *The Queen of Islands and the King of Rivers;* Montgomery, "Union of the Seas," 145–54; "Meeting of Female Industry Association," *Workingman's Advocate,* Mar. 22, 1845; "The Female Industrial Association," New York *Sun,* Mar. 6, 10, 14, May 1, 1845; *Blue Book, Island of Jamaica,* S19, schools.

6. J. M. Cazneau to M. S. Beach, Dec. 27, 1854, Jane Cazneau Papers; J. M. Cazneau to Jeremiah Black, Sept. 18, 1857, Black Papers; Goetzmann, *When the Eagle Screamed,* xvi, 50.

7. Wilentz, "Society, Politics, and the Market Revolution," 59.

8. Anon., "Annexation,"5–10; J. M. Cazneau to M. Y. Beach, Jan. 8, 1850, Jane Cazneau Papers; Merk, *Manifest Destiny and Mission,* 200–1; Goetzmann, *When the Eagle Screamed,* xiii.

9. J. M. Cazneau to William H. Seward, Dec. 30, 1850, Seward Papers; Cora Montgomery, "Our Mexican Border," New York *Tribune,* July 15, Oct. 17, Dec. 11, 1850, Feb. 1, Mar. 6, 8, Aug. 2, 1851; Kinkade, "Jane McManus Storms Cazneau," 23; Nelson, "Mission to Mexico," 227–45; Nelson, "President Polk and the War," 2–95; Cashion, "Women in the Mexican War," 80; Connor and Faulk (eds.), *North America Divided,* 156–57.

10. Connor, *Adventure in Glory,* 88–89; Ann S. Stephens, *The Heiress; an Autobiography* (Philadelphia, T.B. Peterson, 1859), 392–93.

Index

285

C

Y

Z

About the Author

Linda Sybert Hudson was awarded the Texas State Historical Association Caldwell Award in Texas history while studying at East Texas Baptist University. She received a M.A. at Stephen F. Austin State University and a Ph.D. at the University of North Texas. Grants for this research include the John H. Jenkins Research Award presented by the TSHA and the Ottis Lock Research Award given by the East Texas Historical Association. Linda is president of the ETHA and professor of history at East Texas Baptist University in Marshall, Texas.

Colophon

The typeface used for the text is New Baskerville, based on the transitional typeface designed by English printer John Baskerville (1706–1775) in the mid-eighteeth century. The display type is Zapf Chancery, designed by Hermann Zapf in the twentieth century.

Two thousand copies printed on 55 lb. Glatfelter at Edwards Bros., Inc., Lillington, North Carolina.